A
SHORT
HISTORY
OF
ISLAM

S.F. MAHMUD

OXFORD
UNIVERSITY PRESS

OXFORD
UNIVERSITY PRESS

Great Clarendon Street, Oxford ox2 6DP

Oxford University Press is a department of the University of Oxford.
It furthers the University's objective of excellence in research, scholarship,
and education by publishing worldwide in

Oxford New York

Auckland Bangkok Buenos Aires Cape Town Chennai
Dar es Salaam Delhi Hong Kong Istanbul Karachi Kolkata
Kuala Lumpur Madrid Melbourne Mexico City Mumbai Nairobi
São Paulo Shanghai Taipei Tokyo Toronto

Oxford is a registered trade mark of Oxford University Press
in the UK and in certain other countries

ISBN 0 19 577384 5

Second Edition, 1988

Eighth Impression 2004

Printed in Pakistan by
Mas Printers, Karachi.
Published by
Ameena Saiyid, Oxford University Press
Plot No. 38, Sector 15, Korangi Industrial Area, PO Box 8214
Karachi-74900, Pakistan.

To
the memory of
My Daughter
NASREEN

Sur Dynasty, 282. *See also* Sher Shah
    Suri
Suras, the, 19, 23, 24, 25, 31, 51
Suvarov, General, 269
Sweden, 265
Sykes, Sir Percy, 340
Syria, 5, 6, 53, 57, 65, 71, 73, 74, 82, 109,
    130, 133, 142, 145, 169 f., 173, 206 f.,
    223, 226; campaigns in, 28 f., 31 ff.,
    33, 34, 38, 42, 43, 98, 161 f., 165,
    167, 172, 200 f., 236, cf. 303 ff.;
    French Mandate, 337, 355 f.; and
    Russia, 355. *See also* 364, 365, 368,
    376, 382
Szegedin, Peace of, 231

T

al-Tabari, 108, 123
Tabriz, 204, 210, 212, 215, 216, 254,
    256 f., 314, 330
Tadzikistan, 368, 404, 406
Taghlib, Bani, 141
Tahirids, the, 114, 121, 134 f., 142
Tahmasp, Shah of Persia, 212 f. 254,
    280 ff.
Taif, 362
Taiwan, 367
Taj Mahal, 289
Tajuddin Yildiz, 179, 180
Talaat Pasha, 328, 329
Talha, 37, 38
Talikot, battle of, 196 f.
Tangier Statute, 358
Tantia Topi, 320 f.
Tarain, battle of, 178
Tarbila, 274
Tardi Beg, 282
Tarikh-i-Mubarak Shahi, 189
Tariq, 62 ff.
Tartars, 203, 207, 208, 221, 227, 256,
    262, 267, 268
Tashkent, 404
Taxation, 62, 66, 183, 184, 185, 220,
    295
Tehran, 330
Tel-el-Kebir, battle of, 307
Temesvar, 265, 266
Templars, Order of, 169, 173
Tenedos, 260
Theodora, 225
Theodorus, 29
Theophilus, 117, 118

Thrace, 328, 338, 339
Tibb-i-Sikandri, 189
Tiflis, 216, 218, 254
Timur, 173, 188 f., 203, 205 ff., 221,
    229, 274, 275
Tipu, Sultan, 298
Tirhut, 189, 192
Tobacco, 316
Todar Mal, Raja, 282, 287
Tokat, 206
Tokolli, King of Hungary, 263
Toledo, 71 f.
Toulouse, battle of, 67
Tours, battle of, 67 f.
Towly, Mahmud Ould Ahmed, 370
Transjordan, 337, 348, 352, 353 f., 383
Transmigration of souls, doctrine, 113
Trans-Oxiania, 61, 109, 134, 142, 147,
    205, 207 f., 218, 274
Transylvania, 239, 255, 260, 262, 264,
    265
Travellers and geographers, 94, 95,
    110, 146, 152, 247, 272
Tripolitania, 35, 42, 93, 375; Tripoli,
    158, 163, 171, 311; taken by Italy,
    328
Tudeh Party, 342
Tughluqs, the, 183, 185 ff., 190, 195
Tughril Beg, 143
Tughril Khan, 181
Tulunids, 97
Tunisia, 53, 85, 90, 93, 238, 242, 310,
    364, 368, 371, 389; French Protect-
    orate, 299, 311, 312 f., 359 f.
Turan Shah, 161, 168
Turkai, Nur Mohammad, 392, 393
Turkey and Turks, 73, 136, 180, 223 ff.,
    341, 347, 364, 366, 368, 381; Turkish
    bodyguards, 98, 117, 119 f., 129 f.,
    168. *See also* Mamluks; Ghaur
    Turks, 177; Seljuk Turks, 129, 142 ff.,
    154, 204, 223, 224 f.; Ottoman Turks,
    145, 170, 203, 205, 206, 210, 212 ff.,
    223 ff., 270 f., 363; their decline, 244
    f., 253 ff., 300 ff., 308 ff., 336 ff;
    Turkish law, 240, 270 ff., 309 f.;
    literature and language, 202 f., 246
    f., 272 f.; organization of Empire,
    244 f., 269 ff.; World War I, 336 f.;
    Young Turks, 311, 327, 338. *See
    also* 352; Khaljis, Uzbegs, Kemal
    Mustafa, Constantinople, Istanbul
Turkistan, 142, 406, 407

Turkmenistan, 368, 404, 406
Turkomen, of the Black Sheep, 203, 207, 208; of the White Sheep, 208, 209, 210
Tutush, Sultan, 145
Tyana, 61

U

Ubaidullah, 90
Ubaidullah Khan, 275
Uch, 178
Udaipur, Raja of, 294
Uhud, battle of, 16 f.
Ujjain, 180, 183
Ukraine, 255, 262 f.
Ulema, the, 87, 134, 184, 187 f., 191, 284, 286, 293, 300, 323, 333
Uljaytu Khudabanda, 202 f.
Ulugh Beg, Prince, 207 f.
Ulugh Khan, 183
Umm al-Qwaim, 390
United Arab Emirates, 364, 365, 368, 390
United Nations, 345, 348, 349, 351, 355, 357, 362, 381, 384, 388, 393
United States of America, 331, 341, 355
Unsuri, 139
Upanishads, the, 292
Upper Volta, 373
Uqailids, 142
Uqbah ibn Nafi, 53, 61
Urdu, 298, 334, 346
Urmia, Battle of Lake,
Utbi, *Tarikhi-Yamini*, 139
Uzbegs (Turks), 208, 213, 274, 275
Uzbekistan, 368, 404
Uzun Hasan, Amir, 208, 210

V

Varna, 232, 302
Venice, 158, 166, 225, 227; wars with Turks, 231, 233 ff., 238, 241 ff., 254, 258 f., 260, 262, 264 ff.
Vidin, 264
Vienna, 236 ff., 261 ff., Congress of, 312
Vijayanagar, 196, 197, 274
Vikramajit, 290
Viziers, 111, 219 ff., 235, 243 ff., 244 ff., 253, 259, 264, 271; cf. 119; functions of, 243 ff., 271
von Sanders, General, 329
von Stahrenberg, Count, 263

W

Wafd Party, 342, 343
Wahhab, Abdul, 363
Wahhabi Movement, 174, 303, 304, 322
al-Walid, 60, 62 ff., 72
Wallachia, 228, 231, 266, 268, 269, 303, 308
Wasil ibn Ata, 74
Waterloo, battle of, 390
al-Wathiq, 118, 119, 129
Wazir, Nawab of Oudh, 318
Western influence, 309
Wiqar ul-Mulk, 323
Wolesley, Sir Garnett, 307
Women, status of, 23, 75, cf. 281. *See also* 'Harem Rule'.
World War I, 335, 336 f., 340; II, 339 f., 342, 344, 347 ff., 357

Y

Yaghi Sultan, 157
Yahya ibn Ahmad Sirhindi, 189
Yaqub ibn Layth, *see* al-Saffar
Yaqub Shah, 208, 210
al-Yaqubi, 123
Yaqut, 152
Yarmuk, battle of, 29 f., 31
Yemen, the, 1 f., 59, 161 f., 238, 351, 358, 364, 387
Yenikale, 269
Yezd, 204
Yezid I, 54, 55 ff., 71
Yezid II, 67
Yezid ibn Abi Sufyan, 29
Yusuf al-Fihri, 80
Yusuf ibn Tafshin, 91 ff.
Yusuf Zais, tribe, 275

Z

Zab River, battle of, 70, 104
Zafar Ali Khan, 334
Zafar Khan, 183
Zafar Khan (Gujarat), 194
Zaghlul, Saad, 343
Zagim, Husni, 355
Zahedi, Fazollah, 342
Zahiruddin Babar, 190, 193, 197, 274, 275 ff., 284, 297
Zaidis, the, 48, 49
Zain ul-Abidin, 190

Zakaullah, 323
Zamora, 88
Zand Party, 219, 313
Zangids, the, 159 ff.
Zanj Rebellion, 130
Zapolya, John, 237, 238, 239
Zayd, ibn Haritha, 29
Zenta, battle of, 265
Ziauddin Barni, 185

Zia-ul-Haq, General Mohammad, 396, 397, 404
Ziyad ibn Abih, 55, 103
Ziyauddin, Sayyid, 341
Zoroastrianism, 4, 34, 107, 116
Zotts (Jats), 116
Zsitva-Torok, Treaty of, 255
Zubair of Medina, 36, 37, 38
Zuravna, battle of, 262

CONTENTS

page

Preface   ix

1. The Prophet of Islam   1
2. The Orthodox Caliphs   26
3. The Omayyads   53
4. Islam in Spain   79
5. The Abbasids   102
6. The Kingdoms within the Abbasid Caliphate   129
7. The Crusades   154
8. Islam in India   176
9. Islam in Persia   200
10. The Ottomans   223
11. The Later Ottomans   253
12. The Moghuls in India   274
13. Islam in the Nineteenth Century   299
14. Islam in the Twentieth Century   324
15. The World of Islam, 1960-86   362
Index   409

MAPS

page

1. Omayyad Caliphate, 661-750   56
2. Later Abbasids, Minor Kingdoms, Tenth Century   120
3. Mahmud of Ghazni's Empire and the
   Islamic World, Eleventh Century   137
4. The Safavid Empire, Seventeenth Century   211
5. The Ottoman Empire, Early Period,
   Sixteenth to Seventeenth Centuries   245
6. India on the Eve of Babar's Invasion, 1525   276
7. The Moghul Empire in India, Aurangzeb's
   Reign, 1700   facing 296
8. The Islamic World in 1918   326
9. The Islamic World in 1958   354

PREFACE

A Short History of Islam has many aspects. It has been steady as well as stormy, full of disasters as well as astonishing recoveries. It rose out of a semi-barbarous land and touched the heights of intellectual and spiritual glory in a wide world. A rabble, a horde, an unruly and fiercely clannish people welded into an irresistible force by faith, by spiritual pride and moral fervour, by the Word of God and the inspiring leadership and example of a remarkable man, went out of sandy wastes and peopled three continents. The Ummah (the Muslim Community) composed of Arabs, Persians, Berbers, Turks, Indians, Whites and Blacks, beaten now and then, but never completely vanquished, rose in one region or another of the globe and kept alive the light of knowledge, they had garnered from everywhere and never ceased to proclaim that Man has the capacity to reach the stars if he develops his powers. It produced a social order in which slaves became Sultans and were accepted as rulers by others.

It sank and became nearly extinct after 1918, yet its inner vitality remained glowing deep inside it, and today Islam may not be a world-wide force, as it once was, but it is again alive and is making itself felt in world affairs. And this is what has amazed the people of the western world.

Take a look at the explosive beginnings of Islam. By the time the Prophet died (A.D. 632) Islam had taken a firm hold on the Arabian peninsula. But in an astonishingly short time, the volunteer armies of Islam, composed as time went of multitudes of neo-Muslims, conquered Palestine and Syria by 640, Iraq by 641, Egypt by 642, Tripolitania (now Libya) by 647, Persia by 650 and Afghanistan by 661. Tunisia surrendered in 693. Algeria and Morocco were in Arab hands by 705. Sind and Lower Punjab were conquered in 712 and so was Spain. By 732 the advance had reached the middle of France, where it was checked at Tours.

This meant that the *Azan* (the Call to Prayer) was being chanted in Arabic from the shores of Atlantic to the borders of China in the very first century of Islam (A.D. 622-722). And what is marvellous, it is still being called from Indonesia to Senegal and from Sinkiang to Sudan, even though the Central Asian Muslim States are submerged in the Russian cosmos and their voice is mute. What is more, over a million sons of Islam gather at Mecca every year to perform together the Hajj, coming as they do from all corners of the globe.

During all the vicissitudes of time, there have been many catastrophes for Islam. Remember the devastating march of the Tartar hordes in the 13th century and the overwhelming western tide after the eighteenth century. Western domination was slow but it was more insidious. Whereas the Mongols soon accepted Islam and adopted Islamic institutions and their offsprings, the Turks dominated the Mediterranean world for three centuries and were still a force in the eighteenth century, the West remained inimical to Islam to the end. Whereas another, short of the terrible Tartars, the Moghuls, achieved a glory of their own for over two centuries in the Indo-Pak sub-continent and even the British could not smother the aura of Moghul fame, as the cultural supremacy of the Moghuls remained undimmed for another hundred years.

But from nineteenth century onwards, western civilization struck at the Islamic spiritual, cultural, and intellectual roots everywhere and undermined them. Coupled with political domination and scientific progress came their industrial development and commercial exploitation of the subjugated people. The technological advances made by the West and the applied uses of their inventions revolutionized and changed living conditions everywhere, and gave a sense of inferiority to all Eastern people, as to Muslims whether in Africa or Asia.

Yet Islam appears to have survived. It has begun to breathe. The Muslims everywhere are learning the new ways of life without abandoning their own cultural past. An effort is being made to strike a balance between the two opposite (if not antagonistic) spiritual systems, two distinct behaviour patterns, and two almost contrary basic values. The effects of the progress made by western mechanical advancements and technological achievements (even ushering the Atomic Age) which dazzled and even stunned the East, including of course the Muslim World, is wearing off. If Japan, Korea, Taiwan and now China can successfully compete with the West in ingenuity and skill, so can other Eastern people. Consequently the worshipful attitude of most of the newly independent Muslim people is gone and it is being frankly admitted and said that we must move with the times. We must give a new look to our outworn ways of thought and our petrified attitudes of life, without losing the basic values which distinguish us from the West. It has been proved that mere copying of the Western mores would warp one's soul and destroy one's identity. The price to be paid for meretricious progress would be very heavy if not disastrous.

This conscious and deliberate effort of the Islamic World to first, combat the rank secular outlook of the Great Powers (as Iran is doing) and secondly, refuse to be overwhelmed by the power and pelf of the donors of AID, whether economic or military is a good sign. It is a sign of vigour; it is an expression of a vital psyche which has astonished the world. We have begun to realize that AID binds, whatever be its form and we should accept it with care. The world which had finished with the followers of the Prophet of Allah after World War I is seriously pondering over this phenomenal renaissance.

It is true that what we have achieved, in spite of the resolutions of our Islamic Conference, is not yet remarkable, but the work of regeneration has begun, the determination is there and the struggle to attain an honourable place under the sun is on. A few years, even a few decades, are but a moment in the life of nations.

3 May 1987 **S.F. Mahmud**

CHAPTER 1

THE PROPHET OF ISLAM

Arabia. Arabia is the cradle of Islam: the Prophet of Islam was born there; he spoke in Arabic, a language of which the Arabs were very proud and in which they had great gifts of expression and his message was delivered to the Arabs, who spread his teaching everywhere. It is necessary, therefore, to study the country of the Arabs as well as their customs, habits, and their pre-Islamic way of life, in order to understand the effect of the Prophet on them and, through them, on others. The Arabs belonged to a country which was very nearly cut off from the ancient civilized world; a desert encloses the north, and seas border three sides of it; to the north-east flows the Euphrates and in the north-west lies the Mediterranean. The Arabs called it an island—Jazirat-ul-Arab. The Arabs, a branch of the Semitic race, are a very ancient people who have had their own way of life for countless ages and who have been proud of this, and of their birth and origin, their land and its customs. Most of Arabia is a desert, but here and there are valleys in which are pastures for the bedouin, the wandering natives of Arabia. There are also oases, green spots in a wilderness of sands, and even mountains where there is considerable rainfall. Such a place is the Yemen, with which we begin the story of Arabia.

Yemen. The Yemen is a highland country and has a favourable climate. It has its share of rain and its winters are cold. Wheat, millet, and barley are grown in the wide green valleys. On the slopes of its hills are gardens of grapes, figs, apricots, pomegranates, and walnuts; also the famous Mocha coffee, for which the Yemen has been famous throughout the ages, is grown there. Some cattle are kept, too. San'a is the capital. The Yemen has always been the richest part of Arabia, and it is known that in very ancient times it had a well-developed civilization of its own. The Yemen was called Himyar in the days before Islam, and used to trade with the Roman world many centuries before the Prophet was born.

Hadramaut. To the east of the Yemen lay Hadramaut, which was a coastal land. It, too, had historic connections, and must have been a prosperous land, because in its valleys are ruins of ancient cities and canals. The famous frankincense tree, whose gum yielded a perfume which was highly prized in the ancient world, grew in Hadramaut, and the district was mentioned by Herodotus, the ancient Greek historian, writing in the fifth century before Christ. The people were hardy. They grew vegetables, fruits, millet, and barley in the valleys; nowadays they also grow tobacco. They gathered honey, and the bedouin raised flocks. The people loved the sea and traded with the East and the Far East since very ancient times. They went out and settled in East Africa, on the western coast of India, and in Sumatra.

Nejd. Nejd is the raised tableland in the centre of Arabia. To the south and north of it lie two entirely barren areas; in the south is the desert called *Rub al-Khali*—the empty quarter, and in the north is the Nufud desert. Nejd itself is a healthy land, the climate being dry, but invigorating. It has always been famous for its brave tribesmen and its noble horses. It gave birth to a Puritan movement in the eighteenth century under Mohammed ibn Abdul Wahhab. Nejd is now the centre of much activity connected with the production of oil. The entire country except for the Yemen, Hadramaut, and the south-eastern coastal belt, is now called Saudi Arabia.

Hijaz. We come now to al-Hijaz, the most important part of the Arabian peninsula. It lies to the north of the Yemen and to the west of Nejd, and is the most barren of the places we have discussed. It has not the pleasant climate and greenery of Yemen, the comparatively good soil of Hadramaut, the oil wealth of al-Hasa and the eastern regions bordering on the Persian Gulf, or the vigorous climate and the oil deposits of Nejd. Al-Hijaz has its oases, gardens, and orchards at Medina and Taif, but it is in every other way the poorest part of Arabia; and yet it is the most important of all the Arab provinces. It contains the two holy cities of Islam, Mecca and Medina. Even before the coming of Islam Mecca was a holy place, and people from all over Arabia came there on pilgrimage.

Arab Life. Although Arabia contains such widely varied districts, the life of the Arabs was organized in the same way everywhere. They could not build big cities as there was not enough wealth in the land, nor were there enough people. They lived in small groups, held together by the bonds of the family. A few families, presumably the descendants of a common ancestor, joined to form a clan; a few clans of the same origin made a tribe. Every Arab was a member of a family, a clan, and a tribe. They lived together, fought together, sorrowed together, and triumphed together. As there was never enough to eat, neither food for man nor fodder for beast, life was uncertain and dangerous, and tempers were never very cool. At any time, a clan might be raided by neighbours. There was adventure in these raids as well as gain: there was fighting in them too. The Arab fought as often as he could to test his arm, his sword, and his horse. A feud was never a single man's concern; once a member of another clan or tribe had been killed in open fight, in a raid, or even in an ambush, then the whole clan was involved in it for a long time; it might even last for a generation with many people dying on either side, because death had to be avenged. The Arab held life cheap; death was unimportant, so long as he died fighting for his honour. And yet he loved to quote verses, listen to and honour the poets, enjoy poetic contests and hang the winner's verses on the walls of the Kaaba.

Arab Migrations. The Arabs lived in this way for countless generations. Many of them who tired of the sameness and barrenness of their desert home went to the north; for there lay green valleys and broad rivers, and life could be comfortable for a man, even though he had to fight to gain a place for himself. So waves of Arabs went forth to the north-east and the north-west, to Iraq, the land of the two rivers, the Euphrates and the Tigris, and to Syria and Palestine and their green hills and fertile valleys. It is believed that the ancient Akkadians, Chaldeans, Sumerians, and Assyrians who flourished in Iraq long ago came from the desert. In the same way the Phoenicians, the Aramaeans, the Amorites, and the Hebrews who went to Palestine had also been Arabs. Only a century before the birth of Islam an Arab tribe, the Ghassanids or the Bani Ghassan, had gone to Palestine, been converted to Christianity, and had settled in what is now southern Jordan.

Arab Neighbours. Beyond Syria in the north-west and Iraq in the north-east lay two mighty empires: the Byzantine Empire, which was a Christian power, lay to the north-west, and the Persian Empire, called also the Sassanid Empire, lay to the north-east. The Persians believed in Zoroaster, and were mostly Zoroastrians. Both these powers were old civilizations, both were very proud. They rated the Arabs low and called them barbarians; they had little traffic with them except for trade, and even then they did not make friends with them. But these Byzantines and Persians did not like each other either. For a century before Islam they had been fighting with each other; sometimes the Persian Chosroes, as the Persian 'king of kings' was called, had the upper hand and sometimes the Byzantine Emperor. A lot of damage was caused, particularly to trade, since the over-land trade routes to the Far East and to India and China, which passed through Persia, were broken.

The New Trade Route. A different trade route, therefore, had to be discovered, and one was discovered, though it was not very direct, nor was it very new. Part of it was by sea and part by land. The ships from the East came to the Yemen port of Aden in the south where they discharged their cargoes; from there the goods were taken by camel caravans up the coast to Mecca. From Mecca other caravans set out with these goods, as well as the products of Arabia, dates and honey, camel-hair matting, tents, and frankincense. The caravans went to Yathrib, later called Medina, and after a halt and the addition of other goods, continued up al-Hijaz, until they reached the markets and big trade centres of Syria, Damascus, and Aleppo, or the ports of Palestine. This route served the Arabs well. It brought a lot of people to Mecca, and much money changed hands. In the course of centuries Mecca became an important trade depot. Its citizens began to engage in commerce themselves. They went with their caravans to Palestine and Syria, and saw new lands. Mecca and Yathrib were no longer cut off, they became important links in the trade between East and West. Many families in Mecca grew rich. Since money brings prestige to those who hold it and even great prominence if they belong to a respectable or notable family, the tribe which gradually won all this prominence became important in Mecca. This tribe was called the Quraish.

The Quraish. The Bani Quraish claimed to be descended from the Prophet Abraham through his elder son Ismail (Ishmael). In the fifth century, one prominent member of the tribe called Abd Manaf had two sons, Hashim and Abd Shams. Abd Shams was a quiet unassuming man, but his son Omayyah was a very assertive person. He became a rival of his uncle Hashim in duties relating to the care and maintenance of the Kaaba, the sacred shrine of the Arabs. It was not long before the families of these two grew into clans. They were called Bani Hashim and Bani Omayyah. The Bani Omayyah took to commerce and, taking advantage of the trade route through Hijaz, became quite prominent leaders of the commercial group. The Bani Hashim leaned either towards piety or towards the manly sports of hunting, archery, or swordsmanship. Members of this clan also engaged in trade, but not to the same extent as the Bani Omayyah.

Abu Sufyan and Abdul Muttalib. In the middle of the sixth century the leader of the Bani Omayyah was Abu Sufyan, grandson of Omayyah. He was a prominent Meccan, an astute old man, wise, and shrewd in his judgement. The chief of the Bani Hashim was Abdul Muttalib, who had certain important duties relating to the Kaaba. He was respected by all, but in worldly ways and political importance he was not on the same footing as Abu Sufyan. Since all social laws in Arabia were based on tribal customs, the same system prevailed in Mecca. In a clan or a tribe, the headman was a senior member who was a wise leader and a shrewd organizer, and who decided the affairs of the clan or tribe with the assistance of the elders of the tribe. So it was in Mecca, where there was a Council of Elders and a headman. The headman was chosen here as elsewhere, not only for his birth, but also for his qualities, his experience, his seniority, his prestige, and his wisdom. The headman in Mecca was Abu Sufyan.

The Sons of Abu Sufyan and Abdul Muttalib. Abu Sufyan was wise in the ways of the world. He had grown in business and had been many times to Palestine and Syria with his caravans. He had a son called Muawiyah, an able, sober young man, whom he generally took with him. Muawiyah could read and write; he had also learnt to deal with men, and had considerable native shrewdness. Abdul Muttalib had many sons, but the best known of these were Hamza, Abu Talib, and Abbas. Hamza was a great hunter and a mighty warrior. Abu Talib and Abbas were sober men of affairs with good judgement and cool heads. There were two other sons, Abu Lahab and Abdullah. Abu Lahab was an obstinate man of limited intelligence who was mean and revengeful: Abdullah was the youngest son. He was married in 570 while still a young man to Amina, the daughter of Wahb bin Abdalla, a lady of rank. He did not live long, however: he died while on a journey, and soon after his death his wife bore a son, who was named Muhammad.

Early Life of Muhammad (b. 570). Muhammad's mother died soon after his birth. He was then taken care of by his grandfather, Abdul Muttalib. When he was six years old, his grandfather also died. His uncle, Abu Talib, now undertook his care and Muhammad grew up in his house. Little is known of his boyhood, but it is told that as a boy he tended flocks like most Arab boys, though he never played any wild pranks as most boys do. He was quiet and given to thinking even when young. He observed things keenly and tried to understand people around him. He had to learn tact early, because he was an orphan. He tried to make peace between fighting groups of boys, and since he never took part in these clashes and always gave a just opinion when a matter was referred to him, boys began to defer to his judgement. This reputation stayed with him when he grew up. People found that they could trust him; he would stand by what he said. He was always ready to help with word or deed, and he never failed anybody who depended on him. They began to call him *al-Amin*—the trusted one.

Muhammad's Youth. His uncle Abu Talib would sometimes take young Muhammad with him to Palestine and Syria, for he could be trusted with the accounts; he was observant by nature and could give good advice. It did not matter if Muhammad also observed the life of people in that land and listened to their preachers. His uncle knew that Muhammad was a thoughtful young man; when he asked questions, he turned the answers over in his mind. He was interested in what people believed. His grandfather had been the Keeper of the Kaaba and the boy had been in and out of the holy shrine a thousand times. He had looked at people bowing before stones and statues of gods and goddesses. There was a moon-goddess in whom the majority of the Arabs believed called Al-lat. There were two other goddesses called Manat and Uza, and also a god called Hubal, and many more. He had never understood what people found in worshipping these stones or statues, and in believing in so many gods. The Jews and the Christians had their own faiths, but he had found the Jews very rigid and their God stern; they had peculiar rituals and were very intolerant. The Christians believed in a gentler God, but their Prophet was not supposed to be a man at all. He was called the Son of God; the Christians believed him to be God made flesh. Muhammad could not understand how that could be. There was a vague notion among some Arabs that there was one God above all, but nobody seemed to know who or what this meant. Some called him Allah.

Muhammad Marries Khadijah. When Muhammad was about twenty-five years old, he came into the service of a rich Meccan lady of the tribe of Quraish called Khadijah, who was his senior by a few years. He conducted her affairs so well that he soon became her steward, then her manager. She was so taken by his honesty, his industry, and his charm of manner, that she offered him her hand in marriage. Muhammad had never been romantic; unlike other young men, women had mattered little to him so far. Khadijah was certainly older than he, but she had a noble character and she was also very understanding. They were fond of each other, so he consented and they were married.

Years of Contemplation. Muhammad was now free from economic worries. He still managed his wife's business, but he had much more leisure to do what he had always wanted to do: to think, and to get at the root of all these religions and their peculiar practices. Why was man led to worship stones? People believed in evil spirits, he knew, and some even believed in the spirits of trees. What did they find in such beliefs? Obviously man wanted to believe in something, that must be the reason why he could believe in anything. He wanted to understand the 'why' and 'wherefore' of things and he wanted to belong. But a belief was supposed to explain the mystery of life and death, of the heavens and all they contained, the problem of evil, of punishment, and reward. Naturally different people believed in different solutions to this mystery. Where did the truth lie?

Muhammad thought deeply about it all. He talked to others, seeking wisdom from them, but nobody could satisfy him. He would then go out of town and seek a lonely spot where he could think undisturbed. One such spot he found in a cave called Hira, in a hill outside the town, and it became his favourite haunt. He sat there for hours on end and so the years slipped by.

The Revelation (611). One day, when he was forty years old, he was sitting, in a trance, inside this quiet cave when he heard a voice, which seemed to come from nowhere. It called out, 'Muhammad! Muhammad! Muhammad!' It then said, 'Behold! thou art chosen as a Prophet of 'God.' The sound echoed in the cave for some time and Muhammad seemed to hear the words again and again. He could not understand it all, and doubted his senses. He was even frightened. But when a few days later he heard the same voice and with it came a vision of light which seemed to fill the horizon from end to end, he was even more astonished. This vision now told him that it was the Archangel Gabriel himself who had come as a messenger of Allah to His chosen Prophet, Muhammad. He then asked him to read. Now Muhammad was a man of extraordinary talents, but he could not read or write. He was, therefore, bewildered. But the Archangel asked him to repeat after him: 'Read in the name of Allah, thy Creator . . .' The vision then faded.

Muhammad, the Prophet of Allah. After that these messages continued fairly regularly. There were gaps and now the gaps worried the Prophet more than the messages. He was a very honest man, and did not want to deceive himself. He was, therefore, often disturbed, but his wife reassured him, and gradually he was convinced that the visions and voices were not imaginary. This went on for some time. As yet the Prophet had not been asked to start preaching the new gospel, he talked to a few intimates, but that was all. Three years later, however, came the revelation that he was now appointed as a *Rasul* (a messenger of Allah), and he was asked to give this message to his fellow Meccans. This was a very difficult task. He was a simple man, respected in his own circles, but no dignitary of Mecca. He was not rich, nor was he the head of a clan or even a family, and Mecca was no town of backward people; it lay on an international trade route and it was an important trade centre. It was also the seat of a sacred shrine. The head of the Meccan Council was a man of substance; he was shrewd and diplomatic and had a large following, in fact his whole clan was behind him. If Muhammad preached a new gospel, he would be defying the Elders of Mecca. The contest would then lie between Muhammad and Abu Sufyan, that is between an Omayyad and a Hashimite. This was a serious matter, but Muhammad was not deterred.

The New Faith. People complained to Abu Sufyan and to Abu Talib. They asked them to stop Muhammad giving his message, which was: 'Allah is One. He is the Maker and Creator. He is the Giver of Life and the Bringer of Death. There is none like Him. He is Supreme.' He said that people should give up bowing and bending before stones. They should shun idol-worship. God was there to forgive them. He only asked them to be charitable, to be kind, to be forgiving. Allah told them, 'Remember what happened to other people, who thought they could do without God. Are not the ruins of long vanished peoples (Ad and Thamood) a standing testimony to Allah's wrath? Repent, therefore, and seek a refuge with Allah, Who is All-Seeing, All-Knowing and also All-Forgiving!' The thing the Prophet was asked to repeat again and again was the Unity of God. 'There is no god but Allah and Muhammad is His Prophet and Messenger.' This was the rock on which Islam was to be built.

The Opposition. These ideas were simple in themselves, but they alarmed the important people of Mecca. Firstly because, though simple, they struck at the root of their beliefs by denying all the old gods. Secondly, they called on people to break their old loyalties. The aristocrats of Mecca, the purse-proud Omayyads, and also many Hashimites, were not much impressed when they heard that Muhammad, upon whom they had always looked kindly because he was such a harmless man and socially and politically unimportant, was claiming to be the chosen Prophet of God whom he called Allah. They refused to believe this of Muhammad, whom they had known all their lives. They wondered if he was mad. They complained to Abu Talib, the uncle of the Prophet, and asked him to keep his nephew quiet, to stop Muhammad from making trouble. But when Abu Talib spoke to the Prophet, he would take back nothing: instead he began preaching to his uncle. Moreover Abu Talib's own young son, Ali, was one of the earliest and truest believers in the new religion. Abu Talib's persuasive efforts failed. He went back and reported his failure to the Meccans, who now grew angry. They won over a brother of Abu Talib, Abu Lahab, a mean and stupid man but a very obstinate one. Abu Lahab tried abuse and threats; he and his wife persecuted the Prophet, but Muhammad was not daunted. He did not preach openly yet, but went about quietly giving the Word of Allah to the people.

Early Converts. Muhammad's friend, Abu Bakr, had been the first man to be converted, as his own wife had been the first woman and Ali the first boy. A few more now joined the band. The news spread, and people began to be interested, so opposition stiffened. The poorer Muslims were treated badly, but the Prophet consoled them, and advised patience. This went on for some time, and gradually the number of Muslims grew. Hamza, the old uncle of the Prophet, a famous hunter and warrior, openly sided with his nephew, but the little band of Muslims still met in secret until a powerful Meccan, Omar ibn al-Khattab, who was respected everywhere for his strong personality and mature mind, was converted. He was afraid of nobody, and advised the Prophet to come out and preach openly, which he began to do. This made the Meccans more furious than ever. They began to think that Muhammad was

THE DESCENDANTS OF THE PROPHET

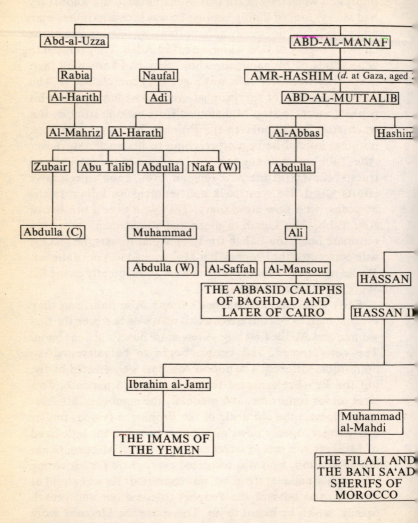

- Abd-al-Uzza
- ABD-AL-MANAF
  - Rabia
    - Al-Harith
      - Al-Mahriz
        - Zubair
          - Abdulla (C)
  - Naufal
    - Adi
  - Al-Harath
    - Abu Talib
    - Abdulla
      - Muhammad
        - Abdulla (W)
    - Nafa (W)
  - AMR-HASHIM (*d.* at Gaza, aged)
    - ABD-AL-MUTTALIB
      - Al-Abbas
        - Abdulla
          - Ali
            - Al-Saffah
            - Al-Mansour

              THE ABBASID CALIPHS
              OF BAGHDAD AND
              LATER OF CAIRO
      - Hashim

HASSAN

HASSAN I

Ibrahim al-Jamr

THE IMAMS OF
THE YEMEN

Muhammad al-Mahdi

THE FILALI AND
THE BANI SA'AD
SHERIFS OF
MOROCCO

(C) Caliph
(W) Wali of Mecca

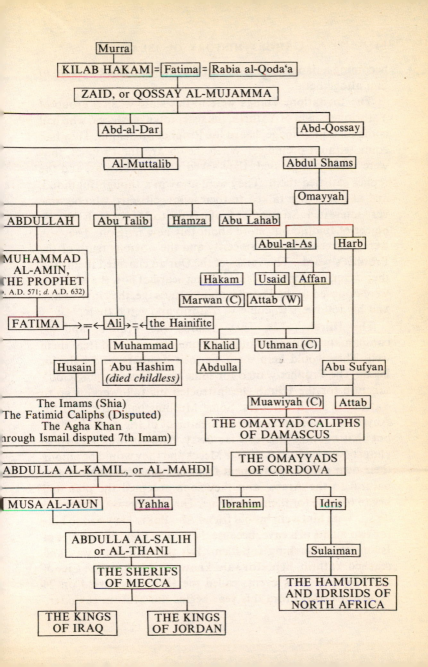

Murra

KILAB HAKAM = Fatima = Rabia al-Qoda'a

ZAID, or QOSSAY AL-MUJAMMA

Abd-al-Dar

Abd-Qossay

Al-Muttalib

Abdul Shams

Omayyah

ABDULLAH

Abu Talib

Hamza

Abu Lahab

Abul-al-As

Harb

MUHAMMAD
AL-AMIN,
THE PROPHET
(b. A.D. 571; d. A.D. 632)

Hakam

Usaid

Affan

Marwan (C)

Attab (W)

FATIMA → = ← Ali → = ← the Hainifite

Muhammad

Khalid

Uthman (C)

Husain

Abu Hashim
(died childless)

Abdulla

Abu Sufyan

The Imams (Shia)
The Fatimid Caliphs (Disputed)
The Agha Khan
(through Ismail disputed 7th Imam)

Muawiyah (C)

Attab

THE OMAYYAD CALIPHS
OF DAMASCUS

ABDULLA AL-KAMIL, or AL-MAHDI

THE OMAYYADS
OF CORDOVA

MUSA AL-JAUN

Yahha

Ibrahim

Idris

ABDULLA AL-SALIH
or AL-THANI

Sulaiman

THE SHERIFS
OF MECCA

THE HAMUDITES
AND IDRISIDS OF
NORTH AFRICA

THE KINGS
OF IRAQ

THE KINGS
OF JORDAN

becoming a danger to them, and they made plans to get rid of him altogether.

The Invitation. Things were in this state when a group of Yathribites, men of Yathrib, the sister town of Mecca, who had come on a pilgrimage, heard the Prophet preaching. They had come without prejudice. When they heard the Prophet, they were greatly impressed; they asked a few questions, and the replies satisfied them. They went away in a thoughtful mood, and at home they talked to their fellow citizens, who became very interested. So another group came to Mecca with the sole object of finding out more about this new religion. They too were impressed by the sincerity and the obvious truth of the Prophet's words. The verses of the Qur'an charmed them, and they eagerly accepted Islam. Having heard of how the Meccans were opposed to the Prophet and his message, they invited him and his followers to come to Yathrib and settle there.

The Hijrah (622). They assured the Prophet and his companions that they would welcome them all and treat them well. They would help them, be their brothers, and fight for Islam. The Prophet waited for some time, but receiving God's sanction for the Hijrah, he instructed his followers to go to Yathrib in small numbers. Some Muslims had left earlier for Abyssinia, to escape the cruel treatment of the non-Muslims, but that country was too far away. Yathrib was known to almost everybody, it was near Mecca and they would be among their own people. Movement from one place to another was natural to the Arabs, and they soon accepted the plan and began to leave for their new home. The Prophet was the last to do so. With him went his old friend Abu Bakr. They had to hide for two nights in a cave, because they knew that the enemies of Islam were searching for them. But they slipped away and reached Yathrib, henceforward known as Medina (the City of the Prophet). This event, called the Hijrah, occurred on 24 September 622. From this year begins the Muslim calendar.

The Prophet in Medina. The Meccans who went to Yathrib and settled there were called Muhajirin (the emigrants) and the men and women of Yathrib were called Ansar (the helpers). From the beginning there was great friendship between the two groups. The Ansar shared their wealth with the Meccans and lived with them; there were many intermarriages too. Soon there was perfect agreement between them, but the task imposed on the Prophet by Allah was still very heavy. Although the Muslims were now free to worship and could preach their religion to others also, they were still too few; they had few alliances with the great tribes of Arabia. The bedouin roamed free. The Meccans commanded the trade routes; they were wealthy and had influence: they were also very hostile. This situation could have daunted many a strong man, but the Prophet was a man of vision. He had great faith in his mission, and in himself. He began to steel the people of Medina for the coming struggle with the Meccans. He was a man of peace, but he was not merely a preacher, he was also a leader of men, a man who inspired them to noble thoughts, but also to noble deeds. Moreover, he had been appointed to play a great role— the role of the last and the greatest Messenger of Allah. He had to take action and to take it quickly, as already fifty-two years of his life lay behind him, and man's days on this earth are short.

Battle of Badr. The Meccans were strong, and proud of their wealth and their position. To fight them, strategy was required. The Prophet decided to strike at the root of these two things. Their wealth depended on their trade with the land of Syria, that is, the Mediterranean littoral, so the trade route to Syria must be cut. The Meccans considered themselves the best of the Arabs in everything, even in valour, so they must be proved wrong. The Prophet sent a small patrol of Muslims with the order that the next caravan to Mecca which was, of course, escorted by fighters, be attacked. As it happened, the caravan was led by the chief man of Mecca, the arch-enemy of Islam,

Abu Sufyan himself. Now Abu Sufyan was a clever man. He had a strong guard with him, but realizing the danger, he sent a swift messenger to Mecca for aid. Meanwhile the Muslims came up under the leadership of the Prophet. They were only about 300 strong, and the Meccans numbered 1,000. These are small numbers, but with these forces one of the decisive battles of the world was fought at Badr in A.D. 623, the second year of the Hijrah. The Muslims were inspired by faith, they never doubted for an instant that they would win. They swept the Meccans off the field. It was a great victory. Many prisoners were taken and much booty, but the Prophet showed great diplomacy and foresight; rejecting vengeful advice, he held the Meccans to ransom and treated them well.

Battle of Uhud (Jan. 625). The defeat at Badr was a blot on the honour of the Meccans of which they were greatly ashamed. So the next year they attacked Medina with a large force which numbered 3,000 fighters. The Muslims could only muster 700 armed men. The Prophet, realizing the seriousness of the occasion, gave strict instructions to his followers. He laid the plan of attack and defence, ordering them to keep to their positions unless told to move; but the inexperienced Muslims forgot all these instructions in the excitement of the battle. They began to fight without plan, and after beating back a flank of the Meccan army, fell on the Meccan camp without making sure that the enemy had been really defeated. The result was that the Meccan reserve, led by a brilliant commander, Khalid ibn al-Walid, came upon them suddenly and scattered them. The Prophet himself was wounded and he fell. A cry rose, 'The Prophet is slain.' This demoralized the Muslims further and many fled. The battle of Uhud ended in a defeat, and the Muslims of Medina were shamed before their Prophet. But the Prophet was no ordinary man; he gathered his men together, read them a lecture, rebuked them for their folly, exhorted them to obey orders in future, and led the chastened Medinites out to face the victorious Meccans once more. He came up with them in the early hours of the next morning. He pitched his camp in sight of them and ordered huge fires to be built. The idea was to show the Meccans that the Muslims had not lost heart. When the day dawned, the Meccans saw the Muslims in their rear going about their morning tasks utterly unafraid, and they were greatly impressed. The Prophet had turned the defeat into victory.

The Jews and Conquest of Islam. After this the Prophet never lost a battle and it was not long before nearly the whole of Arabia came under Muslim rule. After the Meccans, the first people to give trouble were the Jews in Medina and its neighbourhood. Not only did they openly scoff at the Prophet's teachings, but they conspired against the Muslims. They were a united people and rich. The Prophet had to organize a number of *ghazwahs* (holy wars) against them before they were subdued. Before this happened, however, the Jews and the Meccans, allying in a common cause, assembled a large army 10,000 strong and invaded Medina. The Prophet had to dig a ditch round Medina to protect the town. The Muslim resistance was so stubborn, however, that the enemy could not prevail, and withdrew. Now the Prophet turned on the Jews and taught them a severe lesson. The last time the Jews fought Islam was at Khaybar, where, though it was a Jewish stronghold, the Muslims won. It was in this battle that Ali, the young cousin of the Prophet, showed his valour. It was also after this battle that a Jewess, Zainab, put poisoned food before the Prophet, though the Prophet seemed to know at once and spat out the very first morsel. It is believed that the poison was so deadly that it went into his system even in that very short time.

The Pact of Hudaibiya (628). In A.H. 6, or A.D. 628, the Prophet took a large following of Muslims to Mecca for the Hajj or pilgrimage ceremony. The Meccans were no longer disposed to fight, but objected to such a large gathering, especially as many of the Muslims were also armed. This was not strange, as the Arabs were always armed, but the Meccans were alarmed. They refused to let such a large body enter the sacred boundaries. Negotiations were therefore set afoot. After much talk, the Meccans agreed to a truce. A pact was drawn up called the Pact of Hudaibiya. It has been considered a great diplomatic victory for the Prophet, because the Meccans were persuaded to agree to most of the terms of the Muslim leader. According to it, they agreed to the Prophet's right to preach and convert the Arabs to Islam, wherever they be. They agreed to allow the Prophet and his followers to enter Mecca on the occasion of the annual Hajj. The truce was to last ten years. Now that the restrictions on joining Islam were removed, the Arabs began to accept Islam in their thousands. One of the famous converts was Khalid ibn al-Walid, the future great general.

Conquest of Mecca (630). The Meccans then made a mistake. In A.D. 630 they attacked a tribe which was under Muslim protection, and thus broke the truce. The Prophet led a large army of Muslims (10,000 strong) towards Mecca. By now the tide had turned; the Meccans were not strong enough to fight such an army commanded by a general such as the Prophet had turned out to be, and they laid down their arms. Their leader, Abu Sufyan, accepted Islam. His son, Muawiyah, became one of the secretaries of the Prophet. Mecca, the heart of Arabia, now lay before the Prophet. The despised son of that ancient town had come back triumphant, but instead of being vindictive, this strange man was kindness itself. He acted in a way new to the Arabs: he forgave his enemies. He destroyed the idols which lay in the Kaaba, but the first thing he did in the Kaaba was to pray. He gave back the key of the sacred house to the hereditary keepers and told the people to come in peace to him. This conduct delighted the Meccans. They considered this *muruw'ah* (manly generosity) of the Prophet the height of nobility and came forward to enter this astonishing religion which returned enmity with love.

Battle of Hunayn and Conduct after Victory. After the conquest of Mecca, the Prophet should have had a lull as the citadel of opposition was now in Muslim hands, but this was not to be. News came that the pagans were gathering at Taif to make a last great attempt. The Prophet marched against them and faced them at Hunayn. The pagans were desperate and gave a tough fight to the Muslims. The Muslims lost many lives in the battle. At last the unbelievers were defeated and their city surrounded, yet the Prophet did not lay siege to the town. Next year Taif surrendered of itself. There were minor *ghazwahs* besides the three notable ones—Badr, Uhud, and Hunayn. Some of the *ghazwahs* were punitive and some retaliatory, the last was the expedition sent against Tabuk in the north and it is notable because of the action of malingerers. Mention of it is made in Sura 'Tauba', Paras 9-10. No *ghazwah* was undertaken out of lust of conquest. This was so because compulsion in matters of faith is forbidden in Islam. Even in argument the Prophet was asked to 'call men to the path of your Lord with wisdom and kindly exhortation. Reason with them in the most courteous manner. Your Lord best knows those who stray from His path and those who are rightly guided. If you punish, let your punishment be proportionate to the wrong that has been done to you. But it shall be best for you to endure your wrongs with patience'—Sura 'Al-Nahl', vv. 125-7.

Muhammad, Lord of Arabia. By the end of the next year, nearly the whole of Arabia had come under the Prophet's sway. He sent out preachers to every tribe, taught them how to pray, showed them the difference between loyalty to one's clan or tribe and loyalty to an idea. He made great and successful efforts to break the time-old feuds between clans and tribes, and with the force of his personality, his eloquence, his great patience, and his remarkable wisdom, he impressed on the Arabs the ideal of unity and brotherhood. He laid very great stress on the bonds of faith, the loyalty to Islam, and the brotherhood of man. He told them that before Allah all men were equal. He showed them by his own example that the rich and the poor, the mighty and the weak, the man of a large family and the lonely man, were all equal. He himself was a man like them; the only difference was that Allah spoke through him.

The Prophet's Death (632). The Prophet led his last pilgrimage to Mecca in A.D. 631. It was then that the last verse of the Qur'an was revealed: 'This day I have perfected your faith for you, and completed my bounties to you and I have chosen Islam for you as a religion.' The Prophet spoke his last sermon on this occasion and asked men to believe always in Allah, the one God, to avoid setting up other gods, to serve Allah and man, to fight for truth, to love all Muslims like brothers, to give people their rights, to protect the weak, to help the lowly and shun pride. Soon after his return to Medina he fell ill, and after only a few days of illness he died on 8 June 632 (A.H. 10). Thus died the great desert-bred Prophet of Islam who had given a new message of hope to man.

The Prophet's Character. The Prophet was a simple man with simple tastes: his joys and his sorrows were human. Born poor and an orphan, he was never envious of the rich. Essentially humble, he never walked proudly or spoke arrogantly even in the days of his glory. He was always kind in his dealings with others, a friend of the poor, of the lowly, of the beggars, and wayfarers. Understanding and warm in his sympathies, he inspired great love and devotion. Always mild and gentle, he could be angry when people were unkind or harsh. He rebuked Khalid ibn al-Walid when he treated non-believers badly at the fall of Mecca, though they were confirmed wrong-doers and mischief-makers. He loved good deeds and valued good works above pious words. He encouraged his followers to seek knowledge wherever they could find it. Though wiser than most, he always consulted others, if only to give them an impression that they were important. Persecuted for a long period, he forgave his enemies, thus setting his example as a precedent for the ages. Courageous and determined, nothing ever daunted him and he never lost hope in his cause. Always humble before Allah's majesty, although his own name was linked with Allah in the creed of the Muslims, he enjoined on the Muslims the fear of Allah, obedience to Him, and submission to His will. Though he was a man of simple habits, for diplomatic reasons he married several times after the death of his faithful and devoted first wife, Khadijah. He sought alliances with various tribes in order to strengthen the bonds of Islamic relationship with them. He had three daughters and two sons; the sons died in infancy and only one daughter, the Lady Fatima, survived him. She was married to Ali, the cousin, friend, and devoted follower of the Prophet.

Islam the Religion of Man. Apart from other teachings, there are some basic articles of Islamic faith. They all have a definite meaning and purpose. Mere acceptance of them and mere observance do not please God or make anybody a good Muslim. Islamic faith insists on agreement in word and true acceptance of the heart. Islam calls no religion false; God has sent his *Rasuls* and *Nabis* (prophets) to all people. Many prophets, from Adam downwards, were appointed, who preached to the men of their time, but man forgets and adopts other gods. He sets up other deities in place of his worship of the one true God, the Lord of the world. Earlier men were crude folk, they had sometimes to be driven, sometimes to be coaxed. A time came, however, when man reached maturity and a more complete message had to be sent to him which completed and fulfilled what had been partially revealed to earlier prophets. This last prophet was Muhammad.

Basic Articles of Islamic Faith. There are five articles of Muslim faith: the *Kalima* (the creed), the five daily prayers, fasting in the month of Ramadhan, *Zakat* (contribution to the communal fund), and the Hajj. The creed is simple: There is no god but Allah and Muhammad is His Prophet. The Muslim rejects the idea of many gods and believes in the one and eternal God Who raises man to life and lays him down in the dust when his days are over, Who sleeps not nor dies, Who has existed from the beginning and will remain after the end. Muhammad is His creature and His *Rasul*. All Muslims testify to this creed every day. The true word is *abd*. An *Abd* is one who carries out the commandments of Allah in word and deed.

The Muslim is asked to say his prayers in congregation or individually, but preferably in congregational worship, five times a day. He can thus meet his fellow-Muslims daily, stand with them before God, talk to them before or after prayers, keep in close daily touch with them, understand them, and live in harmony with them. Ablutions before prayers make him ready to stand before his Maker. He has occasion to rid his heart of evil thoughts and anti-social impulses five times a day. Truly followed, the Muslim system of prayer is a great force towards the improvement of man.

Once a year he establishes another bond with his fellow Muslims, this time a bond of common suffering, trial, and common restrictions. He fasts for a month, avoids gross habits, evil thoughts, fighting and feuds, thinks godly thoughts, and trains himself mentally and physically to fight the ills of this world. He gains resistance and improves his morale. Fasting is a great asset to Islam.

He is asked to give one-fortieth of his spare goods to the community after he has served his legitimate needs. This teaches fellow-feeling, a social sense, gives him a sense of responsibility, and helps the community. Nothing could be better ordained to forge the bonds of true brotherhood between Muslims than this article of the Muslim faith.

At least once in his lifetime a Muslim must find means to join the Muslims of the world in the pilgrimage to Mecca, which is called the Hajj. He will then have the opportunity of meeting other Muslims, creating new contacts and new bonds. He will widen his sympathies, gain in understanding, and become a true son of Islam, which is a universal religion and which recognizes no barriers of colour or caste, of country or race.

Other Islamic Ideals. A Muslim must always be ready to fight for his faith and for Allah. *Jihad* (holy war) is enjoined upon him, but the cause must be genuine and must truly serve Islam. If he realizes that his services are really needed, then he cannot refuse to serve. Thus Islam requires no conscription or forced fighting. To fight for his ideals is a duty with a Muslim. He must try his best to maintain peace on earth. He must not encourage hatred. He must treat his enemies with consideration, he must not be cruel, and he must protect those who submit to him. He must not force his own religion on them, but must let them serve God as they think best. As they are now his responsibility, he must protect their rights. He has a right to ask for an equal amount of redress from one who has injured him, but if he can forgive he should do so, because forgiveness pleases Allah. He must protect the weak. Allah has made him a guardian of his womenfolk so he must be kind to women and children. He must guide them and look after them, correct them if necessary, but be fair in his dealings with them. Above all, he must remember that Allah is All-Compassionate and Merciful; compassion and mercy are, therefore, God-like qualities and must be cherished.

The Qur'an. The Qur'an is called the Book of Wisdom. The famous Sura 'Ya Sin' begins with these words. It has also been termed the Book of Enlightenment (see opening words of Suras 'Al-Shu'ara', 'Al-Qasas', and 'Al-Naml'). It has also been defined as the Book of Blessing. In Sura 'Sad', Para 23, Allah says: 'We have revealed to you this Book with Our blessing, so that the wise might ponder its revelations and take heed'— v. 29. As to understand it, Abraham, the father of the prophets, is made to pray: 'Lord! Bestow wisdom and understanding on me and count me among the righteous'—'Al-Shu'ara', v. 84. The greatest gift that Allah can bestow on man is wisdom. This is what Allah says in Sura 'Al-Baqarah', v. 269: 'He bestows wisdom on whom He wills. And he who is given wisdom is given the greatest good'.

Allah repeatedly asks us in Sura 'Al-Qamar', Para 27, that we should try to comprehend what He says. This verse is repeated several times: 'And We have made the Qur'an easy for you to ponder over, so why do you not think?

Three Kinds of Verses. The Qur'an has generally speaking, three kinds of verses. First, verses which tell of Allah's Might and Majesty, His One-ness, His Creative Powers and Gifts, His Guidance and Beneficence, His Promises of Bliss for faith and good works, and His Warnings of manifold sufferings for wrong-doing, disbelief, and *shirk*. There are frequent pledges of awards but there are repeated warnings of accountability and reckoning too. As also verses on responsibility, insisting that everyone is responsible for what he does, and will be judged on merit, without favour, and that nobody will carry anybody else's load.

Second, verses that enjoin man to learn from the accounts of the earlier epochs and what the previous law-givers, the earlier leaders of mankind, the prophets of old, gave to generations gone by. Details are repeatedly given of the erring people and their denial of good, and the mistakes man has made down the ages, and how Allah has tried to save him from degradation and destruction time and again. These accounts of ancient times serve as examples as well as a warning. Every nation, every people have been sent prophets who gave them God's message in their own language. Therefore, no people will be judged without the testimony of their own apostle. There are also references to current affairs from which timeless lessons are drawn.

The Moral Code. Third, the Moral Code scattered all over the Qur'an and embedded in significant contexts: chidings, admonitions, suggestions, plain injunctions, and eternal moral principles. Here are a few specimens: The basic principle of goodness is given in Sura 'Al-Baqarah', Para II, v. 177:

'Righteousness (goodness) does not consist in whether you face towards the East or the West. The righteous man is he who believes in Allah and the Last Day, in the angels, and the Scriptures, and the prophets; who for the love of Allah gives his wealth to his kinsfolk, to the orphans, to the needy, to the wayfarers, and to the beggars, and for the redemption of captives; who attends to his prayers and pays the alms tax; who is true to his promises, and is steadfast in trials and adversity, and in times of war. Such are the true believers; such are the God-fearing'.

In greater detail and applicability to everyday life are verses from Sura 'Al-Furqan', Para 19, vv. 63-74: 'The true servants of the Compassionate One, are those who walk humbly on the earth and say "Peace" to the ignorant who hackle them; who pass the night in prayer and on their knees in adoration of their Lord; who say "Lord!" Ward off from us the punishment of Hell, for its punishment is everlasting—an evil dwelling and an evil resting-place; who are neither extravagant nor miserly, but keep the golden mean; who invoke (the help of) no other god (benefactor) beside Allah and do not kill except for a just cause, as manslaughter is forbidden by Allah; who do not commit adultery, because he that does this shall meet with evil—his punishment will be doubled on the Day of Judgement—and he shall abide in disgrace for ever, unless he repents and believes and does good works, for then Allah will change his sins to good actions. Allah is Forgiving and Merciful, because he that repents and does good works truly, returns to Allah; who do not bear false witness and do not lose their dignity when listening to profane abuse; who do not attend like blind and deaf people when the Words of the Lord are read out to them or when they are reminded of them (but listen with care); who say: "Lord give us ease of heart and coolth of eye in our wives and children and make us examples to those who fear you". These shall be rewarded with Paradise for their fortitude'.

Nothing could be less restrictive or more tolerant, and few injunctions could be more persuasive.

CHAPTER 2

THE ORTHODOX CALIPHS

Medina at the time of the Prophet's Death. The Prophet was dead. The Arabs who had newly accepted Islam were disturbed, and wondered what was to happen to Islam and to the new Muslim State of Arabia. Would the Arabs, who had never accepted authority before, remain loyal to the new idea of unity, or would the old loyalties and the old enmities burst forth again? It was a serious problem, realized by many in Medina, the town of the Prophet. They felt that somebody must assume the responsibility of taking over the command immediately. The trouble was that there were a number of men who thought they were capable of controlling the turbulent Arabs; but a man was needed who was honourable, wise, and respected enough to do this.

The Four Groups. People grouped themselves into four major parties. First there were the Muhajirin, who had come with the Prophet. They had been close companions of the Prophet, and had been his friends for a long time. They were all trusted men. Most of them belonged to the Quraish, the tribe of the Prophet. So they thought they had first claim to the honour of succeeding the Prophet. Then came the Ansar, who had an equally good claim. They were men of substance, who had befriended the Prophet at a difficult time and had sheltered him and fought for him. They were tried Muslims. They thought that the successor should come from them. Then there was a small party, a very small party at first, because the idea was foreign to the Arabs, of those who believed that the Prophet's true successor must be his son; and as there was no surviving son, his son-in-law, Ali ibn Abu Talib, who was also the Prophet's first cousin should succeed. Ali had been one of the three earliest converts. He had always fought selflessly and had been greatly loved by the Prophet. The Prophet had included him and his wife in the *Ahl al-Bait* (members of the Prophet's own family).

The last group was that of the old Meccan aristocrats, the clan of Abu Sufyan, the Omayyads, who had been leaders of Mecca before the advent of Islam. These people were rich, knew the world, and had learnt diplomacy. Many of them were educated. A number of them had talent. They thought that nobody was more worthy of leading the new nation of Islam than they, who knew how to lead men.

Election of Abu Bakr. It is not surprising that the people worked fast: something big was at stake. But the Arabs loved their traditions; among them the headman of the tribe was chosen, not on grounds of parentage, but on grounds of seniority, wisdom, and prestige. There were very few men in Medina at that time who were more respected for their piety, their wisdom, and their character than Abu Bakr, the lifelong and trusted friend of the Prophet, who was also his father-in-law. The Muhajirin decided that he should represent them. Omar ibn al-Khattab, who was a very dynamic man and who had a strong personality, spoke for him to the Ansar. It did not take him long to convince the Ansar that Abu Bakr was the most deserving man in Medina to be the first successor of the Prophet, the Caliph of Islam. When these two major groups agreed, the other two parties, which were in a minority, had to accept the decision of the others. So Abu Bakr was elected. There was surprise and even disappointment in some quarters, but no opposition.

Abu Bakr (632-634). The task before the first Caliph was no easy one. The Prophet had not lived long enough to weld the people of Arabia into one nation. Old habits, old customs, old patterns of thought and behaviour take long to die, and there are always some mischievous or wild people in every country. The various tribes had lived separate and independent lives for a long time. Although there were broad groupings among the tribes, it was too much to expect that the people would agree to become one nation in a short time. Many a nation falls apart when a strong ruler or leader dies, and this is what happened in Arabia. Abu Bakr found that a very difficult task was thrust upon him. A number of tribes shook off the overlordship of Medina and refused to pay homage to the new Caliph, or to accept his orders; some of them even denied Islam. This was a serious situation.

Revolt of Musailimah and Sajah. Abu Bakr did not falter. He knew that his work was going to be very difficult, but he was a man who could make a quick decision. The rebels must be subdued. Fortunately for Islam, he had a great general with him, the gifted Khalid ibn al-Walid. He gave him the command of a hastily summoned volunteer army and sent him against the worst of the rebels, Musailimah, who came to be called the *Kazzab* (the Liar), because he claimed to be a prophet. He belonged to the tribe of Bani Hanifah and he had raised his banner of revolt in Yamamah, the central part of Arabia. Musailimah had a large following and had been joined by a woman leader, Sajah, who belonged to the neighbouring tribe of Bani Tamim. These two now married and joined their forces. But Khalid was a general whose like the world has seldom seen. He came upon the combined forces of the two and defeated them at the Battle of Arqabah. Moreover, he taught such a lesson to the rebels that many minor rebellions died down of themselves. Khalid put down one or two other risings, and soon all Arabia was united under the banner of the Caliph of Islam.

Campaign in Syria. Another task now awaited the first Caliph, this was the campaign in Syria. The Prophet had sent messages of goodwill, with an invitation to accept Islam, to the rulers of Persia and Syria. The proud Persian Chosroes had merely turned out the Arab messenger with a few words of contempt, but the Roman (Byzantine) governor of Syria had put the messenger to death. This was an outrage. No honourable monarch treats the envoy of another ruler in such a way. This had happened in A.D. 626. The Prophet had called up a few thousand volunteers and sent them out under the command of his adopted son, Zayd ibn Haritha, in A.D. 630. The raw soldiers of early Islam were no match for the trained and heavily armed Byzantine army, and had suffered a defeat. Zayd had died fighting. The Prophet was busy with the Meccans at the time and later with the Jews. He had died soon after, so the campaign in Syria had not been taken up seriously again. Now that the first Caliph was free of the Arab rebels, he turned his attention to Syria. He organized three small armies and sent them out separately under the commands of Amr ibn al-As, Yezid ibn Abi Sufyan, and Shurahbil ibn Hasanah. Each commander was given 3,000 fighting men. These armies fought a few minor battles with the Byzantines and were successful. The Byzantine Emperor, who ruled a mighty empire from his capital, Byzantium (Constantinople), now sent down a large army under his brother Theodorus. The Caliph soon came to know of this and decided to send over Khalid ibn al-Walid as Commander-in-Chief of the Syrian armies. Khalid was campaigning in Iraq at the time. When he received his orders he took about 900 men with him and made one of the swiftest marches in history. He crossed the waterless desert that separated Iraq and Syria in eighteen days. Thirsty and worn out, but undaunted in spirit, this valiant son of Islam suddenly appeared before the walls of Damascus. His name was well known; his arrival spread panic in the ranks of the enemy.

The Battle of Yarmuk (636). The Byzantines had some Arab allies. A large Arab tribe, the Bani Ghassan, had migrated to Palestine, accepted Christianity, and settled in what is today Jordan, in the sixth century. They had a strong army of their own. The Byzantine Commander-in-Chief now flung these Ghassanids against Khalid's small army. But Khalid was like lightning, impossible to catch. He made such an impetuous attack on the Bani Ghassan that he defeated them in the Battle of Marj Rahit. He then joined the other Arab forces. It was at this time that the Caliph died, but the people soon elected Omar ibn al-Khattab, Abu Bakr's right-hand man, as his successor. So the campaign in Syria went on. The second Caliph, for reasons not understood to this day by many, despatched another Commander-in-Chief over Khalid; he was Abu Obaidah ibn al-Jarrah, a venerable Companion of the Prophet, but no general. He was, however, a wise man. He kept Khalid as the Deputy Commander and the campaign did not suffer. The two armies at last met on the banks of the small river Yarmuk. The day was hot and windy, and dust and sand blew in from the desert. Khalid chose the ground and the day. The northern men of the Byzantine army did not like the situation at all, but they fought bravely, even desperately. It is said that they linked themselves together with chains, but they could not withstand the whirlwind attacks of the Arabs. The new army of Islam, though inexperienced and ill-trained cut down the great Byzantine army, and there was great slaughter. The river ran blood and the army of the Emperor was utterly destroyed. The Muslims had won their greatest battle so far. They had also won a decisive battle. After A.D. 636 Syria was lost to the Christians.

Campaign in Iraq—Death of Abu Bakr. The Muslim army of Iraq though deprived of their commander, fought on, but did not do so well. The Persian army which came against them was heavily armed and vastly superior in numbers, so the Muslims lost an important battle called the Battle of the Bridge. Meanwhile Abu Bakr, the true man of God, had died and Medina was again plunged in sorrow. Fortunately for Islam, however, the great Omar was ready to take over. Everybody knew his calibre. So nobody opposed his nomination by the dying Abu Bakr as his successor. The first Caliph had reigned for two years only, but they had been vital years. He had done three great things: he had won back Arabia and re-affirmed the faith; he had launched the campaign in

Syria; he had begun the compilation of the Qur'an and had the Suras recorded. These three were no mean achievements. He was a quiet man, but a man of firm decisions and sound judgement. His election had been a good choice.

Omar Ibn al-Khattab (634-644)—Conquest of Persia. His successor was, however, a much greater man; a man of great powers, of iron will, of stern justice, of passionate loyalty, and one who had a remarkable gift for administration. He took stock of the situation and gave orders that the campaigns in Syria and Iraq be carried on. It was during his reign that the famous Battle of Yarmuk was fought and won. It was now that the Muslim army of Iraq came into its own under General Saad ibn Abu Waqqas. It engaged the Persians in a mighty battle at Qadisiya. The Persians were led by their Shah-in-Shah, the Chosroes himself, whose name was Yezdjird. The Muslims inflicted a severe defeat on the Persians at this battle. The Persians retreated, and the Muslims pursued them. Madain, the capital of Persia, was attacked and captured. The Arabs entered the town of the mighty Chosroes; they sat and feasted in the palaces of those great rulers. It was not long before the Persians rallied and gave battle at Jalula, but they were again defeated. There were other small battles, and then the Persians pooled all their resources and their Chosroes gave battle to the advancing Arabs for the last time. This was the Battle of Nihavand (641), which laid into dust the glory of the Sassanids. Yezdjird was finally defeated and he fled with a small following. He became a wanderer after this and went to the eastern provinces to lead the life of a fugitive. He died ten years later.

Conquest of Syria. On the Syrian front the Muslims had not stopped at the victory over the Byzantines at Yarmuk. Damascus had fallen in 635 to Khalid the Conqueror. He had been very just in the terms he had given to the conquered, thereby setting a pattern which was followed by later Muslim conquerors everywhere. The terms were approved by Omar, the great Caliph. Khalid had promised that the life and the property of the conquered people would be safe; the new Muslim rulers would look after them, and they would be left to follow their own religious practices. This was because the Muslims never forced their religion on anybody. Allah had declared: 'There is no compulsion in religion,' and few Muslims ever broke this commandment. Khalid also had given orders that the city should not be looted or any houses burnt. In return, he had asked the conquered to pay a nominal tax per head, to which the people had gladly agreed. After Yarmuk, Abu Obaidah, the new Commander-in-Chief, with his deputy the glorious Khalid, went and besieged Jerusalem, the holy city of the Christians and called al-Quds by Muslims. Abu Obaidah led the attack on one side and Khalid attacked from the other. Khalid won his way through. Meanwhile the Christian High Priest surrendered to Abu Obaidah, who was led into the town by him. The two Muslim forces met in the heart of the town. From one side came the dignified Abu Obaidah escorted by the High Priest; from the other came the conquering hero, Khalid. Abu Obaidah told Khalid that the High Priest had surrendered. Khalid said: 'No. We have conquered!' Both were right, because half of the town had been conquered by Khalid. That meant that the conquered part belonged to the conquerors; the other half had surrendered, for which terms were to be different. There was disagreement between the two Commanders, but Khalid was firm in his claim. So the matter was referred to the Caliph at Medina.

Omar's Journey to Syria. Omar the Great decided to come and give his decision in person. He took his camel and his slave and left for Jerusalem, a journey of many days. What a contrast between this humble lord of the Islamic world, who went with one follower to the scene of the conquest, and the later Muslim kings, who were always surrounded by large bodyguards. But the wonderful thing about this journey was the fact that he shared the rides with his slave; now the master would be up and the slave walking and now the slave would be riding and the master walking. It so happened that when they entered Jerusalem, the Commander-in-Chief and his famous captains, as well as the astonished High Priest, saw a curious spectacle: the great Caliph was walking beside the camel and the slave was riding. The terms of settlement were equally wonderful. Omar decided that the half conquered by Muslim arms would be Muslim territory and the half surrendered by the High Priest would remain under Christian authority, though under the overlordship of the Muslim governor of the town. Everybody was satisfied with this arrangement.

Conquest of Egypt. We must now turn to the third front of the wars of Islam in this period, which was Egypt. Amr ibn al-As, a seasoned general, asked the Caliph to give him an army to lead into Egypt. Since Amr knew the land of Egypt and had proved his worth and skill in the wars of Syria, Omar agreed. Amr was given his army and he advanced into Egypt. It was not a large army, having only 4,000 horsemen, but the Muslims were undaunted by large hostile armies. Amr was victorious from the beginning. He first captured the town of al-Farama in eastern Egypt. He next conquered the important town of Bilbays. Soon he came before the walls of the famous fortress of Babiliyun, a very great Byzantine centre. He now felt that he needed more troops. Fortunately Zubair ibn al-Awwam, a leader of the Muhajirin, came up with 6,000 more men. Leaving half his army to besiege Babiliyun, Amr advanced and captured the town of Ayn Shams. Cyrus, the Commander of Babiliyun, grew afraid, and felt he could not hold out long. He asked, therefore, for terms. Amr gave an answer which became famous in history. He said: 'If you wish to accept Islam, you are welcome and your people are welcome. If you do so, you will become our brothers. But there is no compulsion in our religion. If, however, you do not wish to become Muslims, you can surrender and pay tribute. We shall treat you well. If you do not agree, then let us fight it out. Allah will decide.' Cyrus surrendered. Only one town held out; it was the great port of Alexandria in the north. Amr's forces soon swept up to it. The Emperor sent down a large army to help the garrison, but nothing availed. That town also surrendered and the Muslims became the masters of Egypt. For his achievements, Amr was made Governor of Egypt as the great Khalid had been made the Governor of Syria and Palestine. The Muslims found Alexandria fabulously rich. It had been a great seat of culture for centuries. There were many schools and academies there, but it is not true that there was a great library which was burnt by the orders of the Caliph. Many European writers have said this, but it has been proved entirely wrong; the library had been burnt twice before, the last time three hundred years before the Muslims ever set foot on Egyptian soil.

Omar's Achievements. Omar now ruled as the Caliph of Islam over vast lands. Besides Arabia, the Caliphate included Egypt, Palestine, Syria, Iraq, Persia, and Khorasan. All these countries had been conquered within ten years of the Prophet's death. Omar was a wise and far-sighted administrator. He retained in all the conquered lands the same political divisions, the same currency, and the same civil administration. Only the Muslim law now prevailed everywhere. The *Ahl al-Kitab,* Christians, Jews, and even Zoroastrians were termed Dhimmis, which means 'those who are in trust'. Their customs, their religious practices, and their laws were protected. Their lands were not taken from them. The Muslim governors and commanders were asked to live outside the conquered towns; so they first lived in camps, mostly under tents. The Muslim capital of Egypt in those days was a town which grew out of such a camp and was called al-Fustat (the town of tents). Basra and Kufa, the new twin towns of Iraq, also began as tented camps. Omar gave many new things to the nascent Islamic State. He organized the Public Treasury; he settled pensions on the Companions of the Prophet and other noted Medinites; he made sure that the Arabs followed a straightforward code of manners and conduct; he was very democratic and tried to root out superstition. The vast Muslim lands were organized so capably that his name came to be held in the highest respect even in non-Muslim countries. But he had not reigned for more than ten years when he was struck down in the mosque of the Prophet by a freed slave. He was mortally wounded, but even on his death-bed he called a council of the six most prominent Medinites and asked them to elect somebody as his successor. Their choice fell on Osman, the seventy-year-old Companion of the Prophet, who had had the honour of being the Prophet's son-in-law twice. Omar died, and with his death began a train of events which ended in disaster a generation later.

Osman (644-656). Osman ibn Affan was the third Caliph. He came of the family of Omayyah; his election shows that the Muslims made no distinction between the near relations of the Prophet and the relations of the faction which had opposed the Prophet only twenty years before. Osman was a man of substance, having been successfully engaged in business most of his life. He was a generous, warm-hearted man, gentle in manner, and very understanding: a truly venerable person whom everybody respected. He began well. The conquests, which started in the time of Abu Bakr and quickened in the years of Omar, continued for some years. Muslim armies conquered Tripolitania to the west of Egypt. The Muslim navy engaged the Byzantine fleet near Cyprus and defeated it, and Cyprus was captured. A few minor additions were made on the northern borders of Syria and Iraq and the north-eastern flanks of Persia. But then the wave of conquest stopped. The Muslims had a breathing spell. The Arabs, who had been busy conquering and settling in the new lands, now had some leisure. With leisure came thought, and with thought emerged some of the old pagan ideas.

Unrest. One cardinal fact must be remembered—Arab society was built on a tribal system, and each tribe was an independent body of men. There had never been an idea of an

Arab State before and people had never owed loyalty to one supreme head. When Islam gave the Arabs a sense of unity, a new religion, an idea of brotherhood, the Arabs accepted it, but these ideas were long in taking root. What kept old rivalries, old suspicions, and distrust of others down was the glow of the new faith and the glory of the conquests. A strong ruler helped. Everybody respected and even feared Omar. His successor was a very saintly man, but not strong as Omar had been. Moreover he interpreted certain verses of the Qur'an, of which he was a great scholar, too literally; he began to give positions of trust to his own relatives, all of them of the house of Omayyah. He used his judgement in this and he honestly believed them to be competent men. But his opinion was not shared by others. For instance, he removed Amr ibn al-As, the conqueror of Egypt, from his post as governor and appointed his own foster-brother, Abdullah, as governor instead; this Abdullah had at one time incurred the displeasure of the Prophet. Osman also made Marwan ibn al-Hakam his secretary; Marwan had for a time been a renegade. These and similar appointments created unrest. Things became worse because as Osman grew older, Marwan assumed greater powers, and soon he was issuing orders in the name of the Caliph, and these orders were neither just nor free from nepotism or intrigue.

Conspiracies and Rebellion. Soon little groups of interested or designing people began to talk against the Caliph. They said he was being influenced by an evil-minded man (Marwan). It should be remembered that it never took long to inflame the Arabs. Since they were men of action, their reaction to any problem was a practical one, and there was thus open talk in Medina against Osman. Even important Medinites, such as Talha and Zubair did not hesitate to criticize the actions of the Caliph. They asked Lady Aisha, the widow of the Prophet, known as the 'Mother of the Muslims,' to interfere, which that wise lady would not do to such a venerable man as the Caliph. They also asked Ali, the other son-in-law of the Prophet and the head of the House of Hashim, but he said his position was delicate; it was not for him to tell the Caliph what he should do and what he should not do, because in the votes cast by the council of six at Omar's death, Ali had figured second on the list. Moreover, he was obviously the next choice as Caliph. The Arabs had taken decisions so far in a traditional manner and had chosen senior people. By now Ali was in his fifties, and was afraid that if he interfered, Osman might think that Ali considered himself a better man. Ali had a few private words with the Caliph, nevertheless, but Osman, who was now over eighty years old, would not listen to him or anybody. He said he would not abandon the position for which the people had elected him.

Assassination of Osman. When Amr ibn al-As had been dismissed he had not come to Medina, but many of his followers who were veteran soldiers had come to the Prophet's town. Others, more hot-headed than even these, came from Kufa. Malik al-Ashtar, an experienced captain, and Muhammad ibn Abu Bakr, another young leader of the insurgents, now became violent. The situation became so dangerous that even Talha and Zubair withdrew. Ali became alarmed and posted his sons, al-Hasan and al-Husain, the grandsons of the Prophet, with the sons of other prominent Medinites near the house of Osman as guards. But during a temporary absence of these vigilantes, the rioters broke into Osman's house from the back. He was reading the Qur'an at the time, but they struck him down, and his blood was spilled over the pages of the Holy Book.

Ali (656-661). There was an outcry at this deed, and the actors in this ugly drama were themselves aghast at what they had done. Even the people hostile to Osman were shocked. Things could not, however, be left in a state of confusion or there might have been disorder in the Muslim world. Someone had to take things in hand, and there was no difference of opinion, at least not at the beginning, on who was now the most suitable man in the Caliphate to take up the burden of this large state. Ali, son of Abu Talib, was elected unanimously. Ali was a very forthright man who knew no political tricks. He saw the truth clearly, and knew where his duty lay. He considered the Caliphate as a trust; he was not only responsible to Allah for his actions, he was responsible also to the entire Muslim world. He did not, therefore, see any justification in winning over the disturbing factors and the possible leaders of opposition. Indeed it was not yet clear who these were, but there were signs that there would be trouble from three possible sources.

(a)   The Omayyads, a prominent member of whose clan had been assassinated. Their leader was Muawiyah, who had been Governor of Syria and Palestine for over fifteen years.

(b)   The prominent Medinites, such as Talha and Zubair, leaders of considerable reputation, wise old men, who had protested strongly against the alleged favouritism of Osman.

(c)   The extremists, a body of puritans who disliked political intrigues and wanted to live according to a literal interpretation of the Word of Allah.

Risings in Medina and Syria. As it happened, not one, but all three factions became dangerous. Nobody was more unlucky than Ali, the great fighter, the wise counsellor, and the man of God, who had been so near the Prophet; there was nothing but war and disaster in the short period of his Caliphate. The trouble started as a result of Ali's decision to move his capital to a more central place. The decision was wise, but its immediate and ultimate effects were very bad. When he moved to Kufa, the new Arab town in Iraq, he left the discontented elements behind him in Medina. Under his eye they might have kept quiet, in his absence their discontent grew. Ali's next action aroused them further. He removed the unsuitable officials raised to high office by Osman. The prominent Medinites such as Talha and Zubair did not forgive Ali for the fact that he did not select them or their partisans for any high office, so they decided to do something about it. But it was a problem to know what they could do against such a man as Ali who was not unjust, corrupt, or a weakling; who showed no favouritism; who was not unversed in the ways of government, and who had been a prominent counsellor of Omar the Great. They wondered if they could blame Osman's martyrdom on him, although he had had nothing to do with it; they could say that he should have stopped it and his first duty should have been to institute an inquiry. It is possible that they sincerely believed in their cause. They tried to get Aisha, the Mother of the Muslims, on their side. She was a wise lady, but they tried to persuade her that she ought to avenge the blood of Osman. They went to her and told her that Malik al-Ashtar and Muhammad ibn Abu Bakr (her own brother) had been the leaders of the riot which ended in the death of Osman. Malik al-Ashtar was an officer in Ali's army and Muhammad's widowed mother was now one of the wives of Ali. Obviously, they said she must see justice done. Ali would not avenge Osman's death and she must do something about it. At last she was persuaded. She did not like the idea of going to war, but if it was her duty, she felt she must do it.

Battle of the Camel. The result was that Talha and Zubair and other prominent Medinites assembled an army and taking Aisha with them, left for Kufa. Ali soon learnt of their intentions. He was innocent, the world knew that, and it was not proved that Malik al-Ashtar and Muhammad ibn Abu Bakr were the actual assassins. He wanted no bloodshed between Muslims; if the Medinites wanted trouble, they must be stopped. He met the advancing army near Basra in December 656. He tried to persuade Aisha to stop this senseless war, but her counsellors would not agree. The only thing left was to fight. Aisha rode a white dromedary; Ali ordered that she must be captured, because that was the only way to end bloodshed. The Medinites fought round the camel fanatically and the battle is known as 'the Battle of the Camel'. It is said that seventy people died before her brother, Muhammad ibn

Abu Bakr, reached her *mahmil* (litter) and tried to lift her out. At this outrage she cried out, 'What impious hand dare touch the Mother of the Muslims?' Muhammad answered: 'The same whom your mother carried in her womb for many months.' The battle ended in a victory for Ali. Talha and Zubair lost their lives on the battlefield, but Ali treated Aisha with great honour. She was so impressed by Ali's nobility of conduct that she renounced politics. She was sent with an escort to Medina with all honours. In spite of this, nothing was settled.

Battle of Siffin. Seeing that the Medinites could not depose Ali, Muawiyah, who was now a powerful man in Syria, who had a strong army of his own, and was head of the House of Omayyah, decided to try his luck against Ali. He now claimed to be the avenger of Osman's death. It was not, he said, that Osman belonged to the clan of the Bani Omayyah, it was only that he was an innocent martyr and his blood cried for revenge. Muawiyah showed the blood-stained shirt of the martyred Osman to the people, seeking their support, and soon felt himself in a strong enough position to fight. Many people thought that it was a revival of the old rivalry between the Houses of Omayyah and Hashim, but were powerless to prevent it. Muawiyah's army moved east. Ali moved north with his troops. The two armies met at Siffin which lay in north-eastern Syria. Muawiyah had a strong army, but Ali was the better general. Soon Muawiyah found that he could not win, so he thought of a ruse. He ordered his soldiers to tie their Qur'ans to their lances and raise them in the air, which they did. Ali saw through this and told his army that it was a trick, but the soldiers could not cut down men who held up the Qur'an. The fighting ceased.

The Arbitration. Muawiyah now proposed an arbitration; he and Ali should each choose a nominee and leave the matter to them. Ali agreed, because he did not want any more bloodshed, but a number of people in his own camp were not pleased. They said that since Ali was in the right he should not leave such a matter to the arbitration of man. These people belonged to the party of the puritans who disliked political intrigues and wanted to live according to a literal interpretation of the Word of Allah. They said arbitration was for Allah. They also declared that Ali was making a big mistake and would lose their support. After this, they decided to withdraw from Ali's side. Others said that by accepting arbitration Ali had lost all prestige because he thus accepted Muawiyah as his equal although Muawiyah was his subordinate and now a rebel, as he had risen against the Caliph. It appeared to them that Ali had thus tacitly accepted the fact that Muawiyah had a cause, when he had none. What was worse, Ali made a wrong choice. Muawiyah selected a friend of his, the astute Amr ibn al-As, as his nominee; Ali nominated a neutral, Musa al-Ashari. Now Musa, though a famous Companion of the Prophet, was at heart not a great friend of Ali, so he did not advocate Ali's cause as strongly as he could have done. The result was that the arbitrators made a curious decision, they announced that both Muawiyah and Ali should resign. This was really a condemnation of Ali, because Muawiyah was a subordinate who had already rebelled against the Caliph and could not continue in his office. So the verdict was in reality against Ali and he did not accept it. For that matter, neither did Muawiyah. Both armies retreated, and the same state of affairs continued. Ali's loss, however, was double, as Amr ibn al-As openly accepted Muawiyah as the *de facto* Caliph.

The Khawarij Rebellion. The radical puritans now openly left Ali's side and set up as a separate party calling themselves the *Khawarij*, which means seceders or those who have withdrawn. They elected their own Caliph, a Kufan called Abdullah al-Rasibi. It was not long before the Khawarij assembled an army of their own; then they revolted. Ali went against them and defeated them at Nahrawan. Seeing Ali so occupied, Muawiyah sent an army into Egypt and reconquered it. He then appointed Amir ibn al-As as his own Governor of

Egypt and so the land beyond the cradle of Islam was thus practically split.

The Assassination of Ali. Seeing that the Caliphate was divided in this manner, the Khawarij, who had gone underground after their defeat at Nahrawan, now worked out an infernal plot. They decided that Islam was divided because of the differences of Ali and Muawiyah; they also considered Amr ibn al-As to be an evil force. So they decided to kill all three of them. It was planned that all three should be struck down at the same time. The tragedy was that Muawiyah escaped with a scratch, Amr was unhurt, but Ali was mortally wounded. Abdur Rahman ibn Muljam, a fanatic, struck him with a poisoned sword when he was on his way to the mosque. Thus died the last of the great Caliphs and with him died the true concept of a Muslim ruler, one who combined the functions of the Head of State and of Religion; a true representative of the Great Prophet.

Achievements of the Orthodox Caliphs. The four great Caliphs were now dead, and a whole world died with them. After them, the Muslims had many other Caliphs, but except for one or two, there never again appeared a man who was as good, as true, as spiritual as these four. All of them had done something remarkable. Abu Bakr, who came first, won back Arabia for Islam. He started the holy wars and the campaigns which led the Muslims to world empire. Omar the Great was a man of iron, a great personality, a great law-giver, and a great administrator, under whose wise rule Muslim armies triumphed everywhere, and Islam conquered Persia, Iraq, Syria, and Egypt. Then came Osman, a gentle, humane, and generous man, whose great claim to fame is that he had the verses of the Qur'an collected, checked, certified, and codified. A standard version of the Qur'an was thus made and given to the world, which has not changed by so much as a comma since his days. The Muslims conquered Tripolitania in his time and extended into Khorasan. They built a navy and in their first naval battle defeated the Byzantine navy off the coast of Cyprus and so annexed Cyprus. Then came Ali, the great champion of Islam, who had to fight all the four years of his Caliphate, but who never lost a battle, who established a just and impartial rule, who was an enemy of intrigue, of crooked thinking and wrong-doing, who was truly democratic, and who lost his life because he could not compromise with evil. The work of these Caliphs lived after them and the lands conquered in their time have remained Islamic.

Al-Hasan (661). When Ali died, the people of Kufa elected his elder son, al-Hasan, as Caliph. The world of Islam accepted the choice. For some months nothing happened, but then Muawiyah, who had by now been governor of Syria for about twenty years and who had become semi-independent in the last years of Ali's Caliphate and had annexed Egypt to his 'Kingdom of Syria', declared himself Caliph of Islam. He had a compact army under him, was lord of three settled and rich provinces, and had a capable general in Amr ibn al-As to support him. He was also an aggressive man and asked al-Hasan to resign. Al-Hasan, who has been remembered by Islam as Imam Hasan, Imam meaning, 'the leader', was the opposite of Muawiyah. He was kindness itself, gentle, and very good-natured; though calm, balanced, and capable he disliked an office which was envied by others, which caused hatred, led to bloodshed, and was the reason for internal wars. Now Amir Muawiyah wanted power, but he did not want unnecessary bloodshed. When, therefore, he heard that Imam Hasan had decided to abdicate rather than plunge the world of Islam into civil war, he offered to settle a liberal pension on Imam Hasan and the *Ahl al-Bait* (the family of Ali). The offer was accepted and Imam Hasan retired to Medina. There he lived a life devoted to holy living and domestic happiness. His presence and that of his younger brother, Imam Husain, were considered a blessing by the people of Medina. He lived for another eight years, dying in A.D. 669, some say as a result of poison administered by a slave girl in his house. He was a noble man with a cool mind, and a great lover of peace.

Al-Husain. The head of the House of Hashim was now the younger son of Ali, called Imam Husain. He stayed in Medina, and the family pension and grants fixed for the holy family continued. Amir Muawiyah, who was now Lord of the Muslim world, had been Caliph for eight years. He ruled the Muslim lands wisely and well, and he maintained and even increased the prestige of the Muslims in the wider world. Imam Husain led a peaceful life and devoted himself to piety and good works. When Amir Muawiyah died in A.D. 680, Imam Husain had been living with his family in Mecca for some time. Amir Muawiyah, in spite of his political astuteness, made a blunder in his last six months. He nominated his son, Yezid, as his successor, without first finding out whether he would be acceptable to the Muslims at large. He also asked the notables of the court and the nobles who were in the capital at Damascus to vow allegiance to Yezid. Amir Muawiyah enjoyed great prestige, and his courtiers and nobles accepted his orders. Yezid was nominated, and on Muawiyah's death he was proclaimed Caliph. Now Yezid had been a promising man in his youth, but lately he had taken to a life of pleasure. In the early days of Islam this sort of life was considered more than irreligious. In a Caliph it was considered impious and to most Muslims an outrage. The puritans were the ones most disturbed by it. Kufa, a growing Arab town, was crammed with men of various ideas. Many of them had strong views about the duties of Caliphs. They declared that the nomination of a man like Yezid was an insult to God and man.

The Invitation from Kufa. They wrote to Imam Husain and begged him to come to Kufa and guide them and lead them. They said Kufa was the seat of his father's government. He was Ali's son, the grandson of the Prophet, and it was his duty to save Islam. They said that the Muslims of the world and even the future generations would never forgive him if he did not take up the cause of righteousness. Imam Husain wrote back saying that he was friendless, he had no following, he had no money; Yezid was the head of a powerful state, and it would be madness to take up a cause which was so unequal. The Kufans wrote back saying that they were solidly behind him and once he came there, the entire province, as also the whole of Persia, would give him support. Imam Husain consulted Abdullah ibn al-Zubair, the leader of the Meccan Muslims. Abdullah himself had not yet accepted Yezid as a Caliph, and was longing for a fight, and he tried to dissuade Imam Husain. As a precaution, therefore, Imam Husain sent a personal envoy of his own, his cousin, Muslim ibn Aqil, to Kufa, to find out the truth and write to him. When Muslim ibn Aqil reached Kufa, he was welcomed with open arms. He wrote back assuring Imam Husain that everything was all right and advised him to come.

Imam Husain leaves for Kufa. Imam Husain, therefore, left for Kufa towards the end of September 680. He advanced in slow stages and reached the River Euphrates, on whose right bank Kufa was situated, early in October 680. The news of his coming naturally reached the Governor, Obaidullah ibn Ziyad, a second cousin of Yezid. He was a hard man who was ruthless in his dealings. He had already outlawed Muslim ibn Aqil, captured him and his two small sons and had killed them. He now sent a patrol under the command of Hurr ibn Yezid Tamimi, with orders to intercept Husain. Hurr came full of hostile purposes, but after a talk with Imam Husain, became convinced of the purity of his intentions, and instead of opposing him, joined his party. Obaidullah was furious. He now sent a small army under his general, Omar ibn Saad. Omar was a fair-minded man. He was the son of Saad ibn Abi Waqqas, the conqueror of Persia. He brought his 3,000 troops and camped at Karbala where Imam Husain's party had halted.

Commander Omar challenges Husain. He now sent a message to Imam Husain, asking him to surrender. Imam Husain replied that he was a peaceful man, he had committed no offence, done wrong to nobody, and asked why he was being treated in this way. Commander Omar said: 'I am a soldier. These are my orders. I am sorry, but I must ask you to surrender.' Then he added: 'You can, however, vow allegiance to the reigning Caliph and if you do so you can go your way.' Imam Husain had now a vital decision to make; he had to choose between obedience to Allah and obedience to man. He did not consider Yezid fit for the exalted office of the Caliph of Islam. If he were to submit, it would mean he would deny Allah and choose evil. He would then be selling his honour and betraying the trust the Muslims had in a grandson of the Prophet. He did not hesitate. He replied: 'This is a personal matter, between me and Yezid. Permit me to go to Yezid; I will discuss the matter with him. If your orders do not permit you to send me there, let me go back to Medina. If the authorities do not even like that, I shall go to the ends of the Muslim world, to even distant Khorasan with my family. I shall then be out of it all.'

Battle of Karbala (10 Oct. 680). Omar was considering the proposal of Imam Husain, but one of his captains, a fiery and villainous man, Shimr ibn Zil-Joshan, spoke violently against the move, accused Omar of womanishness and treachery, roused his own regiment, and by his violent words and threats of punishment, persuaded the Iraqi army to fall upon Imam Husain's small band. The little group of relatives, friends, and followers, numbering only about a hundred, drew up in battle order. The battle began at about ten in the morning on 10 October 680. There were individual combats between the stalwarts of Imam Husain's party and the Iraqi's in which the Imam's people distinguished themselves. They fought with a heroism unseen even in Arabia before, but the battle was too unequal. One by one Husain's brothers, cousins, nephews, and son died like martyrs around him. Husain laid the dead bodies by the tents. It was now midday, so he said his *Zuhr* prayers, bade farewell to his family, and went to his last fight. He would not strike the first blow and nobody dared to attack the grandson of the Prophet at first. At last, spurred and stung by the taunts of captains like Shimr, the soldiers advanced in a body and attacked him. He fought an epic battle, but at last was so wounded that he fell from his horse. The Iraqi cavalry then trampled him down. They cut off his head and sent it with the rest of the *Ahl al-Bait* to Yezid. Yezid was not pleased by the turn of events, but he received the family with honour. Ali, one of the sons of Imam Husain who had been ill, had survived. Yezid apologized to him and declared again and again that he was not responsible for the tragedy. He said that Obaidullah had exceeded his orders, but nobody has ever believed him. His name is cursed for all times.

Sunnis and Shiites. An account must be given here of the Shiite creed which was to have such influence in later centuries on the history of the Muslim world. The creed is not difficult to understand. It had a political origin, differing from the Sunnis, in considering Ali to be the true heir of the Prophet and Ali's descendants to be the rightful Caliphs or the legitimate heads of the Islamic state. In religion, however, a wide difference arose between the Sunnis and the Shiites. The Sunnis believe that Muhammad was a man like others, except that he was the best of men, and that Allah sent the Word to him through the revelations; that all Muslims are equal and that that man is best in the sight of Allah who follows His Commandments in word and spirit and thus obeys Him most. The majority of Shiites called Ithna Asharis believe that Muhammad was 'appointed' and that his spiritual powers did not die with him. They think that he was sinless and possessed some semi-divine attributes. These spiritual powers and godly qualities were inherited by Ali, then by al-Hasan, later by al-Husain and through him by nine of his descendants who were called Imams. These Imams were all sinless and also 'appointed' by Allah, and they all possessed the semi-divine qualities originally possessed by Muhammad. They were the real leaders of Islam and, since the Sunnis did not recognize them, they committed a great sin. The names of these Imams are as follows: Ali ibn Abu Talib, Hasan ibn Ali, Husain ibn Ali, Ali ibn Husain (Zain-ul-Abidin), Muhammad Baqir, Ja'far al-Sadiq, Musa al-Kazim, Ali al-Rida, Muhammad al-Taqi, al-Naqi, Hasan al-Askari, and Imam Mahdi. The last Imam is believed to have disappeared as a boy, but he is said to be still living, and will appear at a time of great crisis and revive Islam. The idea of the Imamate is, therefore, the crux of the Shiite creed. There are two other major sects of the Shiites, the Ismailis, called the Seveners and Zaidis, called the Firers. The Ismailis believe that the true seventh Imam was the eldest son of Imam Ja'far al-Sadiq who pre-deceased his father but he had been nominated as Imam Ja'far's successor and hence his descendants continue to be the true Imams to this day. The present Imam (the Imam-i-Hazir) being Prince Karim Agha Khan. The Firers believe that the eldest son of Imam Zain-ul-Abidin called Zaid, who died a martyr fighting for his rights against the Omayyads, was the true fifth Imam and his descendants until lately (the Imams of Yemen) were the true Imams.

The Shiite Books and Sects. Since there are such differences between the creeds of the two sects, it is not difficult to understand that the Shiites did not accept the Sunni Books of Traditions or even the Sunni Schools of Law. They had their own divines and their own compilers of Traditions. Four books hold the highest positions in Shiite religious literature. They were compiled however rather late, that is in the tenth and eleventh centuries. The first one is called *Al Kafi fi Ilm al-Din* and was written by the great scholar Muhammad ibn Yaqub al-Kulaini. It contains over sixteen thousand Shiite traditions. The second book is called *Kitab Man la Yadhuruh al-faqih* (Everyman his own Lawyer) and was written by Ibn Musa ibn Babuwaihi, popularly known as Ibn Babuya. This book contains 4,496 traditions. The third and fourth books were written by the same learned scholar who was respected for his learning by both the Shiites and the Sunnis. He was

Muhammad ibn Hasan al-Tusi. His books are called *Tahdhib-al-Ahkam* (Correcting of Judgements) and the famous *Istibsar*. It must be realized that, like all creeds, Shiism has its gradations. There are moderates in it as well as extremists. Those nearest the Sunnis are the Zaidis who believe that the Imams were 'appointed' to their high office by Allah, but were not semi-divine creatures. Next come the Imamis who believe in the Imams being 'appointed', but also believe that the Imams were mortal like other men although they were sinless and the divine light *(Nur)* and power dwelt in them. Then come the extremists, among whom can be mentioned the Druses, some Ismailis, the Qarmatians, the Batinis, and the Nusairids who believe in the Imams as incarnations of God. The extreme Shiites, therefore, had little in common with the other Muslims.

Administrative and Cultural Conditions. Yathrib called after the Hijrah, Medina-al-Rasul and later only Medina, was no town. It was a fairly populous settlement of two or three tribes and their allies and dependants. Of these Aus and Khazraj were prominent. The total number of Muslims who migrated to Yathrib with the Prophet was seventy-two. So small was the number of Muslims at the time of the Battle of Badr, that only 313 *mujahids* could come out to fight. At the Battle of Uhud there were about 1,000 fighters on the Prophets' side. The small settlement was also no trade centre and no agricultural basin, so civic amenities were few. The entire life of the settlement revolved around the personality of the Prophet. The houses were mostly *kucha*. Only some residences of the rich were built of brick and mortar. The mosque of the Prophet was itself a rough and ready affair. Masudi says that it was only in the later half of Omar's glorious Caliphate, that the people began to use stone and costly wood for the erection of their houses. As for civic services like pavements, drains, street lighting, water supply, or medical care, there was yet no concept and no provision. Yet by Omar's time the Muslim

State was already well-organized, though on a semi-military basis.

Administrative Set-up in Omar's Time. In Omar's time, every Arab Muslim was a soldier. A system of almost military communism had been initiated. As Hitti says: 'Omar's policy was to organize the Arabians now all Muslims, into a complete religious military commonwealth, with its members keeping themselves pure and immunized—a sort of military aristocracy'. All Muslims were equal before the law. Omar had no precedent before him and yet he laid the foundations of a democratic state. There were two consultative bodies. One, the General Assembly, which was convened when a general announcement had to be made. Two, a Committee of Elders in which appointments and dismissals of public servants, and even matters of daily importance, were discussed and decided. There was a regular treasury now, called *Bait-al-Mal*. Revenues were called under *Kharaj*—land-tax collected from Muslims according to the fertility of soil and produce; *Jizya*—from non-Muslims in lieu of military service which was compulsory for the Believers (even the Romans called for this tax in their times); *Zakat*—from the rich to be distributed among the needy; and *Ushr*—a land-tax from the Muslims of Arabia only. *Usur* was a custom duty introduced by Omar on horse and camel traders—caravaneers. And lastly, there was the *Mal-e-Ghanimah,* which was really war booty or tributes collected from the newly conquered territories.

Economic and Cultural Affairs. As mentioned above, it was slowly that the Medinites and the Meccans gave attention to good building. It was in Osman's reign that the Companions of the Prophet began to erect mansions and the Principal Mosque was rebuilt with stone and marble. In dress, the Arabs remained conservative and because of climatic conditions, to this day use loose garments. Even the Qur'an permitted women to wear only looser under-dress in privacy. Normally the women wore a long, loose, open-necked shirt over *shalwar,* and a jacket in winter. The head was covered with a big handkerchief which was tied round it. They could attend sermons, take part in warfare, and move in society. This was especially so in Mecca which from ancient times had been an important entrepot, a sort of trade centre on the land route from Aden to Palestine, and beyond. Reference is made to it in Sura 'Quraish', Para 30.

Education. Omar took special interest in education. Ali was his adviser in this sphere as in most other matters. Schools were organized in the towns where theological subjects were taught. It is said that in a school in Syria, where educational traditions had existed since Hellenistic times, there were at one time 1,600 Muslim boys. Kufa and Basra the new towns, gradually became centres of learning. In secular studies, poetry held first place as this had been a favourite form of aesthetic and emotional expression with the Arabs since long. Osman had ordered that mathematics be added to the curriculum.

Terms given to the Conquered. A quotation from Baladhuri will suffice in this respect: 'In the name of Allah the Compassionate, the Merciful. This is what Khalid bin Walid would grant to the inhabitants of Damascus, if he enters therein. He promises to give them security for their lives, property, and churches. Their city walls shall not be demolished, neither shall any Muslim be quartered in their houses. Thereunto we give to them the Pact of Allah and the protection of His Prophet, the Caliphs and the Believers. So long as they pay the poll-tax, nothing but good shall befall them'.

The Greatest Achievement. The greatest achievement of the period of the Orthodox Caliphate was, however, the compilation and standardization of the Qur'an in the days of Osman. From that time onwards it became the Authorized Version. Besides, the Companions began collecting memorabilia of the Prophet and his sayings, which later, after much sifting, were collected into six authentic collections by the Sunnis and later still, into four comprehensive collections by the Shia divines. Many began collecting the legends of the prophets mentioned in the Qur'an, as well as stories of old kings. Muawiyah, for instance, was fond of listening to these legendary tales. Out of such activities grew the science of historiography (history writing—a great Islamic achievement).

CHAPTER 3

THE OMAYYADS

Amir Muawiyah (661-680). We must now go back a little. It will be recalled that Amir Muawiyah was threatening to overrun the eastern part of the Caliphate which acknowledged Imam Hasan as Caliph. It was when the fear of an internal war was quite near, that Imam Hasan decided to give up his office. He therefore retired to Medina and Amir Muawiyah was left unchallenged. He was soon accepted as the Caliph of Islam and he ruled as such for twenty years. He was a very capable ruler and had plenty of experience behind him; he had been governor of Syria for nearly twenty years, and had built up a Syrian army and navy; he had joined Abdullah ibn Abi Sarh, the governor of Egypt, as mentioned before, in the days of Osman (655), and defeated the Byzantine navy in the Battle of *Dhu-al-Sawari* (the Battle of the Masts).

New Conquests. Muawiyah sent his famous general, Uqbah ibn Nafi, with an army to Ifriqiya, which is now divided into three countries, Tunisia, Algeria, and Morocco. Uqbah conquered what is now Tunisia and founded there in A.D. 670 a town called Qairawan. Other generals carried the banners of Islam to Central Asia. Muslim armies completed the conquest of Khorasan, right up to the River Amu Darya, long known as the Oxus; they even crossed the river and raided Bokhara. Then turning east, they entered the country now known as Afghanistan; they had reached Kabul before they halted. In the north of Syria and Iraq, Amir Muawiyah organized a system of annual *ghazwahs* into the Byzantine lands of Asia Minor. These raids were not much more than military exercises to keep the soldiers in trim and give the young officers operational experience. He also erected a line of fortresses along the north-western border. These fortresses were properly garrisoned and from them the Muslims kept the Byzantines at bay. In fact, the Byzantines did not take the conquests of Islam without resistance; they waged a continual war with the Muslim rulers for centuries, until they were slowly driven out of Asia Minor.

Naval Expeditions. Muawiyah was a man with ideas and a shrewd strategist. Though he was not in the same class as Ali as a general, he was a good military organizer. Not only did he create a well-knit, well-trained, and well-equipped Muslim army, he strengthened his navy also, and was audacious enough to attack the Emperor at Byzantium (Constantinople). In 669 Muawiyah sent an army by sea under the command of his son, Prince Yezid. Yezid proved a capable commander and laid siege to the famous town. Many incidents of this campaign have been preserved and they give a fair amount of credit to young Yezid. Here fell a famous Companion of the Prophet, Abu Ayyub al-Ansari, who had been the standard-bearer of the Prophet. He was buried by the walls of Constantinople and though the Muslims lifted the siege and went back, a legend grew up about this holy man. His tomb was visited even by Christians, and to this day it is a centre of pilgrimage. The Muslims attacked Constantinople again in 674, and this time the siege lasted seven years. It was in this war that the Byzantines used liquid fire, also called 'Greek Fire', a mixture of naphtha and phosphorus compounds, which greatly frightened the Arabs. This expedition did not bring in any gains, but it did at least one thing: it established the fear of Muslim armies in eastern Europe. On the way back, the Muslims captured the island of Rhodes.

Achievements of Muawiyah. The reign of Amir Muawiyah was eventful, but it is unfortunate that even historians do not write without prejudice. Most Muslim historians began to write in the times of the Abbasids, when a strong reaction had set in against the Bani Omayyah. Therefore the accounts of this period tend to be prejudiced. In reality Muawiyah was a ruler of note. It is true he was not to be compared with the early

Caliphs, but he was a statesman of great calibre. He tried to establish the Arab empire on sound lines. He did not possess all the virtues of a religious head as well as those of a king, but it will have been seen that he pursued the *ghazwahs* of Islam with vigour. He made Damascus his capital and ruled from there as a great Arab Shaikh. He had a Council of Shaikhs and ordered that all governors of the Arab world should have such councils. He was a very tactful man and used diplomacy and personal charm wherever he could. He stopped the disorder and dissatisfaction, even disloyalty, which was breaking up the unity of the Muslim world. He made the Arabs the dominant people socially as well as politically in the Muslim lands. He knit together the vast Caliphate and centralized the government. The administration continued to work on a Byzantine pattern in the western half and a Persian one in the eastern half, but he reorganized the boundaries and divided the whole Caliphate into many viceroyalties. He had able governors in Amr ibn al-As and Ziyad ibn Abih, who was the son of Abu Sufyan by a concubine and, therefore, a half-brother of Muawiyah. When Muawiyah died he nominated his son Yezid as his successor.

Yezid (680-683). Yezid came to the throne in 680. He had been a capable prince originally and had won repute in the siege of Constantinople. But he was born to the idea of princehood. He was the son of a powerful ruler, who had been successful in all his affairs, and so he considered nobody equal to him. This is not surprising, as he was the accepted Caliph of the Omayyad Caliphate; everywhere his name was read in the Khutbah except at Mecca, the birth-place of the Prophet, and Medina his adopted town. By the time he came to the Caliphal seat, Yezid had begun to live a life modelled on those of the Byzantine princes of the time. He loved to drink, enjoyed mixed company, kept dogs, hunted, and made merry as it pleased him. His behaviour aroused the opposition of the puritan elements of Islam. The story of one of the two heroes of

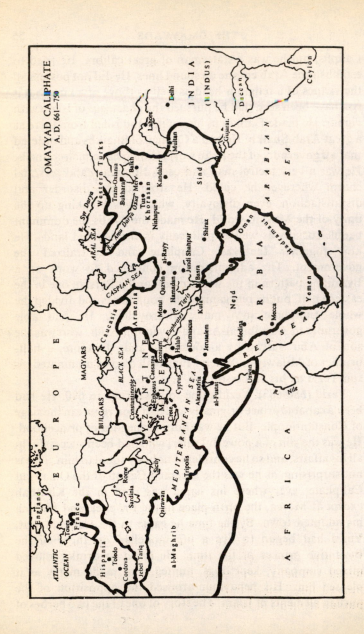

OMAYYAD CALIPHATE
A.D. 661–750

Islam, Imam Husain, who took up the cause of Islamic idealism and refused to submit to force has already been told. He had died in a holy cause and had put new life into the ideology of Islam. The other hero, a smaller man in comparison but a hero all the same, was Abdullah ibn al-Zubair, who was a nephew of Aisha and a grandson of Abu Bakr. He proclaimed himself Caliph at Mecca and soon had himself accepted in al-Hijaz and south Arabia. He then appointed his brother Mus'ab, as governor of Kufa. Obaidullah ibn Ziyad, the governor of Iraq, under whose orders Imam Husain had been done to death, had not improved after that tragic event. He was a cruel man, obstinate and conceited, and believed in harsh measures. It was not long before the Iraqis became tired of this and when Mus'ab ibn al-Zubair claimed a following, a number of people accepted him.

Sack of Medina. Yezid may have been a villain, but he was neither a weakling nor a fool. If there was a rising, he knew it had to be put down. He sent his general, Muslim ibn Uqbah, with an army into Hijaz. Muslim was the son of a famous general and was himself a good soldier. He defeated Abdullah ibn al-Zubair at Harrah near Medina on 26 August 683. Muslim's army looted Medina and some later historians have said that there was a good deal of bloodshed. Muslim then pursued Abdullah to Mecca, but died on the way. He was succeeded in the command of the army by Husain ibn Numayr, who went up to Mecca and laid siege to it. He could not conquer the sacred town, but he did not hesitate to rain stones on the Kaaba itself. For all this Yezid was blamed and quite correctly. It was at this time that Yezid died.

Marwan ibn al-Hakam (683-685). Yezid was succeeded by his son Muawiyah II, who died within a few months. At this death there was great unrest throughout the Caliphate. Abdullah ibn al-Zubair openly proclaimed himself Caliph of Islam. In Syria there was a clash between Arab tribes, because many people supported the Hashimites and were consequently against the Omayyads. Abdullah ibn al-Zubair had appointed Dhahhak ibn Qais as governor of Palestine. At Damascus, the man who was raised to the Caliphate was old Marwan, who had been secretary to Osman. Marwan was a very shrewd man, and it did not take him long to organize himself. He sent an army against Dhahhak and defeated him at the battle of Marj Rahit near Damascus. Another army was despatched to Iraq, as there was trouble there also. The Iraqis had found a leader in a man called Sulaiman, but Marwan's army prevailed there too. Marwan, however, did not live long; he was already over seventy years of age when he came to the Caliphate, and the cares of office were too much for him. He died two years later, but he did a thing of considerable historical importance. He nominated his son Abdul Malik as Caliph after him. Abdul Malik was a great monarch and came to be known as the 'Father of Kings' as four of his sons were called to the Caliphate. In fact the story of the Omayyads is from now on the story of the Marwanids.

Abdul Malik (685-705). Abdul Malik was a very capable man. He knew men and chose his governors and commanders well. He was a good organizer and soon had complete control over the affairs of the state. He realized that the rule of the Omayyads was not yet firmly established. He also saw that nothing satisfied people more than glory and the hope of profit. He bent his mind to both these things. He first selected two men as commanders. Both were gifted in their own way, both made many other generals famous because of the work in which they engaged them. One was Musa ibn Nusayr, whom he made Commander of the western armies and Viceroy of Ifriqiya, the other was al-Hajjaj ibn Yusuf, whom he gave the command of the eastern armies and the governorship of Iraq.

Al-Hajjaj ibn Yusuf—The Fall of Mecca. Al-Hajjaj ibn Yusuf had originally been a school teacher. His dominant nature and gift of leadership were noticed, and he was tried in a small command. He performed his task so well that he was given the task of conquering al-Hijaz as well as Iraq, where Abdullah ibn al-Zubair held sway. Al-Hajjaj decided to strike at the root, and made for Mecca. His reputation had spread and people knew him to be a very hard and determined man. His siege of Mecca is famous in history, because he treated the town as if there were nothing sacred about it. He used all the weapons of war against the sacred walls in a ruthless manner. The Meccans fought with courage and selfless heroism, Abdullah ibn al-Zubair himself set an example of rock-like strength and unflinching determination by fighting to the end, but his bravery could not prevail against the ruthless Omayyad commander. He fell in battle and al-Hajjaj had his head cut off and sent to Damascus. Mecca fell, and with it fell the other strongholds of al-Hijaz, Yemen following suit. The people submitted, and those who could not tolerate the new rulers left for the western front or distant Khorasan, where *ghazwahs* were still being fought and where a Muslim could win glory and a new home for himself.

Al-Hajjaj reduces Iraq. Al-Hajjaj was equally successful in Iraq. Since Kufa was the centre of trouble, he decided to strike there. He took a few trusted fighters with him, and they all went disguised as camel-drivers to the great mosque of Kufa on Friday, at the time of the Juma prayers. Just as the Muslims were getting ready to stand up for the Juma prayer, he leapt on to the *minbar* (pulpit) and threw off his disguise. His loud voice rang out in the utter silence of the faithful. He said: 'People of Kufa, do you know who I am? I am your new governor. I am also a man who can stand very little nonsense! I believe that you require a little blood-letting. You can trust me. I shall cut so many throats that all your thirst will be slaked. Hear me and obey.' The people shook where they sat; nobody dared to say a word. But al-Hajjaj was not a man of words only, he believed in stern examples. He rounded up all those who were suspected of being against the Omayyads, and killed them. Later historians have tried to portray him as a blood-thirsty monster, but he taught a lesson to the Kufans that they did not forget for a long time. It is true that he did not mind shedding blood, but what is sometimes forgotten is the fact that, besides being a good general, he was a very capable administrator. He dug canals, made arrangements for irrigation on a large scale, improved the day-to-day working of the Iraqi government, and made that province one of the richest in the Caliphate.

Conquests in India, Kabul, and the North. Al-Hajjaj was no friend of the opponents of the Omayyads and he believed in drastic ways, but we cannot deny that he was a remarkable man. He organized many campaigns during the reign of Abdul Malik, and his son al-Walid, and not one of them was unsuccessful. Indeed, Islam gained great glory through him. Hearing that Dahir, the Raja of Sind in India was sheltering some pirates who had looted some Arab vessels, he sent an army against the Raja under the command of his nephew and son-in-law, the eighteen-year-old Muhammad ibn al-Qasim. It was not a large army; Muhammad had only 1,000 horses and about the same number of camel-borne troops, altogether not more than 6,000 fighters. Young Muhammad was, however, a fine military commander. He came by land, subduing Makran on the way and pushing through the already conquered Baluchistan. He conquered Debal (a town near modern Karachi), the capital of Lower Sind, in 712. The Raja fled. The people were offered the same terms as were offered everywhere. Toleration, protection, and other honourable terms in return for loyal submission. If the people wanted to accept Islam, they were to be treated as equals. Muhammad ibn al-Qasim then followed the Raja and came up with him near Nirun (modern Hyderabad). The Raja had assembled a large army, 50,000 strong, but Muhammad defeated him again, and the Raja fell in battle. The whole of Sind was now conquered, but Muhammad did not stop there. He fought another battle at Bahmanabad, pushed up to Lower Punjab, and reached Multan. Here too, he was victorious. The entire lower valley of the Indus was now in Muslim hands. Muhammad was, however, not left long in West India. His father-in-law al-Hajjaj having died in 714, he was recalled to Damascus, where after a few years he lost his life as a result of a court intrigue.

Conquests in Central Asia (705-713). Al-Hajjaj had sent another of his generals, Abdur Rahman ibn Muhammad, against the King of Kabul who, though a Muslim vassal, had refused to pay the tribute. Abdur Rahman soon taught him a lesson and Kabul was subdued. Another general Qutaybah ibn Muslim, was despatched with an army into the land beyond the Amu Darya (Oxus). Qutaybah conquered Balkh and Bokhara and annexed all the land around Samarqand. He then turned left and conquered Khiva, the land which became later to be called Khwarizm. In 713 he went beyond Bokhara and conquered Ferghana. The entire region of Trans-Oxiania *(Mawara-āl-Nahr)*, the land beyond the river, was thus conquered.

Conquests in Asia Minor (706-707). Abdul Malik's reign was a reign of conquests. The army of the North had to defend the borders against the Byzantine raiders. Finding the Muslims fighting each other, the Byzantine emperor had sent his troops across the border. For some time the Muslim border troops fought a defensive action, but then Abdul Malik sent a strong army into Asia Minor. It met the Byzantines at Sebastopolis and defeated them. The next year the Muslims captured three important towns, Tyana, Sardis, and Pergamos.

Conquests in Africa. Qairawan had already been founded in Tunisia, but the Berbers of the region had by no means been conquered. In fact, they gave a lot of trouble to the Arab conquerors. They were a vigorous people, who fought well. Hearing of this trouble, Abdul Malik sent an army under Zubair, who had held a command under the famous Uqbah. Zubair defeated a combined army of Berbers and Byzantines. A little later, finding Zubair not too well guarded, the Berbers surprised him and killed him. Even Qairawan was besieged. A new governor, Hasan ibn al-Naaman was then sent to Ifriqiya.

He took back Qairawan, defeated the Berbers, and even when there was another and a stronger rising under a local priestess, Kahina, he crushed the insurgents.

Abdul Malik the Ruler. There is no doubt that Abdul Malik was a very capable ruler. Not only did Muslim arms reach farther in the east, north, and west under him, but a new note was brought into Muslim administration. He was the first Muslim Caliph to strike coins with Arabic inscriptions and to make Arabic the language of the court and the administration. More and more offices were given to Arabs and neo-Muslims. He organized a postal service, and regularized taxation. The Muslims paid *zakat,* but were excused other taxes, which made many people volunteer to accept Islam. These neo-Muslims came to the towns and joined the army as *Mawali* (freedmen). There was some loss of taxes involved, as the soldiers were not only exempted from taxes, but also got a share of the spoils, the regulars being paid a fixed salary; but this move gave large armies to Islam. Abdul Malik also built the great structure at Jerusalem (al-Quds) on the site of the ancient temple (*Haikal*) of the Jews called the Dome of the Rock, also (Masjid-i-Aqsa) a mosque both of which stand to this day as a glory of early Muslim architecture.

Al-Walid (705-715)—Invasion of Spain (712). Abdul Malik was succeeded by his son, al-Walid. Abdul Malik had drawn together and firmly unified the various elements of the Muslim world, but to al-Walid goes the honour of the most spectacular event of the early era of Islam—the conquest of al-Maghrib and of Spain. Hasan ibn al-Naaman, who had pacified Ifriqiya and suppressed the Berbers, was succeeded by Musa ibn Nusayr as governor of Ifriqiya. Musa was a man of vision and had great ambition. It was not long before he opened a campaign in al-Maghrib, the land which is called Algeria and Morocco today. He conquered it and was duly praised by the Caliph. He was now made Viceroy over the entire land to the west of Egypt, which was great honour indeed. Musa had a gifted general called Tariq, who was a freedman. Tariq was appointed governor of the western strip of al-Maghrib, the region which is now northern Morocco. He had his capital at Tangier. To him came one day, a Spanish nobleman, Count Julian, a rebel against Roderick, the King of Spain, who had had difficulty in establishing his authority. In 711 Tariq sailed across the Straits with 7,000 men. He landed at the base of a huge rock, which came to be called after his name, Jabal-i-Tariq or Tariq's Mount. It was later Europeanized into Gibraltar. Seeing that his soldiers and horsemen were afraid of the venture, he played a trick on them. He divided his fleet into two. He hid half the ships beyond the headland and gave secret orders that the other half should be burnt in the night. When the flames leaped up, his camp was alarmed and the sentries came running to him. Many weak-hearted men wrung their hands. Quite a few were deeply disturbed. They asked him what they should do. 'Do?' he asked, 'why nothing!' 'But what shall we do if we have to go back?' 'But why should you go back?' 'Suppose we are defeated?' 'Now, now, my men, that is not like you! Who speaks of defeat? You have no need to go back. This land belongs to Allah why then it belongs to you also. Go and take it. Fight for the glory of Allah and for a home for yourself and your children. Since there is no retreat for you, fight as if you were 70,000, instead of 7,000. You have defeated the enemy before. You will do so even now. Trust in Allah and in your swords. March onward my young heroes!' His men were impressed.

Conquest of Spain. Word was now sent to Musa of what Tariq had done. Such are the failings of human nature, that Musa, the great Viceroy, grew jealous of his own general. Perhaps he did not like an ex-slave, however brilliant, to achieve what his own sons had not done. In any case, he advanced with a large army. But before he could join forces with Tariq, the young general had met the main Spanish forces, under Roderick, who having usurped the throne now summoned up all his resources to fight the Muslim invaders.

He was however out-generaled and out-fought by Tariq and was defeated on 19 July 711. Musa came with his Arabs in June 712, when a greater part of central Spain had also been conquered by Tariq. He, however, conquered the rest of Spain. He captured Medina, Sidonia, Seville, and Merida. It is said that he publicly rebuked young Tariq for having exceeded his orders, but the glory of winning a new prize was already Tariq's, whose name is even today a favourite among Muslims.

Al-Walid and Musa. Something very strange was meanwhile happening in Damascus. Instead of applauding the great achievements of Musa and Tariq, jealous courtiers had begun to poison the mind of Caliph al-Walid against Musa. They said that no subject should be so powerful. They suggested that Spain was too far away. They hinted that Musa would be a fool if he did not proclaim his independence. A man of broad intellect and large sympathies might have rejected all this talk as mere jealousy, but al-Walid was suspicious by nature. He began to pay heed to these malicious hints. He recalled Musa. Musa appointed his son Abdul Aziz as his deputy in the Viceroyalty and moved east. When he reached Damascus, he presented himself to the Caliph at the head of a long procession. He had captive princes, chiefs, and nobles in his train and thousands of slaves bearing on their heads costly presents in gold, ornaments, jewels, and hundreds of precious objects. The Caliph was impressed; he accepted the gifts and received old Musa kindly, even courteously. But he fell ill soon afterwards and his brother Sulaiman, who became the Regent, proved treacherous. He took away Musa's office and kept him about the court without any appointment. He then confiscated Musa's wealth, and later banished him from the court. Musa went to his village to live like an ordinary man and died in poverty. The new Caliph also had Musa's son Abdul Aziz killed. He also recalled Muhammad ibn al-Qasim from India and had him executed. Al-Hajjaj the powerful uncle of Muhammad was dead, so young Muhammad died undefended, an undeserved death. These two deaths were a warning to Muslim generals all over the world. They thought that if the Muslim rulers were so despotic and so ungrateful, it would not be disloyal to safeguard their own interests. It is not surprising, therefore, that in the days of the Abbasids, who came after the Omayyads, it became customary for the generals or governors, to look after themselves and when opportunity offered, to set up as independent rulers, even if it were only in a small way and under a nominal 'protection' of the Abbasid Caliph.

Al-Walid as Ruler. Al-Walid sent many expeditions into Asia Minor. The Muslim forces invaded the provinces of Cilica, and Galatia, which lay in the south of Asia Minor. Al-Walid was a gracious and generous sovereign. He was famous for the beautiful buildings and the many schools and hospitals he erected. He gave liberally to the poor. He enforced justice, correct measures, and a respect for the law. He encouraged the arts of peace, and Arabic poetry began to flourish again in his reign. The Omayyads began building villas on the southern borders of the desert where they retired for rest and where they sent their sons to be trained and educated away from the atmosphere of the court and the towns. Al-Walid added to these villas and beautified their interiors. As firm as his father Abdul Malik, he was much kinder and though not above such human weaknesses as jealousy, he was never cruel. Syria considered him an ideal king and he must be accepted as one of the greatest of the Omayyads.

Sulaiman (715-717). His successor Sulaiman was an unworthy son and an unworthy brother. In his short reign of two and a half years, he did many foolish things. He disposed of two brilliant generals, Musa and Muhammad ibn al-Qasim, and he was persuaded to send a costly expedition against Constantinople at the instance of Leo, a renegade Byzantine general, who betrayed the Muslims in the end, joined the people of Constantinople and, turning upon the Muslims, destroyed their fleet. But such was the prestige of Muslims arms, that the Christian world, instead of being triumphant at the repulse of the Muslims, heaved a sigh of relief that their advance in this area was checked for a time. On the western front, however, al-Hurr ibn Abdul Rahman, the Muslim governor of Spain, who succeeded Musa ibn Nusayr, crossed the Pyrenees and invaded France.

Omar ibn Abdul Aziz. Sulaiman was succeeded by Omar ibn Abdul Aziz, whose honesty, faith, and fervour were of the quality of the earlier Caliphs. Even the severest critics of the Omayyads make an exception of him. He did a few things which won universal praise. Muawiyah had introduced the evil practice of cursing Ali after his Juma Khutbah (Friday sermon). The other Omayyads had followed this evil practice, but Omar ibn Abdul Aziz abolished it. Omar the Great in his zeal had declared all property of the Prophet forfeit to the State, and it had been for some time a point of grievance with the Alids that the orchard of Fidak had been taken from them. Omar ibn Abdul Aziz restored the orchard to the descendants of Ali. He abolished certain taxes on the non-Muslims and was greatly praised for this act at the time, though he deprived the State of much necessary revenue. He was not fond of war or conquest, but even he could not stop the Muslim armies of the west from advancing into France. In 717 al-Hurr made Narbonne in southern France his headquarters and began to operate from there. Omar ibn Abdul Aziz believed in equal rights for all, so he gave equal rights to the Mawali. He lived simply and hardly spent anything on himself. He was not, however, so liberal towards non-Muslims as the other Omayyads had been; but according to the ideas of the time, people even gave him credit for being strict and the Muslim historians do not criticize him for that. The Christian historians have not been so charitable. He did not live long and died after three years on the throne.

Yezid II (720-724). Omar was followed by Yezid II, another son of Abdul Malik. Yezid was an ordinary man, and is remembered for nothing outstanding. It was in his time that things began to go wrong. A Muslim governor revolted and raised his banner in Iraq, but Yezid sent General Maslamah against him and the rising was suppressed. The Muslims began to meet with tough opposition in France and were defeated by Duke Eudo near Toulouse in 721. What was worse, the old feuds between Northern and Southern Arabs broke out again. These two groups had now new labels, Qaisites or Mazharites for the northerners and Kalbites or Himyarites (Yemenites) for the Arabs of the south. The old rivalries began to take new forms and people began to fight among themselves. This evil spread to Spain and even to the advanced bases of the operational forces in France. This internal fighting was soon to spread everywhere and weaken the Caliphate.

Hisham (724-743). After Yezid II, Hisham, another son of Abdul Malik, came to the throne. Two events of his reign are important. Both were harmful to the prestige of Islam, though one of them was at first auspicious. The Muslim armies in France began to advance again under Abdul Rahman ibn Abdullah who succeeded al-Hurr ibn Abdul Rahman. They conquered as they went, and the news of their advance spread terror everywhere. It appeared that the Muslims would conquer France, and if France, why not Europe, The Frankish King decided to call in all his allies and put up a strong fight. He sent word to all the chiefs and noblemen to bring up their contingents. In a short time a large army assembled under his banner. He marched down with it and met the Muslims near Tours.

The Battle of Tours (732). The year 732 was a fateful one for Islam. The Muslims fought with reckless bravery as usual and pierced the steel-clad wall of the Franks again and again. The battle lasted three days. On the third Abdul Rahman was struck down by an arrow. When night fell, the Muslim Amirs assembled in a council; they debated long on whether they should continue or retreat. They saw that the Franks were very strong and had their capital to fall back upon. Their own general was dead. The Muslim line of communication was long. Damascus was over 3,000 miles away and even Spain lay across the Pyrenees. No new reinforcements had arrived. They therefore decided to retreat. At midnight, they struck camp and left. When the Christians woke in the morning, they found no enemy. This was the victory of Tours, which has been called a turning-point in European history. The truth of the matter is, that things were not happy at the centre (Damascus). There were disturbances everywhere and the Caliph could not concentrate on conquests at this time. The Muslim forces therefore paused in their onward march, but they continued their *ghazwahs* in south and east France for a long time. Avignon, which lies to the east, was conquered by the Muslims two years later (734) and they sacked Lyons, which lies in the heart of France in 743. But with the decline in the fortunes of the Omayyads, the advance in France stopped.

Rising of the Alids. What was perhaps more dangerous, as far as the Omayyads were concerned, was the rising of a new movement against their House. This movement started in distant Khorasan. It was well organized from the beginning. The head of this, at first secret organization, was Muhammad the great grandson of Abbas, the Prophet's own uncle. Seeing that some Alids, like Zayd son of Zain ul-Abidin and his son Yahya, had made unsuccessful risings, and had lost their lives in the attempt, he approached the whole thing carefully. He realized that there was considerable pro-Alid feeling among the people, especially in Persia, where people had always believed in hereditary succession. He decided to make use of this feeling and found a talented propagandist and organizer in a young man of Khorasan, called Abu Muslim. With his help Muhammad the Abbasid sent out secret workers and began to win over people for the cause of Ali. All these agents told the people that the world was tired of the Omayyads and that a saviour was to come from the House of the Prophet. The propaganda began to have an effect. Abu Muslim began to send out little black flags as symbols of this rising. This went on for some time, and the movement was greatly helped by the fact that internal feuds and fighting were spreading everywhere in the vast lands of the Caliphate. The Arabs fought among themselves and to the misfortune of Islam they began to fight the non-Arab Muslims, the Mawali, mostly Persian, who claimed equal or near-equal status with the Arabs. Taxes fell, in spite of large schemes of irrigation, which were introduced in Iraq by Abdullah al-Qasri the governor. Dissatisfaction grew apace.

Successors of Hisham. The successors of Hisham were incompetent and helped the decline with their wasteful habits and their love of pleasure. The villas which the Omayyad nobles had built for themselves along the desert's edge now became resorts of pleasure, and some of the remains which stand to this day tell of the luxury and standard of living of these later Omayyads. But this luxury was at the expense of the affairs of the state, which were neglected. This was very harmful to Omayyad interests and completed the ruin of, at that time, the mightiest empire of the world. The later Caliphs even neglected their standing army.

Marwan II (744-750). The last Omayyad ruler was Marwan II. He was a capable man, a good organizer, and a man of action, but he was obstinate and had fixed views. Nor was he very tolerant. He ignored two things. He did not reorganize the central army which had been a powerful weapon in the hands of Muawiyah and Abdul Malik, and he did not take effective measures to put down the internal factions and feuds. The opposition between the Mazharites and Himyarites became deadly. Especially as, by and large, the Mazharites, the northerners, were Sunni and the Himyarites or the southerners were mostly pro-Alid. Their rivalries and fights spread from the lower valley of the Indus in the east, to the Pyrenees in the west, and did much harm to the cause of Islam, which could perhaps have been prevented if timely action had been taken.

Rise of the Abbasids (747). Things were in this state, when Ibrahim al-Abbasi the son of Muhammad al-Abbasi, raised his black banner in the name of the *Ahl al-Bait*. Abu Muslim al-Khorasani was not only a brilliant propagandist, he was an able general too. Ibrahim had another good general in his own brother, Abdullah. The Alids thought it was their own cause, and the Persians believed they were fighting for themselves. They joined the black banner movement. Gradually the rising became general. Nasr ibn Sayyar, the Governor of Khorasan, wrote desperate letters to Caliph Marwan II, to send help, but help took long in coming. The Abbasid troops won victory after victory, and soon they had the whole of Persia with them. There were battles here and there, but by 750 the Abbasids had advanced as far as Iraq. Here Marwan II came up himself with a hastily assembled army and gave battle near the Zab River to the insurgents. He was defeated and fled to Egypt, where he was captured and slain by the Abbasid troops. This was the end of the Omayyads. They had ruled the Islamic world for nearly ninety years, but their end was inglorious.

Abdul Abbas the Saviour and Avenger. Meanwhile, Ibrahim son of Mohammad al-Abbasi had died and his son Abdul Abbas had succeeded him as the head of the Movement. Abdul Abbas was a more forthright man. He came out in the open and declared himself as the promised Saviour. He said he belonged to the House of the Prophet, his great-great-grandfather being the uncle of Muhammad. The Alids felt cheated, but they could do nothing. They went into hiding and refused to give co-operation. When oppressed they formed secret organizations. Another canker, that of secret societies, now attacked the body politic of Islam.

The Abbasid' Revenge. The Abbasids now decided to root out the Omayyads. They therefore took an action which, for sheer brutality has few parallels in history. It happened in Syria, where Abdullah, the Abbasid general, the uncle of Abdul Abbas, was governor. At Abu Futrus, a fortress on the Awja River, he invited all the Omayyad Princes to dinner. The apparent reason was that he wished to make friends with the Omayyads. The banquet was well attended, and many armed guardsmen were present, as was usual. Half-way through, the host made a signal to the captain of the guard, who called his guards in and fell on the unarmed Omayyads. A scene of butchery ensued. Only one prince, Abdul Rahman, realized the danger in time. He grasped his young brother Abdullah, who was with him, made a leap for the nearest window and jumped out of it into the river below. The Abbasids asked the brothers to come back. They promised them life and riches. They swore great oaths that they would do them no harm. Abdullah, who was only twelve years old, turned back. His brother told him not to be a fool, but he was young, the current was strong, and the promises were sweet. He returned and was cut down as he reached the bank. Abdul Rahman escaped, and avoiding all pursuit reached his mother's people in al-Maghrib (Morocco). There he set about building his fortunes again. The Abbasids were now left without rivals and they inherited the entire Caliphate. Abdul Abbas was proclaimed Caliph and was given the title of al-Saffah. It was a well-deserved and appropriate title, as it meant 'Blood-shedder'.

Achievements of the Omayyads. Islamic history has not done justice to the Omayyads. There are several reasons for this. Most of the histories were written in Abbasid times and there was a strong anti-Omayyad bias in those centuries. Amir Muawiyah had not played a very noble role in his claims of vengeance and his fight against Ali. Yezid I, his son, had committed a crime which was of a most despicable kind, and the anti-Ali feeling was deliberately created and fostered by Muawiyah and his successors. Clannish jealousy may also have helped to make the Abbasids so hostile and revengeful. The result is that the achievements of the Omayyads have never been properly assessed by the Muslims.

New Features of the Arab World. It is often forgotten that it was the Omayyads who made the Arabs a world power. The greatest extension of the Muslim State occurred under Walid ibn Abdul Malik. The entire Caliphate was arabicized by Abdul Malik and his descendants. Arabic grammar, Arabic canonical science, Arab historiography, and Arab architecture were all founded in Omayyad times. A new civilization was born in their days. No great creative activity was yet possible, because the Arabs had brought no intellectual background or traditions with them from the desert, but they were keen, they wanted to learn and they did not disdain to sit at the feet of others to do so. They therefore took their time, but what they acquired they made their own; in reality a new society was in formation. The Arabs who had known no superiors and no castes, were now aristocrats. They were the ruling people. Their language was the language of the Caliphate from Bokhara to Lisbon. This social pre-eminence began to change the simple Arab. He began by being a humble student, and ended by becoming the teacher of the world. It was not long before any Muslim who spoke Arabic, believed in Islamic values and who worked for the good of the Caliphate was called an Arab. The domination that the Omayyads gave the Arabs was kept by them for six hundred years, which was a great achievement.

Muslim Society. Besides the Arabs, who naturally formed the top level of society, there were three other classes in the Caliphate: the Mawali or the non-Arab Muslims, the Dhimmis or protected minorities, and the slaves. It is true that most of the high offices went to the Arabs, but it was not long before the Mawali and the Dhimmis began to get, on sheer merit, posts of honour and responsibility. As for slaves, they came from all countries and all nations. It cannot be said that the Muslims took more care of them than of relatives and employees, but they received better treatment than they have ever been given before or since. Many of them rose to positions of the highest trust and great power. In India there was even a slave dynasty. The Bahri Mamluks as well as the Burji Mamluks of Egypt and Syria, as will be seen later, had all been Turkish slaves. Various kingdoms were founded by ex-slaves. It should not be supposed that because the Arab world contained these four classes, they were as rigidly exclusive as the four castes of the Hindu social system. Among the Hindus the four castes divide man from man eternally. A Sudra can never be a scholar, or priest, or warrior, or ruler. This was not so among the Muslims, where the classes were fluid and intermarriage soon put an end to purity of blood or claims of superiority. The Muslims prayed together, fought together, and lived on equal terms. The master could be inferior to the slave, mentally or spiritually, and when it was so, the slave was not denied his rights or due reward. In Islam freedmen or the children of slaves had no stigma attached to them, and the freeing of slaves was the action most favoured of Allah.

Arab Interests. The Arab had a keen mind. He was curious and persistent. Now he had an opportunity to see at first hand the intellectual products of the ancient civilizations of Greece and Persia. He was so hungry for new experiences that his zest knew no bounds. In manly arts, in hunting, in racing and in the skills of the field, he could hold his own against anybody. His love of poetry, of oratory, of good expression was his boast and he turned eagerly to the learning of the older nations. The women were not so secluded as they later became in various lands. They helped in battles, they exchanged verses with their husbands and brothers, they had wit and charm, and many of them were known for their excellent taste and deportment. In short, the Arab was no longer a bedouin, he was now a citizen of the world, and he began to take part in all the activities of a civilized man.

Kufa and Basra. Quite early, as we have seen, two Arab camptowns were founded in lower Iraq. The town of Kufa on the Euphrates and that of Basra south of the confluence of the Tigris and the Euphrates. Gradually these two camps grew into big towns. Great importance was gained by Kufa when Ali chose it for his capital. Soon the two towns, because of their situation as bridges between Persia and Syria and the western world, became important centres of Muslim culture. Most of the great writers, poets as well as grammarians, thinkers as well as canonists came from these two towns. It was here that the science of *Hadith* (Traditions) was founded. Rules for the explanation of the Qur'anic verses, the sifting of the Traditions of the Prophet, the elements of Muslim Law, the beginnings of Muslim sufism all had their beginnings either in Kufa or Basra. The great Muslim mystic and saint Hasan al-Basri (d. 728), as his name tells, was the chief ornament of the religious life of Basra. Very few have ever enjoyed such prestige among his fellow-men as Hasan al-Basri did in his time. Intellectual ferment, thinking about religious practices and religious faith in a rational manner also started at Basra. Wasil ibn Ata was the first Muslim rationalist. He later founded a school of thought called the Mut'azila School which had a great vogue under the Abbasids. All this shows that the Arab mind had awakened fully by the time the Omayyads fell.

The Social Structure. The Bani Omayyah had been a prominent clan of the Quraish even before the advent of Islam. There were among them big businessmen whom wealth gave social distinction. Abu Sufyan had been the head of the Council of Elders which governed the affairs of the market as well as the ceremonies connected with the annual pilgrimage. When the Bani Omayyah came to power under Amir Muawiyah and the Marvanids, they showed the same aristocratic traits in all their dealings with the public, apart from diplomacy. Gradually society came to be divided into the following classes:

(a) The feudal aristocracy (Arab and even non-Arab) which, despite great efforts for its suppression, got a firm footing in Arabia and beyond (cf., Pakistan Society)

(b) The military class (mainly Arabs) encouraged by Omar to balance the feudal aristocracy. This class enjoyed state pensions. (cf., Pakistan).

(c) New converts (the Mawali) who owned neither land nor received any pension. This dissatisfied class joined the Abbasid insurgents later.

(d) Slaves, who were treated like human beings and not like chattels but were still owned by others.

(e) The beggars, the sick, and the incapacitated, who were given financial assistance through Zakat.

Status of Women. The practice of seclusion of women was greatly relaxed under the Omayyads. Even members of the Prophet's family took part in public life. Hazrat Ayesha led the Medinites against Ali in the Battle of the Camel, and in later years, she became the source of many authentic traditions of the Prophet and was often consulted on important issues. Hazrat Fatima during her short life after the Prophet's death took part in discussions on the Caliphate. Hazrat Zainab, her daughter, defended boldly, the holy family after the tragedy of Kerbala against Obaidullah bin Ziyad and even Yezid.

Sukainah, the daughter of Imam Husain, was the leader of the cultured coterie in Medina. During the Omayyad period the old Persian custom of seclusion of women was practised even among the ruling classes as a mark of distinction, but members of the royal households took part in all cultural activities. Among the defenders of the harem institution, one can, however, quote Von Hammer who said: 'The harem is a sanctuary, it is prohibited to strangers, not because women are considered unworthy of confidence, but on account of sacredness with which custom and manners invest them'.

Intellectual Activities and Artistic Efforts. It must be borne in mind that the Arabs brought with them into the wider world, which they conquered rapidly, no science, no art, and no learning. Their studies were confined to theological subjects. Even in India from the days of Muhammad bin Qasim to the times of Sultan Sikander Lodhi (712-1517) the curriculum was confined to religious studies, history, and medicine—subjects which were called *Manqulat* (Traditional). It was Sikander Lodhi who borrowed the Persian precept and introduced some secular subjects which were called *Maaqulat* (Secular/ Rational). The Arabs acquired all their learning from the Syrians, Persians, Egyptians, whether they were Christians, Jews, or the Magi. Thus in the beginning intellectual life in the Omayyad period was not very high.

The swift advance of the Muslim arms over three continents took up most of their time and brought in the wake of conquests, many economic, social, and domestic problems. Yet the Arabs learnt fast. They first polished their grammar as Arabic had to be taught to the conquered people and the Qur'an had to be expounded to the neo-Muslims, and even non-Muslims. So they had to turn their attention to the compilation of dictionaries and the study of linguistics. The search for the true sources of the many Traditions of the Prophet which had begun to float in great abundance, led to methods of research and the beginnings of historiography. The study of Roman law which applied to the conquered non-Muslims, persuaded the Muslims to formulate their own juristic practices (Fiqh). The necessity of building suitable mosques and palaces, worthy of the glory achieved by Muslim arms, made the architects to study prevailing styles of architecture with the result that such magnificent structures as the Dome of the Rock at Al-Quds (Jerusalem) in 691 and the grand Omayyad mosque at Damascus (705) came into being. Al-Walid I rebuilt the mosque at Medina and enlarged and beautified the *Harm-i-Sharif*. He built many schools and hospitals in Syria too. And all along the edge of the desert the princes and noblemen built splendid mansions to which they retired at intervals.

Religious Speculations. Contact with Jews and Christians and the study of Greek philosophers gave birth to much speculation and many groups came up each with its own interpretation of theological doctrines. There was the Qadariya school, believing in Free Will against the Jabariya who stuck to predestination and determinism. Later the Mu'tazila were in great vogue. They (among other things) maintained that the Qur'an was not co-eternal with Allah and that it had been revealed when the time came for it, whereas the orthodox affirmed that it had existed from the Beginning, and was timeless. Another school the Murjites believed in tolerance and said that a sinner remained a Muslim, so long as he continued to believe in Allah, the One and Only, and in Muhammad, as His servant and Prophet. The most intransigent were the Kharijites who had seceded from the Alid cause, because they considered that Ali had done wrong in accepting arbitration between him and Muawiyah since Muawiyah was a rebel, and as such not the equal of the elected Caliph. The Kharijites were the communists of Islam. They forbade the cult of saints and stopped pilgrimages to the tombs of holy persons. They also maintained that it was not necessary for a man to be a member of the Quraish to be elected Caliph. Even a Negro could become a Caliph if he was worthy of that office. There were then the Shiites who were gathering force. Many members of the family of Imam Hasan and Imam Husain made abortive risings and got killed. Many were poisoned by Omayyad agents among whom were Abdalla called Abu Hashim, the son of Mohammad bin Hanfia the elder half-brother of Hasan and Husain. At that time, Abu Hashim was the secret head of the Alid cause. He was poisoned on the orders of Sulaiman bin Abd al Malik. Another secret leader was Muhammad bin Abdullah bin Hasan II bin Imam Hasan killed, who for his piety was called *Nafs-i-Zakia* (the Pure in Spirit). There are two versions about the end of this holy man. Abdul Jabban Al Jaumurd in his biography of 'Harun al-Rashid' says, that he was poisoned, but Ibn Taqtaqa in his famous history 'Al-Fakhri', has recorded that *Nafs-i-Zakia* died, fighting against the forces of Abu Jaafar Mansur, the second Abbasid Caliph, as did his brother Ibrahim bin Abdullah, in another rising.

CHAPTER 4

ISLAM IN SPAIN

Conditions in Muslim Spain. At home, the Abbasids were slashing their way to power and soon they were firmly established. There were risings here and there, but the first two Abbasids put them down with a firm, even a stern hand. In Ifriqiya, however, and much more so in distant Spain, they could not have their way so easily. Affairs in Spain had been in a bad way for quite some time. The Arabs and the Berbers had fallen out. Not openly or bitterly, but they were no longer so closely united as they had been. Moreover, the northern and southern Arabs now worked openly against each other. What was worse, the government of Spain had weakened. The later Omayyads had fallen a prey to intrigue and changed the governors so often that there was little security left in the state. This encouraged the Berbers, who had acquired Kharijite ideas, to rebel in al-Maghrib. The Caliph sent an army of Syrians to subdue the rebels. The Syrian army subdued the Berbers and went on into Spain. These Syrians now formed a block of their own. Their commander, Balj ibn Bashr, watching his opportunity, seized power and proclaimed himself Amir of Cordova. He did not stay long in power, for another governor came and deposed him. More and more governors now succeeded each other, till there were, in all, twenty-three governors in as many years. The state of disorganization into which Muslim Spain now fell can easily be imagined.

Abdul Rahman. Muslim Spain was in this state, when the last Omayyad prince, Abdul Rahman, found his way to Ceuta. He had travelled in disguise all the way from Palestine, accompanied only by a faithful slave. He had braved many dangers and risked his life many times, but he was a courageous and resourceful young man and had successfully overcome all obstacles. Now that he came to his mother's people, he got the help he needed. It was not long before he had a large army under him. He crossed over to Spain and started the reconquest of the Iberian Peninsula. City after city fell to him and at last he defeated the Abbasid governor, Yusuf al-Fihri. Cordova, the capital, fell to him in 756 and after that he was the sole monarch of Muslim Spain. He cut off Spain for ever from the Abbasid Caliphate by founding the Omayyad Amirate of Cordova, and the House of Omayyah ruled in Spain for about three hundred years more.

Abdul Rahman shows his hand. The second Abbasid Caliph, the powerful al-Mansur, was reigning in Baghdad at this time and he did not like the idea of an Omayyad ruler defying him, even in distant Spain. So he selected a governor of his own, al-Ala ibn Mughith, and sent him with a strong escort to take over Spain. He thought that the name of the mighty Abbasid Caliph would be potent enough to make al-Ala accepted as Governor by the people of Spain. He did not realize what type of man Abdul Rahman was. When al-Ala reached Cordova, he had a small army with him, which he had gathered from Ifriqiya, which was Abbasid land. Abdul Rahman defeated him easily, and had al-Ala's head and those of his chief captains and counsellors cut off. He then had a bundle made of the heads, which were preserved. It was wrapped in silk and cloth of gold. To it was attached a letter and it was sent as a present to Caliph al-Mansur. When it was opened in the Abbasid court, al-Mansur was shocked to see the heads of his governor and his counsellors, and exclaimed: 'I thank God that He has put the seas between me and such an enemy.' If the Hashimites did not forget, neither did the Omayyads.

Charlemagne invades Spain. Abdul Rahman had not yet finished with his enemies. The son-in-law of Balj ibn Bashr, the Syrian usurper, now sought help from Charles the Great of France, called Charlemagne. Charles was known as the champion of Christendom. So he welcomed the idea of doing as much damage as he could to a Muslim power, and came with a large army; the more gladly, because he had established diplomatic relations with the Abbasids, and later even became a friend of the great Harun al-Rashid, the then reigning Abbasid Caliph. He brought all his famous knights with him, chief among whom were his nephew Roland, the greatest Christian knight of the times in Europe, his brave friend Oliver and Ogier the Dane. Charles crossed the Pyrenees and fought a number of engagements with the Muslim forces, but he met with very stiff resistance. Things were in this state when word reached him that the Saxons of Germany, whom he had but recently conquered, had revolted. He took a part of the army and went back. The other part he left under the command of Roland, but Roland was asked to withdraw also. This was an opportunity for the Muslims. They pressed on behind Roland and the Franks had to fight many severe rearguard actions. When Roland's army was in the midst of the Pyrenees mountains the fierce mountaineers of the region fell upon him. Roland was now in desperate straits. He was a very brave knight, and he did not want to retreat. He therefore decided to fight. The battle which ensued has been the theme of song and story. It forms the chief episode in the *Chanson de Roland*, or 'Song of Roland', the French epic. The mountaineers were too strong for the brave knights of Roland, who fought like heroes, but were cut down. When Roland was mortally wounded he blew his famous horn. In legend this horn had magical properties. Its call could be heard miles and miles away. The dying echoes of Roland's blast were heard by his uncle Charlemagne who was many miles away. He realized instantly that Roland was in danger. He hurried back, but arrived too late. Roland was dead with his knights. The defeat at this battle of Roncesvalles daunted even Charlemagne and he did not think again of invading Spain.

Abdul Rahman's achievements. Abdul Rahman made no claim to the Caliphate. He called himself Amir and set about making his position secure. He was a very talented man and had progressive ideas. He had repairs done to the towns which had suffered during the sieges and assaults of the last generation; he built canals and developed irrigation; he planted new fruit trees and raised many beautiful new buildings. In 786, he laid the foundations of his finest achievement, the great mosque of Cordova (*Masjid al-Qurtuba*) which was completed in the times of his successors. This mosque was one of the glories of Spanish Muslim art or, as it is sometimes called, Moorish art. Abdul Rahman also made efforts to bring together the warring Muslim groups of the Arabs, Berbers, Syrians, Africans, the neo-Muslims, even the Goths. His efforts were successful and for more than two hundred and fifty years, the Muslims of Spain worked as one people, and as a result, they perfected a civilization which was the finest in Europe at that time and vied with that of the Abbasids in the East. The Arabs of Spain were the teachers of Europe, and the universities of Cordova, Toledo, and Seville served as the fountain-heads of culture for Arab and non-Arab, Muslim and Christian, Jew and Gentile for centuries to come. Abdul Rahman treated the conquered people with as much consideration as they were treated in the rest of the Islamic world. They were not compelled to accept Islam. Muslim Law or customs were not thrust on them. The old, the very young, and the priests were exempted from taxes. In short, a new order of life was set up by this remarkable monarch.

Al-Hakam (796-822). Abdul Rahman died in 788 and was followed by his son Hisham I, who was a good man, given to study and pious works. Hisham's son al-Hakam, who came to the throne in 796, was not so kind or considerate a man as his father and grandfather had been and he did many foolish things. He kept a Nubian bodyguard around him who could not speak Arabic. They were haughty and many of them were not Muslim. There was constant trouble between them and the people and there were a few risings, which al-Hakam put down with such a severe hand that thousands of Spanish Arabs left the country. Many of them took ship and sailed east. They came to Crete, the island to the south of Greece and conquered it. Crete remained under Arab rule for a hundred and fifty years.

Abdul Rahman II (822-852). Al-Hakam's son, Abdul Rahman II, was however, a different man. Truly enlightened, he was a great patron of the arts, and invited and attracted to his court poets, artists, musicians, and singers from other countries. One peculiar thing is associated with this Amir's reign. The fame of Muslim arts and sciences and of the Spanish Muslim universities had spread so far that Christians came in large numbers to study and learn. Arabic became the language of learning. A knowledge of Arabic was indispensable and Arabic books were sought in France and in Italy. The Pope was disturbed and there had to be a reaction. Some Christian fanatics thought of a scheme. They could come to a Qadi's court, apparently to accept Islam, and there in open court would abuse the Prophet and use filthy language about him and his Companions. The obvious punishment for such an offence in those days was death as even now the Muslims cannot tolerate the slightest slur on Islam or the Prophet. Naturally these peace-breakers were tried and put to death, but this did not stop the fanatics. Even some women now joined the movement. They were so brazen in their abusive conduct that the court could make no distinction in their cases. They had to die too. Many people courted 'martyrdom' in this way. Fortunately the movement did not last very long.

Mozarebs and Muwallads. Another disturbing factor rose under the reigns of Abdul Rahman II's successors. The sons of slave mothers, called Muwallads, and the Christians who had accepted Arab ways and were called Mozarebs now started to claim equality of status with the Arabs. Many of these Muwallads and Mozarebs went further. They gave their claims a patriotic colour and proclaimed that they were working for a national cause. They were Spaniards, and there is no doubt that they had every right to fight for their rights. The result was that there were a number of risings which were put down. But these insurgents made common cause sometimes with the minor Christian kingdoms of the north-west and found an ally in the king of Leon in the north. What was worse, a Mozareb of note, a man of talent who had been trained in the Royal household, and held office in the Royal Cavalry and had professed to be a Muslim, calling himself Omar ibn Hafsun, now left the service and went home, where he organized a band of outlaws. He, too, declared that he was fighting for Spain. He raided many towns and harassed the country-side. Gradually he won for himself a considerable area in the south. He even sought the help of the semi-independent Abbasid Governors of Ifriqiya, the Aghlabids, but he failed to get assistance from them. He now showed his true colours, called himself Samuel and openly called all the Christians to him. Things became difficult for the Amirs of Cordova, pressed as they were from all sides.

Abdul Rahman III (912-961). A new champion of Islam was needed at this time and he appeared in the person of Abdul Rahman III, who came to the throne in 912. He was twenty-three years old when he assumed power. He was a gifted man, full of energy and ideas, and set about his task with dauntless courage. It was not long before he had subdued all the territory of the Amirate, and in five years he was supreme Lord of Muslim Spain.

Fights with Fatimids and Christians. Abdul Rahman III had to fight all his life, and he fought valiantly and successfully. Among his chief enemies were the Christians of the north, who were beginning to organize themselves, had a few tiny kingdoms of their own and were determined to fight Islam. Nobody can blame them, for they were fighting for their homeland and their religion. It took them nearly five hundred years to win, though they fought the Muslims whenever they could. His other enemies were a new Muslim power, which had overthrown the Aghlabid rulers of Ifriqiya and become dominant in north Africa. These were the Fatimids, an extreme sect of the Shia who were very zealous and believed in propaganda. They sent their agents into Spain to work against the Omayyad Amirs. The Fatimids claimed descent from Lady Fatima, the daughter of the Prophet and were therefore the declared enemies of the Bani Omayyah. They had underestimated Abdul Rahman III, who was a dangerous person to annoy. He decided to carry the war into the enemy's camp: he had himself accepted as overlord in Morocco and began to operate from there. He also sent a fleet to the Barbary coast (modern Algeria and Tunisia) to attack and harass Fatimid shipping. These attacks and counter-attacks went on for many years.

Campaign against the Christians. The campaign against the Christians of the north, however, was more definite and more important. Ordano, the King of Leon, began the war by raiding the Muslim borders. Abdul Rahman sent a small army against him, but Ordano defeated it, captured the Muslim commander, cut off his head and stuck it on the castle walls of San Esteban, beside the head of a pig. Abdul Rahman vowed in open court that he would teach Ordano a lesson that the Christians would not forget in a hurry. He went north, met and defeated Ordano, captured the important Christian town of San Esteban and razed it to the ground. Ordano sought help from Sancho the king of Navarre, but Abdul Rahman crushed the combined army. He now overran their territories, and a few years later (924) he captured Pamplona, the capital of Navarre, and destroyed it. For many years after, there was peace.

The New Capital (929). Abdul Rahman III now took the title of al-Nasir (the Supporter of the Faith) and resumed the Caliphate of his Omayyad ancestors, setting up his new capital in Cordova. Thus there were two Caliphs at this time in the world of Islam: the Abbasid Caliph in Baghdad and the Omayyad Caliph in Spain. As the defender of Islam, Abdul

Rahman III won great fame, defeating the Christians of the north many times. But once, in 939, he made a mistake. He under-estimated the strength of the allied Christian army of the King of Leon and the Queen of Navarre, and suffered the first defeat of his career. His prestige, however, was high, the strength of Muslim arms was admitted and he lost nothing by this defeat. A truce was signed and friendly relations were set up for a time. When, a little later, Queen Tota of Navarre wanted medical aid for her son, Sancho the Fat, and also help against a usurper, she came to Cordova; Abdul Rahman gave her both.

Achievements of Abdul Rahman III. Abdul Rahman III was the greatest king of his line. He was a great administrator as well as a great builder. He built near Cordova a beautiful palace called *al-Zahra* (the Beautiful) which was considered a marvel of Muslim art. People came to see it from far and near. It was destroyed later by the puritanical Muwahhids from Africa. Abdul Rahman did better with his government. He made it central, strengthened the armed forces, built a strong navy, encouraged industry and made many improvements in irrigation and agriculture. By this time a new middle class of Muslims had grown up which took to industry and commerce eagerly. Only the military commanders sought estates now, the other Muslims had plenty to do. The Christians and Jews had settled down and become part of the Spanish Arab nation. The new Caliph was very tolerant and there was peace and plenty everywhere. The universities of Cordova and other Muslim towns rose to great heights of achievement and population increased, the capital becoming the first town of Europe. This was the Golden Age of Spain.

Al-Hakam II (961-976). After the man of war came the man of peace. Abdul Rahman III's son and successor, al-Hakam II, was one of those rulers who appear only now and then. He is considered a worthy successor to the great Abdul Rahman. Essentially a peaceful man, he devoted the fifteen years of his reign to the pursuit of learning, the spread of scholarship, and the encouragement of science. He expanded the University of Cordova till it became the largest, as well as the finest, seat of learning in the world. The library which he founded contained over 400,000 volumes and he spent untold sums on the purchase of books, manuscripts, and on the employment of learned men and scholars. He was a good scholar himself; thousands of volumes in the University Library bore his marginal notes. The money with which he endowed the university would build many universities today. He was not only a scholar, he took the field against the hereditary foes of the Spanish Arabs, the Christians of northern Spain, and after a campaign lasting eight years (962-970) he forced them to sue for peace. The war with the Fatimids also continued, and there too al-Hakam was successful. He drove the Fatimids out of Morocco in 973 and thus put an end to their power in al-Maghrib. Thereafter, the Fatimids concentrated on Egypt.

The Hajib. Al-Hakam died early. He left a young son and a beautiful and capable queen, who was a princess of northern Spain. When she became the Regent she had to look for capable administrators and found one in Muhammad ibn Abi'Amir, who was a man of great talent. He had risen to high office already by his own ability. She now chose him as her state adviser. After a while he became her chief counsellor. As such he called himself the 'Hajib' (chamberlain). The Hajib took more and more power into his hands, until, in a short time, he became dictator, and as such ruled Muslim Spain for thirty years. To win people to him he showered gifts on the clever men, the Ulema, and the poets. He did one unpardonable thing, however, to which it is said the narrow-minded Ulema forced him: he ordered all the books on philosophy, which al-Hakam had collected at great cost, to be burnt.

Hajib the Conqueror. This side of the Hajib may not have been attractive, but there was another side. He was a great fighter in the cause of Islam. It is doubtful if in the whole history of Muslim Spain there was a greater 'Mujahid'. He strengthened the army and led it against the Christian princes of the north, who had again been raiding the northern borders. He took Zamora in 981, sacked Barcelona in 985 and in 988 laid siege to Leon, the capital of the kingdom of Leon. He took it and razed it to the ground. He then annexed Leon to the Caliphate of Cordova. He even invaded the extreme north-western provinces of Galicia and the Asturias. In all, the Hajib led fifty *ghazwahs* against the Christian princes of the north and in 1002 he died fighting against the Christians with a sword in his hand, to the last.

Successors of the Hajib al-Mansur. The Hajib, who came to be called al-Mansur, which means the Victorious, was also a very able administrator. He held rather old-fashioned views about intellectual pursuits, but in practical matters he was extremely capable. His name had became a terror to the Christian world and when he died there was rejoicing in the whole of southern Europe. The Hajib was succeeded in his office as Chief Counsellor or Chief Minister, first by his son Abdul Malik, later by his second son Abdul Rahman, but they were neither so strong nor so capable as their father. Abdul Rahman was killed by the people of Cordova in a rising. The bodyguard which had been organized by Abdul Rahman III was perhaps behind this rising. This bodyguard now came into power, as similar bodyguards in other Muslim lands did throughout Muslim history. The bodyguards everywhere got out of hand and began to make and unmake rulers. When this happened, whether the rulers were Abbasids, Turks, Ayyubids, or the Sultans of India, the results were unfortunate. In Spain, as all reputable historians of Islam have recorded, a period of intrigue and murder, of double-dealing and political roguery intervened. For a time the government passed into the hands of the Hammudids, who claimed descent from Hazrat Ali and held the government for about thirty years. In time they too became incompetent. The government was then taken over by a

Council of State. The Omayyad Caliphate of Spain now broke up into small states. Mention can only be made of the most important of them.

Kingdom of Seville—Al-Mutamid (1068-1091). The most important of these states was the kingdom of Seville which was founded by the Qadi of Seville. The most notable ruler of this dynasty was al-Mutamid who has elicited high praise from such a discerning writer as Ibn Khallikan. Al-Mutamid was a strong man who ruled with a firm hand, extended the boundaries of his kingdom, set the affairs of the state in order, encouraged learning and patronized the poets and the artists. He was himself a poet of note, and his poems are read to this day. In the last years of his life, he made a political mistake which cost him his kingdom. He allied himself with Alphonso VI, the king of Galicia, against the neighbouring Muslim States. Later he had to fight the rising Muslim power of the Berbers, who were called the Murabits. In this venture he lost everything and was blinded and sent into exile by the victorious Murabits.

The Rise of the Berber powers in al-Maghrib—The Idrisids. Before discussing the Murabits, it is necessary to go back a little and tell of what had been happening in al-Maghrib, because it was there that two Berber powers rose, the Murabits and the Muwahhids, who between them dominated Spain for the next two centuries. Not long after Abdul Rahman I had come into power in Spain, a great grandson of Imam Hasan, more adventurous and more capable than the other Alids, came to the west. He had taken part in a rising against the Abbasids in Medina but had lost. He had managed to escape the slaughter which followed and came to al-Maghrib. He had some followers with him and he used his descent and his cause, the cause of the House of Ali, against the House of Abbas to advantage. In al-Maghrib he found a hearing and soon established a Shiite kingdom (The Idrisids) there. His descendants ruled in this region for almost two hundred years. This was the first dynasty set up by an Alid.

Aghlabids (800-909). The other North African Muslim dynasty during the times of the Omayyads of Spain was that of the Aghlabids. It was founded by General Ibrahim ibn al-Aghlab, who had been sent by Caliph Harun al-Rashid to restore order in Ifriqiya. Ibn al-Aghlab was a capable man. He settled at Qairawan, brought the whole area (half of Algeria, Tunisia, Cyrenaica, and Numidia) under his sway and began to rule as a semi-independent monarch. His descendants were a vigorous set of rulers and became a strong naval power. They built a navy and began to raid the Mediterranean islands and the southern coast of Europe. They conquered Sicily in 902 and then, using it as a naval base, took Malta in the south and Sardinia in the north. They made friends with the Muslim kingdom of Crete and so the combined navies of the Aghlabids, Sicily, and Arab Crete invaded Greece. The Aghlabids arabicized Sicily and laid the foundation of the wonderful Siculo-Arab civilization of Sicily which flourished there for more than three hundred years, even though the Muslims were driven out of Sicily in 1100. Ziyadat Ullah the Aghlabid built a great mosque at Qairawan which stands to this day, though the great *madrasah* which was part of the mosque no longer exists.

The Fatimids in Ifriqiya. The Aghlabids were overthrown by the Ismailis. The Ismaili movement was a secret organization with extreme Shiite views, which believed in its own Hidden Imam and did not care what sacrifices it made or what means it adopted to achieve its ends. Once supreme, the Ismailis destroyed whatever useful social, cultural or religious institutions existed, even if they were Muslim, and then built their own. These Ismailis had already appeared under different names in Persia and Arabia. In Ifriqiya they appeared under a new leader, called Ubaidullah, who claimed to be descended from Lady Fatima, the wife of Ali. He and his followers made their plans and then kindled a rising by which they put an end to the last Aghlabids. The Fatimids built their capital at al-Mahdiya and took over the Aghlabid navy, which they strengthened, making themselves a naval power in the Central Mediterranean. They took over Sicily and Sardinia and made great progress in the cultural, administrative, and agricultural advancement of Sicily. The Fatimids then began to expand towards the east, and by about the middle of the tenth century they had conquered Egypt. They now had a large empire, which they ruled from Egypt for two hundred years.

The Murabits of Morocco — Yusuf ibn Tafshin (1061-1106). The Murabits, who had overthrown the last king of Seville, became a Spanish-Moroccan power. When the Fatimids made Egypt the seat of their power, their governors in Ifriqiya gradually became semi-independent. The weakening of Fatimid control in this region gave the Berbers a chance. They had been ruled by the Arabs for three hundred years. They now began to organize themselves. They found a leader in the head of a religious community, the members of which lived in desert monasteries. A Muslim monastery was called a *ribat*. Hence their title of Murabits (dwellers in monasteries). The leader was Abdullah ibn Yasin who conquered the whole of Morocco. His cousin and successor Yusuf ibn Tafshin founded the city of Marrakesh and made it the capital of the Murabit kingdom. Mention has been made of the mistake of al-Mutamid, the last king of Seville, in seeking alliance with Alphonso VI against the other Muslim states. After al-Mutamid had beaten back his rivals in Spain, Alphonso VI wanted a slice of the kingdom of Seville as a reward. This al-Mutamid would not yield, so Alphonso VI invaded the kingdom of Seville. Al-Mutamid sought help from Yusuf ibn Tafshin. Yusuf came with a large army and in 1086 defeated Alphonso VI who had begun to call himself Emperor of Spain. Yusuf went back after this, but affairs in Seville did not improve. The petty Muslim kingdoms of Spain still fought among themselves. So a strong appeal was made to Yusuf by many nobles to come over permanently and unite all Muslim Spain under him. Perhaps he was tempted himself, and it may be that his own captains wanted to live in the highly civilized cities of Spain. In any case, Yusuf went over in 1090 and brought all of Muslim Spain under him. Al-Mutamid tried to fight Yusuf, but was not strong enough. He was defeated and deported to Morocco as a state prisoner. The Murabits were now masters of half of Spain and a considerable portion of western Africa. Yusuf was a Sunni and acknowledged the Abbasid Caliph of Baghdad as the Supreme Head of Islam. He became a tower of strength for Islam in the west.

Later Murabits—The Cid (1040-1099). Yusuf's son Ali was a devout Muslim. He was also a good ruler. In his time, the Mozarebs, the Spanish Christians, who had taken to Arab ways, and had taken Muslim names besides their own Christian names, who spoke Arabic and lived like Arabs, joined with other Spaniards and began to rebel against the Muslims. They found a great champion in Don Rodrigo Diaz de Bivar, who was a Mozareb himself, had fought for Muslims and had been named by them the 'Cid' or the leader. He now turned against the Muslims, occupied the town of Valencia and became the champion of Christian Spain. He was a gallant fighter and a chivalrous enemy. He fought so cleanly and was so noble in his dealings that he was respected even by his enemies. After his death the Spaniards wrote an epic poem about him called *Cantar de mio Cid* or 'The Song of My Leader'.

The Muwahhids (1145-1212). The Murabits ruled well till 1130, but for the last few years they ceased to be a great power. Incompetent rulers, inner quarrels, the strong opposition of the Christians who were now united against the Muslims, shook the Murabit power. Things were in a bad way, when another Berber chief appeared in north-west Africa. He also was the head of a religious community who, being puritans, called themselves Muwahhids. The leader, who was named Ibn Tumart, organized his community well. He was followed by his able lieutenant Abdul Mumin who became the real founder of Muwahhid power. Abdul Mumin defeated the last Murabit ruler in 1145 and captured all the towns in Morocco. Marrakesh was taken after a siege. He then crossed over to Spain and brought Andalusia under his sway. The Muslims by 1150 had been driven from the upper half of Spain, and except for a small portion of north-eastern Spain, the peninsula was evenly divided between Christians and Muslims. The southern half was called Andalusia and after this time, for three hundred years of varied fortunes, the Muslims never occupied more of Spain than Andalusia. Abdul Mumin, being now master of the situation, extended his domains. He conquered Algeria in 1152, Tunisia in 1158, and Tripolitania in 1160. The Murabits had never conquered the lands of Ifriqiya beyond Algeria, the Muwahhid borders touched Egypt and they did not acknowledge the suzerainty of the Abbasid Caliph. It was the Muwahhids who rebuilt the glory of Muslim Spain.

Al-Mansur (1184-1199) and his successors. The best of the Muwahhids was Abdul Mumin's grandson Abu Yusuf Yaqub called al-Mansur. Abu Yusuf was so powerful a monarch that even the great Salahuddin sought his help against the Crusades, and this champion of western Islam sent 180 ships to Sultan Salahuddin's aid. The Muwahhids shifted their capital from Marrakesh to Seville and, though a puritanic sect, began to build and beautify that town. Abu Yusuf's minaret, the Giralda, stands to this day, though the mosque which stood by its side has gone. He built a hospital in Marrakesh, which was considered the greatest hospital of the time. The Muwahhids encouraged learning and most of the great philosophers and historians of Spain flourished during their time. The last Muwahhid ruler was Abu Yusuf's son Muhammad al-Nasir who was defeated by a strong alliance of the Christian kingdoms of Spain at Las Navas de Tolosa in 1212. After al-Nasir's defeat Andalusia was split up into many small kingdoms. The greatest of them was the kingdom of Granada which flourished till 1492, when the last king of the Nasirid dynasty ruling at Granada was defeated and driven out of

Spain. It was the Nasirids who built the Alhambra in Granada. The Nasirids were very cultured rulers and they held out for two hundred and fifty years against the Christians, who had by now won back nearly four-fifths of Spain.

Muslim Culture in Spain. The Muslims of Spain played a distinct role in history. They built up a civilization and produced a culture which were the finest in Europe in the Middle Ages. They influenced the thought of Englishmen, Frenchmen, Italians, and Spaniards. When the Spaniards were at last successful in turning the Muslims out, they not only killed a phase of civilization, they inflicted irreparable damage on their own country. The Arabs of Spain inspired the whole of Europe, and the treasures in books which they left behind them became the real source of knowledge and learning of the Europeans for centuries. Arab Spain produced as many names in literature, philosophy, medicine, science, history, geography, mysticism, and travel as the Arab world of the East.

Muslim Philosophers. It has been said by the Europeans that the Arabs took what the Greeks had left behind them and only wrote commentaries upon it. This is untrue and unjust. There is no philosopher who does not consider the systems of philosophy which others have propounded before him and philosophy is nothing but finding meaning in the phenomena of this world. To say that everything is derived from the Greeks, or the Indians, or the Chinese, is to deny mental growth and original thinking to mankind. It is true that the Arabs had no literary or philosophic background of their own, but they learnt from all, and whatever they learnt they made their own. They clarified issues which had been left unexplained, and their greatest achievement in philosophy lies in the fact that they tried to reconcile faith with reason. This legacy they gave to Europe, and it is on this basis that Europe built her Revival of Learning. Four great Spanish Muslim names stand out in this field and they all have a high place in the history of thought.

(a)Ibn Bajjah (d. 1138) was a philosopher, scientist, and physician. He believed that the aim of philosophy was to teach man to attain nearness to God and he believed in man's capacity for perfection.

(b)Ibn Tufail, who came after him, was a Muwahhid (d. 1185). He was the chief physician of Sultan Abu Yusuf Yaqub. Ibn Tufail is famous for his outline of the theory of evolution. He believed that man was capable of winning supreme knowledge.

(c)Ibn Rushd (Averroes 1126-1198) lived in the reign of the Muwahhid ruler Abu Yusuf Yaqub and was Qadi of Seville and of Cordova. He is famous for his Encyclopaedia of Medicine. Ibn Rushd was considered by Europe as a master commentator and his liberal outlook recommended him to all. For five hundred years Ibn Rushd's books were text-books in western as well as eastern universities.

(d)Musa Ibn Maimun (1135-1204) was born a Jew in Cordova, but left Spain for Egypt where he became court physician to the great Salahuddin. His fame rests on his effort to reconcile faith with reason. He was a very liberal thinker.

Al-Idrisi (1100-1166). Such was the impetus to learning given by the Muslims of Spain, that it is not surprising that the finest geographer of those days was also a Western Arab. He was al-Idrisi the twelfth-century geographer and maker of maps. He was born at Ceuta in 1100 and his work took him to Sicily. He did his best work under Roger II, the Norman king of Sicily who had succeeded the Fatimids in the dominion of Sicily, but who preserved the Siculo-Arab culture of Sicily.

Ibn Arabi, Ibn Hazm. Among the other famous men of Muslim Spain, mention must be made of the great mystic Ibn Arabi and Ibn Hazm the Qadi. Ibn Arabi was born in 1165 and lived in Seville for a time. In 1202 he went to Mecca for a pilgrimage and decided to stay in Arabia. He was offered a professorship in the University of Damascus, where he taught for the rest of his life. Ibn Arabi taught that Allah was light and the world was an expression of Allah. He also believed that man could perfect himself and approach the Godhead. He wrote a book in which he writes of a journey through the heavens. Scholars think that Dante, the great Italian poet, borrowed the idea of his poem *The Divine Comedy* from Ibn Arabi. The other great name was Ibn Hazm, who was the greatest writer of them all. He wrote about a hundred books and was equally knowledgeable about history, poetry, traditions, and logic.

Ibn Khaldun (1332-1406). The greatest name among the Muslims in the art of writing history is that of Abdul Rahman Ibn Khaldun, a Spanish Muslim by descent. He came much later than the others and was born at Tunis. He took service with the Sultan of Granada in 1361, and in 1382 he went to Cairo and became a professor at the University of al-Azhar. He met Timur, the terror of the world, when he besieged Damascus. The introduction to his history contains ideas about the writing of history which are modern even today.

Ibn Battutah (1304-1377). In the field of travel and observation the greatest name in the Middle Ages is also that of a Muslim of al-Maghrib. It is that of Muhammad ibn Abdullah ibn Battutah. He was born in Morocco and, after finishing his studies, set out on his travels. He covered the entire Islamic world and lived in Delhi alone for seven years in the reign of Sultan Muhammad Tughluq. Ibn Battutah travelled to China and he visited the East Indies. In Africa he crossed the Sahara and visited Timbuktu. His travels provide valuable information about the world of those days and make very good reading even today.

Sicily. A word must now be said about the Fatimids, who rose in Ifriqiya, conquered Sicily from the Aghlabids and then moved to the east and established themselves in Egypt, where they ruled for two hundred years. The Aghlabids had expelled the Byzantines from Sicily by the end of the ninth century and had made Palermo their capital. They had also conquered areas in the south of Italy and had operated from there against Naples and Rome (882-915). At one time they had forced Pope John VIII to pay tribute to them. The Aghlabids had been an energetic people and had quickly introduced the Arab way of life in the island. The Fatimids, when they took over from the Aghlabids, were not behindhand with improvements in any useful field. The Arabs who did most to make Sicily a seat of culture and learning for two centuries and more were a family of Kalbites. When the Fatimids had moved to Egypt, they appointed Hasan ibn Ali al-Kalbi governor of Sicily. Gradually Hasan became a semi-independent ruler and the government of the island became hereditary in his family. During the Kalbite reign Palermo became a great town. Ibn Hawqal, the great Muslim traveller, visited Palermo at this time, and wrote that the town was one of the biggest and the best he had ever seen; that it had 300 mosques and over 300 high-class *madrasahs*. The Normans who conquered Sicily in the eleventh century so appreciated the intelligence, skill and scholarship, as well as the diplomacy of the Arabs, that they retained most of them in office. In fact it was the Normans who accepted Arab ways, dressed like Arabs, spoke Arabic, and stamped their coins with Arabic letters, even stamping the date according to the Hijrah. Arab culture kept its dominant position till the days of Frederick II, the German Emperor who preferred to stay in Sicily, spoke Arabic, had Arabs around him and lived like an enlightened Arab. Sicily gave the best of Muslim learning to Italy and promoted that intellectual awakening of Italy and southern Europe called the Renaissance.

The Fatimids of Egypt. It was in 969 that the Fatimid general Jawhar overthrew the ruling dynasty of Ikhshidids, who had succeeded the talented dynasty of the Tulunids in Egypt. Ahmad ibn Tulun, an Abbasid governor, had become an independent ruler and had made Egypt a strong state, improving administration, building mosques and other important buildings. The Ikhshidids who followed the

Tulunids were not, however, a remarkable dynasty in any way. Then came the Fatimid rule in Egypt. It was General Jawhar who founded the new town of al-Qahirah (modern Cairo) in 973. Jawhar also built the great mosque of al-Azhar and made it into a *madrasah* on a grand scale. Not long afterwards the Fatimids conquered Syria as well as al-Hijaz, and thus became a great power in the Middle East. They now styled themselves Caliphs. Since they professed the extreme Shiite creed, they were intolerant of Sunnis, and even of other Shiite creeds and had no love at all for the Sunni Abbasid Caliph at Baghdad. This divided the Muslim world into three parts: the Sunni West, the Shiite Middle, and the Sunni East. The Sunni al-Maghrib and Andalusia was cut off from both the Middle East and the East. The easy flow of ideas and the sense of unity which had prevailed so far in the Islamic world was thus greatly affected. This split the Muslim world and encouraged Christian Europe to start the Crusades.

Fall of the Fatimids. The greatest Fatimid was the fifth Caliph, Nizar al-Aziz. During his reign the Fatimids had a larger area under them than even the Caliph of Baghdad. Al-Aziz was a great builder and a noted patron of the arts. He constructed mosques, palaces, bridges, and gardens. He was a very tolerant monarch and no non-Muslim was badly treated during his time. The Fatimids had early organized a corps of Turkish slaves as a royal bodyguard and after al-Aziz's death this corps began to grow powerful. Unfortunately for Islam, al-Aziz's successor al-Hakim was deranged in his mind. He did many senseless acts, annoyed the Christians unnecessarily and by his intolerance was mainly responsible for bringing on the Crusades. He was killed in a court intrigue and then the bodyguard came to real power.

Arts and Sciences. The Caliph al-Aziz had founded a Hall of Science (*Dar-ul-Hikmah*), but there was no great outburst of intellectual activity under the Fatimids. Being Shiites, they devoted more attention to their own literature and traditions and scorned liberal pursuits. Consequently not many poets, philosophers, or mystics were born of their efforts to encourage learning. There were, however, a few scientists of calibre in this period. Of them Ibn al-Haytham (Al-Hazen) must be mentioned with honour. He was a physicist and did great work on optics. The Fatimids raised many fine buildings and added to the beauties of Muslim architecture. Fatimid work in pottery, metal-work, and wood was highly prized, and can to this day be found in the museums of the world.

Muslim Spain at its best. Abdur Rahman III—called the Great Khalif was a remarkable ruler and a representative of the excellence in the arts of war and peace achieved by the Muslims in Spain. Quoting Dozy, the eminent historian of Spain, Stanley Lane Poole says: 'He had rescued Andalusia both from herself and from subjection by the foreigner. And he had not only saved her from destruction, he had made her great and happy. Never was Cordova so rich and prosperous as under his rule; never was Andalusia so well-cultivated, so teeming with the gifts of nature, brought to perfection by the skill and industry of man; never was the State so triumphant over disorder or the power of law more widely felt and respected. Ambassadors came to pay him court from the Emperor of Constantinople, from the Kings of France, of Germany, of Italy. His power, wisdom, and opulence were a byword over Europe and Africa and had even reached to the farthest limits of the Moslem empire in Asia. And this wonderful change had been brought by one man with everything against him; the restoration of Andalusia from the hopeless depths of misery to the height of power and prosperity had been effected by the intellect and will alone of the Great Khalif Abd-er-Rehman III'. (*The Moors in Spain*—Chapter III).

Cultural Transmission to Europe. An Arab writer, the famous historian Al-Maqqari said of Cordova: 'To Cordova came from all parts of the world; students eager to cultivate knowledge, to study poetry as well as the sciences, or to be instructed in divinity or law; so that it became the meeting place of the eminent in all matters, the abode of the learned and the place of resort for the studious; its interior was always filled with the eminent and the noble of all countries; its literary men and soldiers were continually vying with each other to gain renown and its precincts never ceased to be the arena of the distinguished, the race-course of readers, the halting place of the noble and the repository of the true and virtuous. Cordova was to Andalusia what the head is to the body or what the breast is to the loin'.

This may sound extravagant as it comes from a Muslim writer but in a recent publication : *Cambridge History of Islam* Vol. II, Chapter 13, the following remarks about the results of the contacts between East and West in Spain and Sicily deserve mention: 'This two-fold aspect, Greek and Arab, of the knowledge which from the XIth century onwards the Christian West had been eagerly striving to acquire, is clear; clear too is the awareness of its hybrid character on the part of the West. This second contact between East and West in the cultural field was a repetition in Europe after the year 1000 of that which had taken place in Mesopotamia and Iraq between Greek and Islamic culture during the third/ninth and fourth/tenth centuries.'....

'Muslim and Mozarabic Spain before its re-conquest by the Christians was the theatre and the most important centre of this new contact. Contacts between the West and Graeco-Arab culture in other Mediterranean areas such as Sicily and Italy were of secondary importance, compared with the intensity and significance of the work accomplished in Spain; and the influence of the Crusades to which at one time it was customary to attribute a considerable share in these scientific and cultural exchanges now appears to have been very slight'. Talking of the role of Sicily in transmitting Arab literary and scientific masterpieces to Europe, F. Gabrieli of the University of Rome says: 'Here the cultural contact between the Cordova Amirate was carried on intensively by Mozarabic and Jewish elements throughout the period of Arab domination and it yielded its best fruits at the time when this domination was declining. We know that translations Arabic into Latin were made in Catalonia from the tenth century onwards and during the first half of the twelfth century Barcelona was the abode of the first translator of those days, whose identity can be established— Plato of Tivoli. Between 1116 and 1138 with the help of an Andalusian Jew, Abraham bar Hiyya, called Savasorda (Sahib al-Sharta), Plato of Tivoli translated Jewish and Arab works on astrology and astronomy, including the astronomical tables of Al-Battani. About this time, the centre of such activities shifted to Toledo, which had been restored to Christendom a few decades before, and had become a beacon of Graeco-Arab-Hebraic culture for the whole of the Latin West. The praiseworthy activities of the learned men who flocked thither from every part of Europe in order to study the treasures of Graeco-Arab philosophy and science were a striking feature of a great part of the 12th century'. And further, Professor Gabrieli says:

Muslim Learning Inspires the West. 'In this way far from being merely the transmitters of the philosophical ideas of antiquity, the Arabs and the Muslims in general, became the teachers and inspirers or else the controverted and confuted adversaries of the West. The chief factors in the transmission of philosophy and the controversies that followed, regarding questions such as the reconciliation of reason with faith, was in reality extraneous to genuine Classical Philosophy, or were at least barely touched upon, but from its distant cousin Islam, Christianity inherited the ideal formulation and the dramatic tension of the problem. The Muslim element was reflected in scholasticism, in medieval apologetics and even elaborated and perhaps adulterated or misunderstood in the philosophy of the Renaissance and the Enlightenment'. *(Cambridge History of Islam,* Vol. II, Chapter 13).

CHAPTER 5

THE ABBASIDS

The Task before the Abbasids. The Abbasid propaganda, the disorganization which resulted from internal strife, the loss of respect for the rulers, increased taxation, the struggle between the Arabs and the neo-Muslims or Mawalis, all combined to make the accession of the Abbasids easier. To their surprise, they found that the later Omayyads had neglected to keep up the strength of their standing army. All these lessons were not lost on the Abbasids. They decided to avoid all these pitfalls, and for a century and a half they succeeded in doing so. This was the period of the great Abbasids and it was in this period that they did their greatest work, the work of building up a living Arab civilization and making the word Arab mean something worthwhile in the world of those days.

The World of Islam (750). A brief survey of the Islamic world makes it easier to understand the picture. Medina and Mecca had fallen out of politics and had become seats of learning and culture. People returned to these early centres of Islam, built villas, and cultivated their tastes in living. Damascus was a great Muslim town, al-Fustat and Qairawan were growing into important seats of government, and Kufa as well as Basra was already noted for its political as well as cultural role. The Arabs had fallen hungrily on the treasures of Greek, Indian, Persian, and Syrian knowledge and every avenue of science was being explored eagerly by them. Whereas they had originally accepted the civil administrative systems of the Persians and the Byzantines, by 750 they had changed them sufficiently to suit their own conditions and needs. The .term Arab was now extended to include all Muslims who lived in the Islamic world, learned its ways, thought its thoughts, and worked for the common good of all Muslims. Never before or after was there such unity of purpose seen anywhere as in the century and a half which were to follow.

The Early Abbasids—Al-Saffah (750-754). The Abbasids inherited from the Omayyads a great empire, from which only Spain and al-Maghrib had been separated. Arab life was still simple, there was yet considerable zeal for Islam, nobody was yet sated with either conquest or government, responsibilities of office or creative work, pomp or glory. The Abbasids were in a position to achieve more because the ground had been prepared for them by the great Omayyads, and the early Abbasids took advantage of this. Al-Saffah, the first Caliph, was a blood-thirsty man. He justified himself by saying that the Omayyads deserved all that could be done to them, but his story is not one to be proud of. The name 'Bloodshedder' in itself does honour to nobody. No doubt he had to take strong measures to make his position secure, as there were a great many risings early in his reign, and these risings continued in the reigns of his successors. Kufa was especially trouble-some. The Kufans would not take al-Saffah seriously, for they had seen the great Ali and his sons al-Hasan and al-Husain, and later Omayyad governors like Ziyad, his son Obaidullah, al-Hajjaj ibn Yusuf, and al-Qasri. They knew what good government was. They had started so many conspiracies and new movements themselves that they knew the worth of the Abbasid propaganda. Al-Saffah therefore used an iron hand in suppressing the reactionaries. In order to impress people he posed as a holy man. On Fridays, when he led the prayers as Caliph of Islam, he wore the mantle of the Prophet. He kept many learned men about him. Every effort was made to persuade the people that the Abbasids were the true representatives of the Prophet's House. It is clear from this, that by now, more emphasis was being put on belonging to the Prophet's House than on being the best representative of the people. The Caliphs were not only the representatives of the

Prophet, they were also the shadow of God. They soon came to be 'appointed'. Nobody thought any longer of electing a new Caliph. The Caliphate became a hereditary possession. This gave great strength to the Shiat-i-Ali, or the Party of Ali, who naturally said that if Caliph-hood was a matter of right, then nobody deserved it more than the House of Ali, especially as represented by the children and descendants of al-Hasan and al-Husain. They further argued that since al-Husain was also a great martyr, his descendants had a greater right. This idea later brought about a great division in Islam.

Al-Mansur (754-775)—The Risings. Al-Saffah did not live long and was succeeded by his brother Abu Ja'far who was a much more capable man, though no less ruthless. Abu Ja'far, who later took the title of al-Mansur, was the real founder of the Abbasid power. He had to meet with a number of rebellions early in his reign. The first was that of his own uncle, General Abdullah, who had defeated Marwan II in the battle of the Zab River, conquered Syria and destroyed all the Omayyads. When al-Saffah died, Abdullah thought he would be the next Caliph, and when Abu Ja'far was appointed, Abdullah, who had been governor of Syria under al-Saffah, marched with his army towards Kufa. Abu Ja'far sent his other general, the famous Abu Muslim, to meet Abdullah. Abdullah was defeated at Nisibin in 754 and died in prison. The other Abbasid general, Abu Muslim, was now a powerful man. He was governor of Khorasan and a proved military commander. Abu Ja'far was uneasy over this; he feared that Abu Muslim, who was semi-independent in his own region, would rebel. Perhaps Abu Muslim had begun to be arrogant. Abu Ja'far sent for him and accused him of treasonable activities. Abu Muslim denied the charges, but he was tried, found guilty, and beheaded. Two obstacles were now out of Abu Ja'far's way. The Alids now made their attempt. Two great-grandsons of Imam Hasan, Ibrahim and Muhammad, organized a revolt at Medina. The Shiites of Hijaz and Iraq flocked to them, but they were defeated. The partisans of Abu Muslim rose in Khorasan, but Abu Ja'far crushed them also. He was now supreme in the Islamic world. He took the title of al-Mansur, the Victorious, and set about making his administration strong and his army ready and effective to undertake 'holy wars'.

The Holy Wars. With al-Mansur began an unending border strife between the Abbasids and the Byzantines in Asia Minor. Unconsciously, the Byzantines and the Abbasids were following an old tradition. Asia Minor had been the battleground of East Europeans and West Asiatics for centuries. The Greeks and Persians had fought over this land. The Byzantines and the Sassanids had fought there for two centuries. Now the later Byzantines and the Abbasids were continuing the struggle of East and West under different names: Christians *versus* Muslims. With the Abbasids, it began as a defensive war. Seeing that the Muslims were at each other's throats, the Byzantines had been harassing the border for some time. Al-Mansur could not tolerate such a thing for long, and sent an army against the Byzantines. The Christians had captured the fortresses of Malatyah in Armenia and Massisah in Cilicia, but the Muslim army soon recovered them. The Abbasid armies were on the march. The army sent to the north advanced into Caucasia, annexed Tabaristan and went along the shore of the Caspian Sea for a considerable distance. The army of the East captured Kandahar and reached the Khyber Pass. In a few years the Muslims had crossed into India and overrun the area now called the North-West Frontier of Pakistan. They even penetrated the valley of Kashmir.

Foundation of Baghdad (762). Al-Mansur had now mastered his internal enemies, and impressed himself on his external foes. There was peace and order in the Caliphate, trade and commerce had increased, and money had begun to flow into the treasury. He therefore turned his mind to other things. In 762 he laid the foundation of a new city on the Tigris which he called Baghdad. For four years hundreds of thousands of artisans, builders, architects, tile makers, masons, stone cutters, carpenters, cabinet makers, and decorators worked to build the city, which was built in a circular pattern. There were three walls round the city, and in the centre stood the Caliph's palaces and halls. The dome of the Audience Chamber (*Diwan Amm*) stood 130 feet high. Baghdad became a great city and was destined to shine for five hundred years as the cultural centre of the Eastern World.

The Barmakis. During Mansur's reign a family came to power which played a prominent role in the reign of four Caliphs. This was the family of the Barmakis, whose head was Khalid ibn Barmak. Khalid was appointed Vizier and his descendants held the same position with later Caliphs. The Barmakis were all able men and gradually became very rich and powerful. Great patrons of art and literature, their name is associated with large endeavours. Ja'far al-Barmaki, the Vizier of the great Harun al-Rashid, figures prominently in the imaginary stories of the *Arabian Nights*.

Heresies. Al-Mansur's reign is also noteworthy for the many heresies which sprang up. These religious movements had ancient roots and could be traced back to the mystery cults popular in pre-Islamic days. In 776 a follower of Abu Muslim rose as a great leader. He wore a veil over his face and called himself al-Muqanna, or the 'Veiled One'. He conquered the province of Khorasan, and led a rebellion of Khorasanis against the Arabs. There was another rising of the Kharijites in north Persia. The Mazdakites, the followers of Mazdak, rose in Jurjan. These movements give evidence of the awakening of the people of these lands. Since they were also anti-Islamic in character, al-Mansur put them down with a very severe hand.

Al-Mansur as Empire Builder. Al-Mansur died in 775, having reigned for twenty-one years. He had many unlovable traits; he was a harsh man and quite unforgiving, but he had vision and great strength of character. He had a high opinion of the office of the Caliph of Islam and lived up to it. He did not seek pleasure, but lived privately, like the Muslims of early times, though for public appearances he adopted the style of the Persian Chosroes. In course of time, however, the Abbasids outshone all other monarchs of the world in magnificence.

Al-Mahdi (775-785). Al-Mansur was followed by his son al-Mahdi who took Yahya al-Barmaki, the son of Khalid ibn Barmak, as his vizier. Al-Mahdi is famous for his wars in Asia Minor. The Byzantines had kept quiet for about fifteen years. When they stirred again in Asia Minor, al-Mahdi acted quickly. He put his young son Harun (the future Harun al-Rashid) in command of the army and sent him on a *Jihad*. Harun proved a good commander and defeated the Byzantine forces on many occasions. He then pursued them right up to the shores of the Sea of Marmara. The ruler of the Byzantine Empire at this time was the Empress Irene. She sued for peace, which was concluded on condition that the Byzantine Government should pay 8,000 dinars annually as tribute to the Caliph of Islam. It was as a result of this campaign that Harun was given the title of al-Rashid (the Orthodox).

Achievements of al-Mahdi. Al-Mansur had built Baghdad. Al-Mahdi filled it with the right people. He was very generous in his patronage of artists, writers, thinkers and philosophers. There was consequently great intellectual activity in his time. Al-Mahdi improved roads, and commerce increased in his time. Travelling became easy and more visitors came to Baghdad. In every way al-Mahdi's reign, though short, was important, because it was a period of vital preparation. Not only was encouragement given to Muslim thinkers and scholars, but even Zoroastrian studies were stimulated. Al-Mahdi was a tolerant ruler, though he did not encourage heresy. When he found that a certain Shaikh, called Ibn Abdul Quddus was preaching doctrines which were a disguised form of Zoroastrianism, he had him promptly arrested and later tried as a heretic (*zindiq*). This stopped all wayward thinking.

Harun al-Rashid (786-809). Al-Mahdi was succeeded by his elder son Musa al-Hadi, but Musa found a strong rival in Harun, his younger brother. The mothers of the two were bitterly opposed to each other, each working against her rival, and the result was that al-Hadi was assassinated. That left Harun sole heir, and he came to the Caliphate to become the most illustrious of all the Abbasids. He ruled for twenty-three years; his reign was crowded with events and with glory for Islam. As the Caliph of Islam he was known to the kings of the East and the West. He exchanged presents with Charlemagne as well as with the Emperor of China. He travelled greatly himself, and though he went on Hajj nine times he lived life fully and denied himself no pleasure. His name appealed to romance writers and he figures largely in the *Arabian Nights*, which book, fantastic though it is, gives some idea of the might and majesty of Harun al-Rashid and the glory of Arab civilization.

War in Asia Minor. The splendour of Harun's reign was increased by the peace and order which generally prevailed over all the Muslim lands. There was, of course, a war with the Byzantines, but that was now an accepted thing. There was one major war with the Byzantines in each reign, sometimes more. As had happened before, the truce was broken by the Byzantines. Mention has been made of the treaty between Irene, Empress of Byzantium and al-Mahdi, the father of Harun. Some years later Irene had been succeeded by Nicephorus I, who was not a very wise man. He was arrogant and had nothing but contempt for the 'infidels'. So he wrote a very rude letter to Harun, rejecting the terms of the old treaty, and not only refused to pay the annual 'peace-money', but on the contrary, demanded from Harun the return of the money paid to him by Empress Irene. Harun wrote a reply which has been preserved in the pages of Tabari, the famous Arab historian. It may be quoted in full, as it gives the reader an idea of the relations between the Emperor of the Byzantines and the Caliph of Islam.

'In the name of Allah the Compassionate and the Merciful. From Harun the Commander of the Faithful to Niqfur, the dog of a Roman!

Indeed I have read your letter, O son of an infidel mother. You will not hear my answer; you will see it.'

He then ordered a number of small armies into Asia Minor. They marched through Asia Minor, captured Heraclea and Tyana, Iconium and Ephesus. Cyprus was attacked in 805 and Rhodes captured in 807. The pride of Niqfur, or Nicephorus, was indeed brought low. He begged for peace and signed a treaty by which he agreed to pay a much larger tribute and in addition a personal tax on himself and each member of the royal family.

Risings during Harun's reign. There were minor risings here and there in Harun al-Rashid's reign. There was one at Medina in 786, which was led by a claimant of the House of Ali. The rising was put down, but Idris, a cousin of the claimant, fled to al-Maghrib and, as related in the last chapter, succeeded in founding a dynasty in Morocco, that of the Idrisids which lasted for two centuries. There was severe strife between the Mazharites and Himyarites in Syria, but this disturbance was put down very effectively by Ja'far al-Barmaki, the Grand Vizier. In Ifriqiya the governor revolted and Ibrahim ibn al-Aghlab was sent by Harun to settle that area. An account has been given of how Ibrahim founded the Aghlabid dynasty of Ifriqiya. The last rising, though separated from the others by about fifteen years, was in Trans-Oxiania, where Rafi ibn Layth, the governor of Samarqand, revolted in 805. Harun took the field against him himself, but fell ill on the way and died while still in Khorasan.

The Fall of the Barmakis. The Barmakis had been powerful during three reigns. In Harun's time their prestige was second only to that of the Caliph. Their patronage of learning, their gifts and presents, their taste and splendour dazzled everyone. The palaces that they built were as good as those of the Caliph. It was no wonder that they had many enemies. They were a talented family and people were jealous of them. So a whispering campaign began against the splendid Barmakis. At last it reached the ears of Harun. The Barmakis were Shiites, and it was reported that they were no longer loyal to the Sunni House of Abbas. Harun had given his sister in marriage to his Grand Vizier Ja'far Barmaki, but in the end even this did not protect him. In 803 the fall of the Barmakis came. Harun turned against them all, confiscated their property and had them imprisoned. Ja'far and his equally famous brother Fadl were put to death. It is said that nothing is so uncertain as the favour of princes. This was very true in the case of the Barmakis.

The Abbasid Way of Life. The Abbasid period saw the peak of Arab achievement. In every walk of life the Arabs were in the forefront of world civilization. Their zest for life, their acceptance of what life could give, their search for possibilities, their keen searchings into every branch of knowledge, their taste in living, in creature comforts, in the standards of conduct, in commerce, in international trade, in dealings with other men, all made a new life for them and made these centuries one of the finest eras in the history of the world. It is no slur on them that they took knowledge from the Greeks or from the others, for the mental heritage of man is there for the whole world. The Arabs took things from everywhere, made the heritage their own possession and then made great advances in literature, philosophy, science, history, geography, the arts and the crafts. The Abbasids made Baghdad the centre of the world and ideas issued from that centre like the rays of a bright lamp. The light shed by Baghdad went to all corners of the eastern hemisphere. The seeds of all that the Arabs achieved were sown in the reigns of al-Mahdi and al-Rashid. They came to flower in the days of the great Mamun, the son of Harun al-Rashid.

The Abbasid Rulers. The Abbasids encouraged learning as very few monarchs ever did; they also made changes in their way of life. The early Omayyads still believed in simple things. Muawiyah was basically the old Arab Shaikh. Many other Omayyads retired periodically from the pomp and glory of imperial life in Damascus and lived on the edge of the desert in simple, rural surroundings. Most of the Omayyad princes were given this early training. This no longer applied to the Abbasids. The Abbasid Caliphs and the Abbasid princes lived magnificently. They early adopted the luxurious Persian style of living and they gradually became more and more influenced by Persian customs. The most important official at the court was the Grand Vizier who was the *Naib*, the Deputy of the Caliph. This Grand Vizier had a status only slightly lower in grandeur than that of the Caliph. There were other viziers too, who had trains of servants, slaves, and hangers-on. The standard of life on the whole was very high and the higher officials everywhere believed in and lived on the grand scale. This bred a love of luxury and ease in them which weakened them and they began to lose their capacity for effort and achievement. Before that happened however, many other events took place which put new life into weakening rulers and weary courts, so that the vigour of the Muslims was not sapped for long.

Al-Amin (809-813). Harun al-Rashid left a number of sons, of whom Mohammad al-Amin, Abdullah al-Mamun and Mohammad al-Mu'tasim are famous. The former was the son of Zubeida, the Chief Sultana, so he had the advantage over al-Mamun whose mother was a Persian concubine. Al-Mamun had, however, the backing of the Persians. Harun had in his own lifetime made certain decisions. He had made al-Amin governor of Syria and Egypt and al-Mamun governor of the eastern provinces with his capital in Khorasan. A third son, al-Qasim, was made governor of Iraq. But Harun had also decreed that al-Amin should succeed him and so al-Amin became Caliph. It was not long after this that the brothers fell out. It came about in this way: al-Amin dismissed al-Qasim, which did not please al-Mamun. What al-Mamun liked even less was the nomination by al-Amin of his own son Musa along with al-Mamun as his successor. Al-Mamun began to suspect al-Amin's motives. He was, however, too far away from the capital and was not sure of his strength so he did not act at once. Moreover, al-Amin had the Arab party solidly behind him. However, al-Mamun was persuaded by his minister and the Persian noblemen to declare his independence. He hesitated for some time, but at last he did so. Al-Amin, as Caliph of Islam, dismissed al-Mamun from office and sent General Ali ibn Isa with an army to reduce Khorasan and subdue his rebellious brother.

General Ali was not successful; in fact he was outgeneralled, defeated, and killed. The second army sent against al-Mamun fared no better. Then al-Mamun's generals Tahir and Harthmah set out against al-Amin. They came to Baghdad, besieged it and conquered it. Al-Amin was captured and killed and al-Mamun was proclaimed Caliph. This civil war lasted nearly four years. Al-Mamun still remained in Khorasan.

Disturbances—Alid Rising. Al-Mamun himself did not have an easy time in the beginning. He had to spend years in putting down one rebellion after another. Some of the chief disturbances must be mentioned, especially as they belong to a pattern which was to repeat itself in many reigns. First, the Alids raised a claimant of their own. They, it must be remembered, were firmly convinced that nobody deserved the Caliphate except one of themselves. All others, in their eyes, were usurpers. There was no difference between an Omayyad and an Abbasid Caliph; one was as bad as the other. To an Alid both were in wrongful possession of the right of the descendants of Ali. Nobody could convince the Alids that

Islam does not recognize such inherited claims. To God that man is nearest and best who obeys Him most and who serves man best. But the Shiites believed in Divine Right, which meant the right of the House of Ali to rule. Hence they rose whenever and wherever they could. In al-Mamun's reign they rebelled in Iraq under a leader named Muhammad ibn Ibrahim. Unfortunately for the Alids they seldom made proper arrangements in men or equipment for a rising; the result was that they were nearly always defeated. This time, too, Muhammad went down before Harthmah. Al-Mamun was a very enlightened man and, seeing that the Iraqis were pro-Ali, he gave one of his daughters in marriage to Imam Ali al-Rida, the eighth Shia Imam, and declared him his heir-apparent. He also changed the colour of the Abbasid flag from black to green, green being the colour of the House of Ali.

Trouble in Iraq. The Iraqis were, however, not satisfied. They first tried to tempt al-Mansur, an uncle of al-Mamun, with the Caliphate, and when he refused they raised Ibrahim, a son of al-Mahdi and another uncle of al-Mamun, to the Caliphate. When this matter was reported to al-Mamun he decided to go to Baghdad from Khorasan in person. Before he could leave, a follower of al-Muqanna, the veiled false prophet of the time of Caliph al-Mansur, arose. This man was called Babak and had some strange ideas. He believed, for instance, in the transmigration of souls and other ideas contrary to Islam. Al-Mamun did not have time to go against the Babakites. He therefore postponed action and hastened to Baghdad. He had not passed Tus, however, when his son-in-law Ali al-Rida the eighth Imam, fell ill. All that was possible was done for him by way of treatment, but Imam al-Rida died and was buried at Tus, which was called Meshhed, the place of martyrdom, after this event. The Shiites were not satisfied about the cause of his death and believed that he had been poisoned and he was therefore a martyr. Meshhed has since that day been a sacred place of the Shiites.

Al-Mamun in Iraq. Al-Mamun came at last to Baghdad. He found the city in a state of ruin. Many fine buildings which had been built at great cost by Harun, al-Mahdi, and al-Mansur had been burnt down. Al-Mamun found it difficult to house himself and his nobles and himself chose to stay in the palace of the one-time powerful Grand Vizier of Harun, Ja'far al-Barmaki. He then set about putting things in order, but was not yet to have peace. A Kharijite rebellion broke out in Khorasan and he sent his able general, Tahir, there with orders to bring peace to the province. Tahir did so, but Mamun found it necessary to keep Tahir in Khorasan, of which province he made him governor. Later the governorship was made hereditary in his family. The family of Tahir became semi-independent after al-Mamun's death and founded the dynasty of Tahirids in Khorasan.

Egypt—Babak and Byzantines. All was not even yet at peace in the Abbasid world. The old rivals, Qaisites and Kalbites, or Mazharites and Himyarites, now began to quarrel violently along the River Nile. The Mazharites, who were mainly Sunnis, had taken the side of al-Amin, and the Himyarites, who had always leaned towards Shiism, had favoured al-Mamun. Whatever the issue, these two parties would find cause or reason to argue themselves on to opposite sides, and their differences were never quiet or passive. They always broke out into open fighting. Hearing that the situation was getting out of hand, al-Mamun sent General Abdullah, who was the son of General Tahir, to establish order. However, before Abdullah had completed his task, the Byzantines, the inveterate enemies of the Abbasids, began to aid and abet Babak, the heretic, who now rebelled in the north-western Persian province of Azerbaijan, and al-Mamun took the field in person. The campaign against Babak lasted four years (829-833), but al-Mamun broke the movement, defeated Babak and drove him out. He then fought against the Byzantines and captured the fortress of Zubra near Tarsus. He was still engaged in this campaign when he died in 833.

Conquests in the Mediterranean. Al-Mamun's reign was full of risings and rebellions, and he would appear to have had neither peace nor time to build up or expand the intellectual centres of the Caliphate. The remarkable thing is that he did. In the Mediterranean, Muslim culture was extended when the pro-Abbasid Arabs, who had been forced to leave Spain by the second Omayyad Amir, al-Hakam, conquered Crete, and the Abbasid hereditary governors of Ifriqiya, the Aghlabids, conquered Sicily, Sardinia, and Malta during al-Mamun's reign. In Sicily Muslim culture came to a state of perfection which made the island a cultural centre for nearly four centuries and one of the three main bridgeheads between the Arab world and Christian Europe, the other two being Spain in the west and Baghdad in the east.

Arab Culture in Baghdad. Al-Mamun has been adjudged great by history because, although his disturbed reign did not last long, he found time to found institutions and collect men and books from all places and set them on roads of achievement or encourage them to do work which made his reign memorable as well as productive. He encouraged the sciences as well as the arts. He built one observatory near Baghdad and another near Damascus. Beside the Baghdad observatory, he built a House of Knowledge, in which scores of scholars worked in various fields. There were dozens of them whose only task was to translate works from Greek, Syriac, Persian and Sanskrit. Independent work was done in literature, philosophy and religious law as well as in the sciences. Al-Mamun was a liberal thinker who believed that all our ideas should be measured in terms of reason. The school of thought he most favoured was the Mu'tazila school which had been founded in the previous century and had done much intellectual work. The Mu'tazilites believed that reason should also be applied to our religious ideas and nothing should be accepted without a rationalistic check or without full understanding.

Al-Mamun as Caliph. Al-Mamun's chief achievement lies in that he tried to liberate the human mind and for this he took all knowledge for his province. He was no mean scholar himself and used to take part in the discussions which were a regular feature of his *Dar-ul-Hikmah.* Al-Mamun had no prejudices and to him the Sunnis and the Shiites were one. He could even tolerate the opinions of Zoroastrians and other non-Muslims. He was not, however, a man without ideals. He could not tolerate heretics, as his prompt action against Babak shows. Nor was he only a scholar, for when occasion demanded he could take the field himself as he did against Babak and the Byzantines. He is chiefly remembered for his humanitarian outlook, for the great intellectual achievements of his time and the impetus he gave to learning. There have been few monarchs who put mind before matter as al-Mamun did.

Al-Mu'tasim (833-842). Al-Mamun died comparatively young and was followed by his brother Muhammad, who took the title of al-Mu'tasim. Al-Mu'tasim's reign was an eventful one. The first thing that happened was the revolt of the Zotts in the lower regions of Iraq. These Zotts were a strange people who had migrated to Persia a few centuries before from India when the Sassanids were emperors of Persia. They were then called Jats and had been settled near the confluence of the Tigris and the Euphrates. In course of time their name changed to Zotts. They had always been a troublesome people. They could not settle down and were rough and violent in their ways and would not keep to anything for long. The Zotts had rebelled under al-Mamun, but the rising had not been a very big affair. Under al-Mu'tasim they organized a revolt on a large scale and began to loot caravans and raid settled areas and towns in Iraq. Al-Mu'tasim had to take strong measures and at last defeated them in 825 and forced them to migrate to the border province of Cilicia in Asia Minor. Many Zotts settled in

Cilicia, but a few bands passed into Europe and took to a wandering life. These are the people who came to be known as the Gipsies and are now found in many countries.

The Turkish Bodyguard. It was al-Mu'tasim who first organized the Turkish Guard. Al-Mamun had formed a corps of Turkish slaves as his personal bodyguard, but all the officers of this corps had been Arabs. Al-Mu'tasim expanded the corps and threw the officer ranks open to the abler of the Turkish slaves. This appeared to be more democratic and was certainly more true to Islamic principles, but it gradually made the bodyguard a purely Turkish body of armed and well-paid men who began to exercise a great influence on state affairs. When the Caliphs became weak the Turkish bodyguard grew uncontrollable and began to take part in court intrigues. Later they became corrupt and gained control of the Caliphs themselves. The same thing had happened in Roman times to the bodyguard of the Caesars, called the Praetorian Guard.

Al-Mu'tasim builds Samarra. Al-Mu'tasim now built a residence of his own at Samarra, a town about a hundred miles north of Baghdad, and soon many more palaces were erected there. Naturally the nobles who wanted to be near the Caliph built their own mansions where the Caliph lived. Mosques and schools were built also. It was not long before Samarra began to rival Baghdad in splendour, except that it never took the place of Baghdad as a great intellectual centre.

War with Byzantines. Babak the heretic had been defeated, but not killed by al-Mamun, and he rebelled again under al-Mu'tasim who sent his Turkish general Afshin against him. As in al-Mamun's time the Byzantines came up with their forces at the same time and Mu'tasim himself led an army against them. The Byzantine Emperor Theophilus had captured the Muslim town of Zibata and razed it to the ground. Zibata was the birth-place of al-Mu'tasim: infuriated, he marched to avenge it. The two forces met near Ancyra where a crushing defeat was inflicted on Theophilus. After that al-Mu'tasim besieged Amorium, the birth-place of the emperor. The siege lasted fifty days, but at last al-Mu'tasim was successful and he razed the town to the ground. Many people were killed and the rest were captured and sold as slaves in Baghdad. The Byzantines were stricken with terror at the revenge of al-Mu'tasim. While al-Mu'tasim was still busy pursuing Theophilus he heard that the Turkish general Afshin had revolted. So he left Asia Minor quickly, and on his return had Afshin arrested and thrown into prison. Al-Mu'tasim now resolved to attack Constantinople by sea and ordered a fleet to be got ready. The fleet set sail for Constantinople, but a terrible storm arose. The ships were scattered and many of them were lost, so the expedition had to be given up; it was a great loss.

Character of al-Mu'tasim. As a Caliph, al-Mu'tasim had the same stature as the earlier Caliphs. He was a man of firm views and quick action. He was not inimical to intellectual or philosophic pursuits and the quickening of the Arab mind that had come to flower under al-Mamun continued under him. He made his name respected by the Byzantines, and Samarra, in his time, was a byword for grandeur. He upheld the dignity of his office and was a terror to non-Muslims.

Al-Wathiq (842-847). Al-Wathiq, who succeeded al-Mu'tasim, was the last of the great Abbasids. He was a very capable ruler, generous in his ways and liberal in his ideas. A great patron of liberal thought, he gave much money to charity and encouraged learning to the full. He was himself an accomplished man and a good musician and composed many melodies. The state was prosperous during his time and industry flourished, the trade between East and West, which was made easy by the Abbasids and had greatly increased, rose to new heights. He was a truly enlightened ruler, though religious controversies raged high in his time, for reaction was setting in.

New Forces at Work. New forces were already at work. The liberalism of the last four reigns, especially that of al-Mamun, had brought about a reaction. There was, in particular, great popular opposition to the influence of the rationalists who were called the Mu'tazila. It was the Mu'tazila who had been the spokesmen of religious thought in the last two reigns and they were encouraged by al-Wathiq. The leader of the reaction was the famous Imam Ahmad ibn Hanbal, the fourth Doctor of Muslim Law. He was so outspoken in his views and he criticized the Caliph so openly that he was imprisoned. There was some restlessness, also, in the Turkish Guard. Al-Wathiq made the mistake of appointing a Turkish officer, Ashnas by name, with whose ability he was impressed, as the Lord Lieutenant or *Naib* of the Caliphate. This was a very high office and was usually given to the ablest nobleman of the state. This was a democratic action and shows how liberal the Abbasids were, but it was an act which brought great trouble to the successors of al-Wathiq, who had to struggle against their own Turkish officers, at whose hands many of them died. Al-Wathiq died young and was succeeded by al-Mutawakkil. With his death the Abbasid power began to decline.

Al-Mutawakkil (847-861). Al-Mutawakkil was a man of a different stamp from the liberal Wathiq. He was a very orthodox Caliph indeed. As soon as he came to power the Ulema, who had not played a very prominent role in the reigns of the earlier Caliphs, came into their own. They protested against the importance given at court to the leaders of the 'Rationalist' (Mu'tazilite) school. Al-Mutawakkil did not need any persuasion to act against the leaders of liberal opinion as he himself did not like or appreciate critical thought. He first liberated Imam Ahmad ibn Hanbal, who was given a welcome in which a great number of people joined. He then started controlling and later suppressing the Mu'tazilite scholars. Many of them were prosecuted and most of them were imprisoned. A large number died at his hands. Al-Mutawakkil was equally intolerant of Shiite opinion and of non-Muslims. It was in his reign that a party of bigots attacked the mausoleum

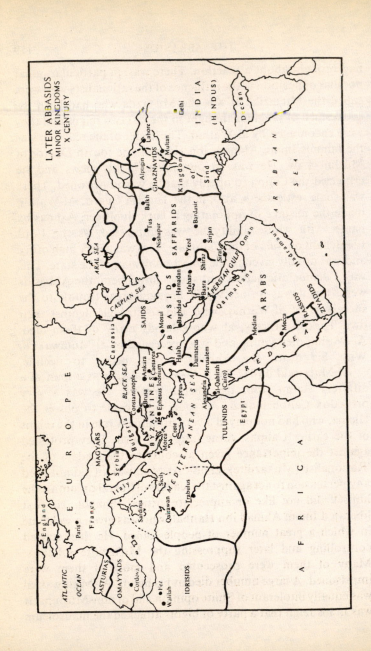

LATER ABBASIDS
MINOR KINGDOMS
X CENTURY

of Imam Husain at Karbala and damaged it. Hearing of the inner disturbances at the Abbasid centre, the Byzantines took heart. They overran the Muslim province of Cilicia in South Asia Minor and attacked and captured Damietta in Egypt. People became very dissatisfied and this gave an opportunity to the Turkish Guard to become turbulent. Al-Mutawakkil tried to shift his capital to Damascus to escape the Guard, but this he could no longer do. He therefore sent for Muhammad, the hereditary Tahirid governor of Khorasan, to subdue the Guard, but before that could happen, the Guard murdered him. With al-Mutawakkil ended the first period of Abbasid rule.

Later Abbasids. The glory had begun to fade after al-Wathiq, but at least al-Mutawakkil held the reins of the government in his own hands. After him the Caliphate lasted for four hundred years, but the Caliphs became less and less powerful as the years went by, until they held but a shadowy existence at the centre. Kingdoms sprang up within the Abbasid Caliphate; great advances continued to be made in all the fields; new towns, new universities, new centres of scientific research and industrial output appeared within the bounds of the Caliphate, but they owed nothing to Abbasid patronage or Abbasid inspiration. There is no doubt, however, that the real foundations for all that happened later were laid by the Abbasids.

Government of the Abbasids. The Abbasid government was well organized. In Islam sovereignty rests in Allah and since the Caliph was the representative of Allah on earth, all authority, spiritual or temporal was vested in him. He appointed a *Naib* to perform certain duties and there were the Grand Vizier and the Council of Ministers. There were departments of Finance and Revenues, of Communications and Excise, of Police and of Defence. Things were properly organized, and for checking weights and measures, and the quality of goods sold, for controlling dealings of businessmen there was a department of

Ihtisab, the Superintendent of Examinations (*Muhtasib*) being a powerful and useful official. The inspectors who went around checking and probing were dreaded by wrong-doers. All these arrangements made for a well-knit society. There was a standing army to protect the frontiers and to maintain law and order, but for *ghazwahs* men were enlisted as and when occasion arose. Most of the soldiers on these expeditions were volunteers and were not paid regular salaries, although they got their dues for the time they served and their share of the spoils of war (*mal al-ghanimah*). The Caliph was more powerful than many emperors, but he was normally approachable and often led the prayers on Fridays; he commanded his troops too. He was therefore the real head of the state.

Great Men of the Abbasid Times. Mention can be made here of only a few great men who adorned the Arab world in the early Abbasid times. All these great men dominated world thought for hundreds of years in their own fields. In philosophy the greatest names are those of al-Kindi and al-Farabi. Al-Kindi was a man of such eminence that the first half of this century has been named after him by the eminent historian of science, Georges Sarton. Al-Farabi is a household word even now. They have become symbols of wisdom and knowledge. In the field of medieval medicine the name of al-Razi was supreme. The books written by him are studied to this day in the East and in the West, and were text books till the seventeenth century. In mathematics the greatest name of those days, and for seven hundred years afterwards, was that of al-Khwarizmi who compiled the first astronomical tables, made algebra into a regular science, and gave arabic numerals to the world. In astronomy the Muslims of those days were pre-eminent. All the observatories were of Muslim origin and such astronomers as al-Battani and al-Farazi were authorities on the subject everywhere. The greatest chemist and analyst of the age, whose empirical methods were used for centuries everywhere, was Jabir ibn Hayyan, a typical product of the early Abbasid era. In geography al-Yaqubi stood above anyone else, and as historians the Muslims of this era are respected to this day. To Ibn Hisham, al-Tabari, and al-Masudi the world owes much of its knowledge of those days, al-Tabari and al-Masudi being in a class of their own.

Muslim Law. Muslim law too was studied and regulated in this area. There are four great names in this field, and their insight and wisdom, their judgement and their interpretation of the fundamentals of Islam have made the basis of all Islamic law. These learned doctors of law were Imam Abu Hanifa, Imam Malik ibn Anas, Imam al-Shafii and Imam Ahmad ibn Hanbal. They were called Imams because they were leaders of religious thought and had vast followings. Of them Imam Abu Hanifa was the most liberal and most adaptable. He saw Islamic law as an organic growth in which changes would be necessary from time to time as new conditions and new social tendencies and ideas grew. He and Imam al-Shafii, who was midway between the liberal Imam Abu Hanifa and the conservative Imam Malik ibn Anas, have the greatest following among the Sunnis today. Imam Ahmad ibn Hanbal believed in the strict interpretation of the Qur'an and the Traditions and did not favour any departures, even in non-essentials.

The primary belief of all these Imams, whose interpretations have made the *Shariah*, was the acceptance of the Qur'an, the Sunnah, the reported conduct, career and sayings of the first four Caliphs and the democracy and brotherhood of Islam.

The Traditions. Muslims became interested in the Traditions of the Prophet quite early, but systematic work on them started only in Abbasid times. In the beginning, the study of the Traditions (*Ahadith*) of the Prophet was the first subject for Muslims. As the Traditions grew in number, people began to think about checking and sifting them. It was not long before the work of scrutiny and examination developed its own rules and gradually these rules developed into a systematic science. The two divines who spent a life-time on this work and whose word came to be accepted only next to the Prophet were Imam Muhammad ibn Ismail al-Bokhari and Imam Muslim ibn al-Hajjaj. These two collected hundreds of thousands of Traditions on every topic and sifted them so carefully that they reduced them to a few thousand in each case. Their great compilations are called *Sahih al-Bokhari* and *Sahih Muslim*. They are accepted as authentic (*sahih*) and they amplify and implement the fundamental laws laid down in the Qur'an. Four other books, the *Sunan* of Ibn-Majah (866), the *Sunan* of Abu Dawud (889), the *Jami'* of *al-Tirmidhi* (892) and the *Sunan* of al-Nasai (915) stand next in popular regard.

Growth and Decline of Intellectual Life. The beginnings made by the Muslims during the Omayyad period bore fruit in the Abbasid times, as some very enlightened princes ascended the caliphal throne. The peak was reached in the times of al-Mahdi, the father of Harun al-Rashid, to the reign of al-Wathiq (775-847). Even al-Mutawakkil the successor of al-Wathiq was broadminded and encouraged liberal thinking but his successors, al-Muntasir, al-Mustain, al-Mu'tazz and al-Mahtadi (861-870) were all just play-things in the hands of the Turkish military commanders who had now become a power behind the throne. Moreover, the ding-dong battle between Sunnis and Shias for official patronage did inestimable harm to the world of learning. Al-Mahtadi, an admirer of Umar bin Abdul Aziz the pious Omayyad Caliph, tried to follow his practice. He cut down extravagant court ceremonials and even tried to free the Caliphate from the grasp of the Turkish military, but got caught in a court intrigue and was murdered. After him the Caliphate entered on a period of decline and as mentioned earlier, a number of principalities got established, which owed only nominal fealty to the Caliph. Naturally, as central patronage diminished learning suffered.

Abbasid Claims. Actually the Abbasids' anti-Omayyad propaganda had been based on the slogan that in Islam there was no difference between an Arab and a non-Arab, between a

Quraish or a neo-Muslim, but as Dr. S.A.Q. Husaini says in *Arab Administration*, this was mere propaganda. 'The Abbasids came to power backed by a strong movement for the revival of the pure and impartial state of early Islam, a revolution which demanded that a Quraish or Salman Farsi (a respected Companion but a Persian by birth), a noble Arab and the Negro Bilal, an ordinary subject and a prince like Jabbah (the Ghassanid Chief) should once again be treated as equals. This was a revolt against the discriminatory practices of the Omayyads and the worldliness of their administration. As creatures of a strong religious revival, the Abbasids laid great stress on the religious character and dignity of their office as an Imamate. In about a century, however, they took the titles of Khalifatullah (Viceregent of Allah) instead of *Khalifatur Rasullah*. In course of time they became *Zillalahi-ala'l-ard* (The Shadow of Allah on Earth)!'

Abbasid Society. The Abbasids had as their helpers, neo-Muslims and non-Arabs. In their struggle for power, the society in their times gradually became cosmopolitan and the old Arab simplicity and aristocratic dignity, bearing, and prestige were lost. There was no pride in Arab blood any more. Persians and Turks began to replace the Arabs in most fields. The mothers of only three Abbasid Caliphs were of Arab descent. The mothers of all the other Caliphs were slaves of different nationalities. This fusion of the Arab nobility with the subject races, the practice of polygamy and concubinage, made for a social amalgam wherein loyalties became uncertain and a hierarchy of officials emerged, a bureaucracy at first Persian and later Turkish which decreased Abbasid prestige and power for good.

Love of Splendour. Moreover, splendour became the chief aim of the rulers and the ruled. Syed Ameer Ali, in his *History of the Saracens*, describes the Caliphal palace thus: 'The imperial *Kasr* was resplendent with inlaid jewels and the interminable halls bore distinctive names according to their ornamentation. The special feature of one of a tree made entirely of gold, with birds perched on its branches, made also of gold and studded with gems. Another, the Hall of Paradise, with its magnificent chandeliers, its inlaid jewels on the walls and ceiling, its colouring and adornments was a perfectly fairy sight'. Such extravagance and luxury do not make for endurance or promote cultural advancement. And inevitably they led to decay and ultimate ruin.

Position of Women. Under the enlightened rulers of the first century of Abbasid rule (760-860) women at first enjoyed a high position in society as Hitti says: 'The early Abbasid women enjoyed the same measure of liberty as their Omayyad sisters; but towards the end of the 10th century under the Shia Buwayhids (of Persian origin), the system of strict seclusion and absolute segregation of the sexes became general' — (*History of the Arabs.*) At first women took part in all affairs of state. They went to war, clad in mail. During Harun al-Rashid's reign Arab maidens went to fight the Byzantinians, on horse back. The mother of al-Muqtadir herself presided at the High Court of Appeal. Even up to the troubled times of al-Mutawakkil, reunions and conversations between cultured women and learned men did not stop. *Kitab al-Aghani* is full of anecdotes of gifted ladies who took part in social functions. Shaikh Shahda (a lady), lectured at Baghdad in mid-Abbasid times on humanistic subjects and Zainab Umar al-Muwayyid had many diplomas given to her by prominent scholars as to her ability to teach law (Fiqh). Taqia, daughter of Abul Faraz was a poet of renown and even gave discourses on Hadith. But in later times as a study of the *Arabian Nights* will show, there was a moral laxity, a loosening of character, a love of intrigue, and a loss of a sense of honour and fidelity which reflects a great weakening of moral fibre.

Industry and Commerce. In that age of conquests, economic prosperity, and intellectual advancement, with observatories and Dar-al-Hikmahs flourishing in a number of places, and great scholars spreading the light of knowledge in all fields, the people lived comfortably. Commercial links with Europe and the Far East had been established. The voyages of Sindbad give in fantasy form, the vast reaches of the Baghdad entrepreneurs. This was the result of the industrial output of the Abbasid Caliphate. In Western Asia special attention was paid to the manufacture of rugs, tapestry, silks, cottons and woollens, brocades, and other luxury items, and they were exported all over the known eastern and western worlds. The swords of Damascus were much in demand in Europe as were the Toledo blades. *Al Maqdisi* gives the following list of exportable items from Central Asia: 'Soap, carpets, copper lamps, pewter wear, felt, cloaks, furs, amber, honey, falcons, scissors, needles, knives, swords, bows, Slavonic and Turkish Slaves'. Manufacture of paper was introduced in the middle of the eighth century into Samarqand from China.

Cultural Activities. H.W. Hazard in his *Atlas of Islamic History* sums up the cultural level achieved by the people in Abbasid times thus: 'Despite this political disintegration (in the 9th century), Arabic culture flourished amazingly, completely out-stripping all rivals. Translations from Greek were accelerated and broadcast, including Aristotle, Hippocrates, Galen, Ptolmey, Euclid, and others. Most of the translators and some of the original thinkers were Nestorian Christians, Jews, or pagans, who flourished in the tolerant court at Baghdad, but outstanding contributions came from Muslims, usually from Persia. Important works in Arabic included geometry, algebra (al-Khwarizmi), trigonometry, astronomy (al-Battani), geography, mineralogy, chemistry, optics, botany, and medicine (al-Razi), among the sciences. And history (al-Yaqubi), biography, philogy, philosophy (al-Kindi), and music, in the humanities. Biographies of Mohammad and his Companions, histories of Arab conquests, route-books and geographies of the Islamic domain, codification of Muslim Traditions and Shafiite and Hanbalite jurisprudence served to stabilize and unify an advanced Muslim culture, which though centred at Baghdad, transcended the frontiers. An important development was the foundation within orthodox (Sunni) Islam of the mystic Sufi movement while Shiite extremists set up Ismaili and Qarmatian communities. Meanwhile the secular arts of poetry and architecture continued to flourish while commerce throve within Islam and with Europe and the Middle and Far East'.

CHAPTER 6

THE KINGDOMS WITHIN THE ABBASID CALIPHATE

Break-up of the Abbasid Caliphate. The power of the Abbasids began to diminish with the death of al-Wathiq, but al-Mutawakkil still held the various parts of the Caliphate together. With his death, however, the Turkish Guard came into power and when that happened the Caliphs became mere puppets in the hands of this guard. It was, therefore, not long before the provinces farthest from the centre began to fall out. Their governors became semi-independent and soon set up dynasties of their own. New adventurers appeared on the scene and carved out little kingdoms for themselves. After them came people from outside, like the Seljuk Turks, or like the Ghaznavids, who built great empires within the wide framework of the Caliphate. Egypt broke away, and governors there became independent monarchs. People with strange ideas, mostly destructive, like the Ismailis and the Qarmatians, began underground movements which ate away the foundations of Islam. The end of this grand era in world history was however, brought about by the dreaded Mongols, who destroyed what centuries of effort had produced. In this chapter is told the story of the centuries which intervened between the death of al-Mutawakkil (861) and the fall of Baghdad (1258).

Successors of al-Mutawakkil—Al-Mutamid (870-892). After they had killed al-Mutawakkil, the officers of the Turkish Guard put first one son of al-Mutawakkil on the throne, then another, but no one lasted long. They then tried other princes of the line, but none suited them for any period, till in 870 they made the last son of al-Mutawakkil Caliph. The new Caliph took the title of al-Mutamid. The Caliphs had for some time been living at Samarra, and al-Mutamid decided to move his capital back to Baghdad to escape the power of the Turkish military chiefs who had set up quarters in Samarra. For some time he succeeded in doing so, but he did not escape other troubles so easily. The Governor of Egypt, Ahmad ibn Tulun, had become independent, and the Caliph could not prevent him, as ibn Tulun was a very strong man. Then the black slaves who had been living in the salt marshes in the delta of the Iraqi rivers organized themselves and, finding a capable leader in Ali ibn Muhammad, revolted.

The Zanj Rebellion. These people called themselves the Zanj and had ideas which today are called communist. They believed in and practised complete equality, held property in common, and had very strict ideas on religion. Their discipline was such that they soon established a good military record and began an offensive campaign against the Caliphate. In 871, they captured Basra and sacked it. They then advanced to the north and conquered a considerable area. At last al-Mutamid sent his own brother al-Muwaffiq in command of a large force. Al-Muwaffiq defeated the Zanj and suppressed the heresy. Meanwhile an adventurer rose to power in mid-Persia: Yaqub ibn Layth, originally a copper-smith and a bandit, but now a leader of some strength. The Byzantines also availed themselves of the opportunity and advanced through Cilicia into Syria. The Abbasid Caliphate was not in a position to stop the Byzantine troops, though the Egyptian army of the Tulunid rulers of Egypt and Syria faced them boldly and beat them back.

Al-Mutadid and Al-Muqtafi (892-908). Al-Mutamid was succeeded by Al-Mutadid, the only memorable event of whose reign was that, the Tulunids having grown weak, Egypt and Syria were annexed to the Caliphate again. After him came al-Muqtafi, who was more energetic. In his time the Byzantines again came up with an army and overran a number of border districts. Al-Muqtafi took the field against them himself, and this was to be the last time that an Abbasid Caliph was to lead his armies against an enemy. Al-Muqtafi beat back the Christians and pursued them. He then went farther and attacked the famous fortress of Adalia in south-west Asia Minor. But he did not have time to capture the town, for a new enemy of Islam rose behind him; the heretical sect of the Qarmatians. Since these terrible people played an important role in Muslim history and did Islam a great deal of harm, and since they were an offshoot of Islam, they must be discussed separately.

Origins of the Qarmatians. The Qarmatians followed an extreme form of Shiism, but during the course of a hundred years since they had broken away from the main branch, they had changed so much that it was difficult to recognize them as Muslims. It all began with a violent difference of opinion among the Shiites about the successor of the sixth Shiite Imam. It must be made clear that the true Shiites did not recognize the Sunni Caliphs as the spiritual heads of Islam, as the rest of the Muslim world did. The Shiites believed that the real leaders of Islamic thought and practice were the descendants of Ali and particularly of Imam Husain. Such descendants were called Imams. The sixth Imam Ja'far al-Sadiq, the great-grandson of Imam Husain, the Martyr of Karbala. Ja'far al-Sadiq had two sons, Ismail and Musa. Ismail was the elder, but he died within the lifetime of Ja'far and after his death people accepted as the seventh Imam the surviving son Musa, known later as Musa al-Kazim. But many Shiites declared that, since Ismail had been the eldest son, Ismail was the seventh Imam, and his son Muhammad should be the eighth Imam. This claim started a split among the Shiites which has never healed. The followers of Ismail have been known as Ismailis and, since they consider themselves in the right and felt that an injustice had been done to them, they began to organize themselves secretly. In course of time they had three leaders who made a great stir in the world. The first was Qarmat, the second Obaidullah, who declared himself the Mahdi in Qairawan and laid the foundations of the Fatimid power, and the third was Hasan ibn Sabah who founded the Assassin Organization. He was the original *Shaikh-ul-Jabal*, the 'Old Man of the Mountains'.

Qarmat. By the end of the ninth century, the Ismailis had found a leader in Hamdan Qarmat. Qarmat was a good organizer. He borrowed many non-Islamic ideas including blind obedience to a Hidden Imam, and he gave very careful schooling to his followers, declaring that they could never find Allah by their own efforts, and that their prayers and good works would never be acceptable to Allah, nor could they understand the meaning of the Qur'an, unless they depended entirely on their secret preceptors, who were superior beings and hence knew the hidden meanings of everything. If the follower gave utter obedience to the agents of the Hidden Imam, he would be permitted to do what he liked and his sins and errors would be forgiven him. Many people accepted these terms and became blind tools of Qarmat, as they later became blind followers of Obaidullah al-Mahdi or Hasan ibn Sabah. After Qarmat's death his successors became heads of the organization. For a time they came into conflict with the Abbasids and were defeated. Their power thereafter decreased in Iraq and Syria, but they found a foothold in east Arabia and began to operate from there, till they became a dreaded power, and ruled in Arabia for a century and more.

Qarmatians in Arabia. In 894, the Ismaili High Command sent Abu Said ibn Bahram al-Tannabi to Bahrain, an island off the eastern coast of Arabia. There he won over a few tribes, gave the Shaikhs certain privileges and soon founded a new state. He chose Mumaniyah (the town of the faithful) as his capital. He and his lieutenants owed allegiance to the Hidden Imam of the Ismailis, but here in the eastern coastal belt of Arabia Abu Said was supreme. He died, but his descendants increased their power. Soon they had a large army of very fanatical followers. They began to raid Nejd to the west and

Iraq to the north, and even al-Hijaz in the distant west. The period of their highest power was 913-943. During these thirty years, they raided where they liked and were not suppressed. In 930 they attacked Mecca and captured it. They took out the Black Stone from the Kaaba and carried it away with them to their capital. They raided even Lower Syria during this time. They held inner Arabia for more than a hundred years.

The Last of the Great Abbasids—Al-Muqtadir (908-932). The last Abbasid Caliph to hold any power was al-Muqtadir. The Caliphate still included Iraq, Syria, Egypt, Persia and Khuzistan, but the treasury was nearly empty. The Caliphs and the nobles had become very extravagant, conquests had ceased, taxes had fallen, trade had diminished, life had become insecure because of such elements as the Qarmatians. Law and order were difficult to enforce, the differences between Sunnis and Shiites had increased and people had begun to lose faith in the order of things. The world seemed to many a place where there was more pain than joy and whatever joy there was was short-lived. Many people joined secret societies like those of the Qarmatians. A number turned to the religious orders and brotherhoods and became mystics. A wave of other-worldliness swept over the Abbasid domains at this time and many famous mystics made their appearance.

The Mystics. The mystics, or Sufis, asked people to fix their minds on the true world, the inner world of Allah, and of light, and consider this world and its values as mere passing shadows. All that tied us to this world was bad, if it was not downright evil. These mystics were good people who had attractive personalities. They appeared to radiate spiritual power and such was their burning faith that they had very large followings. Many of these Sufis were unconventional people. They did not follow all the tenets of Islam, believed more in the spirit than in the form of the Shariah, so they were looked upon with great suspicion by the Ulema and the *Fuqaha* (doctors of sacred law). Some were even persecuted for their teachings, which the doctors of Muslim law and the Muftis did not understand and did not wish to encourage. The most famous Sufi Saints of this period were Khwaja Maruf al-Karkhi of Baghdad (d. 815), Shaikh Bayazid Bustami (d. 875), Shaikh Junaid of Baghdad (d. 920) and Mansur al-Hallaj (d. 922). Mansur is the most famous of them all. He was a much loved preacher, and wandered here and there speaking of Allah's nearness to man and man's understanding of Allah. The Ulema said he presumed too much and because in one of his rapturous moments he had said 'I am the Truth', they declared that he was a blasphemer. They had him arrested and flogged and then finding him 'guilty' had him hanged. But he triumphed in death, for he became a hero of the seekers after Allah.

Kingdoms within the Caliphate—Tahirids (820-872). With al-Muqtadir's death the Abbasid power became secondary to the power of the kingdoms within the Caliphate, although the Caliphs continued to be the Caliphs of all Sunnis wherever they might be. It is necessary therefore to give an account of the kingdoms which broke away from the centre and flourished for shorter or longer periods. The first to establish itself was the kingdom of the Tahirids. This was a kingdom in north-eastern Khorasan with its capital at Merv. It was founded by Tahir, the able general of Caliph al-Mamun. After Tahir, his son Talha became the Abbasid governor of all the lands between Mazandaran and Trans-Oxiania. His brother Abdullah became another famous general under the Abbasids. The Tahirids recognized the overlordship of the Caliph, and paid a nominal tribute, but in internal affairs they were independent. They had their own army, their own government, and imposed their own taxes. They had their own officials too. One of their officials, named Saman, belonged to an old Persian family. There were other members of this family in positions of trust, and gradually they grew powerful. Eventually, in 872 a descendant of Saman, Nasr ibn Ahmad, overthrew the Tahirids and set up the Samanid Kingdom in Trans-Oxiania.

Before that happened another power had come into being in the middle of Persia.

Saffarids (867-908). This power was founded by a talented man of low birth, a man called Yaqub ibn Layth, who had started life as a coppersmith (*saffar*)—hence the name of the dynasty founded by him, the Saffarids. In his youth he had joined a band of outlaws and in time became their leader. He was an unusual man, for, in spite of his being an outlaw, he was not unkind; he was charitable to the poor and helped them in their distress. He robbed the idle rich only and never harmed a good man. His fame spread and the Caliph, hearing of him, made him a general and even made use of him on behalf of the Caliphate in suppressing other outlaws. As a reward the Caliph granted him lands, which Yaqub extended. He became a powerful ruler in all the region between Khorasan and the Persian Gulf and even Sind. He took Seistan and Lower Khorasan from the Tahirids. Al-Saffar even conquered Kabul and it was under his rule that all the region now called Afghanistan accepted Islam. He and his brother Amr were recognized by the Caliph, to whom they owed allegiance. The Saffarids were ultimately overthrown by the Samanids.

Samanids (874-999). As has been mentioned above, Nasr ibn Ahmad the Samanid was the man who rose in Trans-Oxiania under the Tahirids. It was Nasr's brother, Ismail (892-907), who finally drove out the Tahirids from Khorasan. The Samanids like other dynasties considered the Caliph as their suzerain, but were otherwise independent. They extended their boundaries in the reign of Nazr II (913-943) and the entire Eastern Caliphate, east of Iraq, came under their rule. They made Bokhara their capital, and built up Samarqand from a small town to a big city. The Samanids encouraged the Persian language and were great patrons of the arts and the sciences. It was in their times that the three geniuses Abu Ali ibn Sina, the philosopher, physician, mathematician, and scientist; Al-Razi, the philosopher; and Firdausi, the great Persian poet, lived.

The Samanids had the Arabic classics translated into Persian and it was because of their patronage that the Persian language came into its own after a long eclipse.

Ghaznavids (961-1186). The Samanids flourished till the end of the tenth century, but about the beginning of the sixth decade a new power began to rise in Kabul. It was founded by a Turkish ex-slave of the Samanids, a man called Alptigin. He had risen to a high position in the royal bodyguard of the Samanids and had been made governor of Khorasan. After some time he had fallen out of favour and had left with a small army for the eastern provinces. He had gone to Ghazni and founded a small city-state there. His slave and son-in-law Subuktigin, who succeeded him, was even a more capable man. Subuktigin (967-997) became independent and extended his dominions. In the west he conquered Khorasan from the last Samanids and in the east he captured Peshawar. It was on the present borders of Pakistan and Afghanistan that he was attacked by Raja Jaipal of Waihind, who came up with a large army, but was defeated and agreed to pay a large tribute. However, Jaipal went back on his word when he reached Lahore and so Subuktigin invaded Jaipal's territories. Jaipal sent out messages to the other rajas and sought their help. A large army assembled and marched on Subuktigin, but once more he defeated the Hindus. As a result the land to the west of the Indus became Ghaznavid property.

Mahmud the Great (998-1030). It was Subuktigin's son, the great Sultan Mahmud of Ghazni, who made the name of the Ghaznavids famous in Asia. Mahmud had learnt campaigning under his father and knew of the fights between his family and the Samanids on the west and between them and the Shahi kings of the Punjab on the east. Jaipal was now dead and his son Anandpal ruled in the Punjab. He, like his father, refused to pay the agreed tribute and this started the wars between Mahmud and the Shahi kings which resulted in the famous seventeen invasions of India by this great knight of Islam.

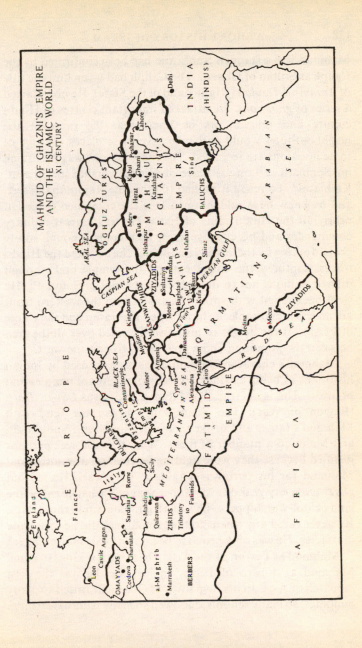

MAHMUD OF GHAZNI'S EMPIRE
AND THE ISLAMIC WORLD
XI CENTURY

INDIA
(HINDUS)

ARABIAN
SEA

OGHUZ TURKS

Delhi
Lahore
Peshawar
Kabul · Ghazni
Herat · Kandahar
Merv
Tus
Nishapur · Isfahan · Shiraz
Sind
BALUCHS
EMPIRE OF GHAZNI'S
M A H M U D

ARAL SEA

CASPIAN SEA

ZIYADIDS

HASANWAYHIDS

B U W A Y H I D S

Sultaniya
Hamdan
Mosul
Baghdad
Kufa · Basra
PERSIAN GULF

Muslim
Kingdoms

Armenia

Damascus
Jerusalem
Alexandria · Cairo
Cyprus

Medina
Mecca
RED SEA

ZIYADIDS

QARMATIANS

FATIMID EMPIRE

BLACK SEA

Byzantine Empire

Minor
Constantinople

BULGARS

E U R O P E

England
France

Italy
Rome
Sardinia
Sicily

MEDITERRANEAN SEA

Mahdiya
Qairawan
Fatimids
Tributary
to
Fatimids

ZIRIDS

Leon
Castile · Aragon
OMAYYADS
Cordova · Zahariatah
al-Maghrib
Marraksh

BERBERS

A F R I C A

Mahmud was a staunch Sunni and had been confirmed by the Caliph as Sultan of Ghazni. The Caliph had given him the title of *Yamin-ul-Daulah* (Right Hand of the State). He now started a series of *ghazwahs*. He attacked important centres of Hindu culture and religion, as he knew that the rajas of the neighbourhood would gather to save these places. Twelve of these invasions are recorded. The most famous was his attack on Somnath, a famous place of Hindu worship in Gujarat, Kathiawar. To reach it he had to cross the Rajputana desert, and he knew he would have to face the combined forces of nearly all the Hindu rajas of India. He was a great military commander and his courage knew no bounds. Though sorely pressed at first by the larger Hindu army, he defeated the Hindu forces, captured the town, entered the temple and, though offered millions not to do so, broke the idol of Somnath. He went back laden with spoil. His exploits on the western front are no less remarkable, as he annexed Khorasan and the whole of Persia. At the height of his power he ruled over all the area between the Jumna in India and the Tigris on the west.

Mahmud's character. Mahmud has been accused by Indian historians of being a raider, a greedy plunderer of temples and of towns. This is not true. To Mahmud, India was *Dar-ul-Harb* (Region of War). The Shahi kings began the feud with Mahmud's father and broke their word both with Subuktigin and Mahmud a number of times. What they did was perhaps justified because they were fighting for their own country, and Mahmud for his part was waging a 'holy war'. He led out *ghazwahs* every year or every other year into what he called the land of idol-worshippers. This was legitimate war in those days. He never razed any towns to the ground, nor did he order any massacres. He was only proud to be known as an 'idol-breaker'.

Mahmud as Patron of the Arts. There are few kings to equal Mahmud as a hero of Islam. In his time he was the first monarch of Asia. In his own town of Ghazni he raised so many buildings, so many schools, endowed so many seats of learning, and invited so many great men to his capital, that he came to be known as the greatest patron of learning in the eleventh century. He it was who encouraged Firdausi to write his famous *Shahnama*, and he spent about 400,000 dinars annually on poets and learned men alone. He established a university at Ghazni and made the famous philosopher, scientist, wit and poet, Unsuri, a professor at this university. Many other poets, among whom Asadi Tusi, the *ustad* of Firdausi, Asjadi and Farrukhi are most famous, were there too. The great al-Beruni also worked for him, but could not agree with Mahmud's powerful counsellor Ahmad ibn al-Maimandi and attached himself to Sultan Masud, Mahmud's son. Utbi, the famous historian, who wrote the *Tarikhi-Yamini* about the Ghaznavids, also worked at Mahmud's court. Few monarchs have had so many writers, wits and scientists at their courts, or enjoyed such prestige and honour in the whole continent.

Mahmud's successors. The successors of Mahmud included famous sultans like the mighty Sultan Masud and his son Sultan Bairam ibn Masud who was famous for his unusual thirst for knowledge. Bairam was very liberal with his gifts and salaries to learned men and he attracted to his court famous men like Shaikh Nizami, the writer of *Makhzan-i-Asrar*, and Sayed Hasan Ghaznavi. It was in Sultan Bairam's reign and due to his patronage that *Kalilah wa Dimnah*, the collection of fables, was first translated from Sanskrit into Persian. The Ghaznavids continued to rule over a diminishing kingdom for more than a century, but were later forced into the Punjab, where the last descendant of Mahmud was the ruler of Lahore in the days of Shahabuddin Ghauri (1186).

The Buwayhids (945-1055). While the Ghaznavids were ruling in the far-eastern part of the Caliphate, in the centre a new power rose to great prominence. The Caliphs themselves were responsible for this power. Since the days of al-Muqtadir, the Caliph had created a new office, that of *Amir-ul-Umara* (Lord of Lords). This title was generally given to the commander of the Royal Bodyguard. This man was therefore the most powerful man in the Caliphate. Under the Caliph al-Mustakfi (944-946) this office was bestowed on a noble of Persian birth, Ahmad ibn Buwayh. When Ahmad was secure in his office, he took the title of *Muizz ud-Daulah*. His had not been an easy appointment, but had been forced on the Caliph. Ahmad's father, the chief of a Persian tribe in the north, had three sons who had small military commands under the Samanid kings. These brothers built up armies of their own and it was not long before they invaded Persia and conquered Isfahan, Khuzistan, and Karman. By 934 they had established themselves at Shiraz and eleven years later Ahmad, the ablest of the brothers, marched on Baghdad. The Caliph's bodyguard fled and since he was helpless he welcomed Ahmad as a protector. Ahmad was given the highest office, that of *Amir-ul-Umara*. Thus the Buwayhids, who were Shiites by creed, began to rule from the centre and the Caliph, who was a Sunni, became their protege.

The Buwayhid Regime. The Buwayhids were able rulers and did a great deal to tighten up the administration of the Caliphate. Trade improved, old industries began to flourish again and prosperity became widespread in the Muslim world. They also made many changes. Since they were Shiites, they began to establish Shiite customs and Shiite festivals and Moharram was observed officially. The Buwayhids openly declared that Ali had been the rightful heir of the Prophet. The *Yaum-al-Ghadir*, on which day (1st Dhul Hajj) according to Shiite tradition, the Prophet had announced at the oasis of Khumm-al-Ghadir that Ali was to be his successor, was celebrated officially. The Buwayhids ruled for just over a hundred years. They had some very cultured rulers among them and made Shiraz, their capital, a second Baghdad.

Adud ul-Daulah (949-983). The greatest ruler of the line was Adud ul-Daulah. In his long reign of thirty-four years he extended his sway over nearly all the Abbasid lands. He married the Caliph's daughter and gave his own daughter to the Caliph in marriage. At the height of his power, he assumed the title of Shah-in-Shah. He was a great builder and was especially famous for the great hospital he built at Baghdad, called after him Bimaristan-i-Adudi. There were twenty-four paid physicians and other specialists on the staff of this hospital. He was such a patron of the arts that he received odes and *qasidas* (eulogies) from most poets of his time. The great Arab poet al-Mutanabbi also wrote in his honour.

Sharaf ul-Daulah and later Buwayhids (983). Adud ul-Daulah was succeeded by his son Sharaf ul-Daulah who, like Harun al-Rashid's son al-Mamun, was an even greater patron of learning than his father. Sharaf built an observatory for the scientists and was a very liberal friend and admirer of men of talent. His son Baha ul-Daulah was not like his father and grandfather, but his vizier Sabur ibn Ardashir built a college in Baghdad in 993 which had a famous library attached to it. Al-Ma'arri, the famous Arab poet, studied at this college. The Buwayhids are noted for great intellectual activity of another kind in their times. A group of radical Shiite thinkers, called the 'Brethren of Purity' (*Ikhwan us-safa*), who wrote a collection of articles called *Rasail* on a variety of subjects, flourished during their times. The later Buwayhids fought among themselves and gradually lost power. Smaller kingdoms arose on the borders and flourished for half a century or so in each case. Some of them produced a sultan or two who made their mark on the times, and nearly all of them helped in the growth of Muslim culture. The Buwayhid power lasted in a restricted form till the middle of the eleventh century when they were at last overthrown by the Seljuks.

Smaller Kingdoms on the Borders (1023-1096). Most of the small kingdoms on the borders were founded by one Arab tribe or another. The first one to arise was the Bani Taghlib who founded the Hamdanid dynasty between Mosul and Aleppo. The most famous of the sultans of this kingdom was Saif ul-Daulah who carried on *ghazwahs* against the Byzantines with great success. His court became for a time a brilliant seat of culture and the great Arab poet al-Mutanabbi worked there. Later a small dynasty was set up at Aleppo by the Bani Kalb. The rulers of this dynasty were fighters and held their own against powerful neighbours for about sixty years. They were called Mirdasids. The Bani Kalb who overthrew the Bani Taghlib, that is the Hamdanids of Mosul, lasted longer, ruling for over a hundred years. One of their rulers was the famous Sultan Muslim ibn Quraysh, a great fighter who extended his kingdom to Aleppo and beyond. Another small kingdom was set up to the west of Mosul at Diyar Bekr by a Kurd, Abdul Ali ibn Marwan after whom the dynasty was called Marwanid. The Marwanids lasted for about a hundred years. Like the Uqailids, who succeeded the Hamdanids, the Marwanids were overthrown by the great Seljuks.

The Islamic World before the Seljuks. When the Turks first made their appearance in Muslim history, the Abbasids had long been in decline. Other kingdoms from the Tahirids to the Buwayhids, to say nothing of the small principalities, had come and were nearly gone. The Arabs were a spent force in Spain and the Berbers were coming to power. The Fatimids had been ruling in Egypt and Ifriqiya for almost a hundred years. There was a peculiar but balanced grouping of Shiites and Sunnis in the Islamic world. The Sunnis were in power in Spain. The Fatimid Shiites held North Africa. There were the minor Arab kingdoms of Syria, Diyar Bekr and Mosul, which were all Sunni, and the Shiite Buwayhids were masters in Iraq and Persia. Trans-Oxiania was all Sunni. Obviously tension existed between these parts and the idea of unity, which was the gift of Islam to the world, was badly shaken.

The Seljuks—Tughril. This was the state of affairs at the beginning of the eleventh century (fifth Islamic century) though earlier a clan of Turks, the Ghuzz, had come from Turkistan into Trans-Oxiania, settled around Bokhara and had accepted

Islam. They preferred the democractic tradition and became Sunnis. Their leader was called Seljuk and they came to be called after their leader, Seljuk Turks. The Seljuks were a very energetic people and soon began to make themselves politically strong in the area. One of their leaders was Seljuk's grandson Tughril Beg, who led his people on a victorious march. He first conquered Khorasan and, after establishing himself there, divided the army into three commands. He commanded the first army. The other two commands he gave to his brothers. All three marched down into Persia, conquering one province after another. The only strong military power in the east at that time was that of the Ghaznavids, but the successors of Mahmud the Great had grown weak by fighting among themselves, and were too busy with their quarrels to take the field against a new wave of conquest. They lost their western provinces to the Seljuks without a fight. The Buwayhids also had been weakened by internal strife and could do nothing against the Seljuks. By 1055 Tughril was master of the eastern half of the Caliphate, and later that year he marched on Baghdad. The Turkish general of the Buwayhids in the capital was al-Basasiri. He fled before the Seljuks and the Caliph thought a deliverer had come. The Seljuks were Sunni and would perhaps respect him more and permit him more power. He therefore welcomed Tughril and in 1056 gave him the title of *Amir ul-Sharq wal-Gharb*, Lord of East and West.

The End of al-Basasiri. Tughril had yet to conquer the northern kingdoms of Mosul and Diyar Bekr. He therefore marched away with his army and reduced those principalities, but in his absence the Buwayhid general, al-Basasiri, who had fled to the Shiite Fatimids of Egypt for aid, brought back an army with him and reconquered Baghdad. The Caliph was terrified. News was sent to Tughril who hurried back to Baghdad. A fierce battle was fought between him and al-Basasiri in which Basasiri's army was destroyed and he was killed. Tughril thus became lord of all the Abbasid lands, except for Syria and Egypt, and he founded the Seljuk Empire.

The Great Seljuks. There were four great Seljuk kings: Tughril, his son Alp Arsalan, his grandson Malikshah and his great-great-grandson, the last great Seljuk, Sultan Sanjar, who lost the empire to a new Muslim power, the Khwarizm Shahs. The Turks were a wild people in comparison with the civilized and cultured Buwayhids but they were more vigorous and better fighters. This has been generally true of all 'barbarians' who have overthrown great civilizations. But the Seljuks began within one generation to rebuild what they had overthrown and it was not long before they themselves were in the forefront of Muslim culture. They became the greatest patrons of learning in the world in their time and set up institutions which advanced the cause of civilization, of which the Muslims were the spearhead at that time.

Alp Arsalan (1063-1072). It was Alp Arsalan (the Lion-Hearted) who made the might of the Seljuks known to the world. He was a worthy son of Tughril the Conqueror. The Seljuk Empire had settled down by the time he came to power and so he could turn his mind to two things, the glory of Islam abroad and the cultivation of Islamic culture within the Empire. The Byzantines, who had grown bold because of the central weakness of the Abbasids and the growth of small kingdoms on the north-western borders, had been waging continual war with the Muslims. Alp Arsalan now took up arms on behalf of Islam, went into Asia Minor and inflicted a crushing defeat on the Byzantine Emperor at the battle of Manzikert and took him prisoner. After this victory the Muslims advanced into the heart of Asia Minor and settled there. Since the days of Alp Arsalan the Muslims have never been dislodged from the heart of Anatolia. Alp Arsalan appointed one of his own cousins, Sulaiman ibn Qutlumish, as hereditary governor of central Asia Minor, which the Muslims called Rum. The Seljuks of Rum continued to rule in that part till the days of the Ottoman Turks. They first made Nicaea their capital, but in 1084 the Seljuks captured the biggest town in the country, Iconium (Konya) and established themselves there. Iconium was the richest and the most beautiful town of the Byzantines in Asia Minor and it became a great city under the Seljuks of Rum.

Alp Arsalan and Persia. Alp Arsalan chose Isfahan as his own capital as he did not want to take over the city of the Caliphs although the Caliph was a mere puppet in his hands. The name of the Seljuk sultan was, however, mentioned openly after that of the Caliph in the Khutbah after the Friday prayers. The Buwayhids had introduced the same innovation (*bidaat*), but the Seljuks never did anything to humiliate the Caliph though they did not give him any power. Alp Arsalan captured Aleppo in 1070 and then conquered al-Hijaz from the Fatimids. So the holy cities of Mecca and Medina came under the Seljuks. One of the sons of Alp Arsalan called Tutush, was appointed governor of Syria and founded the dynasty of the Seljuks of Syria. It was the descendant of Sultan Tutush who faced the fury of the first Crusade. Alp Arsalan was a popular monarch and many *qasidas* written in his honour survive to this day. With the coming of the Seljuks a new wave of interest ran in the Islamic east; people began to show more enthusiasm for life, and art, literature, and science were greatly encouraged.

Malikshah (1072-1092). The greatest of the Seljuks was Alp Arsalan's son Malikshah. A great ruler, a great builder, a great administrator and a great patron of learning, Malikshah was in a class of his own. He built mosques, bridges, canals and caravan-serais along the route to Mecca. The drainage system of Baghdad had fallen into disrepair, and he had it overhauled and greatly improved. The land between the Aral and the Caspian Seas, called Khwarizm, was conquered, and a Turkish ex-slave of Malikshah, Anushtigin, was made governor of the land. It was this Anushtigin who later founded the dynasty of the Khwarizm Shahs, gradually became a mighty power in central Asia and ultimately overthrew the Seljuks. In Malikshah's days great encouragement was given to learning, especially by his very capable, loyal, and famous Grand Vizier, Nizam ul-Mulk.

Nizam ul-Mulk. Seldom has it been the good fortune of kings and sultans to have such an honest and gifted Grand Vizier as Malikshah had in Nizam ul-Mulk. He was a very cultured man, highly educated, and remained fond of studies all his life. He wrote a book on the art of government, called *Siyasat Namah*, a work of great political insight and scholarship. He established the famous university of Nizamiyah at Baghdad. This he endowed so liberally that it supported many learned people. It therefore attracted a large number of people from all over the Islamic world and even beyond. Imam al-Ghazzali, the world-famous Muslim theologian, philosopher, and mystic, was a professor of this university. Nizam ul-Mulk was a friend and patron of Omar Khayyam, the mathematician, astronomer, and poet. Nasir Khusro, the famous Ismaili writer and traveller, also belonged to this period.

Hasan ibn Sabah. Hasan ibn Sabah, who founded the order of neo-Ismailis, called later the Assassins, had been a class-fellow of Nizam ul-Mulk and Omar Khayyam. He now retired to the Elburz mountains and built there an impregnable fortress, Alamut. From there he sent out his secret agents to work out his designs and, if necessary, to kill and terrorize; indeed his activities were the origin of the English word 'assassinate'. The Assassins gave absolute obedience to their lord in return for a promise not only of salvation but of paradise. A foretaste of this paradise was given to the apprentice Assassins in the beautiful gardens and palaces, which formed part of the Alamut stronghold. These Assassins began a reign of terror everywhere and murdered many prominent people who stood in their way, or refused to pay them huge sums of money or obey the orders of the Lord of the

Mountain, the *Shaikh-ul-Jabal* of Alamut. Nizam ul-Mulk at last undertook an expedition against Alamut, but failed to capture the fortress and was assassinated by order of the Shaikh. This was one of the worst crimes of the Ismaili fraternity, for Nizam ul-Mulk was a truly great son of Islam.

Successors of Malikshah. The successors of Malikshah did very little to add to the lustre of the great Seljuks. They quarrelled among themselves and, as a result, divided the mighty empire into various small Seljuk kingdoms. There were Seljuks in Karman, Seljuks in Iraq and Kurdistan as well as the Seljuks of the east. The last great sultan of the line, who showed something of the might and magnificence of the earlier Seljuks, was Malikshah's son, Sultan Sanjar of the eastern Seljuks. He had to fight continuously against a new branch of the Turks who were still pagans. Their leader, the Ghaur Khan, defeated Sultan Sanjar and also the Ghaznavid ruler of Afghanistan. He founded the line of rulers called the Ghaurids. The Seljuks were finally overthrown in 1157 by the Khwarizm Shahs.

The Khwarizm Shahs. When the Ghaur Khan defeated the Seljuk Sultan of the eastern kingdom he made it easy for the Seljuk governor of Khwarizm to become independent. He was called Atsiz and was the grandson of Anushtigin, the first governor. After a time the Khwarizm Shahs became powerful in central Asia, and in Khorasan and Persia. The strongest ruler of this line was Alauddin Muhammad (1199-1220), who captured Khorasan from the Ghaurids, who had by now accepted Islam. He conquered Bokhara and Samarqand and completed the conquest of Persia. In 1214, he invaded Afghanistan and captured Ghazni, with the result that early in the thirteenth century the strongest Muslim power was that of the Khwarizm Shahs. Sultan Alauddin quarrelled also with the Caliph and, defying him, even turned Shiite and elected his own Caliph for central Asia. Alauddin was a good ruler, however, and in his time central Asia became the centre of Muslim culture: schools and colleges sprang up in the Trans-Oxianic cities, trade flourished, and the fame of central Asian wealth went out to other lands. Unfortunately it attracted a new people who were rising in Mongolia. These were the Mongols, who were being hammered into a terrible fighting machinery by their chief, Timuchen. It was this chief of the Mongols who now burst on the world as Genghis Khan, the Scourge of God.

Genghis Khan (1162-1227) and Prince Jalaluddin. Genghis Khan claimed that a border incident, which occurred on the eastern confines of the Khwarizm empire, was an offence against him. He therefore poured his hordes into central Asia. The Khwarizm Shah sent out army after army against him, but could only stop the advancing Mongols for short intervals. Unhappily he was not on good terms with his brilliant son Prince Jalaluddin, against whom interested courtiers had influenced the Sultan. Prince Jalaluddin had the courage of a lion, an astute brain, and great stamina, and he was also a wonderful organizer. He collected an army of his own and attacked the advancing Mongol army. He struck severe blows at them, but could not check their advance, because the Mongols appeared to be countless and Jalaluddin had at best a few thousand men with him. Genghis laid low most of the cities of central Asia, put to the sword hundreds of thousands of Muslims, defeated Alauddin, and conquered the upper lands of the Khwarizm Shah. The only person to oppose him was Jalaluddin, whom he pursued through the valleys of Afghanistan and the defiles of the Khyber Pass. Jalaluddin fought him and the other Mongol armies all the way and sometimes beat them. He was the only man to defeat Genghis Khan in an engagement. Each battle, however, left him poorer in men and material. At last Genghis came up with him near Attock on the banks of the Indus. Here Jalaluddin fought his last battle. He fought desperately, but, seeing his brave companions falling one by one before the Mongol horde, he at last leapt fully armed into the river and began swimming across. It is said that the Mongol archers were shooting at him when Genghis stopped them, saying: 'You shall not kill a brave enemy like that.' Jalaluddin swam across in full armour, reached the opposite bank and, standing there in full view of Genghis, hurled defiance at him. He then went to the court of Sultan Iltutmash, the 'slave' king of Delhi, and sought help from him, but Iltutmash did not want Genghis to invade India, so he refused. Jalaluddin collected a small army and conquered Sind, but left after some time and eventually reached Azerbaijan where he won a small kingdom for himself for a few years.

Hulagu Khan. The Mongols did not enter Khorasan or Persia under Genghis Khan. The conquest of these regions fell to the lot of his grandson, Hulagu Khan, who swept down and laid the entire country waste, burning, killing, and destroying everything that came in his way. The only good thing that he did before he laid Baghdad waste was to destroy the Assassin stronghold of Alamut. It is said that he invited the Caliph to send him troops in the Mongol campaign against the *Shaikh ul-Jabal*, but the Caliph had no troops and the Seljuk rulers of Iraq were too timorous. A number of people had joined Hulagu Khan by this time. Among his counsellors was the famous scientist and mathematician Nasiruddin Tusi, whom the Shiites consider *Muhaqqi-iq-Awwal*, the 'First Establisher of Truth'. Hulagu laid siege to Baghdad and conquered it, and the city of the Caliphs, the seat of Muslim culture, the centre of world enlightenment, was thus destroyed. The libraries were either burnt or the books thrown into the river and beautiful palaces, schools, hospitals, and mosques went down before the Mongol attack. The Caliph and his family were first imprisoned and later most of them were beheaded. Islam received a shock from which it never fully recovered. In appreciation of the conquest of all this region Hulagu Khan was given the title of Il Khan and made ruler of all the regions below the Oxus. He was the founder of the dynasty of Il Khans of Persia which will be discussed in a later chapter.

Arab Civilization. The Mongols had come and destroyed what has been called Arab civilization although it contained such varied elements as the Turks, Persians, Syrians, Arabs, Jews, Berbers, and converts from Spain and Sicily. All of them had believed in the simple and straightforward creed of Islam and all had tried to speed the processes of human thought and stir human consciousness. They had achieved much knowledge and increased the sum total of the mental and spiritual heritage of man. Their works lay stored in libraries, in museums, and in academies, and their spokesmen were scholars, scientists, philosophers, poets, mystics, artists, and the great artisan class which worked in the field of handicrafts. All these things were destroyed by the Mongol hordes. Life became insecure, thought became frozen, and men were discouraged. One indirect advantage, however, came from the Mongol invasions. Men of talent fled into various Muslim countries. Many were killed and most of them were uprooted, but not all of them were destroyed. Two countries gained most in this way. Firstly, Asia Minor and the small world of the Seljuks of Rum, and secondly, the sultanates of India. Before discussing the men who went to these two corners of the Islamic world and began to re-build the structure of Islamic life and thought there, a short account must be given of some of the great men of the later Abbasid times.

Imam al-Ghazzali (1058-1111). The greatest religious thinker of these times and perhaps the greatest name in Muslim theology is that of Abu Hamid al-Ghazzali who was born in Tus (Meshhed) in Khorasan in 1058. He was a great scholar and learnt early to use the logical and rational methods of argument of the Asha'ri School, but he surpassed all theologians in the depth of his insight and the range of his knowledge. He gave the final shape to Sunni thought and such was his stature that even the Shiites considered him the greatest man of the century. He worked as a professor at the Nizamiyah University of Baghdad, but later acquired such mystical experience (illumination) that he became a Sufi. He was a liberal thinker and made no distinctions between Sunnis and Shiites. He cleared Islamic thought of many philosophic difficulties and made it intelligible to the ordinary man.

Great Saints and Founders of Orders. A number of Sufi orders or brotherhoods called *Silsilajat* or *Tariqahs* came into being during this period. These orders were known after the names of the saints whose preachings and precepts gave them shape and purpose. The greatest order was founded by the Saint of Saints, called afterwards *Pir-i-Piran*, Sayyid Abdul Qadir al-Jilani (1077-1168) of Baghdad. This order is called the Qadiriya Order or *Silsila-i-Qadiriya*. There were other orders also, like the Suhrwardiya Order, the Mevlaviya Order, the Rifa'iya Order, the Bektashiya Order, and the Naqshbandiya Order. These all preached devotion to and love for Allah, faith in the *Pir*, salvation by faith, love of truth, independence from the cares of this world, and a life of contemplation and directed action. These orders helped a great deal in saving the faith of people and, though they appeared to be other-worldly, in reality they served to keep up the morale of the Muslims in these difficult times.

Ibn Sina (979-1037)—Al-Beruni (973-1048). The greatest Muslim philosopher, physician and scientist of this period was Abu Ali ibn Husain, known to us as Abu Ali ibn Sina and to Europe as Avicenna. He flourished during the days of the Samanid sultans and for his work in medicine and philosophy he was known as the Great Teacher. His work was used as an authority all over the world for about seven hundred years. Another man of nearly equal stature was Abul Rayhan Muhammad ibn Ahmad al-Beruni who is even today acknowledged as the greatest mathematician of Islam and one of the greatest scholars and scientists of all time. He lived in the times of the Ghaznavids and wrote in the days of Sultan Masud. He was also a Sanskrit scholar and translated many books from Sanskrit to Persian. He measured the longitude and latitude of the earth and gave expert opinion on the axis of the earth.

Omar Khayyam (1040-1124)—Nasiruddin Tusi (1201-1274). Mention must also be made of two great astronomers and mathematicians. Omar Khayyam, who also wrote *ruba'iyat* as a hobby and is now mostly known through the world-famous free translation of his quatrains by Edward Fitzgerald, was a great scientist and the first astronomer-mathematician of his age. His solar calendar is one of the most accurate ever invented, and an achievement of which we can be proud even today. Nasiruddin Tusi's fame has been spoiled by his friendship and alliance with Hulagu Khan. As he was a staunch Shiite some people have even suspected that he had a hand in the destruction of Sunni Baghdad. This could not have been true. Hulagu Khan honoured him greatly and built for him the great observatory of al-Maraghah near Tabriz and collected a large library of books at great expense for him. These books had to be obtained from all over the Il Khan's lands because the Mongols had destroyed the major universities of these regions. For this alone Nasiruddin Tusi's name should be honoured.

Ibn Hawqal—Al-Maqdisi—Yaqut (1179-1229). Some geographers of eminence also appeared during this period of whom Ibn Hawqal the great traveller, who revised the compendium of al-Istakhri, an earlier geographer, and al-Maqdisi, who travelled and researched for twenty years, are famous. Al-Maqdisi's book is the better because in it, for the first time, human geography was made the subject of research. The greatest geographer of them all was Yaqut ibn Abdullah who wrote two dictionaries, one geographical, the other literary. The geographical dictionary, *Mujam-al-Buldan*, was a great achievement.

Literature—The Arabian Nights. The greatest work in literature, and indeed one of the greatest works of art in the world was also an achievement of these times. It is known as the

Arabian Nights. The book actually received its final shape in Mamluk Egypt, but it is a product of these times. It is a collection of fables, fairy stories, romances, tales of adventure, humour and social life of Abbasid times, heightened and made enchanting by a liberal imagination. It is perhaps the best monument to the zest for life which was the gift of the Arabs to the world. It tells, under romantic covering, of the best and the worst that the Arabs possessed in living and thinking. It is not original, for many of the stories are derived from Indian, Persian, Greek, and Egyptian sources, yet they have undergone a magical change in the telling and have emerged as something quite delightful and entirely new.

CHAPTER 7

THE CRUSADES

Christians and the Muslim Middle East. The Arabs had fought two peoples when they had emerged from Arabia: the Christians of the West and the Zoroastrians of Persia. Later they had to fight the Indians of the East too. The first group had much in common with the Muslims. Indeed, the Arabs came to inherit later the intellectual heritage of the Roman and Greek worlds, as the Christians had inherited that of the Byzantine Empire. Thus there was some common ground of understanding between the two, even though they fought for centuries against each other. The fight with the Zoroastrians has already been dealt with; Persia was first arabicized and later completely Islamicized. The struggle with the third non-semitic people, the Indians, will be discussed later. The Christians had been pushed back, but they had begun to recover their position in the west. In Spain they had won back one-third of the peninsula by the end of the eleventh century. However, the Seljuks had conquered Asia Minor which had made the balance even, but had started a new movement. The Seljuks were a rough people to begin with and they were very staunch Muslims. They objected to the frequency of pilgrimages to Palestine and cut off the land route of the European pilgrims through Asia Minor for a time. The land route now lay through Muslim lands, which annoyed the Christians very much.

The Seljuks of Rum and the Fatimids. The Muslim world at the eastern end of the Mediterranean was shaped like a crescent. One horn of the crescent ended near the Sea of Marmara, the other on the other side of Egypt. Palestine lay in the hollow of this crescent. The Seljuks now blocked the northern end and the later Fatimids were proving difficult at the southern end. The result was that the Christians were greatly disturbed and, being now in a position to do something about it, they began a campaign against the Muslims, whom they called 'infidels', the effects of which are apparent to this day. Nearly five hundred years had gone by since the Prophet of Islam had given his message to the world. The power of that message had strengthened the Muslims, and the West had suffered many defeats in these five hundred years. It was now ready to strike back and the protection of the 'holy places' was a convenient excuse.

The Powers behind the Crusades. Many types of people reacted to the 'danger' to the holy places. The first protest came from the Byzantine Emperor. He protested mostly because his Asian dominions were very nearly gone, and a sturdy people, whom it was difficult to dislodge, had come and settled in Anatolia. He appealed to the Pope of Rome, who at this time was Gregory VII, a very powerful Vicar of Christ, who was fighting for supremacy in Europe with the German emperors. He answered the appeal eagerly, thinking it would help him to unite all the Christian powers of Europe under his banner and thus make him the leading power in Europe.

The city states of Italy, Venice, Genoa, and Pisa had large commercial interests in the Middle East. They wanted to help the 'Holy Cause', as they thought they would gain very valuable trade concessions if the Christians got a foothold on the coast of Syria or Palestine. Many knights and the noblemen of Europe who had heard of the fabulous wealth of the East joined the cause hoping to share in the loot. There were also the genuine, sincere zealots who wanted to fight for Christ and overthrow the 'infidels' who had been blackened in Europe's eyes as enemies of Jesus and evildoers of the worst type.

Finally, the Crusades were a sign of the rise of the West after centuries of Muslim superiority, the slow awakening here and there, of a people who had been swamped by Islam. The

Mediterranean Sea had been a Muslim lake for centuries; all the islands in it were Muslim possessions, even the northern mainland contained colonies of Muslims, in the south of Italy and near Marseilles in France.

The Tide turns in the Mediterranean. At last the tide began to turn in the Mediterranean in the eleventh century. The first note was struck by the Italian city-state of Pisa which conquered the island of Sardinia from the Muslims. The Pope blessed the event openly and much was made of it. Then the kingdoms of Castile and Aragon in Spain made a solemn alliance against the Arabs in Spain and began a holy war there in earnest. Priests worked everywhere rousing the people. Now that they thought the Muslim power was weakening they grew in fervour and spoke with greater confidence. The cry rose from every pulpit that the Holy Land must be rescued. The Pope to whom Emperor Comnenus of Constantinople had appealed was dead, but another Pope as strong as Gregory VII, was now in the papal chair. This Pope, Urban II, put the case of the Byzantine Emperor before a combined session of all the clergy at the Grand Church Conference, first at Piacenza (1095) and again, later in the same year, at Clermont. Here the Pope made a great speech which succeeded in rousing the entire Christian world. Soon his cry was taken up in all corners of Europe, but more particularly in France, perhaps because the Pope was a Frenchman. Wandering friars also took up the cause and went from place to place inciting the people. One such friar was Peter the Hermit, who did a great deal of propaganda for the idea of the Crusades.

The First Crusade (1096-1099). Soon a grand army was assembled in France. The leaders of this Christian army were Godfrey of Bouillon, his brother Baldwin, Count Raymond of Toulouse, and the representative of the Pope, Adhemar of Puy. They decided to travel by land and enter Asia Minor by way of Constantinople, partly because Peter the Hermit and a brother friar, Walter the Penniless, had so inflamed the people that a

Christian horde had already gone ahead this way, looting as it went. It had entered the territories of the Seljuks of Rum in Asia Minor and had been destroyed. The leaders of the first Crusade, therefore, wanted to proceed carefully and keep their lines of communications clear. Fortunately for them and unfortunately for Islam, the Seljuks of Rum had split into many small principalities by this time and could not offer them a determined and united front. The Crusaders did not, therefore, have a difficult time. They fought a battle at Dorylaeum, defeated Qilij Sultan, the ruler of the chief Seljuk kingdom in Asia Minor, and took Nicaea, his capital. The Seljuks were pushed back to Anatolia and the Crusaders kept the coastal lands.

Baldwin and Bohemund. The Crusaders now marched south along the western coast of Asia Minor till they reached the kingdom of Armenia which lay at the eastern end of the southern coast. Most Armenians were Christians. They welcomed the Crusaders and joined them, so Count Baldwin, the commander of the first army, took the whole of Armenia and made himself its king. The rest of the crusading army now marched to Antioch where another Seljuk prince, Yaghi Sultan, ruled. He resisted the Crusaders with all his might and his city withstood the siege for eight months. He sent appeals to the Abbasid Caliph and to other monarchs, but the Seljuk Empire had by now broken into many kingdoms, each wary of its neighbours, so no help came from the east. Amir Ridwan, the ruler of Aleppo, came, but arrived too late. One of the captains of Yaghi Sultan, an Armenian Christian, betrayed him. One night this Armenian opened the gate over which he was keeping watch and let in the Crusaders, and the city fell. Kaibuqa the Amir of Mosul, another Muslim ruler, now advanced, but the Christians were in too strong a position now and defeated him also. This prevented the other Muslim Amirates from sending any further assistance. The Syrian population had seen so many different rulers, Fatimids,

Seljuks, Turks, and lords of many kinds, that they had very little spirit left in them. The north of Syria, therefore, formed another Christian principality and Count Bohemund made it his own kingdom, with Antioch as his capital, where he remained.

Raymond and Godfrey. Two leaders were now left, Count Raymond and Godfrey of Bouillon. Count Raymond was determined to win some territory for his own and taking his army, went raiding and destroying. He took the coastal town of Maarrat al-Numan and in a brutal manner killed its population of about 100,000 Muslims. It was a great outrage, but the Muslims were themselves to blame. They were not united anywhere at this time and could therefore do nothing. Godfrey pushed south on his own, asking Raymond to join him as soon as possible. At last on 7 June 1099, the Crusaders' army stood before the walls of Jerusalem, the holy city of the Christians. The siege lasted five weeks and on 15 July 1099, the Crusaders entered the town. So vindictive were they that they killed much of the Muslim population of the town. Godfrey now sent an army to the south to conquer the rest of Palestine, and the Fatimid army, which gave them battle near Ashkelon, was defeated. After this there was no further resistance and Godfrey of Bouillon was proclaimed king of Jerusalem. The coastal towns were attacked by the navies of the Italian city-states, as Venice and Genoa had co-operated by sending their commercial fleets. Since they had helped to conquer the coastal belt they were given ample trade concessions. The entire coastal region from the sea of Marmara to the south of Palestine was now in the hands of the Crusaders. Only one leader, Count Raymond, was yet without a kingdom of his own, but he soon captured the important coastal town of Tripoli and the surrounding area and carved for himself the principality of Tripoli. All the leaders were thus provided for and the first Crusade was over.

Effects of the Crusades. The Crusaders now settled down in the coastal lands they had won from the Muslims. They all kept near to the sea because the Mediterranean was their channel of approach to the West. The East as represented by Islam suffered a set-back. In the age-old struggle between East and West, the East had been victorious for five centuries. Was the West going to push the East farther back? All Europe expected it, but this did not happen. Instead, the Crusaders, seeing the progressive East for the first time from close quarters, were so deeply impressed by Eastern art, culture, and way of life that they began to take to Eastern ways. A strange kind of social relationship grew up. The Christians who had been fed with tales of the wicked Easterners saw for themselves that the Arabs had evolved a civilization which was much superior to theirs. They also found that the followers of Muhammad were truthful, honest, and god-fearing; that they respected Jesus and believed in him as a prophet of Allah. The Muslims had considered the Europeans barbarians and found that the Christian knights had strict codes of honour, that they could fight cleanly, and were keen to appreciate the superior skills and refined products of the Muslims. Friendships thus began to form and commercial relations were set up. The Christians began to build houses like the Arabs, eat Eastern food, like Eastern music, and enjoy hawking and hunting like the Arabs and later with them. They even called their Muslim neighbours to help when they needed aid against an enemy. Thus this mixture of races and cultures produced very good results and many Eastern discoveries found their way to Europe. Gunpowder was one of them, sugar was another, the compass was a third, and so on. This went on for some time.

Zangids (1127-1250)—Imaduddin Zangi (1127-1146). Gradually the Muslim world began to realize that a stranger was in its midst, though it must not be forgotten that the Muslim world was no longer one continuous belt from Kashgar to Cordova as before. This is why the idea of resistance took time to crystallize. Feelings became strengthened and slowly the idea of driving the Christians from the Muslim Middle East began to grow. When such a thing happens the right man also appears. Such a man came from the dynasty of the Zangi rulers of Mosul. Imaduddin Zangi had been a trusted slave of Sultan Malikshah the Seljuk Emperor. He had moved west and had gradually made himself master of the area between Mosul and Aleppo. He was a strong man and a fearless fighter and was soon at grips with the Christians. He first laid siege to the town of al-Ruha which lay on the caravan route from Syria to Baghdad and which was now in Christian hands. The town fell in 1144 after a siege of four weeks.

The Second Crusade (1147-1149). The crusading spirit was yet alive in Europe. The news of al-Ruha's fall was received with concern by Pope Eugenius III; he asked Saint Bernard of Clairvaux to preach another Crusade. The German Emperor, Conrad III, and the King of France, Louis VII, answered the call. They organized the second Crusade in 1147. The armies of the two leaders marched separately, their objective being Damascus which was still a Muslim town. The Crusaders arrived, and besieged Damascus, but they did not succeed in their venture. Damascus resisted them easily and the Crusade proved a failure. The only man who benefited from this attempt was Robert the Norman, King of Sicily, who attacked the Muslim islands in the Aegean Sea and drove the Muslims out of them all.

Nuruddin Zangi (1146-1174). This was a great blow to the prestige of Islam and it was widely resented. A new champion rose from the house of the Zangids. He was Nuruddin, the very capable son of Imaduddin Zangi. Nuruddin succeeded his father in 1146 and immediately set about fighting the Crusaders systematically. His first action was to move his capital from Mosul to Aleppo. In order to have a unified front he took Damascus from its weak Muslim ruler and began to fight the

Christians on a wide front. His father had taken the town of al-Ruha; Nuruddin annexed the entire district of al-Ruha. He captured the Christian governor of the area, Count Jocelin II, and imprisoned him. He then attacked the ruler of Antioch, Bohemund II, defeated him and captured him too. He would not release these two princes till they had paid him a large ransom.

Shirkuh (1164). Soon Nuruddin became a terror to the Christians. He had a capable general named Shirkuh, whom he sent with a strong military escort, as his ambassador to the last Fatimid Caliph of Egypt. Shirkuh was a very able man and won so much favour at the court of the Fatimid Caliph that he was offered the appointment of Vizier which he accepted. He had a nephew called Salahuddin who showed signs of brilliance. Shirkuh did not live long after his new appointment and after his death the Caliph appointed Salahuddin as his Vizier. With this appointment Muslim fortunes began to recover again, because this man was the famous Sultan Salahuddin al-Ayyubi, the great Champion of Islam.

Salahuddin al-Ayyubi (1169-1192). Salahuddin was the son of Shirkuh's brother Ayyub, the commander of Baalbek in Syria under the Zangids. Salahuddin had been well educated. He was a Sunni. He loved Islam and now that he was a powerful minister he resolved to do all he could to root out the Crusaders. For this he had to have a strong army, and a strong army depended on a powerful state. He was the virtual ruler in Egypt, so he set about winning a kingdom, and his time came when Nuruddin Zangi, his overlord, died in 1174. At his death Salahuddin announced that Egypt was now independent. The Zangis came against him with an army, but Salahuddin defeated them at Qurun Hamah and annexed Syria. He then sent his brother Turan Shah with an army into al-Hijaz which he conquered in 1175. He went farther and conquered the Yemen too. After this Salahuddin sent a request to the Abbasid Caliph at Baghdad to invest him as Sultan of Egypt. This the

Caliph was glad to do because it meant the end of the rule of the Fatimids, who had held extreme views even for Shiites. Salahuddin was thus accepted as Sultan of Egypt, al-Hijaz, the Yemen, and Syria.

The Assassins. The Christians became afraid. Here was a new force risen to fight them and the man in command was a military commander of note. They thought of ways and means, and somebody suggested the Assassins. Why not have Salahuddin assassinated? One had only to pay the price and the *Shaikh ul-Jabal* would do the rest. A price was therefore paid and a couple of Assassins went their silent way and attacked Salahuddin, but fortunately he escaped unhurt and the Assassins were caught. The Sultan was furious that the so-called Muslims of the neo-Ismaili order should attack him and he decided to teach the *Shaikh ul-Jabal* a lesson. He led an army against Rashiduddin Sinan, the *Shaikh ul-Jabal* and stormed his fortress so impetuously that he became afraid and sued for peace. Peace was granted to him on the promise that he would never again raise a hand against Salahuddin. To this he had to agree, and he kept his word.

Salahuddin Marches against the Crusaders. Salahuddin now turned to the Christians. He first attacked Tiberias and took it on 1 July 1187. The Christians then collected a large army and came to meet him. The battle which followed was fought at Hittin on 4 July. The Christians were 20,000 strong, but Salahuddin's army was more than a match for them. He fell on them with such fury that he cut them to pieces and captured Guy of Lusignan, King of Jerusalem, whom he treated very courteously. He was, however, very stern with Reginald of Chatillon, a treacherous Christian nobleman, who had broken his word to Salahuddin again and again, ill-treated Muslims, looted caravans of pilgrims, and molested the innocent and the weak. Salahuddin had sworn to cut off his head with his own hand and did so. He then marched on Jerusalem and reconquered it; the town had been in Christian hands for eighty-eight years. In contrast with the behaviour of Godfrey of Bouillon he did not order any killings. After this he conquered the rest of the kingdom of Jerusalem and only Antioch, Tripoli, and Tyre remained in Christian hands.

The Third Crusade (1189-1192). The fall of Jerusalem sent a wave of horror through the whole of Europe. All the kings of Europe rose up to fight for the honour of Christendom, and three powerful monarchs took the lead. Richard the Lion-heart of England, Frederick Barbarossa, Emperor of Germany and Philip II, King of France. Frederick came by land, the others by sea. Frederick was full of enthusiasm, but never reached Syria, for while crossing a river in Asia Minor he was carried away by the current and drowned. Richard I stopped on the way to capture Cyprus from the Muslims and later sold the island to the dispossessed king of Jerusalem, Guy of Lusignan. Philip II therefore arrived first and joined forces with King Guy who came out to meet him. Together they besieged the town of Acre, a Muslim sea port in lower Palestine.

The Fall of Acre (1191). King Guy had been captured by Salahuddin, but had been released on ransom, on condition that he would never again take up arms against Salahuddin. King Guy, however, broke his word as soon as he heard that the kings of Europe were on their way. He got his men together, collected Emperor Frederick's army and joined Philip II. The Crusaders attacked Acre from the sea and King Guy from the land. When Salahuddin heard of this he advanced to the town's rescue, scattering the land forces of the Christians on one side, but the siege continued from the other side and from the sea. Soon Richard came up with his forces and the Christian side grew stronger. The Muslim garrison fought from within and Salahuddin helped from without, but the Christians would not be driven away. Salahuddin appealed to the Caliph and to other Muslim monarchs, but no help came. At last after a siege of two years the town fell. It was a great disappointment to Sultan Salahuddin.

The Terms of Surrender. The Christians said that they would let the garrison go if three of their conditions were accepted:

(a) The Muslims should pay 200,000 pieces of gold.
(b) The Holy Cross, on which the Christians believed Jesus had been crucified, should be returned.
(c) The money must be paid in one month.

A month is a very short time to collect so much money and Salahuddin had not sufficient resources to pay it at once. He sent out appeals again, but distances were long and the time was short. The men of Acre pooled all their resources and Salahuddin helped with all he had, but the month passed and the sum could not be made up. Richard the Lion-hearted then had all the Muslim captives, nearly 3,000 men, killed. This was not a kingly act and has remained as a slur on his name.

Salahuddin's Nobility. Richard's behaviour was in strict contrast to that of Salahuddin, who had set a similar price on the heads of his captives in Jerusalem when he had recaptured the town two years before. Since the poor Christians could not find the money he had let them all go. This example of great-heartedness has seldom been equalled in history. Salahuddin did many such deeds. Chivalry was part of his nature and the European monarchs honoured him for it. Richard I was so impressed by him that he offered the hand of his sister in marriage to al-Malik al-Adil, the brother of Salahuddin. He knighted the son of this brother, al-Kamil, with great pomp and show. They exchanged presents and though they never met there was mutual respect between the leader of the Crusade and Salahuddin. A peace treaty was drawn up between the Christian leaders and Salahuddin in 1192. Its main points were that Salahuddin promised to give free passage to Christian pilgrims to Jerusalem and retained all the lands he had conquered.

Salahuddin's Character. Salahuddin did not live long after this. He died a few months later and his death was mourned everywhere. He had been a great warrior, a fine king, a noble foe, a liberal patron of arts, a learned Muslim, and a great champion of Islam. He had built new roads, improved irrigation, opened and endowed schools and colleges, and built the citadel of Cairo which stands to this day. The Ayyubid University which he organized and endowed in Damascus became a famous seat of learning and flourished for centuries. To Europe he has ever since remained a pattern of chivalry.

Salahuddin's Successors—Al-Adil (1192-1218). Salahuddin's family divided the Ayyubid Empire among themselves. His eldest son, al-Malik al-Afal, chose Syria; al-Malik al-Adil, the ablest of the Ayyubids and brother and lieutenant of the great Salahuddin, got Egypt, but before long he took Syria from the weaker al-Afal. He was a very enlightened ruler and kept diplomatic and commercial relations with many European powers. He ruled for twenty-six years (1192-1218) and maintained the name and glory of the Ayyubids. After him his son, al-Kamil, came to the throne and ruled effectively too, but after al-Kamil the Ayyubids began to quarrel among themselves and gradually became weak. The result of this was that forty years after Salahuddin's death the Christians recovered most of the towns that he had wrested from them.

Fourth Crusade (1202-1204). There were many Crusades after this, but not all were aimed against the Muslims, nor was the object in every case Jerusalem or any other holy city. For instance, the fourth Crusade was aimed at and resulted in the capture of Constantinople, much against the Pope's wishes. The Italian towns had refused to take part unless they were promised large sums of money and other concessions. Moreover, the Crusaders did not behave well at Constantinople. They began to interfere in the local government and took part in all sorts of court intrigues.

Naturally there were reprisals, much bloodshed resulted and the Byzantine Emperor of Constantinople fled to Nicaea in Asia Minor. The Crusaders put a nominee of their own on the throne at Constantinople. There was thus considerable bad feeling in many quarters and it gave the Crusaders a bad reputation. The Pope feared that the action of the leaders of the fourth Crusade would reflect on the entire Christian world, so he tried to recover the papal position and win back some initiative. He began to organize a new Crusade. It took him time, but by 1218 his efforts began to bear fruit.

Fifth Crusade (1218-1221)—Al-Kamil. The Pope needed adequate financial backing for the fifth Crusade, and he asked the Republics of Venice and Genoa to help. They said they would co-operate if the Crusade was aimed at Egypt. Theirs was a frankly commercial interest. They were not interested in crusades as such. They wanted Egypt because the trade to the Far East passed through Egypt and the Red Sea ports. The ruler of Egypt at this time was the Ayyubid Sultan al-Kamil, the son of al-Adil. He, like his father, had kept good relations with these republics and he was surprised to learn that his friendship mattered little to these commercial people. He awoke to the seriousness of the situation when the crusading fleet captured the Egyptian sea port of Dimyat (Damietta). He began to fight back in self-defence and did not let the Crusaders advance farther into the land. Finally, after a struggle lasting two years, he drove them out of Dimyat as well. The leaders of the Crusade were greatly surprised; they had thought that, since al-Kamil was no bigot, he was a weakling. He was actually a very liberal-minded man; he was well read, and knew about other religions. He took part in discussions with the Ulema and the Christian Fathers and is said to have entertained even St. Francis of Assisi when he came to Egypt. But he was a strong military captain and kept up many of the traditions of the Ayyubids.

The Sixth Crusade (1228-1229) — Frederick II and al-Kamil.
The sixth Crusade was quite different in nature from the others. The object was the recovery of Jerusalem, but the leader who undertook it went about it in a peculiar way. He was Frederick II, Emperor of Germany and King of Naples and Sicily. Since he was married to Yolande, the daughter of the last king of Jerusalem, he could be said to have a right to Jerusalem too, even though the town was now in Muslim hands. This monarch was a friend of the Arabs, admired Arab culture, surrounded himself with Arab philosophers and physicians, lived mostly in Sicily, and was not bigoted. The Pope asked him to lead this new Crusade and he agreed to do so, but he fell ill on the way and returned home; a second attempt he postponed for reasons of his own. The Pope was very annoyed with him and, finding his rebukes falling on deaf ears, cut him off from the blessings of the Church. This may have been one of the reasons why, at last, Frederick II decided to go on this Crusade. He embarked quietly and went to Egypt where al-Kamil, the nephew of Sultan Salahuddin, was still ruler, although the latter's cousins, the Ayyubids of Syria, were fighting against him continuously. He therefore made an alliance with Frederick II and promised to give him Jerusalem and a corridor from Acre, the city won by the Crusaders in the third Crusade, to Jerusalem, if Frederick helped him to fight the Ayyubids of Syria. Frederick agreed because it appeared to him to be a good bargain. Frederick II got Jerusalem and al-Kamil a victory over his rivals. Al-Kamil's role in this deal was not very noble and cannot be defended, as it was a betrayal of a cause. It is strange that what Salahuddin had won with such valour his nephew gave away as a present. Seventeen years later, al-Sultan al-Salih, the successor of al-Kamil, engaged the services of a wandering band of Khwarizm Turks and with their help reconquered the city. So Jerusalem, known to Muslims as *Bait-al-Muqaddas,* came back to Islam in 1246.

The Seventh Crusade (1244-1249). The seventh, and last important Crusade was led by Louis, the saintly king of France, in the last year of the reign of al-Sultan al-Salih. St. Louis also captured Dimyat and advanced into the Nile delta towards Cairo. He had chosen the wrong season for this: the Nile was in flood and the region of the delta was one vast marsh. St. Louis's army got bogged down and when al-Salih sent a few regiments against the Crusaders it was not difficult for them to defeat the invaders and capture the leader and most of his knights, many Christians dying in the venture. Al-Salih himself lay dying when this Crusade was being repelled. When St. Louis was brought to him as a prisoner he treated the noble king very courteously and let him go after a month on payment of a ransom. St. Louis left for Syria where he spent some years in repairing the fortresses of the Crusaders. This was the last of the important Crusades. Enthusiasm was now running out and people could no longer be persuaded to rise and leave for the Holy Land on what they now knew was no easy task. Moreover, the power of the Popes was not so great as it had been. Hence, after this, there were no major attempts at the recovery of the Holy Land. Palestine remained in Muslim hands till the First World War in the twentieth century when it was captured by the British from the Turks. A part of it is now a Jewish state.

The Fall of the Ayyubids. Al-Salih died not long after St. Louis's Crusade and after his death his widow, a very capable lady by the name of Shajar al-Durr, ruled for some time till his son Turan Shah came from Iraq where he had gone on a visit. When Turan Shah arrived she handed over the reins of the government to him, but the young prince did not have an easy time. He tried hard to maintain his position, but the royal bodyguard, made up of Turkish slaves called Mamluks, was too strong for him. As with many other Muslim powers, the bodyguard soon made things difficult for the weak descendants of Salahuddin. Turan Shah was assassinated and Shajar al-Durr made Regent, but the power behind her was Aybak the Chief of the Mamluks. Soon the Mamluks came to power openly and the Ayyubid empire passed into the hands of the branch of Mamluks called the Bahri Mamluks who ruled for a hundred and thirty years, making room ultimately for another branch of Mamluks, the Burji Mamluks, who ruled for a hundred and thirty-five years more.

The Bahri Mamluks (1250-1382)—Sultan Baybars (1260-1277). The first line of Mamluks is more important historically, for it produced some great monarchs and two great champions of Islam. One of them, Sultan al-Zahir Baybars was a real sword of Islam. He, the fourth Mamluk sultan, defeated the Mongols and the Crusaders. When Hulagu Khan, after overthrowing the Muslim kingdoms of the Middle East and destroying Baghdad, was marching through Syria to lay Egypt waste, Sultan Baybars came east to meet him and at the battle of Ayn Jalut, on 3 September 1260, inflicted a severe defeat on the Mongols who until that time had been unconquered. Sultan Baybars did not stop there. He turned his attention to the strongholds of the Crusaders and the areas still held by the crusading Franks who had made pacts with Hulagu and were inciting him to come again and conquer the Muslims of this region. Baybars organized yearly *ghazwahs* against the Christian principalities, which had been strengthened by many orders of Christian knights, bands of fearless and determined fighters, who had built their own fortresses in Christian localities and ruled over many towns and districts. The most famous of these orders were the Order of the Knights of the Temple, called Templars, and the Order of Hospitallers. Baybars attacked the stronghold of the Hospitallers at Arsuf in 1263 and conquered it. Next year, he captured Safad, the fortress of the Templars. He was not so charitable towards the enemy as Salahuddin had been. Moreover, he was greatly offended by the cruel behaviour of these Christian knights, who were very bigoted and unforgiving to the Muslims. So, when he conquered Safad, he refused to ransom the two thousand Templars who fell into his hands and had them all executed. It now became his custom that, when he had taken a Christian stronghold, he either burnt it or razed it to the ground and sold the captives as slaves. He was a stern opponent and his enemies feared him. He took the town of Arkad from the Crusaders after a siege of fourteen days and destroyed it. Baybars then led a campaign against the stronghold of the Assassins in North Syria and defeated them. During his reign his generals conquered Nubia, the land lying south of Egypt. He then brought an uncle of the last Abbasid Caliph of Baghdad and installed him as Caliph of Islam in Cairo. This began a second line of Abbasid Caliphs which continued till early in the sixteenth century. These Caliphs did not have any temporal power except over the *awqaf* (religious endowments) and over investitures of the Sultans of the Muslim world. Even Sultan Bayazid I, the Ottoman Sultan, requested a blessing and an investiture from the then Caliph, as Sultan of the Ottomans.

Character of Baybars. Sultan Baybars was a great military commander, but he was much more than that. He was a very fine ruler and did a lot for the Mamluk Empire. He built new roads, dug new canals, strengthened and improved the navy, and organized a quick postal service between Cairo and Damascus. He also erected many mosques and had very liberal views. So much so, that he appointed four chief Qadis in Cairo, each belonging to one of the four schools of Muslim law: Hanafi, Shafii, Maliki, and Hanbali. The custom, which remains to this day, of preparing in Egypt an embroidered covering for the Kaaba and sending it annually to Mecca was begun by Baybars. He established diplomatic relations with many rulers in Europe and even the Far East and made an alliance with the Khan of the Golden Horde, (Muslim Mongols who had inherited parts of eastern Europe and southern Russia from the empire of Genghis Khan).

Sultan Qalawun (1279-1290). Baybars was succeeded by Sultan Saifuddin Qalawun who was a greater enemy of the Crusaders than even Sultan Baybars. His lifelong pursuit was war with the Franks and so effective was he that he conquered the remaining Christian areas one by one. Another order of Christian knights (the Knights of St. John) held the town of al-Marqah which he captured in 1285. He then attacked Tripoli, the town won in the first Crusade by Count Raymond of Toulouse, and conquered it in 1289. He was so victorious in his campaigns against the Crusaders that he came to be known as *al-Malik al-Mansur* (the Victorious Monarch). He was also as fortunate as Baybars in his battle with the Mongols. Hulagu's son Abaga, who was an ally of the Christians and was in correspondence with the Pope and other Christian monarchs of Europe, came at their request to fight the rising power and fame of Sultan Qalawun. Qalawun defeated him at Hims in 1280 and this made the name of the Mamluks a terror to Europeans and Mongols alike.

Qalawun as Ruler. Qalawun was a great lover of Islam and did not find it easy to forgive its enemies. Armenia, where Count Baldwin of Boulogne had established the first Frankish principality of the Crusaders, was still in Christian hands and had allied itself with Abaga against the Muslims. Qalawun therefore sent an army into Armenia and captured all the fortresses which the Crusaders had built. He had these strongholds pulled down and repaired the Muslim fortresses which had suffered during the Frankish occupation and the rule of the Crusaders. He also built a great mosque in Cairo which stands to this day. His greatest achievement was the erection of a hospital in Cairo which was the biggest structure of its kind ever built. He then built a medical school alongside it which had a large staff of experts and such modern arrangements as separate wards for infectious diseases, separate treatment rooms for women and specialist advice in most illnesses. The accounts of this hospital which have come down to us astonish the modern reader.

Successors of Qalawun. The last stronghold of the Crusaders fell in 1291 before Qalawun's son and successor Sultan al-Ashraf. This was the town of Acre, round which had centred all the fighting of the third Crusade and which even the great Salahuddin had not been able to relieve. When Sultan al-Ashraf captured the town he rid Syria of all Crusaders. It had taken the Muslims two hundred years to dislodge them. The good days of the Bahri Mamluks were now over. Al-Ashraf's successor, al-Nasir, did not have an easy time. Under him the Mamluks were defeated by Ghazan, the great-grandson of Hulagu, near Hims in 1299, but when Ghazan came back three years later to deal the finishing stroke to Mamluk power in Syria he was met by a strong Mamluk force and was defeated at Marj-al-Saffar. This was, however, the last flicker of a once powerful flame. The Bahri Mamluks did nothing remarkable after that, and in a few generations grew weak enough to be overthrown by another Turkish bodyguard, also of Mamluks, called the Burji Mamluks, because for a long time they had their headquarters in the Citadel (*Burj*) of Cairo. Al-Nasir was a cultured monarch and a great patron of the arts. Scores of buildings, arches and gardens, and the Nasiriya College of Cairo, which became a great centre of learning, were built by him.

The Burji Mamluks (1382-1517). The chief of the new Mamluk bodyguard was Barquq. He was a strong man and easily overthrew the last Bahri Sultan. The Burjis now set up a new type of government which was not hereditary. It was an oligarchic form of government, the power being held by the military chiefs, and it was not often that the son of a Sultan succeeded him. Since there was much jealousy and intrigue among the chiefs, the Sultans of this dynasty did not reign long. Not that the Burji Mamluks did not produce some strong rulers, but, by and large, they did not achieve as much as the

Bahri Mamluks, nor did they leave any great mark on history. In their time the governors of various provinces were changed so often that people who were entrusted with the task of administration lost interest in their work, since their appointments did not last long. The country was mismanaged and gradually became poorer. This tempted Timur, the Tartar King of Central Asia, and his invasion of Syria finished whatever was left of order and prosperity there. Both Egypt and Syria marked time for almost a century after Timur's invasion. Egypt lived mostly on trade with India and the Far East. Now and then the Burji Mamluks recovered a certain amount of power; one of their achievements was the reconquest of Cyprus which had been turned into a stronghold of adventurers by the Knight Templars and was ruled by the descendants of Guy of Lusignan. These ex-Crusaders had turned pirates and Muslim shipping was not safe in these waters. Sultan Barslay led an expedition against them and took the island. He defeated the knights and led away a thousand of them in chains. After this the Knights of St. John, who held Rhodes, were forced to make peace with Sultan Barslay.

Achievements of the Mamluks—Ibn Taimiya (1263-1326). The rule of the two lines of Mamluks lasted for two and a half centuries and the Sultans, though not learned themselves, encouraged learning as did other Muslim rulers. Under the Mamluks considerable good work was done in the practical sciences, in history, and in the arts and crafts, but, except for a few names, no great thinker or writer of high rank emerged during their days, the great exception being Imam Ibn Taimiya. Taqi al-Din Ahmad ibn Taimiya lived at Damascus where he was professor of Hanbali Law at the university. He was a great scholar, a fearless fighter, and outspoken in argument. He held very strict views and often interpreted the Qur'an very literally. He also held firm views on many other points which to others appeared rather radical. He has been respected by many famous men including Mohammed ibn Abdul Wahhab, the great eighteenth century Puritan of Arabia and founder of the Wahhabi movement. Ibn Taimiya was no mere speaker; he could fight like a soldier and took part in the wars against the Mongols.

History—Ibn Khallikan (1211-1282). Another name of this period was that of the greatest biographer in Muslim history, Ahmad ibn Muhammad ibn Khallikan. He is well known for his biographies of 865 famous Muslims. The book shows great scholarship and has been called the greatest biographical work of the time by every discerning critic. Three other historians, Ibn Taghri-Birdi, Jalaluddin Suyuti, and al-Maqrizi also belonged to this period. They are not so great as the historians of the Abbasid period because their work is derived from older writers, but what they did was useful and invaluable for the history of these times.

Sciences. In the sciences there were a few outstanding names. Ibn Abi Usaibiah (1203-1270) was a famous historian of medicine. His renowned *History of the Sciences* contains the lives of 400 physicians, most of whom were also philosophers and scientists. His work is therefore a dictionary of Arab sciences. Ali ibn al-Nafia, a physician on the staff of Qalawun's great hospital, wrote on the circulation of the blood; al-Baytari was a great veterinarian, Ibn Abi al-Mahasin of Aleppo and Abdul Fadl ibn al-Naqid were great occulists. Hibatullah ibn Jumay, a physician to Sultan Salahuddin, wrote on the influence of the mind on the body and suggested methods of mental healing; a new subject on which nobody had ever written before.

Buildings. The Mamluks, especially the Bahri line, were fond of building beautiful mosques and other monuments. The greatest builder of them all was the Bahri Sultan al-Nasir, who built aqueducts, bridges, parks, gateways, mosques, schools, and *khanqahs* (monasteries). The college, al-Nasiriya, which he built in 1304 is a fine example of Egyptian architecture. The best builders among the Burji Mamluks were Barquq, Qait Bay (whose mosque and school stand to this day), and al-Ghauri. Most of these buildings have a slender beauty all their own, which make this style of architecture a credit to Islam. It can be said with confidence that the Mamluks left their mark on the history of the arts and the sciences.

CHAPTER 8

ISLAM IN INDIA

The Coming of Islam to India. The story of the coming of Islam to India has already been touched upon in Chapter 3. When Raja Dahir of Sind had begun interfering with Arab shipping late in the seventh century, al-Hajjaj ibn Yusuf, the powerful governor of Iraq, had sent his nephew Muhammad ibn al-Qasim with an army, and young Muhammad had conquered the entire lower Indus Valley up to Multan. He had not stayed long in India, but Islam had stayed and since those days Sind and even south-west Punjab had become part of the Arab Empire.

Effect of Early Conquest. The Arab governors of Sind had tried to expand to the east and from time to time had sent expeditions into Rajputana, Malwa, and Gujarat. One such governor was Junaid, and in his time the Muslims overran the upper reaches of the Vindhyas. They even crossed into the Deccan which was ruled by the powerful Chalukyas who stopped the Muslim advance. In the centre the Pratiharas ruled with great might and they too prevented the Muslims from getting a foothold in the central parts of India. The Muslims, however, remained masters of the lands west of Rajputana; they were not yet an Indian power, but they certainly came in contact with the Hindu civilization, and cultural relations developed between the Hindus and the Muslims. The Arabs were keen students and eager for knowledge. They began to study Indian mathematics, the Indian system of medicine, Indian sciences and philosophy, and Sanskrit literature. The result was that Indian ideas and Indian learning were carried across to other Arab countries, to increase the sum total of Arab knowledge. It is recorded that quite early Muslim scholars and scientists came to Benares and other seats of Hindu learning to study astronomy and mathematics.

The Ghaznavids—Mahmud al-Ghaznavi. The real impact of Islam on a large scale came with the invasions of Mahmud of Ghazni. Mahmud came as far as Kanauj and Delhi, but annexed only the Punjab. The Punjab, or more than two-thirds of it, became a part of the Muslim world under the Ghaznavids. Lahore was the provincial capital of the Ghaznavid governors of the Punjab and Upper Sind, and the last Ghaznavid ruler belonged to Lahore and not to Ghazni. Mahmud left a lasting impression on India, an impression which was not confined to the permanent annexation of the Punjab, but lay more in the awe, if not the actual terror, that he and his Turks inspired in the hearts of the Indians. He had beaten them so often, and the fame of his son Sultan Masud and great-grandson Bahram had so spread in India that when the Ghauris came to India, except for the opposition offered by Prithvi Raj, the Chauhan Raja of Delhi and Ajmer, the Indians offered little resistance to the advancing Muslims.

Ghaurids. The people who overthrew the Ghaznavids were the followers of Ghaur Khan, the leader of the Ghaur Turks of whom mention has been made in an earlier chapter. Bahram Shah, the last Ghaznavid king, had captured two chiefs of the Ghaurid Turks, Qutbuddin and Saifuddin, when the Ghaurs had come raiding, and had had them killed. This incident so roused Alauddin, the younger brother of these two Ghaurs, that he collected a large force and attacked Ghazni. Alauddin was a very revengeful and reckless man. Still half a barbarian, he did not care for the glory of Ghazni, its palaces, mosques, university, libraries, schools or *khanqahs*. He attacked Ghazni, conquered it and set it on fire. The great city, one of the biggest in Asia, on which had been lavished the wealth of many countries, burned for seven days. For this wicked deed Alauddin came to be called Alauddin Jahansoz (World-burner). The Ghaurs now assumed power in this area and it was

Ghiathuddin, the nephew of Alauddin, who became the first king of the Ghaurid dynasty proper, though the man who made the Ghaurids really famous was Ghiathuddin's brother, Shahabuddin al-Ghauri, the conqueror of north India.

Shahabuddin Muhammad al-Ghauri (1175-1206). Shahabuddin was the Commander-in-Chief of the Ghaurid forces and a great warrior. He wanted to win for his house a large empire than even Mahmud had been able to acquire. He invaded India first in 1175 and conquered Multan from its Ismaili ruler. He also reached south to Uch, which is now in Bahawalpur Division, and was a very important political and cultural centre in those days. Shahabuddin more than once made the mistake of under-rating the Hindus. Consequently he suffered two defeats in his career at the hands of Hindu Rajas. The first was in a battle with the Raja of East Punjab in 1178. In 1181 he came again and this time secured his lines of communications. He built a fortress at Peshawar. He then attacked the last Ghaznavid ruler of Lahore whom he defeated in alliance with the Hindu Raja of Jammu. Khusro Malik (1160-1182), the last ruler of his line, was taken prisoner and sent to Ghazni in 1182. Shahabuddin then built a fort at Sialkot and thus made his position secure in at least two-thirds of the Punjab.

Shahabuddin al-Ghauri and Prithvi Raj. The battle for India came a few years later, and Shahabuddin al-Ghauri had a much stronger foe to contend with—Prithvi Raj, the Raja of Ajmer and Delhi, and a great fighter. The first time they met, Prithvi Raj had the advantage. Shahabuddin was defeated at Tarain near Thanesar in south-east Punjab and although he fought with great valour he was grievously wounded. His army was discouraged, but one of his captains took him up on his horse and left the field. The Ghaurid soldiers fled; the victory was a triumph for Prithvi Raj and was used as a theme in many Hindu romances and histories. Shahabuddin felt greatly shamed and punished all those soldiers of his army who had turned their backs on the enemy. In 1192 he came again, this time with a stronger force. Prithvi Raj moved forward with many allies and a fierce battle ensued between the Hindus and the Muslims, but this time Shahabuddin al-Ghauri was victorious. Prithvi Raj died fighting, as did many Hindus and this defeat broke the back of Hindu opposition. The only other raja who fought the Muslims after Prithvi Raj's death was his rival, Raja Jaichand of Kanauj, who would not assist Prithvi Raj, but who put up a good fight himself and died fighting. Shahabuddin went back to Ghazni, leaving his general Qutbuddin Aybak behind, but in 1197 he came back in person against Raja Bhim Dev of Gujarat, Kathiawar and defeated him. In 1202 the fort of Kalinjar fell. Meanwhile General Bakhtiyar Khalji had conquered east India up to Bengal. The whole of north India was now in Muslim hands.

The Slave Dynasty—Qutbuddin Aybak (1206-1210). Shahabuddin succeeded to the empire of the Ghaurids in 1203 on the death of his brother, Ghiathuddin, but he did not live long to enjoy his high position. The Khokhars, a war-like tribe in west Punjab, rose in 1205. Shahabuddin came out against them and defeated them, but when he was on his way back to Ghazni he was killed by an assassin. His Viceroy in India, Qutbuddin Aybak, now became king of north India, which angered the other generals of Shahabuddin. Chief among them were Tajuddin Yildiz who became independent in Kabul and Nasiruddin Qabacha who took Multan and Sind. Qutbuddin was too strong for them and, moving against them, subdued them. However, he died in 1210 after a fall from a horse, while playing polo in Lahore. His tomb lies in an obscure lane of that town. Qutbuddin was a great-hearted man, and so generous that he came to be known by the title of *Lakh Bakhsh* (the Giver of Lakhs). He began the construction of a great mosque outside Delhi with materials taken from old Hindu buildings of which only remains have survived at Mehrauli. The Qutub Minar was to be the minaret of this mosque.

Iltutmash (1211-1236). The rulers who came after Qutbuddin were mostly ex-slaves, hence this dynasty is known popularly as the Dynasty of Slave Kings. Two of these kings stand out: Iltutmash and Balban, both of whom left a mark on Indian history. Iltutmash came to the throne in 1211 at the request of the nobles of Delhi. He had been one of the generals of Shahabuddin Ghauri, and he was recognized as Sultan of Delhi by the Caliph of Baghdad and given the title of Sultan-i-Azam. Both Tajuddin Yildiz and Nasiruddin Qabacha gave trouble again, but Iltutmash defeated them both and became the Sultan of all the dominions of Shahabuddin Ghauri. He took Ranthambor in 1226 and in 1230 he reduced Bengal which had cut itself off from Delhi. He conquered Malwa in 1234 and Ujjain in the following year. It was during Iltutmash's reign that Prince Jalaluddin came to Delhi for help, but Iltutmash was afraid of bringing the Mongols into India and so refused him aid. Iltutmash now bent his mind to establishing order in the country, which he did with a firm hand. He completed the building of the Qutub Minar, named after Khwaja Qutbuddin Bakhtiyar Kaki, the Saint of Delhi. The great mosque, Quwwat-ul-Islam, whose arches stand to this day was also begun, but never completed.

Ghiathuddin Balban (1266-1290). Iltutmash was succeeded first by a son, then by his talented daughter Sultana Raziya, but the age was not yet ripe for the rule of women and she had a difficult time. Her nobles rose against her and she died fighting in battle with a sword in her hand. Then another son of Iltutmash, Nasiruddin Mahmud, came to the throne, a pious, well-meaning, and hardworking ruler who depended a great deal on his chief minister and general, Ghiathuddin Balban. Nasiruddin was succeeded by Balban who became a great ruler. Although Balban himself had been minister under Nasiruddin, he had not been absolute master. The country was not therefore as well administered as he wanted it to be, and the treasury was nearly empty. The Turkish nobles had become too powerful and the Mongols raided the north-west provinces again and again. So Balban set his hand to these tasks. He first reorganized the army, strengthened the cavalry, and chose his commanders well. Then he turned to the Rajputs of Mewar who had become bandits on a large scale. They lived in the woods near Delhi and made travelling difficult for everybody. Balban crushed these bandits and went against other outlaws who lived in the land between the Ganges and the Jumna, conquered the fortresses of Kampil and Bhojpur and built his own forts, filling them with strong Muslim garrisons. He now re-allotted lands to the nobles on new terms, kept order among them and soon had complete control of the country's affairs.

Mongols and Bengal. The Mongols had now advanced to the borders of the Delhi Sultanate. They had conquered Kabul and were making almost yearly raids into the Punjab. Balban went north, rebuilt the fort of Lahore and appointed his brave son, Muhammad, as governor of Multan. Another son, Bughra Khan, was made governor of the eastern districts of the Punjab. These two brothers now faced the full fury of the Mongols and beat them back again and again. Unhappily Muhammad lost his life in an ambush; it is said that he was surprised and killed when he was saying his prayers after beating off an attack of the Mongols. This was a great blow to Balban. The governor of Bengal, Tughril Khan, revolted at this time and Balban marched against him. Tughril fled before the angry Sultan; Balban pursued him into the jungles of East Bengal, caught up with him and killed him. He now made his son, Bughra Khan, governor of Bengal, gave him sound advice and left for Delhi.

Balban as Ruler. In his time Balban was the strongest Muslim ruler in the east. His fame spread far and wide and he was visited by many Muslim princes and rulers. He upheld the law of Islam and made Upper India a part of the Islamic world. He had some very learned people around him and the Nasiriya College founded in Delhi by Sultan Nasiruddin was liberally endowed by him. Amir Khusro, the famous scholar and poet, was an ornament of his court and one of his ministers. He himself gave generously to writers and his brilliant son Muhammad had collected the best men of his times around him. This prince had written to Shaikh Saadi, the Persian poet, asking him to come to Multan where he promised to build a large *khanqah* for him. Many famous men lived during Balban's days. Among these, mention must be made of Shaikh Farid Shakar Ganj of Pakpattan, Shaikh Bahauddin Zakariya of Multan, Shaikh Badruddin Arif of Ghazni and Khwaja Qutbuddin Bakhtiyar Kaki of Delhi. Sayyid Maula, another eminent Shaikh, founded a college with a *langar khana* (alms house) at Delhi where free board and lodging were given to students. Sultan Balban's times were therefore a period of great intellectual activity.

The Khaljis (1290-1320)—Alauddin Khalji (1296-1316). The successors of Balban were incompetent people and the Sultanate soon passed into the hands of Jalaluddin Khalji, the leader of the Khalji Turks. He was old, but still a fine military commander. Early in his reign a great army of Mongols invaded India. Jalaluddin went out to meet them and inflicted a crushing defeat on them. The great man of this dynasty was his nephew and successor Alauddin, a remarkable man in many ways. An adventurous prince even before he came to the throne, he had invaded the upper kingdoms of the Deccan and levied tribute on the Rajas there. The only blot on his career is that he was incited by his scheming counsellors to kill his own uncle. Otherwise he left a mark on India which lasted hundreds of years. Alauddin was a man of steel, tireless in war and extremely hard-working in peace. He looked into every department of state and made his own decisions, most of which were for the betterment of the administration. A great patron of learning, he made generous gifts and grants to schools and colleges.

Wars and Conquests. Much happened during his reign of twenty years. He first put down the resistance of the Indian natives, the Rajputs, who used to rebel in almost every reign. His brother, Zafar Khan, held the north-western provinces against the Mongols. In 1311 the Mongol leader, Qutlugh Khan, led a large army into India and, brushing all resistance aside, marched straight on Delhi. Zafar Khan again met the Mongols and fought with such reckless bravery that the Mongols were daunted. Zafar fell wounded in battle, but the Mongols were so impressed by the Khalji resistance that they retreated. They came again a few years later, but were again repulsed and this time so severely that for a time they did not make another attempt. The man who now held the Punjab against this deluge was Ghiathuddin Tughluq, the governor of the province, who for his prowess against the Mongols came to be called Ghazi Malik. Ulugh Khan, another brother of Alauddin, now overran the kingdom of Gujarat and captured its beautiful Rani, Kamal Devi, along with enormous booty. Alauddin himself went against the Rajputs who were giving trouble and captured Ranthambor and Chittor. He then conquered the remaining Rajput principalities of Ujjain, Mandu, Dhar, and Chanderi. The story that he attacked Chittor because he wanted to see its lovely Rani, Padmini, is not true. Alauddin was a very stern man and the pursuit of pleasure was not in his character. In 1310 Malik Kafur, Alauddin's Abyssinian general, went out to the south in order to help one of the Pandya princes who had asked Alauddin for help against a usurper. Malik Kafur had already conquered the kingdoms of the Kakatiyas and of the Hoysala in mid-Deccan. When Kafur reached Madura the usurper fled and Kafur captured the town and took charge of its treasury; untold wealth fell into his hands. With the conquest of the Deccan Alauddin became the first Emperor of India. This empire lasted till the end of Muhammad Tughluq's time.

Alauddin as Ruler. Alauddin was an autocrat and his word was law, though the law of the land was the *Shariah*. At one time he wanted to pose as the spiritual head of Islam too, but his loyal friend the Kotwal of Delhi and a famous Muslim saint persuaded him to confine himself to worldly rule and to his conquests. He refused, however, to let the Ulema interfere in his decisions. At one time he put a ban even on the meeting of the nobles. He was a just man who introduced a rationing system, fixed the prices of goods, regularized the pay and allowances of the soldiers, made stable the revenues of the country and declared black marketing and wrong measures heavily punishable. He even started a police system. All these and many more things made him a most enlightened ruler. Most historians regard him as exceptional.

Successors of Alauddin. His end, however, was not happy. In his last years, he leaned much on Malik Kafur and that crafty man got more and more power into his own hands. It is believed that in the end Malik Kafur poisoned him. Alauddin had been a great military commander and a remarkable ruler, but his successors were unworthy of him. For a time Malik Kafur was dominant and he turned out to be a very evil man. He blinded the sons of Alauddin and imprisoned the Queen Mother, but after a time the nobles rose against him and killed him. Then the last son of Alauddin, Qutbuddin Mubarak, a mere lad, was put on the throne, but he took to low companions and showed debased tastes. He had a favourite, a Hindu convert, who was a man of low caste and very low mentality, named Khusro. Mubarak gradually came entirely under his influence, though on the field of battle he sometimes showed great courage. Khusro intrigued against him and in the end put him to death and himself became king, whereupon he rejected Islam and began to revive Hinduism. He set up idols in mosques, openly insulted Islam, showed contempt for the Qur'an and behaved so indecently that even the Hindus turned against him. The nobles at the court invited Ghiathuddin Tughluq, the hero of forty battles against the Mongols, to come and take the throne. Since there was no Khalji prince left, he accepted the offer.

The Tughluqs (1320-1413)—Muhammad Tughluq (1325-1351). Ghiathuddin Tughluq thus became the first Tughluq Sultan. He was an old man now, but still a great military commander. He reconquered Warangal in Upper Deccan and then East Bengal in 1324. He introduced many reforms and improved the administration which the successors of Alauddin had very nearly ruined. The real genius of this family was the Sultan's eldest son, Prince Juna, who came to the throne after Ghiathuddin's death in 1325. He is known in history as Muhammad Tughluq. It is doubtful if in the whole world there has been a more gifted monarch. A great scholar and a fine linguist, he was a man who could discuss religion, philosophy, mathematics, astronomy, or literature with anybody in the land. As for brilliance of ideas, he had enough to suffice a dozen kings, but it was his tragedy that he lived before his time and people could not keep pace with the rush of his ideas. He adopted many schemes, most of which were excellent, but did not succeed in any. So advanced were his ideas for the men of his time that he came to be called Mad Juna. Ibn Battutah, the great Muslim traveller, came to India in his time and stayed at his court. The historian Ziauddin Barni wrote about his reign. There were many observers of his character and each saw a different man in him. He was self-willed and could be quite unreasonable at times. He became especially intolerant after he saw the failure of his great schemes. Perhaps the truest judgement on him is that he was a very unfortunate man.

Muhammad Tughluq's achievements. His first reform was the re-calculation and fixing of the taxes in the Jumna and Ganges basin. A famine occurred at the time and the people could not meet the taxes. The Sultan saw their misery and gave them loans, dug wells for them, and even took the barren land and tried to till it at state expense. There was nothing wrong with this idea, but the scheme did not succeed. The people did not like to change their ways and this the Sultan would not understand. The Empire stretched to the south of India, and the north had become unsafe because of the Mongol invasions, which still continued. The Sultan decided to move his capital for reasons of state. He selected Deogri, an old town and the ancient capital of many Hindu kingdoms, lying just the other side of the Vindhyas and therefore safe from Mongol attacks. He named it Daulatabad and built new palaces, audience halls, and schools there. He built a broad road from Delhi to Daulatabad and lined it with trees. He lent people money to move their goods to the new capital. Some refused, many accepted the orders with a bad grace; many pleaded some excuse or other. The Sultan had done everything and he thought that the idea was good. Northern India was already a part of the larger Islamic world. He wanted to include the Deccan in that area too. The new capital was more central, but his own people did not see it that way, and the scheme was a failure. It was a very costly failure, and he ordered the capital to be shifted back to Delhi.

Other Events. Money became short, so the Sultan decided to issue token currency. Paper currency was already in vogue in China. The Sultan introduced copper currency, but the people would not accept the coins. Today we mostly use currency notes, which are just stamped paper, but the people then could not understand his idea and this scheme failed too. The Sultan paid back in silver and gold when the people called for money in exchange for their hoards of now useless copper coins. Then the Mongols invaded India and the Sultan went out to meet them. Some people say that the Sultan bought them off. In any case the Mongols disappeared, but the people blamed the Sultan even for this. He now wished to hit back, perhaps at the Mongols. He collected a large army and wanted to send it to the north-west, but was at the last minute persuaded not to do so. On the other hand the Himalayan tribes, perhaps the Garhwalis, the ancestors of modern Gurkhas, began to raid what is now Uttar Pradesh and Bihar. The Sultan sent an army against them, but a great snow-storm came and the Sultan's army perished. People began to say that the mad Sultan wanted to conquer China and had therefore sent an army into Tibet, but this was not true. The result of all these failures was that people began to rebel. He defeated quite a few rebel governors because he was a good general, but many provinces broke away from the centre and became independent. Most governors founded dynasties of their own, which remained in power in regions like Kashmir, Bengal, Gujarat, and the Deccan till the days of the Moghuls, two centuries later.

Firuz Tughluq (1351-1388). Muhammad Tughluq died in 1351 and for some time there was confusion in the land. Then the nobles requested Muhammad Tughluq's cousin, Firuz Tughluq, to take over the throne. Firuz was a god-fearing man. He put the matter before the Qadis and Ulema, and it was only after they gave their *fatwa* (decision) that it was right for him to take the throne that he became king. Firuz did a great deal to pull together the administration and he succeeded to some extent, but he was no military genius and so did not succeed in winning back all the lost territories. Thus the Muslim Empire of India, which came into being at about 1300 in the reign of Alauddin Khalji, became the Sultanate of Delhi again in 1350. The Deccan became independent under the Bahmanis; Khandesh and Gujarat, Malwa and Bengal, and in the north Kashmir all remained beyond his reach. Though he undertook two campaigns to Bengal and even fought twice against the Amir of Bengal, he did not succeed in winning back any lost territory except Sind. On the way east he stopped at a place called Zafarabad and founded the city of Jaunpur there, in memory of his beloved cousin Juna, known as Muhammad Tughluq. However, he fought successfully in Sind and made the Amirs of Sind acknowledge his suzerainty.

Firuz Tughluq's Achievements. Firuz Tughluq was a sound administrator and made the government of his Sultanate strong and efficient. His love of learning was so great that when, in his campaign in Bihar, he besieged and conquered

Nagarkot, and found 300 volumes in Sanskrit, he ordered them to be sent to Delhi and translated into Persian. Firuz Tughluq is famous for his building projects. He built useful buildings, such as tanks, bridges, baths, hospitals, canals, and caravanserais all over the Sultanate. He also built many mosques, and the gardens he laid out are said to number 1,200. He preserved old monuments, among which were two of Asoka's pillars. He purchased slaves and had them trained as artisans, as a 'good work' (kar-i-khair).It is said that there was no Muslim monarch in India before Firuz who did so much for education. The Firuz Shahi Madrasah was the best of its kind. Barni describes it as the most commodious and best staffed college to be found anywhere. It catered for the poor also, giving free board to hundreds. It was once called the 'Glory of the Age', but has long since crumbled into dust.

Timur's Invasion (1398). The successors of Firuz Tughluq were so weak that more parts of the Sultanate broke away. Jaunpur became the seat of the Sharqi kingdom and the central Sultanate shrank into a small kingdom. Things were in this state when Timur, the Tartar conqueror, descended on India. He carried everything before him, defeated every army sent out to meet him and had collected about 100,000 prisoners, mostly Hindus, by the time he reached Delhi. He says in his memoirs that here, in a council, his Amirs advised him to do something about the Hindu prisoners, because a large contingent of Muslim warriors had to be kept to watch and guard them. The prisoners raised Hindu slogans when a battle was being fought and tried to break away. Since Timur was now preparing to meet the Sultan of Delhi's main forces, the council advised him to kill all the prisoners. Timur says he was forced to give the order for this mass execution. He met the Sultan and defeated him, taking away as much gold and treasure as he could. There was much bloodshed in Delhi during the short time of his stay, but Timur blames it on the Hindus. He says he always honoured Sayyids, Shaikhs, Ulema, and the learned professions. However, he took away hundreds of artisans with him and left the country poorer in many ways.

The Sayyids (1414-1451). Timur left a nominee behind him, Khidr Khan, whom he made governor of Multan and Lahore. Since the later Tughluqs were weak and inefficient rulers, Khidr Khan advanced on Delhi and took the capital. As he claimed to be a Sayyid, this dynasty is called the Sayyid Dynasty. He and his Vizier, Taj ul-Mulk, who was an able military commander, had to fight often to maintain their position, but the dynasty continued in power till 1451, although it produced no great monarch. The only memorable event in the years of Sayyid rule was the compilation of *Tarikh-i-Mubarak Shahi*, written by Yahya ibn Ahmad Sirhindi in the days of Khidr Khan's son and successor, Mubarak Shah. It is a memorable historical record.

The Lodhis (1451-1526). The last of the Sayyids was overthrown by a powerful Pathan chieftain, Bahlul Lodhi, who was a capable man. He annexed the Jaunpur kingdom also, fought against the Rajputs, who were rebelling, and made the Sultanate a strong state again. He was a distinguished ruler, a far-seeing man and a fine general. He encouraged learning and made his name respected all over India. He ruled for thirty-eight years.

Sikander Lodhi (1489-1517). The finest ruler of the Lodhi dynasty was Sikander Lodhi, who was a great fighter. He brought Bengal back under the centre and then fought against the Rajas of Tirhut, Dholpur, and Chanderi. He campaigned against the Rajputs till he had reconquered the states of Etawah, Byana, Koil, and Gwalior. He was a good ruler also, being firm and upright in his dealings, and had a clear head. He was seldom caught unawares and could meet any crisis. Also, to his credit, he appreciated the beauties of poetry and music. He was a poet himself and encouraged learning. A great book on medicine called *Tibb-i-Sikandri* was compiled in his reign, mostly based on systems of Hindu medicine. His generosity was so great that scholars came from Arabia, Persia, and even Bokhara to take up residence in Agra or Delhi. His nobles, too, were generous. One of them, Masnad Ali Khan, gave away large sums of money and many stipends to deserving students and left a will that even after his death these stipends should continue.

The End of the Lodhis (1526). His successor was Ibrahim Lodhi who, though by no means a fool, did many foolish things. He quarrelled with his nobles, was either too strict or too lax with them and generally made enemies by his arrogance and intolerance. The result was that the empire so carefully built by the two previous Lodhi Sultans, began to break up, and Darya Khan, the governor of Bihar, became independent. His own relatives began to intrigue and later joined Daulat Khan the governor of Lahore, who, with Rana Sanga, the Rajput prince, wrote to Zahiruddin Babar, the Sultan of Kabul, asking him to come down and help to overthrow Ibrahim. Babar agreed, and defeated Ibrahim Lodhi in the First Battle of Panipat (1526), but disappointed the conspirators by becoming Sultan of Delhi himself, founding the great Moghul Dynasty of India.

Minor Kingdoms—Kashmir (1346-1540). Before the whole period of the Sultanate of Delhi is reviewed, it is necessary to complete the story of Muslim India in the eleventh to fifteenth centuries by an account of the minor kingdoms which had been set up by the Muslims on the break-up of the Empire of Muhammad Tughluq. It is best, perhaps, to begin with the kingdom of Kashmir in the north, which lasted for a long time. It was founded by Shah Mirza, a nobleman of the Frontier province, who took service with the Hindu Raja of Kashmir in 1315. He soon rose to a very high position and, when the Raja died in 1331, assumed the title of king. The dynasty that he founded produced two famous kings, Sikander But Shikan (the Idol Breaker) and his son Zain ul-Abidin. Sikander But Shikan was so called because he could not tolerate idol worship and broke idols whenever he could. He did not compel people to become Muslims, but had no liking for *kafirs*. The result was that many high-caste Hindus left the state. He welcomed scholars, and Ulema who had fled from Central Asia because of Timur's high-handed and autocratic ways and settled in Kashmir. He made his kingdom a strong power. His successor, Zain ul-Abidin, was a man of a different type. He was well educated and very liberal in his views, never forcing anybody to accept his ideas. He knew many languages and was fond of learning. He abolished the Jizya which his father had imposed and recalled the Brahmins who had left Kashmir. He introduced the Panchayat system in villages, made the roads safe from bandits, was firm in his dealings and his justice was known far and wide. A very capable ruler and a great patron of literary activities, he had the *Mahabharata* and *Rajatrangini* translated into Persian and many Arabic and Persian books translated into Hindi. He ruled for fifty years and made his name famous and his country prosperous. The dynasty continued after him for a hundred years or so, but produced no remarkable king. It was annexed to the Moghul Empire in 1540.

Jaunpur (1398-1476)—Ibrahim Sharqi. The next small kingdom was the Sharqi kingdom of Jaunpur, founded by Khwaja Jahan, the governor of the region, after the death of Firuz Tughluq. Khwaja Jahan was a very able man and laid the foundations of his kingdom well. He and his descendants aimed to make their people prosperous and happy and succeeded in doing so. The great man of this dynasty was Ibrahim Shah Sharqi who ruled for thirty-four years. He made Jaunpur famous all over Asia for its university. He filled the place with so many learned people that it came to be known as the Shiraz of India. He built many fine buildings and one of them, the Masjid Atala, which was built out of money given by Atala Devi, a Hindu lady of rank, stands to this day. Another famous king of this dynasty was Husain Shah Sharqi, who came to the throne in 1456. He was an adventurous man, who made a pact with Sultan Bahlul Lodhi of Delhi and, finding himself safe from the west, led his forces into Tirhut and Orissa. From Orissa he returned with a great deal of treasure. In 1466, he attacked Raja Man Singh of Gwalior and humbled the proud Rajputs. The Raja paid him a large sum of money in return for safety. Husain Shah then made a mistake. He quarrelled with Bahlul Lodhi who was a strong man. In the clash that followed Husain Shah lost his kingdom. The Sharqis were a fine family; they set a high standard of kingship and their patronage of learning became a byword.

Bengal (1338-1539)—Ilyas Shah's kingdom. To the east of Jaunpur lie Bihar and Bengal. Mention has been made of the inconclusive war waged by Firuz Tughluq with the ruler of Bengal. This ruler was Ilyas Shah, originally known as Haji Ilyas, a foster brother of Alauddin Ali Shah, governor of North Bengal. Haji Ilyas annexed south and east Bengal and became Sultan of the whole of Bengal in 1345. He overran Orissa in 1352, conquering the country to the west as far as Benares. This led to Firuz Tughluq's campaign against him, though nothing came of it. Ilyas Shah remained independent. He made Gaur in Bengal his capital and raised some very fine buildings there. He was a good ruler and made his kingdom rich. He died in 1357 and was followed by his son Sikander Shah, who was as strong a ruler as his father. Another famous ruler of this line was Ghiathuddin Azam, a learned man who had good artistic taste. He corresponded with Hafiz, the great poet of Shiraz, and exchanged embassies with the Emperor of China. He was also a very clever administrator. His son, however, was not a capable man and was overthrown by his Hindu Vizier, Raja Ganesh; Ganesh's son Jadu became a Muslim and called himself Jalaluddin Muhammad Shah. Jalaluddin did not prove to be a good king and there was a lot of unrest in the land. His son Shamsuddin was worse and at last the nobles rose against him and put him to death.

Later Rulers. After Shamsuddin's death they put Nasiruddin, a grandson of Haji Ilyas, on the throne. Nasiruddin ruled for seventeen years and proved to be a man of ability. He erected some fine buildings at Gaur. His successor, however, was overthrown by the commander of the Abyssinian bodyguard. The Abyssinian rule lasted for about fifteen years. In 1493, the nobles rose again and expelled the Abyssinians, calling Alauddin Husain, an able minister of the state, to the throne. Both Alauddin Husain Shah and his son Nusrat Shah were capable rulers, especially Nusrat Shah. Alauddin conquered Orissa and Bihar and Cooch Behar in Assam. He thus made Bengal a large kingdom and ruled for twenty-five years (1493-1518) to the satisfaction of everybody and the great good of the land. His son Nusrat Shah was very generous and kind-hearted, and yet a masterful ruler. He treated all his relatives kindly and was so unsuspicious of them that it was remarked by everybody. However, they all remained loyal to him, a rare thing in the history of kings. Nusrat Shah's fame had even spread to Kabul, and Babar the Moghul conqueror mentions him in his memoirs as a ruler of note. Nusrat Shah built some very fine mosques and encouraged learning. He was liberal with the Hindus and had the *Mahabharata* translated into Bengali. He died in 1533. His successors were not competent and Sher Shah Suri annexed Bengal in 1539.

Malwa (1401-1562)—Dilawar Khan—Alp Khan—Mahmud Khan. In the centre of India lay the Muslim kingdom of Malwa, founded by Dilawar Khan Ghauri, the governor of Malwa in the time of Firuz Tughluq. He became independent as soon as Firuz died. It was, however, his ambitious son, Alp Khan, who was the most famous ruler of this line. Alp Khan took the title of Hushang Shah, led an adventurous life and had many exploits to his credit. His surprise attack on the Raja of Orissa which he made disguised as a merchant is famous. He took a large sum of money from the Raja before he let him go. He captured Kherla and carried off its Raja. He fought with everybody, even with the Sultan of Delhi and the king of Gujarat. He was not always victorious, but he bore his defeats well. His son was not a strong man and was overthrown by his own minister, Mahmud Khan, who now founded the Khalji dynasty of Malwa. Mahmud was also a noted fighter and his war with the Raja of Mewar is famous. It was a long drawn-out war, and at the end of it both rulers claimed victory and erected towers of victory in their capitals to commemorate the event. Raja Kumba of Mewar built the Tower of Victory at Chittor and Mahmud Shah built a seven-storeyed Minar in his capital, Mandu. Mahmud extended his kingdom and ruled wisely and well. A very efficient administrator, the kingdom progressed under him. He was fond of heroic stories and had men at his court who read heroic tales of all countries to him. He ruled for thirty-four years and was respected widely for his ability in peace and war. He died in 1469. His successors at Malwa were not very important, but they kept their thrones. The kingdom was at last annexed by the Sultan of Gujarat in 1531.

Gujarat (1401-1572)—Zafar Khan. Gujarat, Kathiawar had been a prosperous country for a long time; it had, therefore, always attracted the Sultans of Delhi. Alauddin Khalji conquered it in 1297 and it remained a part of the Muslim Empire of Delhi till 1391. The governor at that time was Zafar Khan, who gradually cut off his relations with the centre, and became independent in 1401. His line produced some very fine rulers. The most famous of them are his grandson, Ahmad Shah, Mahmud Beghara and the last ruler, Bahadur Shah. Ahmad Shah was a good warrior and made many conquests, but he was much more than a general; he was a fine administrator. He built the town of Ahmadabad, observed the law of Islam as it should be observed, made no distinction of caste, creed, or position among his subjects, and was famous for his justice. In his time Gujarat became a great centre of industry and commerce. He ruled for thirty years.

Mahmud Beghara. In 1458, there came to the throne the greatest ruler of the line, Mahmud Beghara, a powerful man. He ruled for fifty years and made his name famous over all the west-Asian countries. He was a terror to his enemies and never gave up an enterprise, nor did he ever lose a battle on land. He put down piracy at sea and captured famous forts like those of Junagarh and Champanir. His most important work lay in his fight with the Portuguese, who were now supreme in the seas to the west of India. He made an alliance with the Burji sultans of Egypt and, with the help of the fleet the Sultan sent him, he inflicted a crushing defeat on the Portuguese in 1508. In 1509, Albuquerque, the Portuguese Viceroy, brought a huge fleet with battleships carrying heavy guns, and Mahmud suffered a defeat. Mahmud then made a treaty with Albuquerque and gave him the site of Diu in Kathiawar to build a fort. Mahmud died soon after when he was still at the height of his fame. A fearless, capable, wise, just, and warlike monarch, he had a forceful personality and was known even in Europe. The last ruler of this line was Bahadur Shah, the grandson of Mahmud. Bahadur Shah also fought with the Portuguese and refused to let them build a factory at Diu. He conquered the Rajput strongholds of Jhalanand, Bhilsa, and Chanderi. He stormed the fortress of Chittor, but quarrelled with Humayun, the Great Moghul, for harbouring some refugees and refusing to surrender them. Humayun invaded his kingdom, defeated him and annexed Gujarat. When, however, Humayun left to prepare for his war with Sher Shah Suri, Bahadur Shah regained his lost dominion. He was later treacherously slain by the Portuguese. The kingdom was annexed by Akbar the Great in 1573.

The Great Bahmani Kingdom. (1347-1526). The principal minor kingdom of India, and one which left the greatest mark on the history of south India, was the Bahmani kingdom founded by Hasan, the Tughluq governor of Upper Deccan, who became independent after Muhammad Tughluq's death and assumed royal honours with the title of Abul Muzaffar Alauddin Bahman Shah. He made Gulbarga his capital and conquered Goa, Dabhal, Kohlapur, and Telingana. He thus became a powerful ruler, his only rival in the Deccan being the Raja of Vijayanagar, the only Hindu kingdom in the whole of India at this time. The cause of the trouble between the two was the Raichur Doab, the valley which lay between the rivers Krishna and Tungabhadra. There was also the rivalry between Islam and Hinduism, between foreigners and Indians. The Bahmani rulers and the Rajas of Vijayanagar fought with each other in every reign and sometimes twice or thrice in each reign. The advantage lay nearly always with the Muslims and they defeated the Rajas many times. They often pursued the Rajas to the gates of Vijayanagar and levied tribute on them. Once a Raja was forced to give his daughter in marriage to a Bahmani king (Firuz Shah, 1397-1422). There is room here only to mention one other Bahmani king, Alauddin II, 1435-1457, and one great man, Mahmud Gawan, the Chief Minister of Sultan Muhammad III.

Sultan Alauddin. Sultan Alauddin was the son of Sultan Ahmad Shah who had been a great fighter and had conquered Warangal and defeated the Raja of Vijayanagar. Alauddin has been mentioned by famous historians like Farishta in very glowing terms. He waged war with the Raja, defeated him twice, and exacted large tribute from him. He is, however, more noteworthy for his interest in education, in buildings, mosques, schools, and orphanages. He also built a great hospital at Bidar, at which many famous physicians worked. He prohibited the drinking of alcohol in his realms, put down idling and vagabondage, and compelled people to live honestly. He ordered his *Kotwals* to see that the people observed the regulations laid down by Islam, and followed Islamic ways himself.

Mahmud Gawan (1461-1481)—Battle of Talikot (1565). The other great name is that of Khwaja Mahmud Gawan, who was a remarkable man in every way; a great general, scholar, statesman, and administrator. He carried the whole government of the kingdom on his shoulders, looked personally into every department and worked extremely hard. When he commanded an army he never lost a battle, and the treasure he collected in his campaigns was incalculable. He captured Goa and all the remaining states in Mid-Deccan. He put down corruption and was severe in punishing evil-doers. He thus made many enemies, and evil courtiers influenced Sultan Muhammad III, who had lost control of his mind through a life of ease and pleasure, against him. In one of his fits, Sultan Muhammad was persuaded to give orders for the death of this most loyal and efficient minister, and he was killed. In 1527 the Bahmani kingdom at last split up into five small kingdoms, those of Ahmadnagar in the west, Golconda in the east, Berar in the north, Bidar in the centre, and Bijapur in the south-west. These kingdoms had a long and prosperous life. They once united to give the Raja of Vijayanagar his worst defeat (Battle of Talikot—1565) and then sacked Vijayanagar which was at that time the richest city in the east. This put an end to the power and glory of Vijayanagar and crushed Hindu aspirations. The five Muslim kingdoms continued to survive, but were gradually absorbed by the Moghul emperors, the last two to fall being Golconda and Bijapur, which were annexed in 1686 and 1687 respectively, by Aurangzeb the great Moghul Emperor.

The Muslim Divines. By the time Babar the Moghul came to India in 1526, India had been a Muslim land for five hundred years and Sind and Multan for eight hundred. India had also been part of the larger Islamic world and actually within the spiritual boundaries of the Caliphate. It was considered by all Asiatics as *Dar-ul-Islam*. Muslim divines and philosophers, scientists and poets, scholars and thinkers came to it from all over the Islamic world and found themselves at home there. The language of culture was Arabic or Persian. There were universities everywhere and great patrons of learning. The Muslim rulers, except perhaps for Sikander But Shikan of Kashmir and Sikander Lodhi, never interfered with the religion, or the culture, or the customs of their Hindu subjects. They treated them with courtesy, engaged them in state work, gave them high offices, enrolled them in the army, appointed them to military commands, and in no way treated them as inferior. All the work of teaching, of creating goodwill, of educating people in the simple and direct message of Islam, was done by Muslim divines like Data Ganj Bakhsh of Lahore, Khwaja Moinuddin of Ajmer, Khwaja Bakhtiyar Kaki of Delhi, Baba Farid of Pakpattan, Shaikh Bahauddin Zakariya of Multan, Makhdum Jahanian Jahan Gasht of Bahawalpur, Shaikh Nizamuddin Aulia of Delhi, Ahmad Sabir Kalyari of the United Provinces, Jalaluddin Tabrizi of Bengal, and Khwaja Gesu Daraz of the Deccan. These great divines spread their light wherever they stayed. The people, both Muslim and Hindus, listened to them and the great majority of conversions to Islam were due to their teachings. All these divines flourished during the earliest times, mostly during the period of the Slave Kings. Nizamuddin Aulia died in days of the Khaljis, and Khwaja Gesu Daraz early in the fifteenth century. They taught the simple faith, the mercy of God, the pleasures of honest dealings, fellow-feeling, the nearness of God, the duties and responsibilities of men in respect to other men, the power of prayer, and the beauties of faith. They were never persecuted and had large followings. They made Islam popular in the country.

The Bhakti Movement. Gradually their simple teachings began to affect Hinduism, which had always been dominated by the few and the privileged, till, in the fifteenth century, there arose a group of *Bhagats* (Popular Saints) in India, Guru Nanak in the Punjab, Ramanand and Kabir in Central India, Chaitanya in Bengal, Dadu in Rajputana, and Nanadeva and others in Maharashtra. All these saints taught of love and goodwill, simple devotion and faith, fellow-feeling and love of man. Their teachings became popular and soon they had great followings. Each of these *Bhagats* became the head of a *Panth* (creed) and these *Panths* produced an awakening in the people. The Hindus began to study their past and improve their present conditions. A century later this movement changed: it created first a literary revival among the Hindus and, two centuries later, a social and political awareness. It resulted ultimately in the eighteenth century in militant groups like the Sikhs in the Punjab and the Mahrattas in West India, and made the Bengalis a cultured and literary people. This movement is ultimately responsible for the creation of a national spirit in the Hindus and the liberation of the Indians from the fear of the Muslims and the awe of the British. The national spirit of the Hindus has, therefore, a long ancestry. It is ironic to note that it can be traced back to the effect of the spiritual teaching of Muslim divines.

CHAPTER 9

ISLAM IN PERSIA

The Il Khans (1260-1349)—Hulagu. The story of Islam now moves back to Baghdad, which, as narrated in Chapter 6, was destroyed by Hulagu Khan and his Mongols. It would, however, be wrong to think that the Mongols were monsters, who only went about killing, burning, and destroying. They destroyed a large part of the Islamic world and dealt a death-blow to Arab civilization, but they did not stay for long in the rubble and ashes of a lost world. The lands south of the Oxus (*Amu Darya*) were bestowed on Hulagu Khan who had conquered them and he was given the title of Il Khan. Thus all lands east of Asia Minor and Syria up to the bounds of India were called the Il Khanate. Hulagu's descendants ruled this area for nearly a hundred years. Hulagu Khan set about restoring order in the lands he had won and building up some of the seats of learning he had destroyed. Mention has been made of how he rewarded the services of, and showed admiration for, Nasiruddin Tusi, for whom he built the observatory of al-Maraghah and the big library attached to it. He adopted the civil administrative system of the Muslims and made changes in it. He left a large empire to his son Abaga, when he died in 1265.

Abaga (1265-1281). Abaga was a Christian and soon made diplomatic contacts with the Pope as well as with some European monarchs. His correspondence with King Edward I of England has been preserved and in it we read that Abaga was being continually incited by the European powers to attack the remaining Muslim states, especially the Mamluks of Egypt, whose Sultan, Baybars, had stopped the advance of Hulagu himself. Abaga led an army into Syria, but as mentioned in Chapter 7 he was defeated. It was during Abaga's reign that

Marco Polo, the famous Venetian traveller, passed through Persia on his way to China. Abaga was a good administrator and the country settled down to a peaceful way of life during his reign. He was succeeded by his son Tagudar, who became a Muslim and took the name of Ahmad. Ahmad exchanged envoys with the Sultan of Egypt, but the Mongol generals objected to Ahmad's acceptance of Islam. They revolted and Ahmad was overthrown and killed. There is irony in this event: Hulagu destroyed Arab civilization and his grandson died for Islam!

Ghazan Mahmud (1295-1304). After an interval of two reigns a new Il Khan, Ghazan, came to the throne. As a prince, he had served as governor of Khorasan. He was the sixth Il Khan. He also accepted Islam and when his generals revolted as they had done under Ahmad, he defeated them. He was a powerful ruler and a fine administrator. He too led a Mongol army against the Mamluks in 1299, but this time the Mamluks were divided among themselves and Ghazan's army was stronger. The two armies met. The Mamluks broke the centre of the Mongol army, but Ghazan used his mounted archers to great effect. The Mamluks had to withdraw and Ghazan won the battle. He now marched on Damascus and besieged it. After a while the townspeople surrendered. Ghazan, being a good Muslim, respected the town and did not harm it in any way. He did not permit his soldiers even to enter it and took particular care that the famous gardens of Damascus were not ruined by his Mongols. He imposed a tribute on the town, left a garrison behind and went back. Ghazan, who now called himself Ghazan Mahmud, had trouble soon after on his northern borders which kept him engaged for a few years. The Mamluks made use of this time and reconquered Syria. When Ghazan was free, he came back with an army. He sent his son Prince Kutlugh Shah ahead of him in command of about 50,000 troops. There was a great battle at Marj-al-Saffar in 1303 and in this battle the Mamluks were victorious.

Thousands of Mongols died and hundreds were taken away as prisoners. This was a great blow to Ghazan Mahmud and it is said that the shame of it killed him.

Ghazan as Ruler. Ghazan Mahmud was a gifted man and belonged to a wider world. He had diplomatic relations with the West and it is interesting that the European monarchs continued to think that Ghazan, like his father Arghun or like Abaga, was a Christian and therefore an enemy of Islam. Perhaps the idea was strengthened by the wars between the Mongols and the Mamluks. Since the Mamluks had rooted out the Crusaders, Europe felt very hostile to them. Many offers were therefore made to Ghazan to join the Europeans against the Mamluks, and also against the Ottoman Turks, who were already a power. Ghazan rejected all these offers because he did not wish to fight against Muslims. His feud with the Mamluks was almost hereditary and had nothing to do with Europe or its diplomacies. As a ruler he was an independent man. He tried to revive all the institutions which the Mongols had destroyed, the schools, universities, libraries, mosques, the arts and the crafts. Up to his time the Il Khans recognized the Great Khan of China as Suzerain. Ghazan broke this connection. He called himself 'Sultan by the Grace of God' and made his own laws. He fixed all the taxes justly and in poorer areas he exempted the peasants from the land revenue; he established the Shariah everywhere and appointed learned and just men as Qadis. He built an observatory and established a school for teaching the sciences. The task of writing a history of the times was entrusted to his learned minister, Rashiduddin. Tablets of law were fixed everywhere, on stone pillars and wooden boards outside mosques and synagogues, in towns and villages and even in pastures. He worked hard to undo the harm done by his ancestors.

Uljaytu Khudabanda (1305-1316). Another great ruler of this line was Ghazan's brother and successor Uljaytu who, originally a Christian, later accepted Islam and called himself

Khudabanda. He conquered Jilan in the north-west and Herat in the north-east. He too fought the Mamluks of Egypt and, like Ghazan, he also had diplomatic relations with the Christian rulers of Europe, by whom he too was incited to attack the Mamluks and the Ottoman Turks. He introduced Turkish as a state language and now both Turkish and Persian came to be used all over this area. Uljaytu raised some beautiful buildings at Sultaniya, a town founded by him. He erected a mighty tomb there, in which he had the idea of burying the remains of Imam Husain, which he wanted to be dug up from Karbala. This was a grand building and stands to this day. It has a dome eighty-four feet in diameter, the largest dome in Persia. After Uljaytu there were no great Mongol monarchs and gradually the Mongol Empire of Persia broke up into a number of minor kingdoms, some of which deserve mention.

The Jalayrs (1336-1411). One of the most important of these kingdoms was that of the Jalayrs, which was founded by the family of Amir Husain Jalayr, the son-in-law of Arghun who succeeded Ahmad, the third Il Khan. The first king of this dynasty was Shaikh Hasan Buzurg who made Baghdad his capital in 1336. He was a strong ruler and made his kingdom powerful. In 1356 he was succeeded by his son Owais who conquered Azerbaijan, Mosul, and Diyar Bekr. Owais was a very capable man and tried to rebuild Baghdad and give it new life. The next ruler was Amir Husain who had to fight with a new Turkish people, called *Kara Kuyunlu* or the Turkomen of the Black Sheep, who had settled to the north of Mosul. He also fought with another kingdom which had sprung up on the remnants of the Il Khan Empire, that of the Muzaffarids of Shiraz. It was during the time of Amir Husain's successor that Amir Timur, the Tartar conqueror, swept through these regions.

The Salgharids (1148-1182)—Sa'di of Shiraz (1194-1281). Another dynasty was that of the Salgharids of Fars which had been founded by one of the chiefs of the Seljuks who had obtained the south-western corner of Fars in 1148. The dynasty accepted the suzerainty, first of the Iraqi Seljuks and later of the Khwarizm Shahs. When the Il Khans came to power the throne passed on the Hazaraspids. The Salgharids and their successors were a self-contained people and tried to make the people of their small kingdom happy. In the reign of one of the rulers, Sa'd ibn Zangi, 1256-1291, there lived at Shiraz, the capital of these kingdoms, the great Persian poet Muslihuddin, who took the pen-name of Sa'di after the name of his patron Sa'd. Sa'di was a great traveller and had an adventurous career. He visited all the countries from Ifriqiya in the north of Africa to Somnath in Gujarat Kathiawar in India in his travels. He went on Hajj fifteen times. He was a great observer and saw and noticed men and their manners, the ways of kings, of those in power, of the lowly and the wayfarer everywhere. He came back and settled in Shiraz and there he wrote his two famous books *Gulistan* (The Rose Garden) and *Bostan* (The Orchard), stories in prose (*Gulistan*) and verse (*Bostan*) which contain practical and moral readings. He also wrote *qasidas* and *ghazals,* which made his name famous all over the world. A great master of prose and poetry, his poems and stories became recognized texts and were used as such for hundreds of years all over the Muslim world.

The Muzaffarids (1313-1393)—Hafiz of Shiraz (1300-1389). After the Salgharids came the Hazaraspids, followed by the Muzaffarids whose dynasty was founded by Sharafuddin Muzaffar who had originally been the governor of Yezd under the later Il Khans. His son Mubarizuddin got the governorship of both Yezd and Fars from the Il Khan Abu Said, son and successor of Uljaytu Khudabanda. Mubarizuddin married the daughter of Shah Jahan the Khan of Karman. By 1340 he had inherited Karman and then conquered Fars and even Isfahan. He was strong enough even to lead an attack against Tabriz, but domestic problems forced him to go back. One of his successors, Shah Shujah was a great patron of the arts and the sciences. He built a university at Shiraz which became a famous seat of learning. A professor at this university was Shamsuddin Muhammad who became world-famous as Hafiz of Shiraz. Hafiz's *Diwan* (collection of poems) was published in 1368, and has been famous for six hundred years. His subject was the beauty of women and nature and he wrote in musical verse of love and its sorrows, of the vicissitudes of life, of God and His Love. He disliked hypocrisy and wrote of sincerity, and friendship, of fortitude and honour. He came to be respected for his mystical insight, and many have called him *Lisan al-Ghaib* (The Voice of the Unseen). The last ruler of the Muzaffarid line was Shah Mansur who fought heroically against the great Timur and in his last battle fought his way to the heart of the Tartar army and attacked Timur in person. He was cut down by Prince Shah Rukh, Timur's son, and Timur annexed the kingdom.

Timur the Conqueror (1336-1405). The Il Khanate was by now a thing of the past and the entire Middle East was divided into minor kingdoms. There was no great Muslim power in the world at this time. The Ottomans, who were to grow into a great people, were as yet building up their power. They were a strong entity already, but their time had not yet arrived. In India the subcontinent was divided into small kingdoms and so was Muslim Africa. There was need in the Muslim world for a great man and a great power, and such a man rose in Samarqand. He was Timur, a descendant of Chaghatai Khan, one of the sons of Genghis who had inherited Central Asia as his Khanate from the colossal empire of the Great Mongol. Timur as a young man was made governor of a district in Trans-Oxiania. He was an extremely able man and gradually rose in power. He became Vizier to the Chaghatai Khan, as the ruler of the Chaghatai Khanate was called. In 1369, Timur conspired with other nobles and overthrew the Chaghatai Khan and so became ruler of Samarqand. He then conquered the rest of Trans-Oxiania, but he was not satisfied with these conquests. He was a man of extraordinary ambition and he dreamed of a world empire like that of his ancestor Genghis. In reality, Timur was a remarkable man, although it is not easy to justify his overrunning so many Muslim lands and causing so much destruction. He had a marked trait of cruelty and did not hold life sacred. He was ruthless in his anger and ordered many massacres during his career. He destroyed more than he ever built and his passion for collecting the best skilled workmen, artisans, designers, and craftsmen from all the lands he conquered from Delhi to Damascus and carrying them off to Samarqand in order to build a great town there, made all the countries poorer and is perhaps responsible for the decay of art in the Muslim world. One cannot, however, deny that Timur had great powers, great military ability, and great force of personality. He never lost a battle and was remarkably brave. If he was a hard taskmaster, he at least never spared himself and nothing, he declared, was dearer to him than the honour of Islam.

Timur's conquests. Timur led an expedition almost every year from Samarqand and these yearly campaigns brought under his sway Khorasan, Kabul, West India, Persia, Iraq, Syria, and Asia Minor. His empire stretched from Delhi to the Sea of Marmara. He was provoked to the conquest of Asia Minor by the Ottoman Sultan Bayazid I. The Ottomans had been fighting the Byzantines for a century and they had won a large empire for themselves. Sultan Bayazid had heard of Timur and feared that he would have to fight him one day. As a precaution, therefore, he decided to extend his power in Asia Minor where there were many small principalities at this time, some of which were vassals of Timur. Bayazid conquered them all, Karman, Kayseri, Tokat, Sivas, and Kastamuni. Some of the rulers fled to Timur's camp and sought his help. Undeterred, Bayazid invaded the country of the Armenian chief of Erzinjan, who was a vassal of Timur. Timur took it as a challenge to his prestige. He therefore led his forces westward.

In 1400, he conquered Sivas, captured Ertughrul, son of Bayazid, who was governor there, and had him and his entire garrison killed. In 1402 he came again and Sultan Bayazid went out to meet him, but he did not bring a very strong force with him. Timur defeated him easily and took him prisoner. Bayazid died in captivity. Timur had by this time conquered Syria in the extreme south-west and Delhi in the extreme south-east. In 1405 he thought of conquering China. He assembled a large army and marched into Central Asia, but he fell ill after he had reached the borders of China and died.

Timur's successors—Shah Rukh (1404-1447) and Ulugh Beg. Timur had nominated another son to succeed him, but in a short time Prince Shah Rukh, who had been governor of Khorasan, became lord of the Timurid Empire and reigned in undiminished glory for forty years. He was a worthy successor to the great Tartar. He tried to rebuild the social and cultural life of Persia and the Middle East, so badly broken up by the Tartar invasions under his father. He concentrated especially on the cities of Khorasan, Merv, and Herat. He sent his son Prince Ulugh Beg to Samarqand and made him governor of Trans-Oxiania and thereafter never interfered with that part of his empire. This brilliant Prince Ulugh Beg, therefore, ruled on his own and raised Samarqand to a great height as a centre of culture and the sciences. As a patron of the sciences, Ulugh Beg has seldom been surpassed. He built an observatory at Samarqand which stands to this day, and the astronomical tables associated with his name were considered for centuries the most accurate tables in the world. Shah Rukh himself was a great builder and his wife Gauhar Shad raised a mosque at Meshhed which is still the glory of Persian architecture. Shah Rukh's court was the finest and most splendid in Asia at that time. He exchanged embassies with many countries, including the Grand Khanate of China. As a fighter too, he was equal to the best. Many times, he defeated the Turkomen of the Black Sheep, who were becoming powerful. He died in 1447 and was succeeded by Ulugh Beg, but in his time the Uzbegs rose from the steppes of Central Asia and swept into Trans-Oxiania. They even attacked Samarqand and looted it. Ulugh Khan was greatly shocked at the destruction wrought by the Uzbegs and did not live long after this, being succeeded by his son Abu Said in 1452.

Abu Said (1452-1467) and The Turkomen of White Sheep. Abu Said was a true Timurid and won back the great Timur Empire from the Indus to the Euphrates, but towards the end of his reign a new Turkoman tribe made its appearance in Diyar Bekr. They called themselves Turkomen of the White Sheep. Under their leader, Amir Uzun Hasan, these Turkomen conquered Kurdistan and Armenia and even tried to expand to the west, but the Ottomans defeated them in 1461. Uzun Hasan, therefore, turned to the east and began to overrun the lands of the Timurids. He was a skilled military commander and it was not long before he invaded Persia, overthrowing the Turkomen of the Black Sheep, who held him up for a short time. Abu Said, the Timurid emperor, marched against him, but was defeated. Uzun Hasan therefore annexed Azerbaijan and Persia. The Timurid empire broke up after this. Uzun Hasan was succeeded by his son Yaqub Shah who was a wise ruler and gave peace and prosperity to his territories. He was also an enlightened king, but his successors were less able, and confusion began to prevail in the newly founded Turkoman empire. Things continued in this state for some time until a Persian called Ismail Safavi overthrew the Turkomen and founded the great Safavid empire.

Eminent men before the Safavids—Jalaluddin Rumi (1207-1273). Great harm had been done to the Muslim lands by first the Mongols and then the Tartars. For two and a half centuries there was little progress. The universities had been destroyed, books which were the treasure-house of knowledge had been lost, men of talent had either been killed or scattered, and the continuity of cultural progress had been broken. Great writers now appeared only in the corners of the Muslim world, such as Sa'di and Hafiz in Shiraz. Another great poet, perhaps the greatest mystic poet of Islam, was Jalaluddin Rumi, who made his appearance in Asia Minor. Jalaluddin's father had fled from Khwarizm when the Mongols had overrun central Asia. He was a learned man and had found asylum with the Seljuk Ruler of Konya, Prince Alauddin, who made him a professor at Konya University. Jalaluddin was then a boy. After his father's death Jalaluddin, who was only twenty-three years old, was offered the professorship. He was a very learned man and very popular as a teacher, but he came under the influence of the great mystic Shamsuddin of Tabriz and was converted. He then became a Sufi and wrote a series of narrative poems which were collected and published as the *Masnavi*. The *Masnavi* has been called the greatest Persian collection of poems and perhaps the finest literary work of the Muslim world. Sir Muhammad Iqbal, the modern poet of the East, considered Rumi his spiritual guide.

Historians. Two great names and a few others appear in the realm of history writing. One is that of Alauddin Juwayni who was secretary to Hulagu Khan himself and saw things at first hand. His work is called *Tarikh-i-Jahan Gusha*, and it tells the story of the Mongols and their achievements. The other man was Rashiduddin Fadlullah, the minister of Ghazan Mahmud, who was a very learned man. Rashiduddin wrote *Jami ul-Tawarikh* (The Complete History). This book covers a vast amount of ground and tells of the history of Persia from before the coming of Mongols. It is greatly valued for its sober tone and careful treatment. An account of the romantic and chivalrous Prince Jalaluddin also exists. It is the *Story of Jalaluddin Khwarizm* by Shihabuddin Muhammad of Nisa, who was a secretary of Jalaluddin. Another historian of note was Mirkhond who wrote in the later half of the fifteenth century at the court of Amir Husain of Herat, about the period of the later Timurids and the Turkomen of the White Sheep.

His work is called *Raudat-us-Safa* (The Garden of Purity). He introduces many anecdotes to make his narrative interesting.

The Safavids (1500-1736)—Ismail I (1500-1524). The fifteenth century had ended, the Ottomans had conquered Constantinople and were now a European power, but there was no successor to the Abbasids, the Il Khans or the Timurids in Asia. The Moghuls of India had not yet come to power. A family of dervishes was, however, gaining prominence in the extreme north-west of Persia, just below the Caspian Sea. This family was to found the line of the great Safavid dynasty of Persia. They first became prominent under Shaikh Safi al-Din of Ardabil (1252-1334). He was a holy man and founded an order of dervishes which followed the Shiite creed and spread in the north-west of Persia. One of the descendants of this holy man was Shaikh Junaid, head of the order in the mid-fifteenth century. He married Amir Uzun Hasan's sister, and since the Turkomen of the White Sheep soon overran Persia, Shaikh Junaid gained very powerful relatives by this marriage. His son Haidar married a daughter of Amir Uzun Hasan and began to organize his followers on the lines of the knightly brotherhoods of Europe. He made them wear red caps, and so they came to be known as Kizilbashes (Red Caps). Haidar now became the chief of his order. Being ambitious, he tried his strength against Yaqub Shah, the Turkoman king, but was defeated. One of the sons of this Haidar was named Ismail. He was a very enterprising young man; when he went into hiding he secretly organized his order on firmer lines, and after Yaqub Shah's death in 1497 he came out and made open arrangements for battle. He was a good military commander and had tremendous influence over his followers, who fought for him with great zeal, so when he led them against the Turkomen of the White Sheep he won the battle of Shurur and took Tabriz, the capital of the Turkoman kingdom. He started a war of conquest and was soon master of the whole of Persia. He then conquered Iraq, Mosul, and Diyar Bekr, in fact the entire

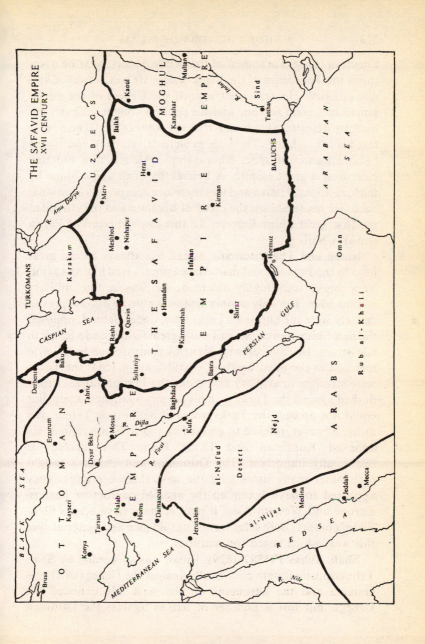

THE SAFAVID EMPIRE
XVII CENTURY

MOGHUL EMPIRE

UZBEGS

TURKOMANS

THE SAFAVID EMPIRE

BALUCHS

ARABS

OTTOMAN EMPIRE

BLACK SEA

CASPIAN SEA

MEDITERRANEAN SEA

RED SEA

PERSIAN GULF

ARABIAN SEA

Rub al-Khali

al-Nufud Desert

Nejd

al-Hijaz

Oman

Karakum

Multan
Kaoul
Kandahar
Sind
Tatthau
Balkh
Herat
Merv
Kirman
Meshhed
Nishapur
Isfahan
Hormuz
Hamadan
Shiraz
Karmanshah
Resht
Qazvin
Sultaniya
Baku
Basra
Derbent
Tabriz
Baghdad
Mosul
Kufa
Diyar Bekr
Erzurum
Kayseri
Halab
Homs
Damascus
Jerusalem
Tarsus
Konya
Medina
Jeddah
Mecca
Brusa

R. Indus
R. Amu Darya
R. Dijla
R. Firat
R. Nile

kingdom of the Turkomen of the White Sheep. Next he overthrew the Turkomen of the Black Sheep. He was, however, still not satisfied. He next went against the Uzbegs of the north. Ismail had great fervour and his soldiers fought selflessly for him. He defeated Shaybani Khan, the Amir of the Uzbegs, who lost his life fighting. The Uzbegs were driven back and Ismail became master of upper Khorasan too. He was now supreme ruler over a great empire. A Persian by birth and a Shiite by faith, he spoke Persian and was therefore accepted as a national hero. He made Shiism the creed of his state and thus founded the first great Shiite Empire. To this day the creed of Persia (Iran) is Shiism.

Ismail and The Ottomans. Ismail has always been a great hero to the Persians and many have even revered him as a saint. Very brave and highly talented, he was a fine military commander. The only people against whom he did not prevail entirely were the Ottoman Turks who, under Selim I, opposed the new Shiite power. Selim I was a great fighter and a terror to Christians. He came up with his army against Shah Ismail who met him at the great battle at Chaldibran in 1514: the Turks were stronger in artillery and broke the Persian ranks. Ismail dashed against the Turks with his cavalry again and again, but could not prevail; the Turks won and Selim took Tabriz. His army, however, refused to go farther and so Selim retired. He annexed Kurdistan and Diyar Bekr. This incident is historically important. The Ottomans and Persians fought each other many times over the next three centuries. They appeared to have taken up the age-old conflict of Eastern Europe and Western Asia. It may perhaps have been a Shia-Sunni conflict. Both sides wasted untold men and material over this war, which lasted for centuries.

Shah Abbas I (1587-1629). Ismail was succeeded by Shah Tahmasp who fought continually against the Uzbegs of Trans-Oxiania and the Ottomans on the west. He defeated the Uzbegs, but lost a number of battles against the Ottoman

Sultan, Sulaiman the Magnificent. It was in Shah Tahmasp's time that Humayun, the exiled Moghul emperor, came to Persia for aid, which was given to him when he became a Shiite. Shah Tahmasp began to rebuild Persia: the new pattern of the Safavids began with him, and came to flower in the reign of his grandson, Shah Abbas I, called the Great. Shah Abbas was a man of ideas and of vision. He wanted to bring back the glory of ancient Persia to his land, and since the Persians had at last a Persian dynasty and a Persian variation of Islam, their own language and their own culture, they recovered a degree of enthusiasm which gave them new life. Shah Abbas began his work systematically. Seeing that the Kizilbashes were getting headstrong, he organized another order of fighters, called 'Friends of the Shah' and thus had a new body of men on whom to depend in a crisis. Remembering that the Turks had had the advantage in the wars in the last two reigns, he reorganized his army with the help of two English adventurers of talent, Anthony and Robert Shirley. He was now ready for anybody, but his traditional enemies were the Uzbegs and the Turks.

War with the Uzbegs. The Turks, however, anticipated him by striking first. They invaded Persia under General Farhad Pasha in 1587. There was a battle near Baghdad and the Persians lost. The Turks captured Tabriz again and annexed the land from Georgia to Luristan. In spite of this, the Shah bided his time, especially as the Uzbegs were giving trouble in Khorasan. The Uzbeg king, Amir Abdullah II, was a very enterprising man who had conquered the entire area of the two rivers from Farghana in the east to the Caspian Sea, and to Astrabad and Gilan in the west. He had then captured Herat and Meshhed in Khorasan. He now came down and captured Nishapur Sabzwar, Isfahan and the whole of Khorasan. In 1597, however, Shah Abbas took his new army north and fell on the Uzbegs with such fury that he broke their entire military strength and drove them from Khorasan. He then turned on the Turks. In 1603 he marched to the north-west, took back Tabriz, and captured Erivan, Shirvan, and Kars. At the great battle of Lake Urmia he defeated the Turks. He next reconquered Mosul, Diyar Bekr, and Mesopotamia, and returned home triumphant. It was a great day for Persia, and there were nation-wide rejoicings. The ancient rivalry of Turan and Iran, of Turk and Persian, was decided in Iran's favour. A great champion was born. Prayers were offered to God. A few years later (1612) a peace treaty was drawn up which was very favourable to Persia. And in 1616, when the Turks came again with a strong army and besieged Erivan, the Persians fought back and repulsed the attack. Again, in 1618, the Turks had to go back after an unsuccessful attack and when, some years later, they ventured again and came as far as Baghdad, they achieved little. Hostilities now ceased and there was peace between the two nations. Shah Abbas had saved the honour of Persia.

Achievements of Shah Abbas. Shah Abbas was a great ruler, not only in military matters, but also in administration. He improved the communications of his empire, built caravanserais and bridges throughout the land: some of the roads he built still exist. He then chose Isfahan as his capital and made it a garden-city, unlike any other. The palaces and other buildings, mosques, *madrasahs*, and religious academies that grew up there were the marvel of the age. Travellers from other countries went back full of praise. The encouragement he gave to the crafts alone, to pottery, to weaving, carpet-making, tiles and other things, bore such fruit that Persian goods became world famous. He tried to make the Persians into one nation, and to that end popularized the Shiite creed. He declared Meshhed, with the tomb of Imam Ali al-Rida, a sacred place and went regularly on pilgrimage to it. Once he walked 800 miles to Meshhed for this pilgrimage. He was liberal to non-Muslims and was popular as a great monarch even outside his country. Due to his encouragement, Persian arts, crafts, and culture had great influence over the whole

Islamic world. Only one thing eluded him: he could not inspire great poetry. There was no renaissance of Persian poetry under him or under any of the Safavids.

Successors of Shah Abbas. The successors of Shah Abbas were not of the same mettle and it was not long before 'harem rule' began to cast its deadly influence over state affairs. Intrigues weakened the power of the Shahs and there was internal strife throughout the empire. The Turks watched the growing unrest in Persia and shortly after Shah Abbas's death, Murad IV, the Ottoman Sultan, invaded Persia, penetrating as far as Hamadan which he sacked. In 1635 the Turks took Erivan and Tabriz, and in 1638 they took Baghdad; when peace terms were at last discussed the Turks gave back Erivan and Tabriz, but kept Iraq and with it Baghdad. From then on Baghdad remained a part of the Turkish Empire and remained so for nearly three hundred years, to be lost, along with the rest of their empire, in the First World War. Things went on in this state for quite a long time, but early in the eighteenth century the last Safavid king went to war with the Afghans whose ruler, Mir Vais, was a staunch Sunni and opposed the extreme views which were prevailing in Persia at that time. He refused to pay tribute to the Safavid Shah Husain, and when the Shah sent an army against him, he defeated the Persians easily. For a time, things went well, but the second Afghan ruler after Mir Vais, Mir Mahmud, invaded Persia in 1722. He won a great victory at Gulnabad and then marched on Isfahan. Shah Husain abdicated, his son Tahmasp escaped to Mazandaran with a view to raising new forces. The Afghans now became masters of Persia and remained so for a few years.

The Afghans—Mir Mahmud and Ashraf Shah. When the Afghans were lords of Persia, Peter the Great was Czar of Russia. He was a remarkable man and a fierce fighter. His one dream was to make Russia great. The best way open to him of achieving this ambition was to attack the Muslims, who were showing signs of weakness everywhere—in the Turkish

Empire, as well as the Persian. So he took the excuse of helping the Safavid cause and invaded Persia from the Caucasus. He took Derbent in 1722, then Resht and Baku. All these towns lay in lower Caucasia which had been in Muslim hands for centuries. Tahmasp II, the Safavid Shah, promised to yield to him Shirvan, Daghestan, Gilan, Mazandaran, and even Astrabad, if Peter the Great helped him to drive out the Afghans. The Turks now took action. They took Tiflis in 1723. There was for some time an alliance between Russia and Turkey. The Turks said they wanted Tabriz, Hamadan, and Karmanshah for their efforts against Persia. The Czar agreed and the Turks took these towns (1724-1725). The Afghan rulers were themselves having trouble at Isfahan. They were Sunnis and comparatively uncultured. The Persian nobles were proud of their culture and their past; they obeyed the new rulers, but always with an air of superiority. The Afghans were short-tempered. They called the airs and graces of the Persians insolence, and punished the people justly as well as unjustly. This made matters worse. Hatred grew on both sides. Things were at this stage when Mir Mahmud died. He was succeeded by Sultan Ashraf Shah, who was a more understanding man. He tried to meet people half-way, and was considerate and tactful, but the Persian nobles were suspicious and did not co-operate. He did not, however, lose heart. When the Turks came in 1727 he defeated them and in the peace treaty which he signed with the Sultan he yielded a little territory, but was acknowledged as Shah of Persia. The following year, however, in 1728, Tahmasp came back with a powerful ally, Nadir Kuli Khan, the chief of the Afshar tribe of Turks in upper Khorasan. Tahmasp and Nadir Khan began their march, and conquered Meshhed and Herat and then went straight to Isfahan. They defeated Ashraf Shah first near Isfahan, and again two years later in 1730 near Shiraz. Ashraf Shah left the country, but was killed on the way back to Kandahar and the Safavids came back to power.

The Afshars—Nadir Shah (1736-1747). Nadir Kuli Khan was now the chief Minister and Commander-in-Chief of the Shah. He married the Shah's sister and became very powerful. Nadir was a great warrior: Islam had not seen his like for a long time. After defeating the Afghans he turned to the Turks and drove them from Hamadan, Karmanshah, and Tabriz. The Abdalis, who had come to power in Kabul, had been giving trouble and Nadir marched against them. In his absence, Shah Tahmasp made a foolish attempt to fight the Turks, but was defeated and lost the towns recently conquered by Nadir. Nadir, angered by the loss, returned to the capital and deposed the Shah. He then put the eight-month-old baby son of Tahmasp, Abbas III, on the throne and himself became Regent. He remained Regent for four years, until the little Shah died. The nobles offered the throne to Nadir. He was a Sunni and accepted the offer, though he made one condition—that the state religion should be changed to Sunni-Islam. The nobles agreed, and during his entire reign Nadir Shah made unsuccessful efforts to bring back the Sunni faith to Persia. He did not, however, fail in other things. He restored the glory of Persia and extended the Persian Empire.

Nadir Shah the Conqueror. The military campaigns of Nadir Shah read like a romance. Such energy, such military leadership had not been seen in the Islamic world for a long time. He did not forget what Russia or Turkey had taken from Persia during the short Afghan regime. He attacked Russia first, and his campaign was so successful that he recovered Mazandaran, Astrabad, and Gilan, but while Nadir was fighting the Russians, the Turks, who had made an alliance with Russia in the previous reign, invaded Persia. Nadir returned to meet them; in the battle of Kirkuk, which followed, he was defeated. He did not pursue the war at this stage, because there was a rising in Trans-Oxiania, but he made a treaty with Russia. He promised to give the Czar all the Persian areas in Caucasia, such as Baku and Derbent, if the Russians helped him against the Turks. The Czar agreed, and in 1735 Nadir met the Turks at the Battle of Baghavand and defeated them. He now took back Tiflis. Finding himself, for the time, safe in the west he marched into Trans-Oxiania and conquered Balkh. He then went to Kandahar and took it. The next year, 1739, he captured Kabul, Peshawar, and Lahore. Muhammad Shah, the Moghul Emperor of India, sent an army against Nadir, but it was defeated. Nadir then took Delhi, sacked it, and massacred the inhabitants. He emptied the Imperial Treasury and took the famous Peacock Throne, besides untold wealth. He left behind him a broken government. The wealth that he took, however, turned his head. He conquered Sind later that year and annexed the treasuries of that province also. He went back, but stopped at Kandahar to display his loot. The jewels and precious stones, to say nothing of golden ornaments, thrones and canopies, tents and other material that were spread before his eyes dazzled him. On his return to Persia he had a palace especially built to house his treasures. He spent hours and sometimes days viewing his wealth. It is said that this made him a miser and changed him considerably. Many even go so far as to say that he was never the same man again, though he carried on his wars and his conquests. In 1740 he conquered Khiva and Bokhara and so extended the boundaries of his empire further.

Nadir's Character. Nadir was a great general and a conqueror in the old tradition, but he was no great administrator. One mistake that he made was his obstinate conviction that because he was so powerful he could change the creed of his people. His efforts did not succeed and he only created discontent. Then the wealth of India made him a miser and, instead of spending it on improving his country, he hoarded it. At first, after his return from India and as a sign of victory, he remitted all taxes for some time, but when he found that the treasury of Persia was getting empty he imposed them again. A great man in many ways, he was not consistent in his dealings and was given to bad temper. The only thing he retained to the end was his military genius. Even in 1745, when the Turks invaded Persia again, he met them and won a great victory over them near Kars. There was at last peace between the Muslim powers, but in 1747 Nadir was killed by one of his own tribesmen.

The Zands (1750-1794). The Afshar dynasty did not last long after Nadir's death. A grandson, Shah Rukh, lost his throne to a Shiite rival who defeated him and had his eyes put out. The prince escaped, blinded as he was, and making his way to Khorasan, established himself there. He ruled in that province till 1796, an example of talent, courage, and resourcefulness. The Abdalis became independent in Afghanistan. In Persia two parties contested for power for some time, the Zand party led by Karim Khan, and the Qajar party. Karim Khan succeeded and became the Shah. His strength lay in the south, so he moved his capital to Shiraz. He was a good ruler, kind and yet firm and he brought back prosperity to Persia. He gave certain concessions to the British to open factories at Bushire (1763) and Basra (1770). After his death, there was some unrest, but after a few short reigns Lutf Ali Khan came to the throne (1789). He was a fine man and had many kingly virtues. But the Qajars, were growing in power, and in 1794 he had to try his strength with them. The Qajar leader, Agha Muhammad, defeated him and put an end to the Zand dynasty. He then set up the Qajar dynasty, which ruled in Persia till 1925.

Persian Administration. A word must now be said about the civil administration set up by the Persians and their cultural institutions. The administration in all Muslim countries was very similar. The Sultan or the Shah, as before them the Caliph, was the supreme head. He had his *Naib* or *Vakil* or Grand Vizier with him. Under vigorous rulers the forces were always led by the ruler or his son. So there was seldom a separate Commander-in-Chief. The Sultan or Shah was also the Chief Judge, though there was always a Grand Qadi to perform that function. The Grand Mufti (*Sadr us-Sudoor*) was the interpreter of the Shariah and therefore the legal adviser of the Shah. There were then viziers in charge of various departments, as of Finance or Posts and Communications or Police. Under the Safavids there was a Royal Seal-bearer also, and a Master of Ceremonies. These officials formed the Council of Ministers. The provincial governors had to be given great powers, because communications were not well developed. The governors therefore had their own councils. They commanded the forces always and were heads of the civil administration too, though they could appoint Faujdars to small military commands and deputies as civil administrators. The governors collected their own revenues and sent a certain percentage to the capital. The chief sources of central revenue were land taxes, taxes on merchants, tributes from vassals, booty in war, customs, tolls and excise. The Shah had a source of personal income in the presents made to him when he granted an audience. The country was thus well organized.

Persian Products. The Persian industries were well developed and many goods were exported. Persian carpets, fabrics, glassware, pottery, and miniatures were greatly in demand. The fame of Persian textiles, especially, was so great that European monarchs took to wearing Persian dress at times. Charles II of England often wore Persian dress, and so did his nobles. The French, too, loved Persian goods and decorated their persons and their houses with the products of Persian industry. The velvets, satins, silver and gold-thread work produced in the reign of Abbas I are shown in the museums of the world to this day. The carpets of those days still preserve their beauty, and in designing them the highest artists of the day helped the weavers. Shah Abbas was so fond of pottery, of which he had a beautiful collection, that he invited hundreds of families of potters from China and induced them by generous presents to settle in Persia. Persian pottery then began to rival the best pottery in the world. Enamelled glassware had been an industry developed even before the Safavids. A Venetian nobleman, Clavijo, who travelled to the court of the great Timur in Samarqand, wrote an account of the wonderful things he saw at the Tartar court and in the Tartar capital. One of these marvels was enamelled glassware, the art of which has been lost to the world since those days. The tiles that the Persian kilns produced have seldom been surpassed. The art of glazed tiles, of plain and vari-coloured (*haft-rangi*) designs spread even to India. The Persian style of architecture influenced the Moghul style greatly, and Persian artisans were in demand everywhere. Persian poetry influenced Turkish poetry in the west and Urdu poetry in the east.

Persian Arts. Much has been said of the glories of Persian poetry. It is unfortunate that, perhaps because of religious zeal, no great poet appeared in the Safavid times. There was, of course, a great deal of poetry, but emphasis had shifted from theme and subject, from emotion and concept, to language and form, and great skill was acquired by the Safavid poets in writing verses of varying lines and flexible metres, so that poems could be written in various geometrical patterns. It is obvious that, when inspiration is forced to such ready-made patterns, great work cannot result; this is what happened to Persian poetry. But in painting and architecture Persia performed wonders. A national style had already emerged in Khorasan under the Timurids. Shaikh Junaid began the movement by illustrating the great Persian classics, such as the *Shahnama* or the *Romances* of Nizami. He was followed by the famous Bihzad, who had a school of his own at Herat between 1480 and 1507. Bihzad made painting more natural and gave it a delicacy and colouring it had not previously possessed. The Safavid school was led by Sultan Muhammad and his more famous pupil Rida Abbasi, the court painter of Abbas the Great. Rida Abbasi also designed fabrics. His association with the court, however, gave to his style a softness and languidness which became worse in the seventeenth century and finally killed good painting in Persia. In architecture, from the days of Uljaytu, Shah Rukh and his wife Gauhar Shad, to Shah Abbas, who built such grand structures as Masjid-i-Shah in Isfahan, and the palaces of Chihil Sutun, Talar Ashraf, and Hasht Bihisht, there have been buildings of which any country could be proud.

CHAPTER 10

THE OTTOMANS

The Origins of the Ottomans—Ertoghrul. The Turks accepted Islam in the ninth or tenth century while they were still in Central Asia. They began to push their way south in the eleventh century. One branch, headed by Tughrul, descended on Persia, and in 1055 took Baghdad. Another branch, that of the Ghaurs, took Kabul and built the Ghaurid Empire. Later another minor branch passed through Persia and Iraq and settled for a time near the upper reaches of the Euphrates during the Mongol invasions. At this time the Muslims were still fighting for their religion against the Crusaders. Volunteers were needed on all fronts, in Asia Minor as well as Syria. Many Turkish bands roamed in this area and some of them won small principalities for themselves which they held during the period of the Il Khans. One such band of Turks was led by a Turkish chieftain called Osman. His Turks were therefore called Osmanlis (later Europeanized into Ottomans). Osman having lost his life in one of the many skirmishes which their wandering life led them into, his son Ertoghrul took service with the Seljuk Sultan of Konya, Alauddin II. These Turks were good fighters, and so the Sultan decided to use them against the Byzantines. He made Ertoghrul the feudatory lord of the district of Sogund on the southern slopes of the Sea of Marmara and gave him the task of defending the border. Ertoghrul died in 1289, and the leadership of the tribe as well as the lordship of the border district passed to his son Osman.

Osman I (1290-1326). Osman is considered the founder of Ottoman power and his name is held in the highest esteem by the Turks to this day. His ambition was to see his people great. He knew what the Seljuks and the Ghaurs had done; why should not his own people, therefore, achieve as much? The obvious target was the crumbling Byzantine Empire. He had to look to the west for his empire and in order to do that he also had to make his people strong. He had to outfight the Byzantines, overcome their remaining strongholds in the west of Asia Minor—the old town of Brusa, for instance, or Nicodemia—become an independent ruler of even a small Emirate and then win a foothold in Thrace across the Sea of Marmara. Osman and his son Orkhan did all these things. To Osman flocked many Muslim adventurers, the guilds of merchants, even Jews, and, strengthened by these, he launched a series of *ghazwahs* against the Byzantines. He conquered the town of Melangnore, named it Karjahisar and made it his capital. He then besieged the important stronghold of Brusa which fell in 1326, the year of his death. Osman became Emir of his small state and announced his independence. He inspired his Turks with a great ambition and left with them a legacy of effort and heroic endeavour. He was succeeded by his son Orkhan I.

Orkhan I (1326-1359). Orkhan I buried Osman's body in the church of Brusa Castle with great ceremony, and since that day the church, which was made into a mosque, became the burial place of the Sultans of Turkey. Orkhan conquered Nicodemia and established the first Turkish school there. Daud al-Qaysari, a learned man of merit, was made the principal of the school. Orkhan carried on the tradition of his father, defeated the Byzantines at Philokrene in 1330, captured the old town and took over the schools and industries there. Like a true nation builder, he let none of the old Greek institutions die: he made them his own and ran them on Islamic lines. He now reorganized the army and made a very able general, Kara Khalil Jandarli Khairuddin Pasha, its head. He introduced foot soldiers in the Turkish army, which had so far only consisted of cavalry. He also built a new corps, called the corps of *Jan-nisars* (faithful unto death) which later became a first-class corps, the first in the Turkish army for valour as well as for utter loyalty. Its members came to be called Janissaries. The corps was recruited originally from the sons of Christian subjects who were given a special training and had a high standard of living as well as of education. Many of these lads became famous generals, all of them having been brought up as Muslims. They were fanatically loyal to the Sultan and were considered his special troops. The *Janissaries* played a straightforward role for about three centuries, but later deteriorated.

Orkhan and the Byzantines. The Byzantine Empire by this time was greatly reduced. First the Seljuks and now the Ottomans had taken away the Byzantine parts of Asia Minor. The power of the Byzantine Emperor in south-eastern Europe was threatened by the growing power of the Serbs. The Bulgars were also advancing. The republics of Venice and Genoa had taken possession of a number of Aegean islands. At this time, on the death of Emperor Andronicus III (1341), his widow Anna became the Empress with a co-Regent by the name of Cantacuzene. They disagreed soon afterwards and Cantacuzene made an alliance with Orkhan I, by giving his daughter, Theodora, in marriage to him. He asked in return for the loan of 6,000 troops. Cantacuzene defeated the Empress with the help of the Turkish cavalry and was accepted as emperor, with his wife as co-empress. Two years later in 1349 the Serbs came down against Byzantium and the Emperor and Empress of Constantinople begged for more Turkish troops. Orkhan helped again with 20,000 foot and horse. Six years later Cantacuzene fell out with Empress Anna's now grown-up son, John Paleologus, and again asked his son-in-law for help. This time he gave Orkhan the fortress of Tzympe on the European side of the Hellespont as payment. Orkhan put his son Sulaiman in charge of the fortress and gave him a strong garrison. Sulaiman was a very enterprising young man. Taking advantage of an earthquake which damaged the fortress of

Gallipoli, Sulaiman took possession of that stronghold also. Cantacuzene protested, but Orkhan said that another fortress, and that a damaged one, was not too great a return for the help so often rendered. This did not suit the Emperor at all; he was alarmed and appealed for help to his fellow-Christians, the kings of the Serbs and the Bulgars, who refused it. This made the Byzantines very bitter against Cantacuzene who, they said, had betrayed them. They labelled him a traitor and made him abdicate. John Paleologus now tried hard to dislodge the Turks from these fortresses, but could not do so, for the Turks had come to stay and are still there, although six hundred years have passed. When Sulaiman died, of a fall from his horse, Orkhan grieved terribly. He died in 1359, a year after the death of his favourite son. He was a good leader, a great organizer, a fine administrator, and a true nation-builder.

Murad I (1359-1389). Orkhan was succeeded by his second son Murad, who had seen service in Anatolia where he had conquered Angora. On Orkhan's death the Anatolians revolted with the help of the *Akhis*, the guild of merchants. Murad hurried back and put down the revolt. He then went over to Thrace and chose Demotika as his headquarters. From there, he opened a series of campaigns against the Balkan princes. He took Adrianople in 1365 and made it his capital, cutting off Constantinople from the rest of the Balkans. He then conquered one small Balkan principality after another. His generals, Evrenos and Lala Shalin, captured the fortresses of Tchorlu and Kirk Kilisse. The Byzantine Emperor now came up with an army, but Murad defeated him at the battle of Eski Baba. Philippopolis was then captured. He pushed forward and conquered all the area up to the Balkan Mountains. Murad thus became a terror to the Balkan people, and Shishman the King of the Bulgars agreed to pay him tribute.

The First Crusade against the Turks. The Crusades were over. Syria had been won and lost, and a century had passed since the last stronghold of the Crusaders in Palestine had been captured by the Mamluks, but the Pope was the spiritual head of western Christendom and could still exert great moral pressure. So when the Byzantine Emperor appealed to him for help, Pope Urban V sent out the old call to the crowned heads of Europe. There was the same response. Everybody asked what sort of people the Muslims were. Even the Mongols could not destroy them, even the Tartars could not finish them, and now they rose again, this time in another corner of Europe. When the Crusade assembled, King Asmodeus of Savoy was elected leader and came with a fleet and an army. He took Gallipoli, but the Turks attacked him and drove him out. This was the end of the Crusade, but it was by no means the last of the Crusades against the Turks. The Balkan powers now joined together and under the command of the king of Serbia attacked the Turkish positions. A great battle was fought in 1371 by the River Maritza. The Serbs and their allies were defeated and Murad annexed Macedonia. He now began sending out raids even into Albania and Greece and became so powerful in the Balkans that John Paleologus, the Emperor of Constantinople, became almost a vassal of the Turkish Sultan.

Further Conquests—Battle of Kossovo (20 June 1389). Murad's generals, especially Khairuddin Jandarli and Haji Ilberzi, were as good as their Emir. They undertook campaigns and it was not long before they made new conquests. Sofia, the capital of Rumelia, was taken in 1385 and Nish in 1386. The Turks became so powerful by these conquests that King Lazar of Serbia also became a vassal of Murad I. The Italian Republics now began to woo Murad for trade concessions, and the Republic of Genoa was the first to arrange a trade treaty with him. The next year, 1388, Venice followed suit and got permission to pass through the Sea of Marmara and trade with southern Russia and the Caucasian seaports on the Black Sea. The Bulgarian Czar, Shishman III, even though he had allied himself with Murad by giving him his sister in marriage, was now forced by the remaining Balkan powers, the Serbians and the Bosnians, to make one more effort to stop the advances of the Turks. He raised a large army, and the Christian allies won a battle at Vidin against the Turkish general Lala Shalin; but soon after, Ali Pasha, the son of General Khairuddin Jandarli captured the towns of Tirnova and Shumla. Now came another alliance and all the Balkan States joined against the Turks. The Serbs, the Bulgars, the Bosnians, and the Wallachians came down under the command of King Lazar of Serbia. On 20 June 1389 a great battle was fought at Kossovo. The Turks broke the ranks of the allies and inflicted a crushing defeat on them. Murad died fighting, but his son, Prince Bayazid, carried on. King Lazar was killed in the battle and the war ended.

Murad's Achievements. Osman may have been the father of the Ottomans, and Orkhan may have founded the kingdom, but the man who made it an empire was Murad I. He was a great conqueror and he dealt such blows to the Balkan peoples that the name of the Turks became a household word in Europe. Courage, determination, and resourcefulness were his chief characteristics. He was also a good diplomat. What he did not win by conquest, he obtained by treaty or alliance or purchase. He married his son Bayazid to the daughter of the Emir of Kermia and so got a portion of the state in dowry. He bought a part of the state of Hamid and enlarged his dominions in Asia Minor. In war he was the terror of his enemies and in his time Turkish forces crossed the Danube. His army was the best in Europe and he left a tradition of honour and glory which his descendants cherished for a long time.

Bayazid I (1389-1402). Prince Bayazid succeeded Murad and showed all the courage of his ancestors. He followed up the victory of Kossovo and compelled Stephan, the new king of the Serbs, to ask for peace. He entered Wallachia (modern Rumania) at the head of his army and compelled its Prince to pay him tribute. All Bulgaria now came within the growing Turkish Empire. Bayazid's son, Prince Sulaiman, captured Tirnovo and the fortresses of Nicopolis, Vidin, and Silistria.

This brought the Turks up to the borders of Hungary and the Sultan sent an army into Hungary too. In the south his fleet began to attack the Aegean islands. Unfortunately for him, he also took Philadelphia, the last Byzantine stronghold in Asia Minor, and this made him think of annexing the whole of Asia Minor, with the results already described in Chapter 9. Before that happened however, Bayazid had laid siege to Const-antinople. This siege lasted eight years (1391-1398). During this time he made and unmade emperors, but he could not capture the town, as the Christian powers of Europe now raised another Crusade against the Turks with King Sigismund of Hungary as leader. All the Balkan rulers, and knights from England, France and Germany joined the Crusade. The Pope stood behind them all. The commercial states of Venice and Genoa helped. The Crusaders met the Turks in battle on 25 September 1396 at Nicopolis, but were utterly routed and the Turks cut the crusading army to pieces. The Turkish army now invaded Greece and conquered it as far as Corinth. This was the zenith of Bayazid's power. Flushed with this victory he met Timur with inadequate forces, was defeated and died in captivity. There was war among his sons after his death, but after a few years of internal strife, in 1413 Prince Muhammad was victorious.

Muhammad (1413-1421). Muhammad only ruled for eight years, but he did not waste any of them. The first job he undertook was to restore order in the Ottoman Empire. The Balkans had taken heart at the war between the successors of Bayazid and had risen here and there. But when Muhammad became Sultan he put down all these risings with a firm hand, though the Venetians, who had become mortal enemies of the Turks by this time, attacked Gallipoli and captured it. Muhammad's navy was not strong enough to fight the Venetian fleet and so he made peace with Venice. Another problem arose, however; a heretic who posed as a Muslim, claimed to be the Messiah. This was Badruddin Mahmud, who began a movement on the western coast of Asia Minor and won a large following for himself, with ideas of a socialist nature. Sultan Muhammad sent a force against Badruddin, but it was defeated. Another expedition also failed, so Prince Murad, the Sultan's son, was now sent with an army, the Beylerbey of Rumelia (Commander-in-Chief of European Turkey) Bayazid Pasha assisting him. They crushed Badruddin's forces and rooted out the heresy. On Muhammad's death Murad succeeded him.

Murad II (1421-1451). Murad was still a youth when he came to the throne. The Christians thought he would be easy to overthrow. The dream of destroying the Turks was cherished by the Europeans for centuries. The Emperor of Constantinople found a tool in Mustafa, who was alleged to be a son of Sultan Bayazid and thus an uncle of Murad. He gave him troops and money and incited him to rebel. Mustafa attacked Murad, and defeated him near Adrianople. But Murad had the solid support of Asiatic Turkey behind him, so he retreated to Asia and mustered his army: soon he was strong enough to chase Mustafa, defeat, capture, and hang him. He was very angry with the Emperor who had been behind this plot, and he attacked Constantinople, but the Emperor sent word to Venice and the Venetian fleet came and attacked Murad from the rear so that he had to raise the siege. The Venetians even captured Salonika from the Greeks, allied with them and began to attack the Turkish positions, whereupon Murad sent his fleet against the Venetian possessions in the Aegean Sea. The Turks took Salonika in 1430, but they did not stop there. They went ahead and conquered Epirus and most of Albania. At this time there was some trouble in Venice, the state of Milan having invaded Venetian territory. The Venetians therefore withdrew and left Murad II as victor.

John Hunyadi, the Champion of Hungary. Murad was now full of enthusiasm. He sent an army into Hungary, but did not time his expedition well. The people of Hungary had discovered a leader of their own. This was John Hunyadi, who possessed many fine qualities. He was very popular with his fellow countrymen, who loved to fight under his command. John Hunyadi thus had an army devoted to him, and full of zeal he led them to victory against the Turks (1442). The news of this victory was welcomed all over Europe, the Christians being glad to hear that there was at last a leader among them who could defeat the Turks. They therefore thought that it was a good moment to prepare for another Crusade. The Pope was hopeful too and sent out his agents everywhere. All the Balkan nations responded. The Hungarians, Bosnians, Wallachians, and Serbians were already there. The Poles, too, joined the holy cause and John Hunyadi led the Crusade. He took Nish and advanced on Sofia. Murad was in two minds. His forces had already been defeated once. Here was a very much bigger army and he had not yet had time to organize a strong resistance. If he fought now he might be defeated again. He took a bitter decision and negotiated for peace. The Peace of Szegedin was drawn up in 1443. By it, Murad surrendered Serbia and yielded Wallachia to the King of Hungary. The peace was to last ten years. It was a wise action, but it broke Murad's heart; he felt so ashamed that he abdicated and retired to Anatolia, leaving the throne to his fourteen-year-old son.

The Crusade of 1444. Europe rejoiced. The Pope was over-joyed and thought that the Turks were finished. The Christian monarchs ignored the treaty; perhaps the Pope persuaded them to break it and to carry on with the Crusade. The King of Hungary brought them all together and led his large army into Bulgaria. The Venetians agreed to join, but said they would send their fleet to join the Crusaders at Varna. It was a national crisis. The Crusaders advanced, the Empire was in danger, and the Turkish nobles sent the terrible news to Murad, begging him to come back. Murad, leaving his retreat, crossed over to Adrianople and took command of the Turkish army. There was great enthusiasm among the Turks and they were no longer afraid. Murad met the Crusaders at Varna and the Turks routed them. Vladislas the King of Hungary fell in battle. In 1448, John Hunyadi came again with another large force, but Murad met him at the second Battle of Kossovo on 17 October and defeated him. He thus won back all his territories and once more the name of the Sultan became a terror to all Europe.

Murad II as Ruler. Murad II was a very popular Sultan and he had many lovable qualities. He was utterly devoted to the Ottoman Empire, was a great military commander, and a learned man. He was patient, just, and merciful in his dealings. He encouraged learning and had many Arabic and Persian classics translated into Turkish, which was now becoming popular and in which good prose and poetry were being written. Murad was a religious man, but he was not unkind to non-Muslims. His treatment of Christian prisoners won him international respect. His word was accepted everywhere, as it was known that he never broke it. Murad was one of the finest of the Ottoman Sultans.

Muhammad the Conqueror (1451-1481). There now came to the throne one of the greatest Sultans of the Turks, Muhammad II, who became known as Muhammad Fatih, that is, Muhammad the Conqueror. He was only twenty-one when he came to the throne, and he reigned for thirty years. He set himself the task of conquering Constantinople, which had stood many sieges and had defied the forces of Islam since the days of Amir Muawiyah. Although the emperor was a Turkish vassal and paid tribute, his city was open to all Europeans and especially to the Christians of eastern Europe, who had been fighting the Turks for a hundred and fifty years. The previous Sultans had built a castle on the Asiatic side of the Bosphorus, on the point nearest to Constantinople called Anadolu Hissar. Anadolu is Anatolia, the name the Turks gave to their possessions in Asia Minor; hissar means fortress. Muhammad II now built a strong fortress opposite Anadolu Hissar, on the European side. He called it Rumeli Hissar; Rumeli meaning

Europe to the Turks. When the fortress was ready, Muhammad began one of the most famous sieges of the later Middle Ages.

The Conquest of Constantinople (1453). There were 10,000 soldiers in the old city. The Venetians and the Genoese brought supplies to the besieged, daring even the Turkish navy which was supreme in those waters. The city was protected from the eastern side, because the Byzantines had prepared a heavy iron chain, which they fixed in the mouth of the Golden Horn harbour so that no ships could pass the barrier. Muhammad II pounded the strong city walls from the west and the north, but the energetic garrison repaired the breaches quickly. Muhammad was undecided whether to approach the city from the south or the east. Should he try to remove the chain? That could not be done, because the guns on the city walls were trained on the mouth of the harbour. If only he had ships on the other side. Could he build some ships on the other side? No, because there were no shipyards there. Could he carry light ships from the Asiatic side? They could be set on rollers and moved from one side of the tongue of land to the other. Could the experiment be tried? He consulted his naval engineers. They said they would try and he promised them great rewards. They came back and said, 'Yes, we think it is feasible.' Seventy light ships were built and dragged overland to the Black Sea. There they were floated, equipped with supplies, guns, ammunition, and soldiers. This small fleet sailed up and attacked the ancient town from the rear. This stratagem broke the back of the besieged. From the western side Muhammad made such an attack that he broke through the walls and entered the old city. The last Emperor, Constantine, was killed, and there was much bloodshed, but the Venetian and Genoese ships saved many Christians. At last the mighty town of Constantinople fell. Its fall had little political importance because the Turks had been masters of the Balkans for a hundred years, but the victory had other values. The city had stood for an old culture; it was the centre of the Orthodox Church and the seat of an ancient line of emperors. It contained a great Christian cathedral—Sancta Sophia—and it was very dear to all Europe. There was great distress, therefore, throughout Europe. The scholars who fled from the town took away with them ancient literary treasures and enriched all Europe, but the Europeans never forgot this loss, nor did they ever forgive the Turks. From that day everybody's hand in Europe was against the Turks. One by one every European nation fought them and the fight went on for four and a half centuries. The Christians avenged themselves in Spain, where they began to storm the last Muslim kingdom of Spain at Granada, till it fell in 1492.

Muhammad the Fatih. Muhammad did not win his title of 'Conqueror' only by capturing Constantinople. He had many conquests to his credit. John Hunyadi still made raids into the Turkish lands, so Muhammad in his turn besieged Belgrade, the capital of Serbia, in 1456. Hunyadi died at this time, and Muhammad pushed on with his conquests. He annexed Serbia by 1458, and Bosnia and Herzegovina between 1458-1461, and many families in these regions accepted Islam. During these years the Turkish fleet took the Aegean Islands. Albania, however, stood out under Sikanderbeg, a leader of note, who was helped at every step by Venice and Genoa. After Sikanderbeg's death in 1467, however, Albania was conquered. All these conquests made Europe anxious; another wave of Muslims was trying to conquer Europe from the East. Venice was especially concerned. The Ottomans had taken all the Aegean islands which had belonged to the Byzantines, and had cut the trade route to the Black Sea ports on which depended much of Venetian sea trade with Russia. The Pope was alarmed, so he raised the old cry 'Christendom in Danger' and tried to raise another Crusade: he even got some response. Hungary was prepared to fight, so was Venice, but nothing came of it. The Turks were, however, annoyed and they hit back. Dalmatia and Croatia were invaded in 1469: then in 1470, Negroponte, a Venetian port on the Adriatic, was annexed.

The Venetians made an alliance with Persia and induced the Shah to invade the Turkish dominions from the East. The Persians came up, but the Turks defeated them at Erzinjan in 1473 and then turned on Venice. They captured quite a few towns in north Albania. The Venetian fleet attacked Scutari, so the Turkish fleet sailed up the Adriatic and attacked Venice itself. This made Venice tractable and a peace treaty was drawn up to end this disastrous war. The Turks kept the towns in upper Albania, Negroponte, and the Aegean Islands and gave back the other towns. Venice agreed to pay 10,000 ducats to the Sultan annually, for permission to trade in the Black Sea.

Muhammad as Ruler. Muhammad the Conqueror was as great an administrator as he was as a conqueror. When he conquered Constantinople he permitted the Christians and the Greeks to remain in the city and even kept the Greek Patriarch, Gennadios, as the Religious Head of all Christians in Turkish lands; he also recognized the Armenian Church. He now planned a new palace, a new school for training of royal slaves, and a new training system. The Grand Vizier was permitted a palace of his own where he received foreign diplomats and representatives, before presenting them to the Sultan. His palace was called *Bab-i-Ali*, the Grand Gate, or, as it came to be known in Europe, 'The Sublime Porte'. Muhammad was full of energy and had great determination, but he was also a cultured man and devoted to the arts. A great admirer of Islamic studies, he had a special love for Persian poetry. He admired Greek culture too, and once received the tribute from the old city of Ragusa in Greek manuscripts. He made laws, founded colleges, built mosques and hospitals, and was sufficiently progressive in outlook to encourage the study of the sciences. He took great pleasure in the company of learned men and was acknowledged in the whole of Europe as a remarkable man. His portrait was painted by the Venetian painter Bellini.

Selim I (1512-1520). Muhammad was succeeded by his son Bayazid, who was not a fighter like his father though he had as great a love for things of the mind. In his reign the Venetians attempted to establish a base in Cyprus and fight the Turks from there, but the Turkish Naval Commander, Kamal Reis, defeated them in a great naval battle. The Turkish navy took Lepanto, Modon, and Koron on the west coast of Greece. The Turkish army invaded the Venetian mainland and raided as far as Vicenza. This was a great moment for the Turks, and Venice now sued for peace. In Bayazid's last years, his sons rose against him and in the civil war which followed, the Crown Prince Selim, was victorious. Selim proved a great warrior. He defeated Shah Ismail of Persia, and then turned to Syria. There the Burji Mamluk Sultan, Qansawh al-Ghauri, a friend of Shah Ismail, came to meet him with a large army, but Selim defeated the Mamluks at Marj Dabiq, on 24 August 1516. Qansawh died fighting and Selim annexed Aleppo and Damascus. The new Mamluk Sultan refused to accept Selim as his overlord, so Selim invaded Egypt and took Cairo on 22 January 1517. The Burji Mamluk Empire was conquered and Tuman Bey, the last Sultan, was executed. A Turkish Governor-General was appointed and left in Cairo with a garrison. The internal administration was, however, left as it was. The Sharif of Mecca surrendered. Selim thus became master of a large eastern empire, but he died on his way back. He had ruled for eight years only, but he had become famous and the whole of Europe rejoiced at his death. The Crusade that Pope Leo X was preparing against the Turks was given up. Selim was a great military commander and also a cultured man. He loved poetry and was himself a poet. He captured the last Abbasid Caliph of the Second Line in Cairo and took the robes of Caliphal office from him. He carried them to Constantinople, now called Istanbul.

Sulaiman the Magnificent (1520-1566). The greatest of the Ottoman sultans, Sulaiman the son of Selim, succeeded him. He was a great ruler in many ways, a conqueror who reached Vienna and besieged it. He did not take the town, but his power was established. He was a statesman, courted by every European monarch, a ruler who made the Turkish Navy mistress of the Mediterranean. He faced combination after combination of Christian powers and beat them. He fought Persia and annexed Iraq. For the glory of his court, for his power and splendour, he is known to history as Sulaiman the Magnificent. His only weak point was the influence held over him by his favourite wife, a Russian slave girl, Roxelana, who bore him a son, and prejudiced him against his elder son Mustafa, who suffered because of his father's attitude towards him.

Battle of Mohacs (1526). The first event of Sulaiman's reign was the final conquest of Egypt. The government of the new possession was now reorganized and a greater control was assumed by the Turkish Governor-General. Sulaiman's next concern was Hungary. He advanced on Belgrade in 1521 and took it. He began to send yearly expeditions into Hungary and Austria. In 1526 King Louis of Hungary came out to meet Sulaiman with a large army and the Turks met him in the famous Battle of Mohacs. It resulted in a great victory for the Turks, King Louis dying in battle. The Turks moved farther north, took Ofen, and then returned. There was now civil war in Hungary between Prince Ferdinand, the Hapsburg heir-apparent and ruler of Austria, on the one side and John Zapolya, the popular leader of Hungary, on the other. Zapolya sought alliance with Sulaiman and the Ottoman Sultan gave him his friendship and went to his aid.

Siege of Vienna and Rhodes. Two years later Sulaiman retook Ofen and moved on to Vienna. He besieged the famous city in September 1529 and kept assaulting the town for six weeks, but winter came on and there was so much rain and snow that the Turkish army found it difficult to move. Heavy guns could not be brought up. Things were in this state when Prince Ferdinand made an offer: to pay tribute to Sulaiman (now a great power in East Europe) if he accepted him as King of West Hungary. Two years later Sulaiman agreed, but he made Zapolya the ruler of East Hungary, paying annual tribute to Sulaiman the Magnificent. Europe was greatly alarmed at this aggressive policy of the Sultan. He next attacked the island of Rhodes, the headquarters of the Knights of St. John, who had been attacking Turkish shipping and making the mouth of the Aegean Sea a dangerous area. The Turks captured the island, although the knights fought bravely. Sulaiman the Magnificent made a grand gesture to the defeated knights: he let them depart in honour with all their arms and belongings. This noble treatment won great respect for the Sultan in Europe.

Khairuddin the Admiral. Sulaiman now turned his attention to his navy. He appointed as his admiral Khairuddin Barbarossa (the red-bearded), a famous corsair who had been in the service of the Bey of Tunis. Khairuddin was already a terror to all Christian shipping. A great naval captain, his boldness was proverbial. He sailed very fast and always arrived at a place before he was expected. As a champion of Islam on the sea, he had no rival. Sulaiman's offer was accepted by him and he immediately set about justifying his choice. His first achievement was the conquest of Tunisia for his new master, and then, outwitting the Italian admiral Andrea Dorea, he raided Sicily and southern Italy. At this, Venice declared war against the Turkish Empire with the aid of the Pope, who organized a new anti-Muslim league and, giving up the idea of Crusades at long last, called his new combination of Christian kings, a Holy League. Charles V, the Hapsburg Emperor, and Venice joined him. This gave Khairuddin a chance. He attacked the Venetians and defeated them in the Battle of Prevesa in 1538. Venice sued for peace and paid a large indemnity. The Sultan now built a Red Sea fleet, and soon the Turks conquered Yemen and Aden and the Turkish navy sailed right up to the Persian Gulf and the coasts of India.

Hungary Again. John Zapolya died in 1540 and Prince Ferdinand broke his word to Sulaiman by marching into East Hungary and annexing it. This was a challenge to Sulaiman, and he took it up at once. He marched north and occupied Buda, the capital of Hungary. Since Zapolya had left only an infant son behind him, Sulaiman placed his own governor in charge of East Hungary. Finding Sulaiman too strong for him, Prince Ferdinand begged for a truce in 1547 and even when he succeeded his father as emperor, Ferdinand continued to pay tribute. When John Zapolya the Younger grew up he was given Transylvania. Sulaiman kept Hungary for himself.

Sulaiman as Ruler. Sulaiman died in 1566. He had ruled for forty-six years and was one of the most famous, certainly the most powerful of the monarchs of his time. As a result of his wars with Persia, he added Mesopotamia to his empire, which now extended from the borders of Persia in the east to the borders of Algeria in the west, and from near Vienna in the north to Aden in the south. His last years were saddened by the intrigues of his wife, Roxelana, but he had made the Ottomans a world power. Though not so great a military captain as Murad, Selim I or Muhammad II, he was a very fine military organizer and a good tactician and was generally successful in his campaigns. He was never harsh or cruel in his dealings with his enemies. He chose his generals well and perfected his army and navy. Resolute, just and firm in his dealings, he was liberal in his views and sympathetic as well as generous to those who deserved reward, but he could be very strict in punishment, when he thought it was indicated. He could not tolerate incompetence or irresponsibility in anybody, general or vizier, and he was very hard on those who were disloyal to the state. He gave land to those officers and men who fought bravely and settled them in strategic places. The only condition he imposed on them was that they must bring up troops or horsemen in times of war to help the Sultan and fight for the empire.

Sulaiman was a cultured and well-educated man and kept a daily journal of his campaigns. He was also a very liberal patron of the arts, and built mosques, *madrasahs*, colleges, hospitals, bridges, and other useful buildings. He reformed the Turkish laws and is known in Turkish history as the Law-Giver. There was peace in Turkish lands in his time and he was loved everywhere as a great ruler.

Selim II and the European World. Sulaiman's death was followed by a struggle between Selim and Bayazid, the two elder sons of Sulaiman, the first of whom won. Selim was an intelligent ruler, though fond of drinking. He inherited the energy of his fore-fathers, however, and the intelligence of his famous father, though perhaps he did not have his sense of proportion or his statesmanship. The world that Selim had to face was a little different from that his ancestors had encountered. Great things had been happening and there had been two major events in Europe. A religious revolution had taken place, called the Reformation, in which many Christians had protested against the religious authority of the Pope and had fought for liberty of religious thought and liberty of worship. These Christians broke away from the Roman Catholic Church, organized their own Churches everywhere and came to be called Protestants. During this time, the fifteenth century, there was a general reawakening of interest in ancient learning and new literature came into being. This movement has been called the Renaissance, or re-birth of learning. The New World had been discovered and first the Portuguese, then the Spaniards, and after them the English had wandered all over the globe making new discoveries. All these things had given the Europeans great confidence in themselves and a broad outlook. They were making conquests in Asia and America, and their navies had become very powerful.

The Battle of Lepanto (7 October 1571). Selim had been helped in his struggle for the throne by a rich Jew, Joseph

Nassi, a refugee from Italy. In return Selim made Nassi Duke of Naxos and admitted him to his Councils. There were two European powers with whom the Turks had been fighting, the Hapsburg Emperor and the Venetians. The Emperor ruled over Austria, Hungary, Spain and southern Italy. Venice was a strong commercial state and a maritime power in the eastern Mediterranean. Selim's Grand Vizier, Muhammad Sokolli, a wise man, advised the Sultan to befriend Venice and fight the power of the Hapsburg emperor, Maximilian. Selim, however, took Nassi's advice and chose to fight Venice. At this time, Venice, which had agreed to give up Cyprus, refused to do so. Nassi was very anxious to get Cyprus as he wanted to settle the Jews there, and he advised the Sultan to declare war on Venice. Selim did so and annexed Cyprus in 1570. This threw Venice into alliance with Spain. Both these powers were supported by the Pope who now organized a new Holy League. The Christian allies combined their navies and made them into a great armada. Don John of Austria was put in command of this fleet, which sailed for Turkish waters. It came up with the Turkish fleet near Lepanto, a port on the western coast of Greece, in the Gulf of Corinth. The Turkish fleet was commanded by Ali Pasha, an arrogant nobleman, who owed his position to influence at court, rather than to merit. A strong wind was blowing from the sea. His captains advised Ali Pasha to keep to his positions and wait for the Christian fleet to come up. Ali Pasha was, however, too opinionated a man to listen to good advice. He said he could fight the Christians anywhere and beat them too. He therefore ordered the fleet out into the open sea. The Christian fleet had 208 ships with six huge war galleons. They had the advantage of the wind. A great battle ensued. It was a crusade and the Christians fought as they had not fought for years. There were great losses on both sides and the Christians won. The Turkish fleet was destroyed. Only one squadron, belonging to the Beylerbey of Algiers, escaped. The

Battle of Lepanto was hailed as a great victory and the whole of Europe rejoiced. It has come down in European history as one of the decisive battles of the world.

What Happened After. It was thought that the Turkish fighting power was crippled and the Turkish navy gone. Europe rejoiced in that idea for a whole year, but their pleasure in the Turkish disaster was short-lived. Selim was not, as a rule, a very energetic man, but he now made a supreme effort. He collected all his resources and sent for his new admiral, Dragut, who had been a lieutenant of the great Khairuddin Pasha. He ordered a new fleet of ships to be built, as strong as the one recently lost, if not stronger. The Turkish shipyards worked night and day for a whole year, and by the end of the year they had built a fleet larger than the one lost through the obstinacy of Ali Pasha. The Sultan made Dragut the Supreme Commander of this new fleet and asked him to chase the allied Christian fleet, which had meanwhile wasted its time. People have blamed Don John for not pursuing the Turks and conquering Morea (lower Greece) at least, but Don John was not to blame. The rivalry between the Spaniards and the Venetians and the difference in their policies were responsible for the delay. The Spaniards wanted to conquer North Africa, at least Algiers and Tunisia (which were a Turkish dominion), but Venice wanted to recapture Cyprus. They both really believed that they had finished the Turkish navy for ever. A year later Admiral Dragut, the dreaded lieutenant of the terrible Khairuddin Barbarossa, sailed up with a fleet which appeared to be much stronger than the original Turkish fleet. It was certainly stronger and the new admiral was no stupid nobleman, but a great naval captain. He chased Don John right up the Adriatic, and the allied commander avoided a fight. Dragut now sailed to the west and recaptured Tunis in 1573. The Venetians saw that their dream of capturing Cyprus had vanished. They made a separate peace with the Sultan, and seeing that the Turkish navy was stronger than before, gave up all claims to Cyprus and agreed to pay an indemnity of 300,000 ducats. This money went towards paying for the new navy. Dragut now roamed over the Mediterranean at will. He raided the coasts of Spain, of France, and of Italy. Sardinia and Sicily came in the way of his annual raids. Dragut collected much booty this way and many slaves. His other purpose was to show that the Mediterranean was still a Turkish sea and that nobody could challenge the Sultan's power in it. Soon the European powers forgot their victory at Lepanto.

The Grand Viziers—Muhammad Sokolli. Muhammad Sokolli, the Grand Vizier, was important not only for his wise statesmanship and skilful direction of the administration of the empire, but also because he was the first of a line of Grand Viziers who dominated the empire for a century and conserved its strength. The Sultans from now on became weaker, and their weakness took the form sometimes of obstinacy, sometimes of foolhardiness, but mostly of weakness of character. The blood of Osman was running thinly in the veins of the Sultans by this time. The Turkish Sultanas (Queen Mothers or Queens) were mostly Christian slave-girls or wives and they began to interfere in the activities of the state. Moreover, the Sultans took to a life of ease. They had everything they wanted. Conquests had now ceased, as Europe was fully awake and with the new scientific advances being made the European armaments and military equipment were getting stronger and better than those of the Turks with every decade. The Sultans, therefore, began delegating more and more of their powers to their Grand Viziers. Muhammad Sokolli was the first of them. Fortunately for the empire he was a gifted man. He had ideas and worked for the glory of Islam. He was the first man in Europe who thought of cutting a canal at Suez to join the Mediterranean with the Red Sea. In the north, he proposed that the Don and the Volga, the two Russian rivers, be joined by a canal. His idea was to build a fleet of small but swift ships and reach the Caspian Sea from the north to attack the traditional Turkish enemy, Persia. The Turkish Empire was by now a great power. The Turkish navy commanded four seas, the Black, the Mediterranean, the Red, and the Arabian. Muhammad Sokolli used his power in improving communications, in making administration more efficient and making the empire a rich state. He succeeded in all these attempts, and the reign of Selim II, which ended in 1574, saw Turkish power at its zenith. His reign, however, is a landmark in Turkish history, because it was the end of the Grand Period of the Ottomans. After his death the Sultans remained powerful for another century, but gradually their strength was sapped and they found themselves faced with internal disturbances and external foes whom they found increasingly difficult to overcome. Their power began to decline. The decline was slow in the seventeenth century, then more rapid in the eighteenth.

Organization of the Empire. The Head of State in the truest sense was the Sultan. He was the head of the Government, head of the army and the navy, head of religion, that is of Shariah, and he was the supreme judge. Later the Sultans became Caliphs also, so that they became the supreme voice in all matters of religion, not only for the Ottoman Empire, but for all Muslims. This gave them great prestige and moral support in the days of Turkish decline, when the sultans needed this extra support. In the centuries just discussed, the Sultan was an autocrat whose word was law, who made and unmade noblemen and commoners and who was obeyed (like Caesar in the olden days) in all the Turkish lands. The only difference was that the Sultan remained a man and never made claims of any superiority as the Caesars had done. Then came the Grand Vizier, who was given great powers and who acted as a Prime Minister. The Ministers were heads of departments, but more powerful than the Ministers were the Beylerbeys. A Beylerbey was the supreme military commander of an entire area. There were originally only two areas, Rumeli and Anadolu (Europe and

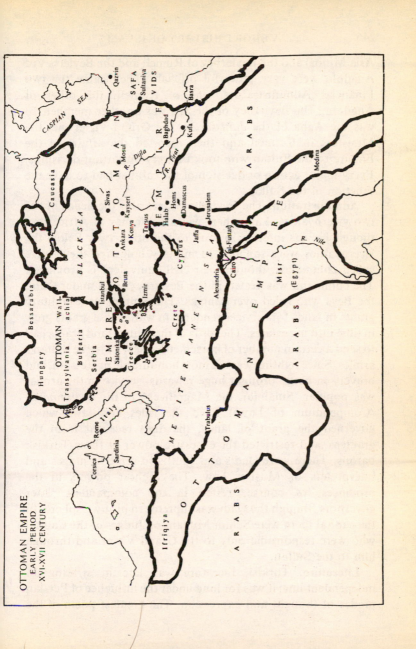

OTTOMAN EMPIRE
EARLY PERIOD
XVI–XVII CENTURY

Asia Minor) and the Beylerbey of Rumeli and the Beylerbey of Anadolu were very powerful officials. Then came the two Financial Administrators, one of Rumeli, the other of Anadolu. The Beylerbey of the Sea was another member, so was the Agha of the *Janissaries*. The Grand Vizier met the Ministers in Council and then reported the affairs of the Empire to the Sultan who took the very important decisions. Every major action or decision of the cabinet had to have the sanction of the Sultan.

Administration. The Beylerbeys were also the heads of the two viceroyalties. Later there was a Beylerbey of Africa too, though he was inferior in rank to the other two. Below the viceroyalties were sanjaks. In military language they were called commands, though their civil equivalent is provinces. The command was vested in the Beylerbeys and under them, the Beys who ruled over sanjaks. The Sultans gave military grants in lands for services rendered in war. These grants grew in time into big estates. The lords of these huge land grants had to send a certain number of horsemen for service in the Sultan's armies. Since fighting was the most honourable profession, and bravery in battle brought huge rewards, service in the armies was popular. Sulaiman the Magnificent in his *Qanunnama* (Compendium of Laws) fixed the rules and laws which governed the grant of lands, the dues received from the grantees, and restricted the excessive power of these Turkish barons. There were Qadis and Muftis to serve as judges and interpreters of Muslim Law. The highest powers in the provinces, of course, rested in the commanders, later governors, though the Qadi was supreme in his own sphere. In the capital there were Senior Mullahs or Judges of the Capital who were responsible only to the Grand Vizier and through him to the Sultan.

Literature. Turkish literature was late in striking an independent line; it was for long under the influence of Persian modes of thought and expression. The greatest poem of the times of the Seljuks of Rum, the immediate Turkish forerunners of the Ottomans, was the great *Masnavi* of Maulana Rumi, which was written in Persian. The first Turkish poem of any significance was the *Mevlidi Sherif* of Sulaiman Chelebi, which was a long *na't* in praise of the Prophet. The first Sultan to be interested in literature was Murad II, who gathered round him poets, philosophers, and learned men, though the first national note was struck by writers after the times of Muhammad Fatih. Four poets of the early period are notable: Fuzuli (d. 1562), Baqi (d. 1600), Nefi (d. 1635) and Nedim (d. 1732). The poetic forms which were attempted by these poets were the time-honoured *ghazal*, *qasida*, and *masnavi*. A *ghazal* is a poem of about nine to fifteen verses, on an erotic, philosophical, or mystical theme. A *qasida* is generally a eulogy in honour of a great man, king, or conqueror. A *masnavi* is a narrative poem which deals with the theme of love or of mysticism. The first book of prose was Admiral Piri Reis's *Book of Travels*. This book contains remarkably accurate descriptions of the Mediterranean lands and others visited by him in his naval expeditions. Turkish literature was well developed by the time the period of the Great Turks ended.

Growth and Decline. We must now review the rise and fall of the Turks as a whole. First nibbling at the Greek petty states in West Asia Minor, the Osmanlis under Orkhan I began their advance into Eastern Europe. This was towards the middle of the fourteenth century. Soon they made their headquarters at Adrianople and fought their way gradually into half of Eastern Europe as well as the Southern regions of Russia right upto Crimea. The wars of conquest remained unchecked for two and a half centuries, a very long period, the crest having reached in the days of Sulaiman the Magnificent. The ebb began in the next (seventeenth) century and continued till weak and vacillating Sultans, intriguing viziers, interfering Sultanas, the mistresses of the Seraglio (Harem), luxury and ease began to sap the vigour of the once hard and almost invincible Turks.

Other Causes of Decline. Two other factors added to the weakening of the 'Grand Turk'. One, the route via the Cape, cut the commercial enterprises of the Turks, because the products of the Far East, which had gone via Aden upto Syria and beyond, long since parts of Turkish Empire, or by sea along the Red Sea were now annexed by the Europeans, the more the imperial income diminished, the more luxurious became the habits of the ruling class and corruption and bribery increased. The second factor was the advances made by the European powers in scientific warfare and their resolve to join forces and start a regular crusade against the Turk, whose name was both a terror and an anathema for the ordinary European. In addition was the retaliatory vindictiveness of Russia, half of which had been under Tartar rule since the march of the Mongols in the thirteenth century. It had been only towards the end of the fifteenth century that Iran IV called Iran the Terrible threw out the Tartar Yoke from his Duchy of Moscar, by expelling the Tartar Resident at his court.

The Turks' Administrative Capacity. Actually the Turks had already performed an administrative miracle. Cut off from the Central Asian Steppes, their source of manpower, by a hostile Persia, menaced from the north and the west by the Christians, their sovereignty over the Mediterranean Sea challenged by the combined navies of the European powers, now in the ascendance after the expulsion of the Moors from Spain, the discovery of America a source of immense wealth, the mastery of the seas by Portugal, Spain, England, and later the Dutch, the Turks began to run short of fresh blood. Polygamy alone could not cope with the war drain. They had found it in the system of taking young boys from the subject races and conditioning them by intensive training, good pay, and honours. The Turks thus built an almost invincible fighting force in the *Janissaries*, who served them loyally for two centuries till privileges and power spoiled them too, and they got out of hand and had to be destroyed, as mentioned above.

Attitude of Early Rulers. Simple horsemen in origin, warlike and vigorous, the Turks and their leaders originally lived as a team, the ruler following the habits and the old customs of people, thus maintaining a fatherly attitude towards his followers. It was not till the days of Bayazid I, who was defeated by Timur, that blight of the Middle East, that the Turkish Amir, assumed the title of Sultan. For a whole century (fourteenth) the ruler and the ruled had been parts of a single body. The Sultan continued to sit amongst his viziers and discussed the affairs of State with them in open court. It was in the sixteenth century, in the days of Sulaiman the Magnificent, that he took to seating behind a window listening to the discussions of his cabinet. After that the Grand Vizier reported the decisions of the Council to the Sultan, to get his approval. The affairs were multifarious as the Turkish Empire spread over three continents, even though the empire had been divided into semi-autonomous villayets (provinces). The entire empire was linked by the Barid (Communications) department which also served as secret service. Trade had flourished and conquests had filled the exchequer. This state of affairs lasted for four centuries (fourteenth to seventeenth).

The Learned Ones and Cultural Activities. So much for the military and administrative genius of the Ottomans, but it has been said that in the cultural field their contributions were poor. This is the result of two centuries of anti-Turk propaganda by the crusading Europeans. The Turks, it is true, like the Arabs had no cultural past. Winding their way through Timurid lands and finding a shelter in the Seljuk world of Asia Minor, these Turks like the desert-bred Arabs picked up whatever they could, wherever they found it. They were as eclectic in the languages they used: Turkish, Persian, and Arabic, and if necessary, Greek. They made use of all of them. Asia Minor had for ages been the meeting place of various cultures, Byzantine, Greek, Seljuk, and Persian all making a very fruitful mixture. The Osmanlis benefited from this cultural reservoir.

The Ulema. The class of the Ulema played a great part in the formation of their outlook. The Ulema were Islamic in birth and by training. They were either Arab or pure Turks, and were held in high esteem. Gradually they became a privileged and even a sacrosanct class and their profession became almost hereditary, so much so that even their children came to be addressed as 'Young Ulema'. Although these Ulema became important functionaries of State, they never could supersede the military. The Bektashi order of Sufis had helped the Osmanlis with men and material in their early days. They had got merits for them and had joined in the *ghazwahs* with zeal. They long held an important niche in the body politic, till they began to interfere in State policies.

Advances in Learning. The Osmanlis were great admirers of learning from the very beginning, at least as they settled down in their fiefs below Marmara and they did not disdain to learn from others. Mosques and *madrasahs* had been built even by the first chieftains, perhaps, as a reflection of the centres of learning at Konya and other places that they had seen in their wanderings. Some of these mosques, especially at Brusa stand to this day. Attached to these mosques were *madrasahs* where free education was imparted. The curriculum was mostly of a religious nature as everywhere else in the Islamic or non-Islamic world except, perhaps, in China, where educational tests had been held for the selection of civil servants for a thousand years. Those boys who wanted to go in for higher studies were sent to Egypt. The school at Iznik became especially important because of the association of Shaikh Edebali, the father-in-law of Osman, with it. There were other learned savants besides. Names of such scholars as Dursun Faqih and Chanda-ali Kara Halil have come down in history. After the conquest of Constantinople in 1453 wonderful mosques and *madrasahs* were built in and around Constantinople. Sultan Selim I, the father of Sulaiman, built one at Adrianople and Sulaiman himself was responsible for the magnificent Sulaimania Mosque. To the *madrasahs* attached to these mosques flocked students from near and far and great teachers like Aksarayli Jamaluddin and Saaduddin Taftazani graced the staff. Taftazani's commentaries are used to this day. Under Sultan Mohammad Fatih, Mulla Khusrev distinguished himself by his books on Muslim Jurisprudence (Fiqh).

Cultural Activities. Science in the Ottoman lands was represented mostly by medicine. The first stone-built hospital was raised by Sultan Bayazid I in 1401. In the *madrasahs* attached to the great mosques, medicine was regularly taught. The fame of skilled surgeons, especially in the field of opthalmology reached Central Europe. Names like Altingizadeh, Kahwejizadeh Ahmad, Ali Ahmad Chelebi, and Vesim Abbas became famous for works on medicine. But the most valuable work done by the Turks was in historiography. They first wrote their annals in the Persian ornate style, popular in those days, but soon Turkish historians struck their own vein. Ashiq Pashazadeh of the reign of Bayazid II, and his contemporary, Neshri, in his *Jahan Numa* wrote simply, objectively, and with scientific accuracy, that is without eulogistic embroidery. The Turks also found their own style in architecture. Combining Byzantine and Persian-Seljuk styles, they raised structures which have elicited praise ever since from the best art critics of the world.

Conclusion. This brief account may be ended with a quotation from Julius Germanus's article on 'The Role of the Turks in Islam', in *Islamic Culture*, Vol. VII, 1933. Germanus says: 'The Turk was a soldier and administrator, a judge and guardian of law and order. His only riches consisted of real estate or the salary he drew for service. The Christian subjects took to the more profitable pursuits of trade and soon enriched themselves to such an extent as to arouse the jealousy of the Muslims, whose sons bled to death on the battlefield in the defence of the State. The Christians were exempt from military service and the heaviest burden was borne by the Muslim Turks and these Muslim Turks sustained their burden with a heroism, with a sincere obedience to the Word of God worthy of admiration. They were the bravest knights of Islam and perpetuated its culture, its taste in art and literature and its aspect of life, when no other Muslim race was able to withstand the onslaughts of Europe. They with their achievements have shown an example of endurance and will-power which if rightly understood and followed on the cultural path must inspire other Muslim peoples with self-consciousness and self-reliance'.

CHAPTER 11

THE LATER OTTOMANS

The Decline of the Ottomans. The rise and fall of Muslim powers tends to follow a general pattern. A vigorous people find a corner for themselves somewhere and expand. They gain in power in the first few reigns, then remain in a state of balance for another period and later lose their vigour, take to a life of ease, are influenced too much by the old order of things which they had overthrown, intermarry with the conquered races, lose their individuality and are overthrown. It happened in Spain and in Persia, it happened in India and it was happening to the Ottomans. A period of decline was about to set in. The Sultans were now mighty autocrats. There was no earthly power to check or restrain them. They had reached the limits of expansion and, as had happened to the Arabs in Spain, the Ottomans were confronted with newly risen nationalities. The Sultans were mostly the children of Christian wives or concubines and did not hold the early ideas of Muslim superiority which their forefathers had held. They had everything they wanted, therefore they left the affairs of state to either dominant Queen Mothers or strong Grand Viziers.

For a time, capable Grand Viziers pulled the Sultans out of trouble and confusion but after that there were no capable Grand Viziers left. The *Janissaries* began to get restive. Like all royal bodyguards they realized their importance and began to misuse it. For some time they held power in their own unruly hands and then a strong Sultan had to fight it out with them. In the struggle the Sultan was victorious, but he won only by destroying the *Janissaries* which left the Turkish military power weaker. The European nations began to rise. For a century the Ottomans fought them back with varying fortunes, but then Russia took upon herself to fight for the Christian nations which were subject to the Ottomans. This put the balance of power against the Turks; they began to lose and gradually they became weaker. They lost one province after another, till by the end of the eighteenth century they were a ghost of their former selves. Western Europe then began to call the Sultan the 'Sick Man of Europe'. This began the third phase of their power, which is the period of the Fall of the Turks.

Murad III (1574-1595). The Turks did not become weak suddenly. They were a mighty power when Murad III came to the throne. He was the eldest son of Selim II who recovered his naval power so dramatically after the disaster of Lepanto. Murad III was a serious young man and gave promise of becoming a great sultan, but he had two strong-minded women beside him; his mother, the Sultana Nur Banu, and his wife, Safiya, who was an Italian lady. These two ladies gave him no peace. They interfered constantly in state affairs and it gradually came to be known in European capitals that the Sultan was under the influence of the ladies of the harem. This encouraged the Europeans, who began thinking of ways and means of doing some damage to the Turks, whom they disliked more than they had disliked the other Muslim people who had pressed them hard in the past. They could not call up a Crusade or a Holy League this time, so, led by Venice, they persuaded the Safavid Shah to attack the empire. Shah Tahmasp sent his army across the border and war broke out, but he died soon afterwards. His son Muhammad Khudabanda was a weak king who could do little and the war became a leisurely affair. The Turks were still vigorous, so they came and attacked Persia from the Caucasian side and took Tiflis in 1577. In 1579 they built a great fortress at Kars. A few years later, in 1585, they took Tabriz. The war went on with no further major events and in 1590 the two powers concluded a peace in which the Turks gained Georgia, Azerbaijan, and Shirvan. Their borders now touched the Caspian Sea.

Austrian War—Muhammad III to Osman II (1595-1623).
The Turks had strengthened their position in southern Russia during this period, and the chiefs of lower Ukraine had become vassals of the Sultan. This annoyed the Austrian Emperor very much. A border war had been going on between Turkey and Austria for some years though peace had been declared in 1580, but after ten years a new war broke out in which Prince Sigismund Bathory of Transylvania joined the Emperor. The Turks were not as strong as they had been in the previous century, and the war lingered on. Meanwhile Murad III died and his son Prince Muhammad, the son of Queen Safiya, came to the throne. He was too much under his mother's influence to do anything remarkable, but he had enough strength of character to rise to the occasion at a critical moment in the Turko-Austrian War. The Austrians fell out with the Prince of Transylvania and a Hungarian nobleman, Stephen Bocskay, offered alliance to the Sultan. The Sultan promised him the Principality of Transylvania and he joined the Turks. Even then the combined Austro-Hungarian forces were very strong. It was only when they reached Varuna that pressure was put on Muhammad III, who had not so far resisted them, to take the field. He led the Turkish army, still a strong force when commanded well, and the enemy began to fall back. They surrendered the Turkish positions captured by them and retreated behind the Danube. The armies met at Kereoztes on 24 October 1596, in a battle which went on for three days and which, on the third day, ended in a great victory for the Turks. The enemy lost 30,000 soldiers on the field of battle. The war continued, but at last, in 1606, the Treaty of Zsitva-Torok was signed. The Austrians left east Hungary, but they ceased to pay tribute to the Sultan for the western half of Hungary. The Sultan was no longer the strong power he had been in Eastern Europe.

Internal Revolts. The Ottomans could perhaps have reasserted themselves in mid-Europe but internal revolts reduced their fighting strength. A *Janissary* general, Abdul Halim Kara Yaziji, revolted in upper Syria. He besieged the town of Edessa, and in order to appease him the governorship of Amorsia was offered to him. This encouraged him. He attacked the governors of Damascus in the south and Baghdad in the east and defeated them. He died in battle, but his brother carried on after him. The Sultan now tried to use tact. He sent for this new leader and when he and his chief followers were in Istanbul, he put pressure on them and sent them to fight the Austrians near Buda, which was being besieged by the Turks. The 'rebels' died fighting for their country, but the risings and revolts went on. The Kurd leader, Janbulad, governor of Klis near Aleppo, also revolted, so did Prince Fakhruddin the Druse leader in Lebanon. When the Sultan had settled his affairs in Eastern Europe he sent an army against Janbulad, who was defeated, but fled to Prince Fakhruddin who gave him shelter. The Druses, a fanatical sect, had the advantage of their native hills and resisted the Sultan's forces effectively. The other minor risings in Asia Minor were, however, put down.

The War with Persia. The Ottoman Empire was now on the decline. At the same time, both in central Europe on the western borders and in Persia on the eastern, strong powers had arisen. The Hapsburg Empire was getting stronger in Central Europe and the Safavids of Persia had now a great ruler in Shah Abbas, who reorganized his army and led them to victory against Tartar and Turk. He defeated the Turks at Lake Urmia and took Baghdad, Mosul and Diyar Bekr: he had already seized Tabriz, Shirvan, and Kars. Later he took Georgia and Azerbaijan from them. The Turks had been having things their own way with Persia so far and it was the turn of the Persians to hit back. From then on the Muslims of the Middle East fought against each other almost intermittently and were never united again. Political difference hardened into racial and religious hatreds and the age-old rivalry of Turan and Iran was spread from India to the ends of the Muslim world.

Murad IV (1623-1640). The Turko-Persian War flared up again after the death of Abbas the Great. A vigorous young Sultan, Murad IV, came to the throne. He did not like the idea of Baghdad being in Persian hands and gave orders for the invasion of Persia; but the *Janissaries*, the chief regiment of the Sultans, revolted. They had grown so powerful now and so uncontrolled that they refused to obey the orders of the Sultan. The young Sultan did not know what to do. He consulted his Grand Vizier, who advised him to take a strong line. But if the Sultan was to suppress these unruly troops he needed a loyal body to help him. Murad decided to raise such a body. He first raised new troops in Anatolia and with their help severely punished the leaders of the *Janissaries*. Then he stopped further recruitment of Christians to man the *Janissary* regiments. When the commanders of the *Janissaries* protested, he dismissed these commanders and disbanded the discontented regiments. He then reorganized the army and strengthened it. He led it into Persia and penetrated far into the country, taking Hamadan in 1630. A few years later he recaptured Erivan and Tabriz, and in 1638 retook Baghdad. Peace was declared, and a treaty was drawn up between the rival Muslim powers. According to its terms, Murad IV gave back Erivan to the Persians, but retained Baghdad.

Murad, the last strong Sultan. Murad IV was the last of the strong sultans. He asserted himself early, broke free from harem influences, took strong measures against the *Janissaries*, and re-established the power of the Ottomans in the East. He was strong, as his ancestors had been, and, though he did not rule long, he achieved much. He was the last of the sultans to take the command of his army in person. He was not as remarkable a monarch as many of his ancestors, but he made his name respected. He died in 1640, soon after the conclusion of his long war with Persia, and left behind him a strong army.

He had been assisted by his very capable Grand Vizier, Kara Mustafa, who continued in his office in the reign of Ibrahim, Murad's brother and successor, who came to the throne in 1640.

Kara Mustafa. Ibrahim was under the influence of his mother and his three wives, who all banded together to rule over him. Fortunately the Grand Vizier, Kara Mustafa, was an able administrator and a loyal servant of the state. He had helped Murad in reorganizing the army and the navy, and had rooted out corruption and incompetence in so doing. He had thus made a great many enemies among the *Janissaries*. Since Kara Mustafa had also introduced reforms in the system of taxation, he had raised enemies among the civilian officers too. When the strong hand of Murad IV was removed, the *Janissaries* and the civilians joined hands. They began working on the Queen Mother, the old Sultana, whom they won over. She persuaded her son, Ibrahim I, to put away Kara Mustafa. Ibrahim had little strength of character, so he agreed, and ordered the death of the Grand Vizier. Two years after Murad's death Kara Mustafa was killed.

The War with Venice (1645-1664). In 1645 another war started with Venice, a persistent rival and enemy of the Turks. The Venetians had joined every combination against the Ottomans and fought them for centuries. They were not as strong now as they had been, but neither were the Ottomans so dominant. The Turks had beaten the Venetians so often that they had no respect for them. In spite of the great reverse of Lepanto, the Turks were still a great power in the Mediterranean. The last stronghold of the Venetians was Crete, which lies in a very good position at the mouth of the Aegean Sea, and which guarded the commercial navy of Venice. The Turks who had captured almost all the islands of the Aegean, decided to conquer this island too. A Turkish fleet sailed for Crete in 1664 and made a landing. The large island was poorly garrisoned and the Turks met with little resistance, even when they came up to Candia, the capital. There the Turkish advance halted. The Turkish people believed that the failure to continue was due to poor leadership, perhaps to corruption. They felt that the Sultan was too much influenced by his harem, and that his lack of interest in the affairs of the country had prevented the army from taking Crete. Feelings began to run high and interested parties fanned these feelings. The result, in those days, was inevitable; there was a palace revolt and the Sultan was killed. No solution was found, however, for the problem of the Turkish reverses and lack of determined policy.

Harem Rule and its evils. Harem rule now became the chief factor in the administration and lasted a long time. Its worst feature was the sale of offices. Ranks and positions, commands and offices were sold by the Sultana and the group of intriguers at the court. Efficiency, honesty, and ability were not valued. Influence, bribery, and corruption ruled the day. Those who paid high prices for their offices repaid themselves at the expense of the people when they took charge of their appointments. They cared little for good administration or the welfare of the state. The group of influential people at the court who were chiefly to blame for all this were the officers of the *Janissaries*, because they stood behind the sellers of offices and other corrupt practices. They were still strong and were ruthless in their dealings. People were afraid of them. When any effort was made by an honest vizier or Sultan or statesman to dismiss these corrupt commanders or their subordinates the dismissed personnel became outlaws and formed into bands. They then roamed the countryside and set up strongholds of their own. Thus lawlessness began to increase, and slowly but surely the name of the Sultan began to lose its awe for the people.

The Koprulu Grand Vizier—Muhammad Koprulu (1656-1661). The Europeans watched the downward path of the Turks. They had their spies at Istanbul. Most Turkish nobles had Christian wives. The wives had Christian relatives and

European contacts. News of events did not therefore take long to travel. The eternal enemies of the Turks, the people of Venice, were the first to take advantage of this state of affairs. They began to push back the Turks from the Dalmatian coast on the eastern side of the Adriatic. Then they grew bolder; they sent a fleet into the Aegean. This fleet sailed right up to Paros near the Dardanelles, engaged the Turkish fleet there and defeated it. This alarmed everybody at the court. The Sultan (Muhammad IV, 1648-1687) was a minor. A strong leader was required. Fortunately for the Turks Muhammad Koprulu, an able statesman, was at the court. The post of Grand Vizier was offered to him, but he would not accept it unless he was given power to do what he thought was for the good of the Empire. The Sultan had to agree. Muhammad set about cleaning the court of corruption and intrigue, his measures were drastic and he stood no nonsense. When he found that the *Janissaries* were creating trouble, he seized the ringleaders and had them executed. If a court favourite stood up against him he had him killed. When he found the treasury empty he asked the rich nobles to 'lend' money to the state or took money from the Sultan's own treasury and said it was a loan. He was ruthless, but very efficient. Soon he took up the war with Venice. The Turkish Empire was very large and had great resources. It only needed a strong ruler and efficient administration. When Muhammad Koprulu took charge he found he could easily beat back the enemies of the Empire. He took the islands of Lemnos and Tenedos from the Venetians. In eastern Europe, George Rakoczy rose against the Sultan in Transylvania, but was defeated by the Turkish army. Muhammad's death in 1661, after five years as Grand Vizier was a great loss to the Empire.

Ahmad Koprulu (1661-1678). His son Ahmad Koprulu succeeded him as Grand Vizier. His father had put the administration into good shape, Ahmad followed his father's policy and used his brains. No very harsh measures were now needed. He was therefore tactful and firm; he cajoled the Sultan and outwitted his enemies. He was a fine diplomat and often used negotiation and even compromise to sort out the affairs of the Empire. What alarmed him, however, was the state of the Turkish army. The Turks, who had been considered unconquerable for three centuries, were finding that the Christians were fighting better and were better equipped. Moreover the European nations had so far fought the Turks separately. Now they began joining their forces, exchanging generals, and pooling their resources. The Turks were not the stern and fearless warriors of the days of the early sultans. Three centuries of conquest and ease had taken their toll. Persia had cut them off from Central Asia, their source of new recruits. The Europeans were making discoveries and new inventions which increased their power. Political alliances were opening new ways for them and they were finding that the Turk could be met and beaten.

The Great Siege of Vienna (1663). The first event of Ahmad Koprulu's Vizierate was the great siege of Vienna by the Turks, an expedition which was undertaken because the Hapsburg Emperor was causing trouble. George Rakoczy, Prince of Transylvania, had revolted against his Suzerain, the Sultan, and had been deposed. The Sultan had put Apafy in his place. This choice was not liked by the Hungarians, who appealed to the Emperor. This was a heaven-sent opportunity for the Emperor, who seized it eagerly. He refused to recognize Apafy. This meant that he refused to recognize the Sultan's suzerainty in Transylvania. The answer was war, and the Turks mobilized. On the European side, the Pope sent round his usual summons and most of the European powers responded. Even Louis XIV of France, who was himself an ally of the Sultan, asked his German allies to give 20,000 troops to the Austrian Emperor. The Turkish army moved to the north and carrying everything before it reached the gates of Vienna. The Emperor became afraid, accepted the offer of 20,000 German troops from Louis XIV, and even asked the King of Sweden to help. When the imperial general Montecucculi came against the Turks in the Battle of St. Gotthard on 1 August 1664, he had a united European army under him. It was a new Crusade, although it was no longer labelled as such. The Turks had not been prepared for such an array. They fought long and with their usual bravery, but they were outmatched and defeated. A peace for twenty years was now concluded between the Emperor and the Sultan. According to it the Sultan agreed to let Transylvania choose its own leader. This was the beginning of the slow decline of the Sultan's power. He lost no territory, but the blow to his prestige was severe.

War in Crete and Poland. The Turks now were continually at war on one front or another. The Europeans did not leave them alone for long. The Venetians had been pestering them in the Aegean Sea and the Turks had decided to take Crete. The island had been invaded. The Venetians had asked for help from France and Austria. A French fleet arrived with 7,000 troops, but the Turks were not dismayed. The island fell and the Cretans surrendered the capital in 1669 after a long siege. A treaty was signed after this, and Venice was permitted to have three fortified posts on the island. Three years later, a new war began. The Ukraine (now in the U.S.S.R.) was at that time a part of Poland. The Muslim Tartars of the Crimea and the Cossacks had raided it for centuries. In 1668, Doroshenko, the Cossack chieftain, who had so far been a vassal of the Polish king, accepted the overlordship of the Sultan. The Poles then began to raid Turkish lands. The Turks returned the attacks, and advanced as far as Lemberg in Little Poland. At this time a national hero of Poland, John Sobieski, came on the scene. He overthrew the weak Polish king and became King of Poland in 1674. He is known for his great campaigns against the Turks. He fought many battles, but was not always victorious. At first he conquered Podolia, in southern Ukraine and then, crossing the Dniester in 1676, he advanced into Galicia. But at Zuravna he was encircled by the Turkish forces and defeated. He had to sign a treaty with the Sultan, by which he surrendered Podolia as well as the Ukraine.

Kara Mustafa (1678)—War with Russia (1677-1681). A great misfortune now befell the Turkish Empire: Ahmad Koprulu died. An eminent administrator and a powerful force behind the throne, he had upheld the prestige of the Sultan. He was succeeded by his brother-in-law Kara Mustafa, an ambitious man, headstrong and self-willed, who made wrong alliances and brought new wars on the Empire. He made an alliance with Tokolli, the King of Hungary, against Emperor Leopold I. This brought on a war with Austria. In the north, the Cossacks, perhaps encouraged by Poland and Russia, started raiding Turkish lands. The Cossacks were Russian subjects and when the Turks punished the Cossacks, Russia intervened. There were no victories on either side, but Russia had the advantage in the few exchanges, so, when the Treaty of Radsin was signed, the Sultan had to surrender the Ukraine to Russia and give trading rights to the Cossacks in the Black Sea. This was a bitter concession because the Black Sea had been a Turkish sea for centuries.

War with Austria (1682-1689). War with Austria followed this war with Russia. It lasted eight years and was very expensive. It drained the Turkish Empire of men and money. New factors had come in. The early Sultans were no more, and Europe was reaping the fruits of her scientific discoveries and inventions. The opponents of the Turks, therefore, were better equipped and had larger resources. The Turks, on the other hand, were not advancing with the times. They had vigour in them yet, but that was all. Kara Mustafa led the Turkish army against Austria in 1683 and besieged Vienna. This was the last siege of Vienna by the Turks and was a severe attack. The Turks laid mines under the city's foundations and blew up part of the walls. The Austrians had a brave commander in Count von Stahremberg, and he was soon helped by Charles of Lorraine with an army from the west and John Sobieski from the north.

Again the Europeans were united against the Turks. The siege continued, but negotiations were at last begun, and an armistice was signed. The Sultan lost no territory because the Turks were still strong enough to inspire fear, but this was the last time that they advanced so far north. Even this treaty did not last long, as the Pope was not satisfied, and a new Holy League was formed. Venice was persuaded to join Austria, Russia, and Poland against the Sultan. The King of France, who was still an ally of the Sultan, persuaded the Poles to leave the League, but the Austrians invaded European Turkey, with a strong army, conquered Croatia in 1684 and advanced on Budapest in 1686. The Venetians invaded Morea (southern Greece), and the Russians besieged Azov in Crimea. The Turks had to fight on all these fronts. It was a colossal task which very few powers could stand. In 1687 the Turks fought the second Battle of Mohacs, but times had changed. Their fortune was on the wane and in this battle, in spite of brave resistance, Charles of Lorraine defeated the Turks. This defeat lost the Sultan the whole of Hungary. Panic spread: in Istanbul Muhammad IV was deposed and his brother Sulaiman III made Sultan, but luck did not turn. The Austrians continued to advance, taking Belgrade and then Vidin. There was now a revolution in the Vizierate. Kara Mustafa was dismissed and Mustafa Koprulu, the younger brother of Ahmad, was made Grand Vizier.

Mustafa Koprulu. Mustafa Koprulu succeeded in steadying Turkish affairs. He was a capable man and began putting things in order firmly. He made improvements everywhere. The finances of the empire became better, the army was strengthened and the morale of the troops went up. Soon they began to hit back. They drove the Austrians out of Bulgaria, recaptured Belgrade and regained Serbia and Transylvania. At the Battle of Salem Kemen (August 1691) Mustafa Koprulu defeated Louis of Baden and, though Mustafa died at this battle, the Turkish army pushed on. The Turks thus won back their lands in eastern Europe. The new sultan, Mustafa II

(1695-1703), was also an energetic ruler. He took command of the army himself and captured Temesvar, the capital of the Banat of Temesvar in Eastern Hungary.

The Heroic Fight of the Turks. This recovery of the Turks, however, was short-lived. It was the lull before the storm and the storm which now broke over the heads of the Turks raged for nearly a century. They recovered many times, but were beaten down again and again, in spite of the heroic fight that they put up. Faced with superior armies, better generals, coalitions and alliances, with almost the whole of Europe against them, they fought back and yielded, only to spring up again. Their final defeat was due not to lack of fighting quality, but to inner political weakness, old ideas, fear of change, poor adaptability, and corruption at the court.

Eugene of Savoy and the Treaty of Karlowitz (1699). At this time the Christians of Europe had a great general in Prince Eugene of Savoy, who was now sent to the eastern front. He fought many times against the Turks and never lost a battle. His first victory was at the Battle of Zenta in September 1697, where he routed the Turkish army and destroyed it. On the north-eastern front of the Turkish Empire, in the Crimea, Czar Peter the Great of Russia was besieging Azov, which he at last captured. The Turkish fortunes were at a low ebb. The European allies met and thrust the Treaty of Karlowitz (January 1699) on the Turks. By it Turkey lost half of her European Empire. Austria took Hungary, except for the Banat of Temesvar and also Transylvania, Croatia, and Slavonia. Venice was given Morea, Crete, and most of Dalmatia. Poland got Podolia. Russia retained Azov, although the Czar was not satisfied.

Czar Peter has a Set-back. Ten years later a dramatic incident occurred in Europe. Charles Gustavus of Sweden (Charles XII), annoyed by the grand schemes and manner of Peter the Great of Russia, invaded Russia, but after a few small victories was defeated by the Russians at the Battle of Poltava

(1709). Being a friend of the Sultan, he sought refuge in Turkey. There he began to advise the Sultan to make another attempt against the Russians and finally persuaded him to ask Russia to give back the lost territories of Charles XII. The Czar of course refused. The Turks who were smarting under the disgrace of the Treaty of Karlowitz began to mobilize. The Czar moved down with a large army, but the Turks met him in Bessarabia in the north and laid a trap for his forces. They surrounded him near the River Pruth and would have caught him, if he had not bribed the Vizier who commanded the forces, and escaped. This gave an advantage to the Sultan, and by the Treaty of the Pruth which followed in 1711, he regained Azov.

War with Venice and Austria. The eighteenth century was the worst period in the history of the Turks, during which they suffered defeat after defeat, and dishonour after dishonour. It opened with war with Venice and Austria caused by a revolt in Montenegro, which had been taken by the Venetians. This gave the Turks a chance and they attacked Venice and reconquered Morea and Crete, but this brought Austria against them, and with Austria came Prince Eugene of Savoy. He defeated the Turks again at the Battle of Peterwarden in 1716, conquered Temesvar, and a year later advanced farther and captured Belgrade. The Turks offered to negotiate and the war ended with another humiliating treaty—the Treaty of Passarowitz (July 1718). By it the Turks lost Temesvar and surrendered Northern Serbia and Little Wallachia.

Domestic Troubles. Their misfortunes abroad were matched by their domestic troubles within the empire. The Safavids had lost their throne to the Afghans, and Prince Tahmasp, the last Safavid, was making desperate attempts to regain his throne. He made his headquarters in the extreme north-west of Persia and raided the Turkish borders again and again. The Sultan began preparations for a campaign against Tahmasp, but his *Janissaries* broke into a revolt. They deposed him and put his nephew Mahmud I on the throne, but the anarchy spread and there was chaos at the court for two years. It was only when the *Janissaries* were rounded up and killed in thousands that order was restored.

War with Russia—Treaty of Belgrade. The Turks soon had other troubles, this time with Catherine, the Czarina of Russia, but in the war with Russia (1736-1739) they had the advantage. France, an ally of the Sultan, asked him to protest to Russia against her designs in Poland. It would have been wiser for the Turks to have remained neutral for some time to recover their strength, but they were good fighters and felt that the Europeans had been unfair in their continuous alliances against them. Moreover Russia was being offensively aggressive. The Russians were anxious to have an outlet in the Black Sea and once more started hostilities against the Turks in Azov. Both the Crimea and the Volga Basin had for centuries been the homes of the Tartars, who were Muslims. At one time the Tartars were a power in Russia. In the thirteenth to fifteenth centuries the Grand Duchy of Moscow was not a strong state and had for long paid tribute to the Tartars. It was only after the reign of Ivan the Terrible in the sixteenth century that Moscow had become independent. Ever since then the Russians had been pressing down on the Tartars. The Volga Basin had been lost to them, the Crimean Tartars had come under Turkish domination and it was the Sultan who fought the Russians in this region. So when the Russians attacked Azov again the Turks resisted strongly. Eugene of Savoy was now dead and the Turks found that they could defeat the Austrians easily in Eastern Europe. The war ended in the Treaty of Belgrade, by which the Turks got back Northern Serbia, Belgrade, and Azov.

The Derebays. The Turks were not, however, destined to enjoy peace even now. There was a great internal disturbance, this time in Asia Minor, where the descendants of military fief holders, now called the Lords of the Plains, or Derebays, began to set up small semi-independent principalities of their own, refusing to pay revenue or send levies to the Sultan when asked to do so. This was a recurring disease of the Muslim body politic. When the centre weakened, the outlying provinces or strong governors became independent till a new central power rose to weld all the parts into one empire again. The rule by one strong man never gave the people a chance to think collectively of a state to which they owed loyalty. The democratic idea that sovereignty rests in the people was unknown. The empire was strong when the Sultan was strong and weakened with weak rulers. Wars with Persia, which extended over centuries, sapped the strength both of Turkey and of Persia. These wars were the result of ancient rivalries between Tartars and Persians or differences between Sunnis and Shiites, but the result was that neither country benefited by these wars; they exhausted both.

Catherine of Russia. The Europeans became involved in two wars at this time, the War of the Austrian Succession and the Seven Years War. These wars were bitterly fought, and gave Turkey a chance to recover. Fortunately, she had a capable Sultan, Mustafa III and a very capable Grand Vizier, Raghib Pasha. Raghib Pasha made strenuous efforts during his vizierate, which lasted seven years (1757-1763), to improve the finances of the Empire, and to reorganize the army; he also had time to subdue the Derebays who had created unrest in Anatolia. This peace, however, did not last long. It was disturbed by the Russians and their terrible Czarina, Catherine the Great. She began by invading Poland. The Poles fought back, but were outmatched and defeated again and again. Many of them fled into the Turkish Empire and in pursuing the Poles the Russians raided the Turkish borders. The Sultan hesitated to go to war as he was not yet strong enough, but France now prevailed upon the Sultan to commit a major political blunder; to declare war on Russia. The Czarina acted as if she was waiting only for this chance. She moved her armies into Moldavia and Wallachia. She then sent her fleet, in which she had many British officers, from the Baltic to the Aegean. The Turkish navy was no match for such a fleet, and in the Battle of Chesme, in 1770, the Turkish fleet was defeated. The Russians capped this by conquering the Crimea, and continued to move farther into the Turkish Empire. They would not have stopped, but a revolt occurred in Russia in 1773 called the Revolt of Pugachev. This made the Czarina call a halt to her armies and the treaty, which was signed at Kuchuk Kainarji (1774), was in Russia's favour. By it, Turkey lost the districts of Kinburn, Yenikale, and Kertch in the Crimea. The Tartars of the Crimea were encouraged to become independent though they were told that they could still continue to revere the Sultan as a Caliph. Moldavia and Wallachia were returned to Turkey, but Russia was accepted as the Protector of the Christians in Eastern Europe. She insisted that she should be permitted to build a church in Galata, the part of Istanbul where the Christians lived.

Alliance of Austria and Russia (1781). There was now a new understanding between Russia and Austria. They agreed to do all in their power to drive the Turks out of Eastern Europe, to restore the medieval Greek Empire of Byzantium and, when liberated, the Greeks were to have as their Emperor Catherine's own grandson, Constantine. The Austrians were to have the western half of the Balkans. Working on this understanding, Catherine annexed the whole of the Crimea in 1783, but was still not satisfied and conquered Georgia in the Caucasus too. When Turkey rose to defend her frontiers, Austria joined Russia. The Russian generals Potemkin and Suvarov marched into Moldavia and Wallachia and annexed them. The Turks were not yet fully recovered after their recent wars and their internal troubles over the Derebays, and the Russians easily fought their way to the Danube. The Turks fought well but with little success. They no longer had the strength to fight the Russian army successfully. At last, in 1791, Prussia, fearing again that Russia would become too powerful in Eastern

Europe if unchecked, moved Austria to stop the war, and the Treaty of Sistova was signed. Turkey was now at the mercy of the European powers, but because of mutual jealousies among them she had a better deal than she expected. Belgrade was given back to Turkey in return for a portion of Bosnia which Austria accepted. A year later (1792) Russia was persuaded to sign the Treaty of Jassy. As a result of these negotiations, Russia took Oczakov in the Crimea and returned Moldavia, Bessarabia, and Wallachia to Turkey. The river Dneister was declared to be the boundary. This was the position at the end of the eighteenth century.

The Turkish Government—The Sultan-Caliph. The administrative structure of the empire must now be considered, and the achievements of the Turks in the two hundred years of their history discussed in this chapter must be determined. The Sultan was by now known also as the Caliph of Islam and was, as such, the religious head of the Muslims, although not of all Muslims. Originally the Osmanlis were merely chieftains. Orkhan had called himself Amir and it was Bayazid I who had chosen to be called Sultan. Muhammad Fatih was styled Sultan of the Worlds (*Sultan ul-Barrain wal-Bahrain*). It was only after Selim I had conquered Egypt that the mantle of the Prophet, hitherto worn by both the lines of the Abbasid Caliphs, came to Constantinople. But the actual Caliphate was assumed by the Sultans only in the eighteenth century when they found their power going and their hold on the people weakening. The Persians never acknowledged them as such, as they believed that the Caliphate could only descend through the House of Ali; the Indian Muslims were followers by courtesy only.

Organization of the Empire. The Sultan-Caliph, being the supreme, temporal and spiritual head of the empire, delegated many of his powers to others. As early as the days of Muhammad II, the *Qanunnama* laid down the duties and responsibilities of the higher officials of the state. The Grand Vizier came to be the *Naib* or the Deputy of the Sultan. In the days of the weaker sultans he was the head of the state. The Grand Vizier had sessions with the heads of departments almost every day. This council of his functioned very much as a cabinet functions today, with the difference that the ministers were appointed by the Sultan and were responsible to him and were not the representatives of the people as is the system in most of the democratic countries today. The empire was divided into three viceroyalties; Rumelia, Anadolu, and Africa, which were, as in the days of the earlier Ottomans, under the command of the Beylerbeys.

The Civil Service. The Shariah prevailed in the country, though from the beginning the Osmanlis had their own common law. The Turks trained their civil servants very carefully and had a systematic course of instruction for them extending over years. There were thousands of students attending such schools, and the first course lasted seven years. A successful candidate was called *Danishmand*. He could now join any profession he liked: he could be a teacher or a magistrate, but, if he wanted to become a Junior Mullah, he had to take the advanced course, which lasted another seven years. For higher posts there was always an interview, and even higher standards.

Religious Orders. Religious life was well organized too. In few Muslim countries have the religious orders had such popularity as in Turkey. Three or four orders especially were very powerful. They were purely spiritual in character and did not at first interfere in politics. The three orders most popular were, first the Mevleviya Order, established by Maulana Jalaluddin Rumi, the famous mystic poet. This order came to have a ritual of dancing in ecstasy; its followers were called the 'dancing *dervishes*'. The second order was the Bektashiya Order which had some common features with both the

Christians and the Shiites. The Bektashis did not believe in formal worship and their mystics did not always follow the ritual of Islam. This order found great favour among the *Janissaries*. The third order was the Naqshbandiya Order of which something has been said earlier. This order made a great impression in India in the sixteenth century and gave rise to such great persons as Mujadad Alf Sani and Shah Wali-Ullah. Gradually the religious orders in Turkey began to get worldly, and the heads of the orders began to acquire property and become corrupt. Thus the orders which in the beginning helped to give guidance to the social and moral life of the Turks contributed in the end to their decline and downfall.

Turkish Culture. Turkish traditions have mostly been military and the Turks have always been a practical people. They were good builders, good law-givers, and good organizers. Politically they organized their society on the *millat* system, under which they interfered very little in the cultural, social, or religious life of the many communities in their empire. They gave them all, whether Bulgars, Serbs, Armenians, or Druses, their own laws. If the Turks had moved with the times they would have kept their empire together for this reason alone. In literary culture they followed Arabic and Persian patterns, mostly Persian. Arabic dominated their law and Persian their literature for centuries. Gradually their own forms began to emerge. They were encouraged in this by far-sighted Sultans. At first all Turkish poetry was written in the form and style of Persian poetry and it took the Turks a long time to break with this tradition. In prose they formed a new style fairly early. In 1679 Evliya Chelebi wrote his *Chronicles of a Traveller*. It was an original work, based on his travels and campaigns in Europe. In it he gives a good description of the social and economic conditions of the empire. The finest poem was one written by Shaikh Ghalib (1757-1790), called *Husn-o-Ishq* (Beauty and Love). It is an allegory of divine love and was written by the then head of the Mevleviya Order. Among historians of this period the chief names are those of Sa'duddin, who wrote *Taqut-i-Twarikh*, 'Crown of Histories', in the seventeenth century, and Naima who wrote his *Tarikh* in many volumes.

CHAPTER 12

THE MOGHULS IN INDIA

Minor Kingdoms of India. By the end of the fifteenth century there were many Muslim kingdoms in India, of which the Lodhi Sultanate of Delhi was the strongest. In the Deccan, the great Bahmani kingdom, after a two-century struggle with Vijayanagar, was divided into five small kingdoms which had vigorous lives of their own. These kingdoms, especially those of Golconda and Bijapur, kept the Muslim faith and preserved Islamic culture for two centuries more. A small kingdom in Kabul early in the sixteenth century was, however, soon to become a great empire. The man who was to accomplish this was Sultan Zahiruddin Babar who established the Moghul civilization which flourished in India till the middle of the nineteenth century and is seeking a revival today in Pakistan with new Western influences lending it vigour and scope.

Zahiruddin Babar (1482-1530). Babar was a descendant of Amir Timur and had inherited the small Timurid kingdom of Ferghana in Central Asia. When he came to the throne he had only one ambition, shared by all Timurid princes, namely to become master of Samarqand. In pursuit of this ambition he fought many battles and lost his kingdom many times. In 1504 he ventured into what is now called Afghanistan and conquered Kabul. In 1505 he entered India by the Khyber Pass, then turned south to Kohat. From there he crossed over to Dera Ghazi Khan and then to Tarbila in Multan. It was only a raid, but it gave him an idea of the country.

Babar's other Ventures. Then an event occurred in the west which kept him occupied for some years. The Timurid princes of Trans-Oxiania had a terrible enemy in the Uzbeg Turks of the north-east and Babar had suffered at their hands as had many other princes. Their present leader Shaybani Khan led the Uzbegs far, and conquering Central Asia they crossed into Khorasan. The Timurids had not been able to fight the Uzbegs, but Ismail, the new Safavid Shah, defeated them. The Timurid princes recovered their principalities and Babar's cousin, Mirza Haidar, did the same for Babar's kingdom of Ferghana. Babar now went north with his army, captured Bokhara and Samarqand and at last sat on the throne of his great ancestor, Amir Timur. This glory did not last long; a few years later the Uzbegs rose again under a new leader, Ubaidullah Khan, an uncle of Shaybani Khan. Babar lost Ferghana again, and even his cherished Samarqand. He returned to Kabul and his other dream, the conquest of India.

First Clash with Lodhis (1523). In 1519 he crossed the Khyber Pass again and conquered Bajaur where lived the tribe of Yusuf Zais. He also crossed the Indus and annexed Bhera. Alam Khan the uncle of Sultan Ibrahim Lodhi of Delhi, joined him, and some other nobles came to him, asking for Babar's help to overthrow Ibrahim. Babar also received messages from Rana Sanga, the Rajput ruler of Mewar. When Sultan Ibrahim heard of this conspiracy he sent an army under General Bahar Khan to Lahore. Babar met the army and defeated it, and to the surprise of the Indian princes he annexed Lahore and captured Dipalpur. Alam Khan now offered the kingdom of Lahore to Babar in return for help to overthrow Ibrahim Lodhi. Babar agreed and gave a battalion of horse and two capable generals to Alam. He himself went back to Kabul, as the Uzbegs were threatening his northern borders. Alam Khan marched down and besieged Delhi, but Ibrahim Lodhi easily dispersed Alam Khan's army.

First Battle of Panipat (1526). This repulse did not please Babar. He had finished with the Uzbegs and made ready to deal a blow at Ibrahim Lodhi himself. He marched with an army from Lahore early in 1526 and met the combined Afghan army, led by Ibrahim, on the field of Panipat. Here, on 21 April, the famous First Battle of Panipat was fought. It was the new

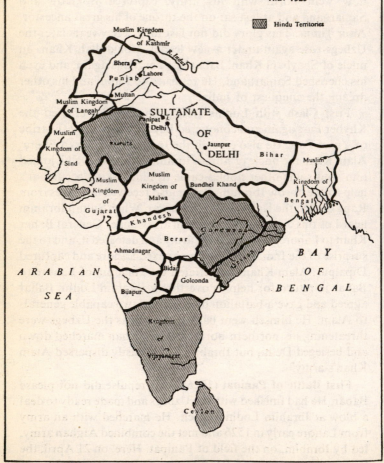

INDIA ON THE EVE OF
BABAR'S INVASION
A.D. 1525

⫽⫽⫽ Hindu Territories

Muslim Kingdom
of Kashmir

R. Indus

Bhera
Lahore
Punjab
Multan

Muslim Kingdom
of Langah

SULTANATE

Panipat
Delhi

RAJPUTS

OF

Muslim
Kingdom of
Sind

DELHI

Jaunpur

Bihar

Muslim
Kingdom of
Bengal

Muslim
Kingdom
of
Gujarat

Muslim
Kingdom of
Malwa

Bundhel Khand

Khandesh

Berar

Gondwana

Orissa

BAY

Ahmadnagar

Bidar

OF

ARABIAN

Bijapur

Golconda

BENGAL

SEA

Kingdom
of
Vijayanagar

Ceylon

world fighting the old. Babar had guns with him; the Sultan had only war elephants. Babar's generalship and his superior armaments won the field and Ibrahim died fighting. Babar moved down to the capital immediately and occupied it; he also captured Agra. Rana Sanga now assembled the entire Rajput strength of the region and accompanied by the Rajas moved towards Babar. It was a huge army and Babar found that his soldiers were showing signs of panic. He had a dramatic personality and decided to make a gesture. He was fond of drink, but he broke all his cups and vessels, poured out all his wine and vowed never to drink again. He declared that God would accept this sacrifice and help their cause. His soldiers took heart, and when the armies met at Khanua on 16 March 1527, the Moghuls fought with a fearless bravery that broke the ranks of the valiant Rajputs. Rana Sanga died fighting and his Rajputs were defeated. This was a decisive victory. It made Babar King of Central India, as he had already conquered the Doab. He next went east, met the combined armies of the Afghans near Patna and inflicted a severe defeat on them. In three years Babar became master of a vast area; the Rajputs being beaten as well as the Afghans. Both of them rose again, the Afghans in the next reign and the Rajputs a little later, but by then the Moghuls had established themselves. They stayed as a major power in India for two hundred years and as a dwindling one for another century, during which period they built up a civilization which made a mark in the world.

Babar's Character. Babar died a year later at the age of forty-eight, but he had been a ruler of one kingdom or another for more than thirty years. Into these years he had packed more adventure, more enjoyment, more keen observation, and more achievement than many people thrice his age. He was an unusual man. Strong in mind and body, he impressed himself on everybody he met. He left a record of his adventures and his views in his memoirs, which for freshness, frankness, and shrewdness of observation have not been surpassed.

Humayun. He was succeeded in 1530 by his eldest son Humayun who ruled for ten years. This prince, though brave, active, and a good general, inherited, besides a freshly won empire, a host of troubles. There were the troublesome Afghan nobles on the one side, the simmering Rajputs on the other and, worst of all, his three treacherous brothers, who for meanness and disloyalty have seldom been equalled. He had confirmed the appointments of his brothers; of Kamran, as governor of Kabul and Kandahar and later even of the Punjab. This was an unwise decision because it cut off Humayun from his recruiting grounds. Another brother, Askari, was governor of Sambhal; a third, Hindal, of Alwar. In return the brothers hindered him at every step and betrayed him in his hour of need.

Humayun's Campaigns. His downfall was due to the opposition of the Afghans. Mahmud Lodhi, a prince of the House of the Lodhis, raised the banner of revolt in Bihar, which was a stronghold of the Afghans. In 1532 he marched with his army to the west and captured Jaunpur. Humayun met him near Lucknow and defeated his Afghans in the Battle of Dadrah. One of the rebel Afghan leaders was Sher Khan of Chunar. So Humayun went to Chunar and laid siege to it. But Sher Khan was a clever man. Seeing that he was not yet strong enough to fight, he submitted and offered the services of his son Qutub Khan to Humayun with a following of 500 horsemen. Humayun accepted the offer and withdrew. Another Lodhi claimant Alam Khan, the uncle of Ibrahim, an old intriguer, had gone to Gujarat and had sought refuge at the court of Sultan Bahadur Shah of Gujarat. Also at Bahadur Shah's court was Muhammad Zaman Mirza, a brother-in-law of Humayun, who was intriguing against the emperor. Humayun demanded the surrender of both these persons from Bahadur Shah, but that monarch considered it dishonourable to give up people who had sought shelter with him. So Humayun marched west with his army and when he reached Gujarat he found Bahadur Shah fighting the Rajputs at Chittor. He waited for Bahadur Shah to finish his *ghazwah* against the non-Muslims before attacking him. Bahadur Shah was no match for the Moghul army and Humayun conquered in this campaign both the western kingdoms—Malwa and Gujarat. He made his brother, Askari, Viceroy of Gujarat and himself stayed in Malwa to put things in order. It did not take him long, but even this short time was enough for the Afghans in Bihar to consolidate their position. The time spent in the west cost Humayun his empire.

Sher Khan. The Afghans rose under Sher Khan. A brilliant man in every way, Sher Khan had come up by personal effort, great determination and unusual ability. His father Hasan Khan had been a *jagirdar* in the kingdom of Jaunpur, but Sher Khan had become a counsellor of the ruler of Bihar and later his Deputy Governor and the guardian of the young king. In a few years he had become the most powerful man in the kingdom, had married the Lady of Chunar and made the fortress of Chunar a real stronghold. By defeating the Lohani Afghans of Bihar who had sought aid from Mahmud Shah, the king of Bengal, Sher Khan now became paramount in Bihar. So he took the throne and assumed the title of Sher Shah Suri. He also invaded Bengal where Mahmud Shah was taken unawares and, finding himself no match for Sher Shah, surrendered considerable territory to him.

Humayun and Sher Shah. It was at this stage that Humayun decided to take action and march against Sher Shah. He stopped on the way to besiege Chunar, but Sher Shah was away in Bengal. Humayun followed him. Sher Shah easily eluded him and when the Moghul Emperor reached Gaur, the capital of Bengal, Sher Shah made a swift counter-march and moved west with his army and occupied Jaunpur. Meanwhile the rains came in Bengal and Humayun's army was caught. Thousands fell ill. Humayun made a great effort, pulled together what he could and marched back in pursuit of Sher Shah. The two forces met at Chaunsa in June 1539. Sher Shah's army was fresh and he easily defeated Humayun's exhausted forces, although Humayun escaped to Delhi. Here he asked help from his brothers, but found that none of his brothers was prepared to give him any aid. Humayun was in desperate straits. He collected what forces he could and met Sher Shah for the last time near Bilgram. He had no army and Sher Shah defeated him easily. Humayun fled first to Agra, but finding no hope of reinforcements there, went to Lahore. Sher Shah occupied Agra and Delhi and sent a small army after Humayun. In Lahore, Humayun found no help either. His brother Kamran refused to do anything and so Humayun left for Multan, then for Sind, with a small following.

Humayun in Exile. History has been unkind to Humayun. It is true that he had neither the resolution nor the high-mindedness of Babar nor the brilliance of Sher Shah, but he was certainly no dreamer. He had determination and a high purpose of his own and although he became an exile he did not give up. While in Sind in 1541, he married Hamida Bano, the daughter of Shaikh Ali Akbar Jami and his young wife joined him in his wanderings. Next year a son, Akbar, was born to them at Amarkot, a small town in Upper Sind. After a few months Humayun left with his dwindled escort for Kandahar where his brother Askari was the ruler. Askari waylaid him and captured Prince Akbar, Humayun escaping with his young wife. He left for Herat, and from there went to the court of Shah Tahmasp whose father, Shah Ismail, had been a great friend of Babar. Humayun sought aid from him and Shah Tahmasp, taking a little time to consider, decided to help him with 14,000 horsemen. By mid 1545, therefore, Humayun was back in Afghanistan. He now laid siege to Kandahar and captured it. Even then he was kind to his treacherous brother Askari, perhaps because he had treated the baby prince well. From Kandahar, Humayun marched to Kabul which he captured. Kamran, who came up with an army, was defeated and so within five years of his defeat at Bilgram at the hands of

Sher Shah, Humayun was master of Afghanistan, the country, from where, twenty years before, Babar had left for India. Humayun continued to have trouble with his brothers and his fortunes varied, but he gradually overcame them. He forced Askari to leave for Mecca on a pilgrimage and Askari died on the way. Hindal died in a skirmish in 1551. Kamran fled to the Punjab, but was captured on the way and brought before Humayun, who ordered his eyes to be put out. He too was despatched on a Hajj and died in Mecca a few years later. Humayun was now free to turn his mind to the reconquest of India.

Sher Shah Suri (1540-1545). In India, meanwhile, Sher Shah Suri had done remarkable things. From Bengal in the east to the Indus on the north-west, the entire area acknowledged him, in fear and respect, as its Emperor. When the Ghakkars of north-west Punjab revolted he marched swiftly against them and effectively defeated them. He reconquered Malwa and taught a lesson to Raja Puran Mal of Chanderi for dishonouring Muslim women, which made even the Rajputs afraid. Later, when Rana Maldev, the ruler of Mewar and head of the Rajput confederacy, began to extend his power at the expense of the neighbouring states, Sher Shah marched against him too. He met the Rajput hosts near Ajmer. The Rajputs had a larger army and fought with reckless bravery, but Sher Shah was a better general. Their ranks broke and fled. It was a great victory and the Rajputs were subdued for a generation.

Sher Shah's Achievements. Sher Shah did not live long. He ruled for only five years, but into these five years he crowded such work and such administrative measures that he has been acknowledged as a very remarkable monarch by every historian who has written about this period. A great general and a fine strategist, Sher Shah never lost a battle. But it was as an administrator that he really shone. He divided the empire into *sarkars* and *parganas*, and organized an efficient civil service. He made periodical transfers of his officers so that the officials should not become lazy and their work stale. He himself checked the work of all the departments at the centre. His revenue system was a wonderful achievement. He had the land properly measured, and fixed the land revenue direct with the cultivators. It was this system which was later taken up and developed by Raja Todar Mal, the revenue minister of Emperor Akbar. Sher Shah built roads and caravanserais; the great trunk road from the Indus to Eastern Bengal was his work. He organized the police system and made each village headman responsible for law and order in his area. Sher Shah was a just ruler and was respected by Muslims and Hindus alike.

Humayun's Return. Sher Shah was succeeded by his son, Salim who continued to rule on the lines laid down by Sher Shah. The empire remained settled during his reign of nine years and nobody disturbed him. Humayun was meanwhile building up his strength at Kabul. His time came when Salim Shah died, as the next Sur monarch was not a capable man. The Moghul army marched on Lahore in February 1555. Humayun defeated the Sur army near Sirhind and captured Delhi. He was proclaimed Emperor of India again. He had been away fifteen years. Humayun, however, died within the year, when his son Akbar was only thirteen years old.

Bairam Khan—Second Battle of Panipat (1556). He left as guardian of the young prince his trusted general Bairam Khan. Akbar himself was away in the Punjab so Bairam Khan hurried to him and crowned him, in a small village, called Kalanaur, now in Gurdaspur District, East Punjab. Bairam Khan may have crowned Akbar, but there was as yet no empire. Adil Shah Suri, the last Sur King of India, ruled in Central India and other Sur princes held Bihar and Bengal. Sind and Multan had broken away. Hemu, the chief minister of Adil Shah, a mean and ambitious man, moved north with the Sur army, occupied Agra and marched to Delhi. The Moghul governor of Delhi, Tardi Beg, came out to meet him, but was defeated. Hemu marched on Delhi and, forgetting his loyalty to Adil Shah Suri, had himself crowned King of India as Raja Vikramjit. Hearing that Bairam Khan was advancing, Hemu marched north, at the head of a formidable army. The two forces met on the battlefield of Panipat on 5 November 1556 and the Second Battle of Panipat was fought. Bairam Khan defeated Hemu, who was killed in the fight, and reoccupied Delhi and Agra where he crowned Akbar as emperor again.

Akbar (1556-1605). There was still much work to be done and Bairam Khan set out to do it. Gwalior and Ajmer in the west and Jaunpur in the east were annexed by 1560. Bairam Khan was not only the guardian of Akbar in these years, he was also the Regent. He was head of the army and also of the civil administration. He was kept so busy that he had to neglect Akbar, for whom he found a good tutor, Mir Abdul Latif. But Akbar was not interested in studies and learned little. All he acquired from his tutor was a very liberal attitude towards all religions. He was already married and surrounded by many strong-minded ladies. His mother, the Empress Hamida Bano, was one, and his foster-mother Maham Anga, a lady of very determined views, another. Akbar grew up into a self-willed young man and learned all the manly skills; he could shoot, ride, fence, and hunt; he loved good company and liked intelligent talk. The court was dominated outside by the Chief Mufti and the Shaikh ul Islam who pressed orthodox views on him. His companions told him Bairam Khan was becoming too strong. Maham Anga openly said that Akbar was a weakling and declared that he was unfit for his office if he could not reduce Bairam Khan's power.

Akbar and Bairam Khan. Akbar was only eighteen when he was persuaded to dismiss Bairam Khan. He wrote to Bairam and proposed that as he was old and tired and needed rest, he should go to Mecca. Bairam Khan was astounded, but he was a very loyal man so he submitted. Unfortunately Akbar was also persuaded to send Pir Muhammad, a personal enemy of Bairam Khan, as his escort. This made Bairam Khan suspicious and he revolted. He went to the Punjab and raised an army, but had no time or resources to raise a large one. Akbar defeated him in a battle near Jullandur. He was brought before Akbar as a prisoner, but Akbar remembered Bairam Khan's services and his loyalty to Humayun. He forgave him, gave him money and another escort and sent him away to Mecca. An old Afghan soldier joined his caravan and one night entered his tent and stabbed him. Bairam Khan's widow and his small son, Abdul Rahim, were sent back to Delhi where Akbar brought up young Abdul Rahim himself, and, when he grew up, made him a noble of his realm. Later he made him *Khan-i-Khanan*, a Grand Noble.

Akbar Becomes Independent. After Bairam Khan, Maham Anga tried to control Akbar, but her influence did not last, nor did that of her son Adham Khan. She even joined with the *Sadr-us-Sadoor*, Shaikh Abdul Nabi, but by this time Akbar had grown up. All that the Ulema of the court and Maham Anga's party succeeded in doing was to make Akbar suspicious of the Ulema. He began to doubt the loyalty of his so-called well-wishers and he lost reverence for the Shaikhs and the Maulanas who wanted to use him for their own ends. Adham Khan, who had bungled an expedition in Malwa, was recalled. He was a foolish man and banked too much on his mother's influence. One day he went too far, Akbar became angry and had him killed. This broke Maham Anga's heart and she died.

Akbar's reign. Akbar was now independent, perhaps too independent. He began to think for himself, both religiously and politically. He found that on the one hand the Ulema were so narrow-minded that they could tolerate no difference of opinion, and on the other every reign had trouble from the Rajputs. They had fought his grandfather Babar, under Rana Sanga, they had fought Sher Shah under Maldev. They were now becoming powerful again. There were a number of smaller Muslim kingdoms in the east and south who combined in one group or another to fight the centre. He decided to work out a policy of his own. He would first show all of them, the Ulema, the Muslim rulers of the border kingdoms and the Rajputs, that he was stronger than they, that he was master. He would then reduce their power. He followed this policy throughout his reign. He defeated the Rajputs in a series of campaigns. Jaipur submitted in 1562. Akbar married the daughter of the ruler, and made her father and brothers nobles at the court. He conquered Bikaner and Jaisselmer and married the daughters of these Rajput princes also. Only one Raja stood out, Rana Partap, the son of the Rana of Udaipur in Mewar. He fought on for a number of years, but was defeated at Haldighat in 1576 and died in exile. All Rajputana was by now allied to Akbar and he had also conquered Bengal. His half-brother, Mirza Muhammad Hakim, who had been Governor of Kabul, had revolted, but had been defeated. Akbar conquered the flourishing kingdom of Gujarat, and annexed Khandesh, the small Muslim kingdom between the Narbuda and Tapti. It contained the famous fort of Asirgarh, which was called the Gateway to the South. He now sent Abdul Rahim, the son of Bairam Khan, with an army against Ahmadnagar, which was under the regency of a very determined lady, Princess Chand Bibi. Neither Abdul Rahim nor his fellow commander Prince Murad made much headway against her. A few years later when Chand Bibi had retired from politics, the Moghul forces succeeded in defeating the Ahmadnagar forces at Supa in 1597, and the capital was stormed in 1600. The kingdom became a Moghul dependency. Akbar had succeeded in two of his three main objects. He had long since become the undisputed and paramount power in Upper India. The Rajputs were allied to him and his family by marriage. Most of their rulers were Nobles and some even Grand Nobles of the Realm. The border kingdoms had all been annexed. Only three kingdoms of the Deccan remained, and they took another hundred years to surrender, the last one falling in the reign of Akbar's great-grandson Aurangzeb.

Akbar's Religious Reforms. Akbar's third object was to reduce the power of the bigoted Ulema. For this purpose he organized weekly debates between leaders of various religions and various religious denominations in the *Ibadat Khana* that he had built for the purpose. Here Sunnis, Shiites, Roman Catholics, Protestants, Jains, Buddhists, Brahmins, Zoroastrians and philosophers met in long wordy combats, each tearing the arguments of the others to pieces. Akbar took part in these debates himself. When he found that the debaters showed neither sobriety in argument nor moderation in debate, and every creed had certain indefensible practices and beliefs, each party being bigoted in the extreme, he lost faith in them all. Or it might be said that he discovered that there was truth in all religions. Unfortunately for Islam, the Muslims who took part in these debates were very rigid in their outlook and narrow in their views. So Akbar now began to think of a creed which could contain the best elements of all the religions he knew. Perhaps he was encouraged in this extra-liberal notion by a learned man, Shaikh Mubarak, who had joined the court with two gifted sons Faizi and Abul Fazl. In any case, Akbar was self-willed enough to propound a new doctrine called Dini-i-Ilahi, of which he called himself the Head. Only a few courtiers accepted the new faith and only one Hindu, Raja Birbal. Most of the powerful nobles excused themselves. Gradually the faith became unpopular, and the idea was dropped by Akbar. Only one relic of this faith remained. People continued to prostrate themselves before the Emperor.

Results of Akbar's Policy. It has been debated whether Akbar ever lost faith in Islam. It is true that he was not a strict Muslim and that he tolerated many Hindu customs and practices which may have been due to his political policy, but he never denied the main articles of Islam and he died a Muslim (though some have doubted this). His political policy, which aimed at reconciliation of the Hindus and was very popular in his day, resulted in encouraging the Hindus and discouraging, even suppressing, the Muslims. The Hindus would not let the Muslims build any new mosques in their areas, slaughter cows or eat anything on the days when they kept fasts; they themselves ate openly during Ramadan. The Sikhs and the Rajputs gained power and proved to be great obstacles in the way of Akbar's successors. His only lasting reforms were the land reforms which were derived from Sher Shah's revenue system, elaborated by Raja Todar Mal and his Muslim colleagues.

Akbar's Character. Akbar was a wise ruler in other ways. He built up the Moghul Empire on firm foundations and encouraged the arts of music, dancing, painting, architecture, and poetry as few sovereigns have done. He was a brave man, famous for his love of the chase and of personal combat, a good general and a good judge of military commanders. His understanding of human problems was exceptional and the awe he inspired in people was remarkable. Though not learned, he surrounded himself with brilliant men and took great interest in the affairs of the state. He was cool in judgement and just in his decisions and his failings were due to his idea that the Hindus and Muslims could mix and become one people. He forgot that both religions are very exclusive and there is nothing in common between them. He failed to realize the liberal and rational principles on which Islam is built and thought he could take liberties with people's faith. In so doing he set in motion a train of ideas, which, a few generations later, overthrew the empire which he had so carefully planned.

Jehangir (1605-1627). Akbar was succeeded in 1605 by his son Prince Salim, who took the title of Nuruddin Jehangir. He had the support of the orthodox party and in the first few years of his reign he tried to uphold the honour of Islam, to maintain justice and to extend the boundaries of the empire. Early in his reign he had trouble with the Sikhs, whose Guru helped a rebel prince named Khusro. Jehangir put down the rebellion and punished the Sikhs, but they made it a religious cause and became hostile to the Muslims. From then on they continually rebelled against the Moghuls.

Nur Jehan. In 1611 Jehangir married a lady named Mehr un-Nisa (Nur Jehan), the widow of a Persian nobleman called Sher Afgan, who had a jagir near Burdwan. Sher Afgan had died in a rising which had taken place in 1607 and Mehr un-Nisa and her baby daughter had been sent to Delhi as royal wards. Four years after her return she attracted Jehangir's attention and he married her. She was a beautiful girl of great intelligence, and became a notable queen. Later when Jehangir's health began to decline because of excessive drinking and his mind became clouded, it was Mehr un-Nisa who, as Nur Jehan, ruled India with the help of her able brother Asaf Khan, Chief Minister at Delhi.

Wars with Rajputs and the Deccan. As in Akbar's reign and in all later reigns, there were continual wars between the Moghuls and the Rajputs on the one side, and the Moghuls and the Deccani kingdoms on the other. The war with Ahmadnagar started first. Ahmadnagar had agreed to pay a tribute in Akbar's times, but in Jehangir's reign the Sultan of Ahmadnagar had a very capable general and minister in Malik Ambar, who refused to pay the tribute. Malik Ambar was a good guerrilla captain and resisted the Imperial army effectively. He began to draft the hardy Mahrattas into his regiments and gave them excellent training. This training helped them in the reign of the next Emperor, Shah Jehan, because by then they had found a leader of their own in a chieftain called Shahji Bhonsle. With two generations of excellent guerrilla training behind them these hillmen made an effective rising in the reign of Aurangzeb. By then, they had a brilliant leader in Sivaji, son of Shahji Bhonsle.

Nur Jehan and Shah Jehan. Prince Khurram, the son of Jehangir, was sent against Ahmadnagar and the Rajputs. He was successful in both his assignments and was made a Grand Noble of the Empire, with the title of Shah Jehan. Later there was some difference between Nur Jehan and Shah Jehan, especially when she began to favour another son of Jehangir, Shahryar, who had been married to her daughter by her first marriage. Shah Jehan, who had been made Viceroy of the Deccan, was deprived of his office and when he revolted, General Mahabat Khan was sent against him. Since the Prince had inadequate forces he was twice defeated, but later there was a reconciliation. Nur Jehan was, however, very self-willed, and quarrelled with Mahabat Khan, though he proved too strong for her and captured Jehangir near the Jhelum. Nur Jehan then settled her quarrel with Mahabat Khan, but not long after, Jehangir, who had been ailing for a long time, died and Shah Jehan became Emperor. Nur Jehan was given a royal pension and she retired from politics.

Shah Jehan (1628-1658). Shah Jehan was welcomed as the new Emperor. He was known to be a good military commander and a capable administrator. He had been a successful Viceroy of the Deccan and soon showed that his reputation was justified. He reorganized the finances of the country and improved the administration with the help of two very talented men, Asaf Khan, his father-in-law, who was his Chief Minister, and Mahabat Khan, his Chief Military Commander. He had therefore a comparatively peaceful reign which he devoted to beautifying Delhi and Agra. He had a passion for building and spent millions on raising magnificent structures like the Taj Mahal, and the Moti Masjid of Agra, the Juma Masjid and the Red Fort with its Diwan-i-Am and Diwan-i-Khas of Delhi, and the Naulakha and Shish Mahal in Lahore Fort. These buildings have no parallel for beauty and grandeur anywhere in the world.

Wars in Deccan. The war in the Deccan, which had been going on since the days of Akbar, continued. The Governor of the Deccan at this time was Khan Jehan Lodhi an Afghan leader, who was not loyal to Shah Jehan. He began taking large payments from the Nizamshahi rulers of Ahmadnagar who, though tributaries of the Emperor, were always conspiring against the empire. Khan Jehan Lodhi even surrendered the Balaghat fort which had been won by Shah Jehan when he was campaigning against Malik Ambar. So Mahabat Khan was appointed Governor of the Deccan and ordered to proceed against Ahmadnagar. Khan Jehan Lodhi fled, and making common cause with the Bundela chieftain, Vikramajit, organized a revolt. The rising now became general and Golconda and Bijapur joined in. The Decannis had a capable guerilla leader in Shahji Bhonsle, so Shah Jehan came down himself to command the operations and in a series of campaigns the Ahmadnagar forces were defeated and cut down. Ahmadnagar fell in 1632 and the kingdom was finally annexed to the empire. But Shahji Bhonsle continued to fight with the help of Bijapur troops. Shah Jehan therefore sent an ultimatum to both Golconda and Bijapur, ordering them to stop helping Shahji Bhonsle: Golconda obeyed but Bijapur continued to fight until Adil Shah, the Sultan of Bijapur, was forced to submit. He had to pay an indemnity of Rs. 2,000,000 and also agreed to pay annual tribute to the Moghul Emperor. Shah Jehan went back to Delhi leaving Prince Aurangzeb as Viceroy of Deccan.

Shah Jehan's Character. Shah Jehan now ruled in peace. He had trouble with the Persians over Kandahar, but the Moghuls failed to recapture the town, because the Persian army was now equipped with artillery and the Moghuls were weak in this respect. If Shah Jehan and his successors had modernized their army, the history of India might have been different. As a ruler Shah Jehan was very successful. He made the country prosperous, and agriculture and industry improved, though it is said that many regions became depopulated as the people, finding the land becoming poorer, moved to the towns to seek work in the industries which were springing up. Shah Jehan was a good Muslim; he abolished the prostration in court introduced by Akbar, protected the rights of the Muslims in

Hindu areas and was just, even liberal, to the Hindus. The high offices of the State and all cadres of nobility were open to the Hindus and military commands continued to be given to capable Rajput commanders. Shah Jehan had one weakness; he was very fond of his son Prince Dara Shikoh and his daughter, Princess Jahan Ara. In his eyes, Dara Shikoh could do no wrong. In spite of the fact that Dara Shikoh remained at court on various pretexts, keeping a deputy in his viceroyalty in the north, he was never reprimanded. Shah Jehan was the greatest builder among the Muslim rulers of India and also the greatest patron of the arts. The tomb of Itimad ud-Daulah which was raised in Agra in Shah Jehan's time is a gem of Moghul architecture.

War of Succession. Shah Jehan fell ill in 1657 when he was sixty-six years old. His four sons, Dara Shikoh, Shujah, Murad, and Aurangzeb had been ruling in the north, east, west, and south respectively. The only one near him was Dara Shikoh. News of his illness spread everywhere and two princes took immediate action. Shujah in the east and Dara Shikoh in the centre. Shujah proclaimed himself king, struck his own coins and moved with his army towards Delhi of which Dara had taken control. Dara sent an army against Shujah and defeated his forces, so Shujah went back to Bengal. Murad now began to negotiate with Aurangzeb who had not moved from the Deccan. Dara sent General Jaswant Singh to the Narbuda with an army to intercept Aurangzeb if he made a move. Meanwhile Dara arrested Isa Beg (the representative of Aurangzeb at court) and confiscated his property. This made Murad and Aurangzeb move quickly. They met at Dayalpur on the Narbuda, and Jaswant Singh advanced to meet the two brothers. A battle ensued and Jaswant Singh was defeated. Shah Jehan was by now better, and advised Dara to do nothing, thinking that he could control the situation. But Dara was arrogant and did not listen to his father. He took an army and moved south against Murad and Aurangzeb. A great battle was fought between the brothers at Samugarh on 29 May 1658. Murad fought most valiantly; Aurangzeb did well also and Dara was defeated. He went back to Agra, but was too ashamed to face his father and the same night left with his family for Lahore.

Aurangzeb. Aurangzeb now marched on Agra and occupied it. Shah Jehan expressed a desire to meet Aurangzeb, but word had reached the latter that Shah Jehan was unfriendly to him. In fact, Shah Jehan was already writing to Mahabat Khan, who was in Kabul, to help Dara Shikoh against Aurangzeb. So Aurangzeb kept away from his father, though he sent his son Prince Azam Jah, with gifts and apologies. Unfortunately for Aurangzeb, the counsellors of Prince Murad began to whisper to him that the real victor of both the battles in which he and Aurangzeb had taken part was Murad, which was partly true. Why then they asked, should Aurangzeb issue orders? Murad was convinced of his own excellence and began to win over nobles and captains to his side. Soon he had a force 20,000 strong. Finding that another war was imminent, Aurangzeb had Murad arrested and sent to Gwalior as a state prisoner. Dara collected a force and gave battle again, but was defeated at Deorai. He fled to Sind and then left for Kandahar, but was captured on the way and sent to Delhi. Here he was tried as an apostate, found guilty, and beheaded. His apostasy is in doubt, but there is no doubt that he was even more liberal in his views than Akbar. He was a scholar of very liberal views, and considered the Upanishads equal in spiritual truth and wisdom to the Qur'an. Shujah was defeated at Bahadurpur near Benares and captured and he too was sent to Gwalior. He became an addict to opium there and died of an overdose in 1662.

Emperor Alamgir—Early wars. Aurangzeb was now crowned Emperor of India with the title of Alamgir. Shah Jehan lived on for a few more years, but was kept as a state prisoner in the Agra Fort. He was looked after well and had no complaints. He was attended by Princess Jahan Ara and a large number of servants. Aurangzeb consulted him on various occasions and accepted his advice as that of a *Murshid*, but never restored him to the throne. Aurangzeb's reign was the most glorious of all the Moghul reigns. There were many conquests. Assam was conquered by Mir Jumla in 1661, Mir Jumla, who was very old, died in this campaign and Mir Shayista Khan, the uncle of Aurangzeb, was appointed governor of Bengal and Assam. He cleared the delta of the Brahmaputra of pirates and captured Chittagong. Mir Shayista Khan governed these provinces for thirty years and made them rich. In the north the Pathans organized a rising under an Afridi leader, Akmal Khan. Aurangzeb himself moved against Akmal and brought the Pathans to order and they gave no further trouble to the Moghuls.

Hindu Revolts. The Hindus had grown very powerful during the long reign of Akbar and during the liberal regimes of Jehangir and Shah Jehan; so much so, that both Jehangir and Shah Jehan had been obliged to protect the civic rights of Muslims in areas where Hindus were in the majority. Since the Hindus were a majority in almost all parts of the country, they had a certain amount of power over the Muslims. For instance, they did not let Muslims build new mosques, or sometimes even repair old ones, but they accepted no restriction of the erection of new temples. These temples had *patshalas* attached to them and in these *patshalas* the pundits held classes, as the Muslim Ulema did in their mosques or khanqahs. Muslim boys of the locality were encouraged to attend classes in these *patshalas* and here they were taught things contrary to Islamic laws. When these matters were reported to him, Aurangzeb issued orders that this practice was to stop. He also ordered that the indiscriminate building of new temples should cease. The existing ones should stay, but no new temples should be built with *patshalas* since they encouraged anti-Muslim feelings, which were already on the increase in the country. The Bhakti

movement, which had at first been a spiritual movement had by
now given birth to national movements and military orders.
The Sikhs and the Mahrattas were cases in point. At
Aurangzeb's attempts to protect Muslim culture there was
widespread resentment. Many groups became violent. The Jats
of Central India rose in 1669, but were suppressed. In 1672 the
Satnamis revolted. These Hindus held extreme views about
Islam and were violently anti-Muslim. Their revolt was also
suppressed and many Satnamis died.

The Sikhs. Then the Sikhs under Guru Tegh Bahadur began
a Holy War against the Moghuls. The Moghul forces met them
and repeatedly defeated them, but the Sikhs took to guerilla
tactics like the Mahrattas. Tegh Bahadur was captured in one
fight and later tried for treason. He was found guilty and
beheaded. This made the Sikhs even more angry. They rose
with greater violence under their last Guru, the famous Gobind
Singh, who was a capable military leader. He reorganized the
Sikhs, but even he could not prevail against the Imperial army
and was defeated. He went into hiding and, after many
adventures, escaped to the region of Hyderabad, Deccan. He
built a Gurdawara at Nander on the Godavari in 1705. Here he
died at the hands of a Pathan fanatic in 1708, a year after
Aurangzeb's death.

The Rajputs. In 1679 the Rajputs rebelled, Raja Jaswant
Singh had died and Aurangzeb had ordered that his baby sons
should be brought up as imperial wards and that the Jodhpur
State should be administered for their benefit. The Rajputs
distrusted this royal favour and they decided to oppose the
order. They attacked the escort taking the babies to Delhi,
killed the captain and took the babies away to the Raja of
Udaipur who now declared himself the champion of the
Rajputs. Aurangzeb took the field personally against the Raja,
who had collected all the Rajputs under him, and defeated
them. The Raja sued for peace, was forgiven and made a Noble
of the Empire. He had, however, to surrender the forts of

Mandalpur and Bandhnor to Aurangzeb. The Rajputs gave no more trouble.

The Jizya. Throughout his early reign Aurangzeb had had nothing from the Hindus but distrust, criticism, disloyalty, and revolts. He became convinced that the Hindus were treating him as if he were an intruder, a foreigner, and unworthy of their loyal regard. Since to submit to all their practices was to permit irregularities against Islam, and he was a good Muslim, he decided that he should treat them as non-Muslims had been treated everywhere before. Since he could not depend on them for war service, those who did not fight were again made subject to the tax, called the *jizya* (1679). The Hindus were angry at this order, but since they had brought it on themselves, Aurangzeb did not cancel it. He ordered that the ceremony of *darshan*, whereby the Emperor showed his face in the morning to a waiting multitude, should be abolished. He turned the court musicians out, declaring that the court was the Emperor's council-chamber, his court of justice, his audience-hall, and not an amusement park. He also abolished the custom of being weighed on birthdays. He worked hard all day and expected others to do their duty. All his reforms, which were aimed at simplification and were meant to improve administration, were considered by the Hindus as anti-Hindu and expressions of bigotry. He was told by his counsellors what the others thought, but he insisted that, since he was the Emperor, he would not pander to frivolity or ignore disaffection.

The Mahrattas and Sivaji. The Mahrattas, who had fought under Shahji Bhonsle in Shah Jehan's time, now found a leader under Shahji's son Sivaji, who began to organize them and to raid Moghul territories, as he had been doing with Bijapur lands. The earlier attempts of Moghul armies against Sivaji failed, so when he looted Surat in 1664, Aurangzeb sent Raja Jai Singh with a picked army against him. Jai Singh soon defeated Sivaji and captured most of the Mahratta strongholds. Sivaji was clever and negotiated a truce with Jai

Singh, who was deceived by his friendliness, and promised to get him made a Noble of the Empire. Sivaji was taken to Delhi and presented to the Emperor. On being made a Noble with the rank of 5,000 horse, he pretended to be insulted, escaped, and returned to the hills where he began to organize himself on a grand scale. Raja Jaswant Singh, who was now sent against him, had never been completely loyal to Aurangzeb, so he temporized with Sivaji. Meanwhile Sivaji grew strong. He began to ask for the title of Raja and Jaswant Singh even recommended this concession. Aurangzeb agreed, but Sivaji never kept faith. Though he had now become a liege of the Emperor, he continued to harass Moghul lands, waylay pilgrims, and loot towns. In 1670 he broke with the Moghuls openly, reconquered all his forts and in 1674 had himself crowned king. In 1677, with the help of the two Brahmin ministers of the kingdom of Golconda, Manna and Akna, who aided him openly, he ravaged the kingdom of Bijapur. He died in 1679 and was succeeded by his son Sambaji. Aurangzeb now moved against the Mahrattas himself as nobody else seemed able to succeed against them. He found that the states of Golconda and Bijapur helped the Mahrattas actively and provided shelter and refuge to them when they were driven out of their strongholds by the Moghul army. He therefore decided to attack these states first. He began the campaign first against Bijapur because it was nearest to the Mahratta lands. He conquered it in 1686. Next year Golconda was also annexed and he now turned against the Mahrattas. He conquered all their forts, defeated and captured Sambaji in 1689 and took away his young son Sahu as a hostage, but treated him well and brought him up like a prince. The Mahratta menace passed and Aurangzeb ruled peacefully for another eighteen years.

Aurangzeb's character. Aurangzeb was a man of extraordinary character; he had always impressed people. His resolution, his bravery, his honesty of purpose, his devotion to duty, his love of Islam, his modesty and his scholarship were

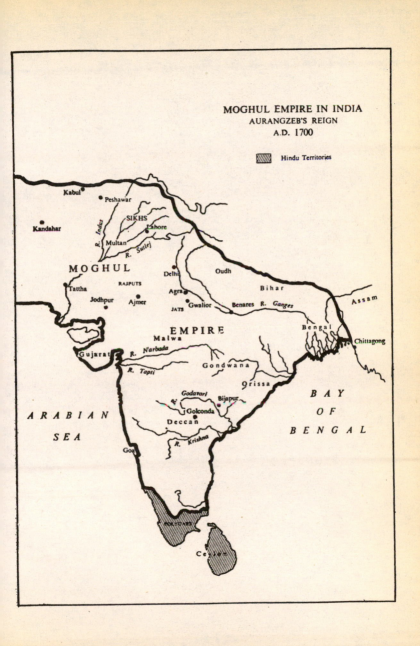

MOGHUL EMPIRE IN INDIA
AURANGZEB'S REIGN
A.D. 1700

▨ Hindu Territories

Kabul
Peshawar
Kandahar
SIKHS
R. Indus
Multan
Lahore
R. Sutlej
MOGHUL
Delhi
Oudh
RAJPUTS
Tattha
Jodhpur
Ajmer
Agra
JATS
Gwalior
Benares
R. Ganges
Bihar
Assam
EMPIRE
Bengal
Malwa
Chittagong
Gujarat
R. Narbada
R. Tapti
Gondwana
Orissa
BAY
Godavari
Bijapur
OF
Golconda
Deccan
BENGAL
ARABIAN
SEA
R. Krishna
Goa
Ceylon

acknowledged by all. During his viceroyalty of the Deccan he had shown the quality of his administration. Painstaking and methodical, he attended to most things himself. It pained him to see the heritage of Babar and Akbar slipping out of the hands of the Muslims. He was a very just man and spared neither himself, his sons, nor his subordinates. He had a high respect for his office, as the head of an Islamic State, and did not let anything stand in the way of the establishment of the just rule of the law. He had, perhaps, no sense of humour and was certainly not given to frivolity, but he had a high regard for duty. His name was known all over the world and his fifty years of absolute monarchy made the name Grand Moghul a byword in every language. He has been blamed for his policy against the Hindus. It is forgotten that the Hindus were rising from a centuries-old sleep and were claiming more than any monarch of that age or even of a later age could give them without a fight. The Sikhs and Mahrattas, when they rose against the Emperor, were rebels against him and he treated them as such. The Deccani States had been fighting against the Moghuls for three reigns. An end had to come to this long struggle, and it came with the victory of the stronger power. Aurangzeb's policy would never have been questioned if his successors had been powerful: he has been blamed for their weakness.

Successors of Aurangzeb. Aurangzeb was succeeded by his son, Bahadur Shah I, whose short reign, like the reigns of the next few emperors, is famous only for wars with the Sikhs and internal dissensions, court intrigues, inefficiency, and corruption. Within twenty years of his death the outlying provinces broke away from the centre. Asaf Jah Nizam ul-Mulk, the Viceroy of Deccan, became independent and founded the State of Hyderabad. Saadat Khan, the Nawab of Oudh, became an independent ruler. Alivardi Khan, the Nawab of Bengal was almost independent by 1740. The Rohillas carved a small kingdom in the upper reaches of the Ganges. Sind broke away soon afterwards. Muhammad Shah, the Emperor of Delhi, became notorious for loose living and the pursuit of pleasure. Nadir Shah, the warlike ruler of Persia, invaded India and sacked Delhi. He left nothing in the treasury when he went back. After him Ahmad Shah Abdali, the founder of the Abdali kingdom of Afghanistan, made North India his battleground and looted it at will. The Mahrattas rose in the south-west and the British East India Company in the east. The Third Battle of Panipat between the Muslims and the Mahrattas on 17 October 1761 resulted in a victory for Abdali and finished the Mahrattas as an imperial power. The British had won the Battle of Plassey in 1757 against the Nawab of Bengal and another battle in 1764 at Buxar established their power in North-East India. In the south, Hyder Ali, a brilliant soldier of fortune, won for himself a kingdom in Mysore. He came into conflict with the British, but held his own against them. His son, Sultan Tipu, was even more gifted than his father. He realized the danger of foreign domination and devoted all his energies and resources to fighting the British, though he was unsuccessful, as no other Indian power supported him. He died the death of a hero, fighting the British at the Battle of Seringapatam, in 1799. At this time the Sikhs produced a remarkable leader in Ranjit Singh, who won for himself a kingdom in the Punjab. The Emperor became a figurehead. He was attacked by the fierce Rohillas and rescued by Mahadoji Scindhia, a Mahratta chief, whose protégé he became, Mahadoji Scindhia becoming the Lord Protector. From this unworthy position Shah Alam, the blinded Emperor, was rescued by the British, who made him their pensioner, leaving him only the title of Emperor and the Red Fort of Delhi. Thus ended the power and glory of the Great Moghuls. Their achievements in civil administration, architecture, painting and music, their culture, the Urdu language that was born during their times, and the consciousness that the Muslims were a separate cultural entity have remained.

CHAPTER 13

ISLAM IN
THE NINETEENTH CENTURY

The World of Islam—1801-1900. The nineteenth century was an unhappy one for Islam. Muslim power declined everywhere and Muslim prestige became a thing of the past. The Ottomans still had an empire, but in Europe they were only tolerated because no one power wanted the other to have a major share of the spoils. The West European powers were determined that Russia should not swallow up Turkish lands and get possession of the Dardanelles. The Persian lands, now in the hands of the Qajars, were lost or mortgaged to foreign powers in pursuit of quick industrial progress. A new minor power emerged in Egypt under Muhammad Ali, but not long after his death Egypt became the plaything of the European powers too. India was already British. France seized Algeria and established a protectorate over Tunisia and finally Morocco; France and England absorbed the Muslim states of West and Central Africa. The coastal states of East Africa, South Arabia, and Malaya nearly all went to the British. When the century ended, Europe had completely dominated the Muslim world. The only thing that the Muslims gained in this clash of the West and Islam was that they began to think in democratic terms and the concept of the Rights of Man began to emerge among them. A few vital personalities like Sayyid Jamaluddin Afghani in the Middle East and Sir Sayyid Ahmad in India appeared on the scene and made the Muslims aware of the battle they were losing. They called on them to go forward and meet the challenge rather than to withdraw and be engulfed altogether. Slowly the Muslims began to awake and the common man began to have a voice. The Caliphs and the Sultans had had their time; now the man in the street was beginning to take a hand in the affairs of the state.

The Ottoman Empire—Napoleon in Egypt. The Sultan who was ruling at this time was Selim III (1789-1807). He was a man of ideas and wanted to reorganize the army on modern lines, to review the treaties with European powers, to overhaul the system of taxation in the empire and to reduce still further the power of the now corrupt and almost ineffective Corps of *Janissaries*. He welcomed the advice of the French Ambassador, General Sebastian, on some of these matters, but the Ulema and the *Janissaries* opposed him at every step and all his ideas came to nothing. Things were in this state when Napoleon arrived in Egypt, and, defeating the Mamluk forces of this Ottoman province, occupied the country. The British Admiral, Lord Nelson, came after him and destroyed his fleet in the Battle of Aboukir Bay. Napoleon, cut off from France, decided to move to the east. He led his army into Palestine, but was stopped at Acre. The British fleet followed him and stiffened the resistance of the garrison of Acre to such an extent that Napoleon was forced to retreat. Moreover, plague broke out in his camp and his supplies were dangerously low. Napoleon had to abandon his dreams of conquering an empire in the east. He went back to Egypt, where, leaving the French forces under the command of General Kléber, he outwitted the British and escaped to France. General Kléber was as cut off from France as Napoleon before him, and began to negotiate with the Sultan. By the convention of El-Arish in January 1800 he agreed to leave Egypt if the Turks helped him to evacuate his troops. A year passed, however, before the British permitted the return of the French troops to France. Egypt was then restored to the Sultan under the Treaty of Amiens (1802).

Rising of the Serbs—The Russians. After this the Balkan nations began to rise one after the other and, aided and abetted by the Europeans, succeeded in winning free from the Turks. The first to rise in a national movement were the Serbs, who, fired by the writings of patriotic writers like Rajich and Obradovitch, organized themselves under the popular leadership of George Petrovich (Kara George) and drove out the *Janissary* garrison of Belgrade in 1806. The Russians came to their support by invading the northern borders of the Ottoman Empire. This made Selim III more unpopular than ever and the *Janissaries* forced him to abdicate. Mustafa IV, who was now put on the throne, did not last long, and two years later Mahmud II, the last prince of the line, was made Sultan-Caliph. He did not have an easy time, because the *Janissaries* at the centre and the Derebays in Anatolia gave him a lot of trouble. He spent some years of his reign in suppressing these two elements. Meanwhile the Russian armies captured a number of towns and things might have gone worse for the Turks had not Napoleon invaded Russia in 1812. A treaty was therefore signed between Turkey and Russia at Bucharest by which Russia gave back to the Sultan the areas recently conquered. But this was only a temporary lull and after Napoleon's downfall the Russians attacked the Turks again.

Serbia and Greece. Meanwhile the Ottoman armies had suppressed the revolt of the Serbs and George Petrovich was forced into exile. After Napoleon's downfall, however, the Serbs rose again, this time under a new leader, Milosh Obrenovich. So determined was the nationalists' resistance that the Sultan was forced to acknowledge Obrenovich as Hereditary Prince of Serbia. The success of the Serbs encouraged the Greeks, who began to organize a national front of their own. They were helped by volunteers and funds from many European countries. They rose against the Turkish garrisons in the Morea and cut them to pieces. The Turks were so angry at this outrage that they killed many Greeks in Istanbul. One of the victims of this mob fury was the Greek Patriarch of Istanbul. On hearing of his death the Czar sent an ultimatum to the Sultan asking him rudely to restore the Greek Church and give guarantees for Christian life and property. Diplomatic relations were cut off after this, but Count Metternich, the Chancellor of Austria, and Lord Castlereagh,

Foreign Secretary of Great Britain, came into the breach. They told the Czar that it was wrong to encourage revolutions—the recent French Revolution had done enough harm, they said, and no one knew what the Balkan revolutions might lead to. This stopped the Czar for a time but the Greeks went ahead with their nationalist activities. The Sultan sent a fleet against them, but it was stopped by the newly organized Greek fleet. The Turks then invaded the mainland. There was much stiff resistance, but at this time the Greek nationalist party was split and this slowed up their activities. The Sultan asked Muhammad Ali his powerful Governor of Egypt, to send across his fleet to help, and Muhammad Ali did so under his son Ibrahim. Meanwhile the Turkish army under General Rashid Pasha captured the much contested fortress of Missolonghi. This event roused the whole of Europe. After this, the European powers (England, France and Russia) began to aid Greece openly. Unfortunately for the Sultan the *Janissaries* were hindering him at every step. So he decided to form a new corps. He organized a new guard and with its help suppressed the *Janissaries* in June 1826. This time he made such a good job of it that their power was destroyed for ever. The Sultan was free of the *Janissaries* now, but his military strength was weakened.

The European Powers and Russia. At this stage the European powers asked Muhammad Ali to withdraw his forces. They also asked the Sultan to stop fighting and on the Sultan's refusal they sent their fleets to the Aegean Sea. Ibrahim's fleet was surrounded and destroyed at Navarino. The Sultan called it an act of unwarranted aggression, but nobody cared. The Sultan had no real power now and had to submit. Even this did not improve matters. Now Russia entered the war actively. Her troops crossed the Danube and, though the Turkish garrisons fought all along the line, the Russians took Varna on 12 October 1828. A conference of the ambassadors of the European powers was held in London, and they decided that Greece should be declared independent though still a tributary of the Sultan. Even this did not stop the Russian army. It advanced to the very gates of Istanbul, taking Adrianople in August 1829. Again luck came to the rescue of the Sultan. Disease began to spread in the Russian army. Moreover, the Czar knew that the European powers would not let him take Istanbul. He therefore came to terms with the Sultan in the Treaty of Adrianople, by which the Russian border came down to the Danube, and Russia occupied Moldavia and Wallachia for five years. The Turks were asked to leave these two provinces, their forts were razed to the ground and all traces of nearly four hundred years of occupation were removed.

Muhammad Ali's Claims. Seeing the Sultan so weakened, Muhammad Ali became over bold and asked for Syria as a reward for his recent services. When the Sultan did not agree Muhammad Ali sent his son Ibrahim with an army to Syria. Ibrahim captured Acre on 27 May 1832 and the rest of Syria in another month. Defeating another Turkish army at Alexandretta on 29 July, he advanced into Anatolia. The Sultan's resources were so poor that he could offer no resistance. He appealed, in vain, to England. Ibrahim defeated another Turkish army at Konya on 21 December 1832 and marched towards the Dardanelles. Russia now sent a military mission to the Sultan and at this England and France became alarmed. The European powers met in another conference and the Sultan was 'advised' to yield Syria to Egypt. Muhammad Ali, however, also wanted Adana, and after more negotiation Adana went to Egypt.

Mohammad ibn Abdul Wahhab—The Wahhabi Movement. Muhammad Ali now became a powerful monarch, though he still accepted the Sultan as a suzerain. He organized his army and navy on modern lines and began to negotiate with Great Britain to open a railway to Suez. He was building up his country when a new force appeared in Arabia. In the eighteenth century a great man named Mohammad ibn Abdul Wahhab had been working and preaching in Nejd. He was a man with a new mission. He was very learned and had a puritanical bent of mind and in his beliefs followed Imam Ibn Taimiya. Ibn Abdul Wahhab revolutionized Islamic thought in Arabia and preached a truer observance of the spirit of the Qur'an and the Sunnah. His teaching won over the chief of Dariyah in Nejd, Muhammad ibn Saud. The House of Saud has ever since been the champion of this movement. The followers of Ibn Abdul Wahhab grew, and after his death, those of his son. The House of Saud also grew in importance with the movement. It was not long before the Saudis came into conflict with the Sharifs of Mecca, the hereditary governors of al-Hijaz. The Wahhabis invaded al-Hijaz and Iraq with the purpose of putting an end to what they said was mere idol-worshipping, but which the Sunnis called veneration of the Saints. In 1801 the Wahhabis captured Karbala and pulled down the dome on the tomb of Imam Husain. Two years later they conquered Mecca and the Sharif fled to Jeddah. Prince Abdul Aziz, the Saudi ruler, was killed by a Shiite fanatic at this time and was succeeded by his son Saud ibn Abdul Aziz.

Saud ibn Abdul Aziz (1803-1814). This prince of the House of Nejd was a remarkable person. A very capable man, he had much in common with the old Muslims. A patriarch in every way, he established a rule which reminded people of the old days. He offered the Sharif the governorship of al-Hijaz, on condition that he acknowledged him as his suzerain and abolished all customs and some other taxes. When the Sharif refused Prince Saud captured Medina. The Wahhabis turned out the Turks and pulled down all the beautiful domes over the tombs of the saints. The Wahhabis now advanced into Palestine and attacked Damascus in Syria and Najaf in Iraq. The Sultan, in his capacity as Caliph of Islam, appealed to Muhammad Ali of Egypt to stop the destruction that the Wahhabis were causing everywhere. Muhammad Ali sent his son Tusun with an army in October 1811, but the Wahhabis defeated him a number of times. Not for another three years did the Egyptians make any progress. It was only after the untimely death of Prince Saud in 1814 that the Egyptians began to make headway. Prince Saud died leaving a name for chivalry, justice, personal charm, eloquence, bravery, and strict adherence to the Qur'anic laws that has not dimmed with the passage of time. After his death, Muhammad Ali sent Ibrahim to Arabia and gradually won back all the lands in the al-Hijaz and the north that had been conquered by the House of Saud.

Muhammad Ali of Egypt. Muhammad Ali was now powerful enough to declare his independence. The Sultan could no longer maintain his position as the supreme Sultan-Caliph. He tried to negotiate an offensive and defensive alliance against Egypt with Great Britain, but the Prime Minister, Lord Palmerston, did not agree. The British were interested in Egypt themselves. It had strategic importance for them, as it lay on the route to their eastern empire. The Sultan then tried to coerce Muhammad Ali. He sent an army into Syria and his fleet to Alexandria. The army was defeated by Muhammad Ali's son Ibrahim at the Battle of Nezib in June 1839, and the Turkish fleet went over to Muhammad Ali. The European powers took the initiative again and met at London to draw up the Treaty of London. By this treaty they acknowledged Muhammad Ali as hereditary ruler of Egypt, but of Syria for his life-time only. He was made to give up Crete, northern Syria and al-Hijaz to the Sultan, also the Turkish fleet. This was more than the Sultan could have expected, but it showed one thing. The Ottoman Empire existed on sufferance from them on. The Caliphate was a shadow and the Sultanate a mockery. Muhammad Ali now devoted all his time to the improvement of his country. He built a new harbour at Alexandria and joined it by a canal with the western arm of the Nile. He encouraged the growth of cotton, opened new schools and began to introduce western civilization into the country. The revenues increased and the treasury began to show surpluses.

Successors of Muhammad Ali. His successors tried to follow in his footsteps, but did not have his intelligence. Muhammad Said, the Khedive who came to the throne in 1854, was a liberal man who made many improvements, tried to abolish slavery and reduced the monopolies. The title of Khedive had been conferred on his father by the Sultan. It was under the next Khedive, Ismail, who reigned from 1863 to 1879, that Ferdinand de Lesseps, a French engineer, completed the construction of the Suez Canal. Many new schemes were also completed, including railways, roads, bridges, irrigation canals, telegraphs, and harbour works for which the Khedive had borrowed very largely from European capitalists. The upper Nile valley was conquered in 1870 and the Sudan in 1874. General Gordon was Governor-General of the Sudan from 1874 to 1879. But the Khedive had borrowed too much money and he had to sell out his shares in the Suez Canal Company to pay his debts. These shares were purchased by the British. When the creditor countries began to clamour for payment, the Khedive had to agree to the appointment of two Controllers of Finance in Egypt, one British and one French. This created a lot of unrest and the people began to say that the Khedive was pledging the country to the foreigners.

The Nationalist Movement. Western education had brought in new ideas of nationalism and democracy, so a nationalist movement began to strike root. At this time a remarkable man appeared in Egypt. He was Sayyid Jamaluddin Afghani, who had been working in many Muslim countries and had been awakening the Muslims from lethargy and a sense of defeat. He taught that the Muslims must meet the challenge of the West, by adopting what was best in Western civilization and by bringing out the finest values in their own civilization. Muslims must realize that progress was not the birthright of Western nations only. Others could learn and take their place in the march of time. Soon a party of progressive people was organized and began to demand a constitution from the Khedive. So strong was the demand of the people that the Khedive appointed a nationalist ministry under Mahmud Sami. This was, however, not the end of the movement. There was a conspiracy in the army led by Egyptians against Circassian officers. The Khedive got alarmed and appealed to England for help. This gave an opportunity to the British, who first bombarded Alexandria and then landed their forces under Sir Garnett Wolesley. Sir Garnett defeated the Egyptian army at Tel-el-Kebir and the British occupied Cairo on 15 September 1882.

The Mahdi of the Sudan. This occupation was resented far and wide, but it stirred up the people of Sudan most, especially as a Sudanese religious leader, by name Muhammad Ahmad, had strong views about the foreigners. He had a great following too. In order to impress himself on his people, he claimed that he was the promised Mahdi. He had organized a resistance movement against the Egyptians first, but when he found that in Egypt the British had come to matter more than the Egyptians, he turned all his wrath against the British. He fought a number of engagements with the Anglo-Egyptian forces and at last besieged Khartoum, the capital. General Gordon sent for help, but it arrived too late. The Mahdi captured Khartoum and General Gordon was killed. This event was received with great indignation in England, but for some time nothing could be done, and the Mahdi became the ruler of the Sudan. He did not live long, and in June 1885 he was succeeded by his Khalifa, Abdullah. The Mahdists remained in power in the Sudan for another thirteen years. In 1896, however, the British Government sent General Kitchener to suppress the movement. Kitchener was a very able man. Securing his line of communications, he proceeded against the Mahdists in a cautious manner. The Mahdists always fought recklessly, but they could not succeed against modern weapons. Kitchener defeated them at the Battle of Omdurman on 2 September 1898, and took Khartoum on 3 September. The Muslims thus lost two states to a European power, Egypt and the Sudan.

Turkey. Meanwhile the quality of the Sultan-Caliphs had not improved. They remained narrow and conservative. They were afraid of new ideas and did not wish to part with their dwindling powers. According to them, they were not only the temporal, but also the spiritual heads of the Muslims and as such the Sultan-Caliph was God's shadow on earth. No Muslim should therefore disobey him and his word was law. But new ideas were working everywhere; their expression was not yet very strong, but they were there. Abroad, the European powers were meeting in one convention after another to decide on and delimit the boundaries and the powers of the Sultan. Russia had a gentleman's agreement with Great Britain over the break-up of the empire. As a first move, the Muslim population of Wallachia, Moldavia, Hungary, and Serbia was forced out of these countries and sent to the Ottoman lands. The Sultan protested, but nobody listened to him. The European powers had already decided to take over various parts and provinces of the Ottoman Empire when it broke up. The Czar made the second move. He declared to the Sultan that he wished to be considered officially the protector of the Greek Orthodox Churches in Turkish lands. The Sultan could not agree and at this Russia sent across her armies, which occupied the Danubian Principalities still under the Turks. The British and French were not prepared for such a quick move. They feared that, if not checked, Russia would take Istanbul and thus get a passage into the eastern Mediterranean. When, therefore, the Sultan appealed to them for help, they agreed. The result was the Crimean War, which lasted from 1853-1856. It was fought mostly in the Crimea, although the Turkish army under General Omar also won the Battle of Oltenitza in South Rumania on 4 November 1853, against the Russians. There were three noteworthy battles in this war, the Battles of the Alma River, of Balaclava, and of Inkerman. At these battles the advantage lay with the Allies. It was at the Battle of Balaclava, that the famous Charge of the Light Brigade occurred. Florence Nightingale, the renowned head of the Nursing Mission, also worked in the Crimea during this war, which the Allies won.

The Hatt-i-Humayun. Since the Allies—France, England, Austria and Sardinia—had helped the Sultan at this critical time, they persuaded him also to listen to the voice of the people and give them a constitution. In it they also asked him to give civic rights to the Christian subjects of the Sultan. These reforms were called Hatt-i-Humayun. Many evils, like torture, were abolished. Since the Sultan had agreed under this edict to give rights to his people and treat the Christians on nearly the same footing as his other subjects, the Sultan's European allies drew up the second Treaty of Paris (March 1857) by which they admitted Turkey to the Concert of Nations. They also forced Russia to surrender the mouths of Danube and Bessarabia to the Sultan. She had to give up Kars in Caucasia and was also made to give up the idea of being Protector of the Christians in the Ottoman Empire. The Black Sea was declared a neutral area. Sultan Abdul Aziz (1861-1876), who now came to the throne, was an enlightened man and during his time many progressive events took place. Western influence had increased after the Crimean War. An American Mission opened Robert College at Istanbul and later a women's college was also opened. Loans were floated and railroads were built. Turkish writers, like Namik Kamal, began to translate such progressive authors as Rousseau and Montesquieu, and liberal statesmen like Ali Pasha and Fuad Pasha came to power. The Imperial Ottoman Bank was founded. First the Academy of Galata Serai (1868) and then the University of Constantinople (1869) were instituted; the School of Law was founded in 1870. The Sultan visited Europe in 1867, being the first Sultan to go abroad. On his return the Turkish Code of Civil Law was framed. The Sultan also gave a commission to a German firm to build a railway connecting Istanbul with Hungary. By the opening of the Suez Canal in 1869, the Ottoman Empire was put on the main trade route to the East; this greatly increased her prosperity.

Sultan Abdul Hamid and Midhat Pasha. Better days seemed to be coming for the Turks. In 1872 Ali Pasha, the Vizier, prepared a scheme for the reorganization of the empire which was progressive and even generous. It promised the Balkan peoples provincial autonomy. But the Balkan peoples were dreaming of complete independence and did not agree. Moreover, Russia did not like Turkey to make any scheme which included the Balkans as a future part of the Ottoman Empire. Meanwhile the grand schemes of improvement and national reconstruction, for which a great many loans had been floated, made the country heavily indebted, as they had done to Egypt, and were doing to Persia in the east and Tunisia in the west. It appeared that the Muslim countries in their haste to become modern were spending too much of other people's money, without adequate provision for eventual returns. A financial collapse was about to occur when a gifted statesman, Midhat Pasha, came to power. He had a very fine record as an administrator in Bulgaria and Iraq. He planned to make a National State with rights for everybody, a constitution, and the democratic machinery that any modern state needs. The Sultan-Caliph, whom everybody considered so progressive, now opposed Midhat Pasha. Midhat Pasha was, however, too powerful and his associates deposed the Sultan. After a first wrong choice, the new Sultan, Abdul Hamid II, came to the throne and Midhat Pasha was accepted as Leader of the Reform Party. On 23 December 1876, the new constitution was proclaimed. It provided for the following things: (a) indivisibility of the Turkish Empire, (b) liberty of the individual, (c) freedom of conscience, the press and education,

(d) equality of taxation and (e) a parliamentary form of government. Unfortunately for the Turks, the new Sultan-Caliph was a narrow-minded and obstinate type of man, who still believed in his supremacy, his autocracy, and his Caliphhood. He prorogued the Parliament and dismissed Midhat Pasha. He provoked everyone; the progressive Turks, the Balkan peoples, and the European powers. There were risings everywhere. The Cretans rose in 1878, the French occupied Tunisia in 1881, and the British took Egypt in 1882. The Armenians revolted in 1890 and their rising was so harshly suppressed that it provoked Europe again. The Bulgars began to raid Macedonia.

The Young Turks (1896-1908). Since the Sultan was deaf to the voice of the times, the progressive Turks organized themselves into a Young Turk Movement. These Turks had mostly been educated in the West and held liberal views. Not all of them were in Turkey; in fact many of them had been banished from Turkey for their advanced views. But contacts were made and these men, whether in France or Switzerland, England or Italy, in Salonika or Anatolia, now joined in support of the views of their political idol, Midhat Pasha. These liberals joined with the Christians of the Empire, the Armenians and the Macedonians. Again the Sultan, who was completely blind to what was happening in the world outside Turkey, banned the movement, and began to persecute the liberals. The movement went underground, but their work continued, and, though the Young Turks could not stop the disruption of the empire, they at least gave hope that they might be able to save something out of it when the crash came. This they did, twenty years later.

Al-Maghrib. At the beginning of the nineteenth century the Turkish Empire had included loosely in her dominions the North-African provinces of Algeria, Tunisia, and Tripoli. The local Beys had long been semi-independent, but they owed fealty to the Sultan whom they still considered as their suzerain, though the entire area had sadly deteriorated. The people of the coast were engaged in piracy and the slave-trade, and shady traffic of all kinds. The interior had gone back to tribalism and only a pretence of modernity remained. There was no political consciousness, no education, and no modern ideas of self-determination. Ignorance and poverty ruled over the whole country. Yet the country had possibilities; it had once been the seat of powerful governments and states, from the days of Carthage and Rome to the days of the Fatimids and the Muwahhids, and even when the Turks had conquered the region.

Interest of Europe in Al-Maghrib. When the Congress of Vienna was held after the downfall of Napoleon, the European powers authorized the British to take action against the Barbary Pirates, as the Muslim Corsairs of Algeria were called. The British wanted the Mediterranean safe for their ships. It was therefore clear that they would take action soon. The following year a British fleet bombarded Algiers and forced the Dey, as the ruler of Algiers had come to be called, to accept their terms; piracy was stopped. This was the beginning. In 1827, the Dey annoyed the French Consul, who reported to his government. The French Government asked the Dey to apologize and when he refused, a French Expeditionary Force was sent over: it overran the country and deposed the Dey in 1830. The tribal chiefs now met to elect a leader. They elected Abdul Qadir of Mascara, and this Chief fought the French for ten years. In 1844, Marshal Bugeaud finally defeated Abdul Qadir and the French now occupied Algiers, gradually extending their power into the interior. By 1870 they had conquered the whole of Algeria. At first a military rule was established because of the unsettled state of affairs, but in 1879 the civil government took over.

Tunisia 1881. Tunisia had remained free, but the Bey of this country wished for quick progress and began to borrow large sums of money from France and Italy. The money was spent, as in Turkey, Persia, and Egypt, on constructive schemes of development, but these schemes did not pay dividends quickly and the creditors began to protest. They made representations to their governments and asked their rulers to intervene and do something. The governments were not unwilling to help. In fact in all cases the governments were only too eager to take action. An International Financial Control was therefore imposed on the Tunisian Government in 1869. In 1878, the British offered the French a free hand in Tunisia if the French did not object to the British occupation of Cyprus, which they had obtained by treaty with the Sultan, on payment of an annual tribute of £92,800. Nobody was to blame for this except the Muslims, who seemed to be doing everything wrong. Even after the French concessions in Tunisia, the situation did not improve, because the Italians and the French began to quarrel over their own share of the spoils. In 1881, because of a border incident in which some Tunisian tribesmen were involved, the French forced the Bey to accept French Protection. The Turks protested strongly, and even England and Italy protested, but the French gave only diplomatic answers. A little later, the Tunisians rose under Ali ibn Khalifa and this gave the French the excuse to take over Tunisia completely. In 1883 Tunisia finally became a French Protectorate.

Persia—The Qajars (1796-1925). By the end of the eighteenth century the Zand dynasty had run its course, and a new power had emerged in Persia with the Qajars, whose leader Agha Muhammad ascended the throne in 1796 as the Shah of Persia. He conquered Khorasan and established a rule of force in Persia. He was not a popular monarch and was assassinated the following year. The new king was Fath Ali Shah, the nephew of the first monarch. He was a much more acceptable man, though by no means wiser. He tried to make his country prosperous by giving concessions to the Europeans, and soon European influence increased. The British persuaded him to go to war against the Abdalis of Afghanistan to recover

Kandahar, which the British said had been a Persian province. The real reason was that the Abdalis had become a power in the north-west of India, which the British had marked for their own. This move of Persia involved her in a long and expensive war with Afghanistan. What was worse for Persia, Russia began to advance into her northern provinces. In 1800 she annexed Georgia, and four years later, she came as far as Gilan. Persia sought help from France and Britain and they sent their military missions, but Russia continued to advance. At last in 1813, she forced on Persia the Treaty of Gulistan, by which she took Derbent, Baku, Shirvan, Shaki, and Karabagh in Caucasia.

Persian Alliances. Persia, in a desperate situation, selected England as her ally. England promised that if Persia cancelled all treaties with powers which were hostile to her, she would lend aid up to £150,000. But this treaty cost Persia a lot. It annoyed Russia, who invaded Persia again and defeated her forces at the Battle of Ganja, taking Erivan and Tabriz. In the treaty which followed she took Erivan and Nakhchivan, but gave up Tabriz, making Persia pay an indemnity.

Muhammad Shah (1835-1848). Fath Ali Shah died in 1835 and was succeeded by Muhammad Shah. This monarch was even less capable than Fath Ali Shah. He tried to play Russia against England, though he had been helped to the throne by both these foreign powers. The result of his efforts was that the British Military Mission left Persia. There was a war with Turkey on the west and Afghanistan on the east, both of which were inconclusive, but they weakened Persia further. The Treaty of Erzerum in 1847, however, ended her dispute with Turkey.

Nasiruddin (1848-1896). In 1848 Nasiruddin Shah, who was the best ruler of this dynasty, came to the throne. He was lucky to have a man of ideas and great energy in Mirza Taqi Khan, who was his Chief Minister. Mirza Taqi believed in progress; he wanted to introduce reforms in the country's finances and her army, but he also wanted a constitutional government, which did not please the Shah, who therefore dismissed him in 1852, and all the good that Mirza Taqi had tried to do was undone. The Czar now threatened the northern borders again. Having annexed Lower Caucasia, his troops began to advance to the Syr Darya valley. Meanwhile Britain changed her policy with regard to Afghanistan. She wanted now to be friendly with her because she had succeeded in helping a British nominee to the Afghan throne. She was therefore displeased, because Nasiruddin continued the Persian war with Afghanistan. When Nasiruddin refused to agree to a peace with Afghanistan, British troops captured Kharek island in the Persian Gulf and occupied Bushire and Mohammarah. The Treaty of Paris in 1857 at last put an end to this tension and the Shah was now forced to accept Afghanistan as an independent state.

Babism and Baha'ism. A notable event of Nasiruddin Shah's reign was the rise of a new religious leader and a new creed in Persia. It began with the founder, Sayyid Ali Muhammad, claiming that he was the *Bab* (the Gate) through which men had to pass to contact the promised Imam (the Mahdi). Later he claimed to be the Imam. Later still, his followers accepted him as a manifestation of God. In his book, the *Bayan*, he claimed that he had received revelations. He sent out his missionaries everywhere and soon began to gain followers. One of the converts was the gifted poetess, Qurrat-ul-Ain, whose poems were full of force and passion. The movement grew so strong that the Shah was forced to take action. He arrested both the *Bab* and Qurrat-ul-Ain, and the *Bab* was killed in prison by one of his fanatical disciples who could not bear to see the sufferings of his 'Imam'. This death made the *Bab* a martyr, and strength was given to the movement by Bahaullah, the successor of the *Bab*, who was less fiery than his master, but more persuasive. Bahaullah gave a new twist to Babism, admitting elements of many religions into his creed and preaching universal understanding. He too was banished from

Persia, but his movement and ideas spread in many countries and today there are followers of his teaching, known as Baha'is, in many countries.

Nasiruddin's Measures. Nasiruddin now began to develop his country. He wanted first good communications, a railway, a postal system, and telegraphs, so he gave a concession to Baron de Reuter, a British subject, to develop communications. The money spent was to be paid out of the customs of Persia. In 1889 the Baron opened the Imperial Bank of Persia to discover and exploit the mineral wealth of the country. The Shah also gave a concession to the British to grow and sell tobacco. In 1878 he organized the Cossack Brigade, a Persian force, officered mostly by Russians. Nasiruddin even went to Europe on tour, where he met Sayyid Jamaluddin Afghani whom he persuaded to come to Persia. Jamaluddin was welcomed by the educated people of Persia with open arms. Here, as in Egypt, his ideas were accepted by the intelligentsia. But his ideas were progressive and alarmed the Shah who sent him out of the country, although the influence of his ideas remained. Jamaluddin set people thinking wherever he went. Nasiruddin may have done a little good by bringing in the Europeans, but many of his people thought that he was selling the country and so in 1896 there was a rising against him in which he was assassinated.

Jamaluddin Afghani. The greatest single force in the reconstruction of Islam in the nineteenth century was Sayyid Jamaluddin Afghani, who was born in Hamadan in Persia, but was taken as a boy to Afghanistan, where he grew up. A man of exceptional ability, extraordinary gifts and great personality, he became a friend of Amir Dost Muhammad of Afghanistan. In 1870, some time after his friend's death, he moved to Istanbul, where his ideas made a great impression. He was liberal in his ideas and asked his listeners to build their future on Islamic thought, but to keep their minds open to new ideas and new forces. He was a great believer in *Ijtihad*, the adaptive principle of Islam, which has kept and can keep Islam a living force. He also believed in Pan-Islamism. He said that the Muslims must understand the West, before they could meet the challenge of the West. He became very popular with the progressive element in Istanbul, and the Sultan was persuaded by the orthodox to send Jamaluddin away. From here he went to Cairo and then to India, stimulating Muslim thought there also. In 1883 he left for Paris, where he issued a paper with the assistance of Muhammad Abduh. This Muhammad Abduh became later a great force in Muslim Egypt and is one of the four or five great sons of Islam of the early twentieth century. In Paris, Jamaluddin met Shah Nasiruddin, who brought him to Tehran. When he organized a Reform Party there he was asked to leave. Jamaluddin left for Baghdad and later went to London. He attracted followers wherever he went, for his personality was magnetic and his arguments stimulating. Finally he returned to Istanbul where he lectured at the university till his death in 1897.

Muzaffaruddin (1896-1907). Muzaffaruddin, who succeeded Nasiruddin in Persia, went further in floating loans. He began to give concessions to Russia as well as Britain and soon there was great rivalry between the two powers, who tried to outbid each other. In 1892, in return for a loan, the British took the customs of the Persian Gulf as security, and in 1900 Russia gave a larger loan to the Shah for which she took the rest of the country's customs. There were other loans and gradually the country was seriously indebted. In 1901 Mr. W. K. D'Arcy, a New Zealander, was given an oil concession for sixty years. It was this concession which ultimately became the Anglo-Iranian Oil Company. By the time the Shah died the country's finances were completely in the hands of foreigners, and he was merely a puppet with little or no power.

India—The Punjab. Muslim India had nearly disappeared by the first quarter of this century. The provinces had broken away, the governors becoming independent. The Sikhs had risen in the Punjab after Abdali had left and divided the province into many parts. The Muslims were suppressed and a reign of terror was established in the province. Muslims were forbidden to say their prayers, or to call out the Azan in the villages. Neither life, nor honour, nor property was safe. Very little heed was paid to authority, and law and order did not exist. The state of things was so bad that this period of mis-rule has been called 'Sikha-Shahi', which means anarchy. Then came Ranjit Singh, a leader of remarkable qualities. Cool, capable, and diplomatic, he united the Sikhs under him, built a strong army and established himself in the Punjab, the Frontier Province, and in Kashmir. He withstood the advancing power of the British and was respected by them. The British knew the calibre of the man and did not advance beyond the River Sutlej. After his death the British did not find it difficult to advance into the province. They fought a number of battles with the Sikhs and after two of them, Sobraon (1846) and Chilianwala (1849), the British annexed the Punjab. They sold Kashmir, which was a mainly Muslim province to one of the nobles of Ranjit Singh, Gulab Singh, for Rs. 9,000,000.

Oudh—Discontent in India. The British had by mid-century become masters of nearly two-thirds of the country. Between their possessions in the east and the centre lay the kingdom of Nawab Wazir of Oudh who had been acknowledged as a sovereign by the British earlier in the century. By the Doctrine of Lapse introduced by Lord Dalhousie, the British East India Company could annex any state if the ruling prince died without an heir. By this convenient rule many principalities 'lapsed' to the British. Some of these 'lapsed' lands were the territories of the Peshwa, especially the kingdom of Satara and the Mahratta States of Jhansi and Nagpur. The richest of these 'lapses' was Nagpur, with a territory of 80,000 square miles. Now came the turn of the kingdom of Oudh. The British found that the kingdom was mis-governed and that the court was corrupt. Lord Auckland had even warned the king as early as

1837 that he must improve. Lord Dalhousie now considered it high time that the Company should take over the burden of this state too. He may even have thought of pensioning off the king, but the directors of the Company ruled otherwise. The kingdom was annexed in February 1856. The Company now ruled over nearly as much of India (without Sind and Burma) as the British ruled later, but the policies of aggressive Governor-Generals like Wellesley and Dalhousie had created great dissatisfaction. The Nawabs and Rajas felt humiliated and insecure, as the Hindu princes were even denied their religious right of adoption. Unrest was increased by the people who were thrown out of employment when the states were annexed. The work of the missionaries, who with the backing of the Company had their own 'Mission Compounds' all over the country, had made both Hindus and the Muslims unhappy and suspicious.

The Revolt of 1857—The Mutiny. The annexation of the kingdom of Oudh was the last straw. It was the last relic of the Moghuls, and the Talukdars (big landowners) of Oudh, both Hindus and Muslims, were greatly upset by the disappearance of their last link with the past. Moreover, discontent had been spreading in the Company's Indian regiments. Restrictions which interfered with the religious principles and sometimes ran counter to the faith of both Muslims and Hindus, had made the Indian soldiers—the sepoys—revolt a number of times. There had been mutinies in 1824 and 1852 among regiments which were detailed to go abroad. In 1844 some regiments had refused to go to Sind. The quality of British officers was deteriorating; the new officers had less and less sympathy for and understanding of the sentiments of the Indians. All these elements combined to make the sepoys very restless. The political events affected them further. Many soldiers came from Oudh, mostly recruited for the Bengal regiment. The spark, however, that lit the fire was the introduction of the new Enfield rifle. The cartridges which were used in these rifles were greased with animal fat. It was rumoured that the fat was either of beef or bacon. This upset both Hindus and Muslims and the sepoys refused to use the cartridges. When forced to do so, a sepoy killed a British officer on parade on 29 March 1857 at Barrackpore in Bengal. Soon the troops began to mutiny everywhere. At Meerut some mutineers were degraded and badly handled, and the men rose and killed their officers. They did so in other places too. They now advanced on Delhi crying that the British were finished. Bahadur Shah, who had never dreamed of an active military life, was pulled out of seclusion and hailed as emperor.

A 'National' Movement. Soon the rising became general. In Jhansi, the Rani, who had been deposed, rose against the British. Nana Sahib, the adopted son of the last Peshwa, rose in Cawnpore. Everywhere the people joined into bands and started burning, looting, and killing the British. Only two powers in India stood by the British, the Sikhs in the Punjab and the Nizam of Hyderabad in the Deccan. Among the sepoys the Gurkhas also remained loyal. In distant Afghanistan Dost Muhammad, the Amir, remained friendly. The rest of India wanted to throw off the British yoke. The Hindus wanted to restore the Peshwa and the Muslims the Moghul line of kings. Unfortunately, they had no leader of outstanding quality or organizing power and the movement had no central core. There were three storm centres; Delhi, Central India (Jhansi), and Oudh (Cawnpore and Lucknow). The British army had therefore three targets. Sir John Nicholson moved with a British force against Delhi, General Havelock, later helped by Sir Colin Campbell, worked in Oudh, and Sir Hugh Rose led his troops against the Rani of Jhansi, who was holding out with the help of Tantia Topi, an officer of the Nana Sahib. All three succeeded after initial failures and setbacks. Sir John Nicholson entered Delhi on 14 September 1857, the Emperor was captured, and later tried and banished to Rangoon. Oudh was reconquered by March 1858; Jhansi was taken in April

1858. Tantia Topi continued fighting in guerrilla fashion, but was betrayed and captured in April 1859, and hanged. The revolution, which began as a mutiny and developed into a general movement, ended miserably for lack of organization and leadership.

The Crown and India. The Crown took over the government of India on 1 November 1858 and the Company ceased to exist. The Queen proclaimed that the Indian princes who had stood by the Company in the recent disturbances would retain their boundaries and the treaties made by them with the Company would be honoured; there would be freedom of religion, the customs of the Indians would be respected and protected, the right of the Indians to hold office would be conceded, the peaceful industry of India would be encouraged, and the government of the country would be organized for the benefit of the Indian people. Many of these promises were kept.

The Reaction of the Muslims. The Hindus and the Muslims reacted differently to the new state of things. The Hindus accepted the new order and began to adapt themselves to the new circumstances. When the British opened schools they sent their children to the new schools. If only low paid and subordinate jobs were first offered to the Indians they accepted the subordinate jobs. If in the new industries set up by British capital they could only get humble positions they did not disdain these positions. After all, the new industries required raw material, and somebody had to supply this material, so they bent their minds to commerce. They began to shed their insularity; they started going to other countries, even getting education abroad. In a generation they made a position for themselves in administration, in industry, and in commerce. They had an enlightened leader in Raja Mohan Roy of Bengal. The Muslims sulked; they would not co-operate. Their Mullahs considered everything British anti-Islamic. The new education was bad because it made people non-believers; service under the British was bad because the British were enemies of Islam;

trade was bad because you had to borrow and lend, and taking interest was forbidden. They saw no difference between usury which is forbidden by Islam and ordinary interest which is legitimate profit on a business undertaking. Going abroad was extremely irreligious because everybody ate bacon and ham there and nobody drank water, only wine. These prejudices kept the Muslims backward for a whole generation in education, industry, and trade and kept them from absorbing democratic ideas and developing a political consciousness.

Sir Sayyid Ahmad. The greatest force in Muslim India in this century was the personality of Sir Sayyid Ahmad Khan who undertook to uplift an unwilling people from the depths. The Muslims had worked themselves into a blind alley. They would not accept a foreign power, they would not co-operate with the British socially, they would not accept new ideas and they refused to be educated in any but the outworn classics of Persian and Arabic. Sir Sayyid had therefore four tasks before him: (*a*) to reconcile Indian Islam to modern ways, (*b*) to make the Indian Muslims accept the British as a sovereign power, (*c*) to stop them considering the British and the Christians as untouchables, (*d*) to educate them on modern lines. He succeeded in this four-fold programme of reform. His first attempt was to reconcile the Muslims to the British. For this purpose he wrote in 1860 his *Asbab-i-Baghawat-i-Hind* (Causes of Revolt in India). Next year he followed it by *Loyal Muhammadans of India*. He even wrote *Tabyin-al-Kalam*, a commentary on the Bible, to reconcile the Christians and the Muslims on religious grounds. He wrote other pamphlets also, even one on 'Rules for eating with the People of the Scriptures'. His work in convincing the British that they should not continue to suspect the Muslims and thus block their progress was as valuable. The British were greatly disturbed by the Wahhabi movement in India which had become militant and involved not only the two brothers from Patna (Inayat Ali and Wilayat Ali), but also Sayyid Ahmad of Bareilly, Ismail Shahid of Delhi, and thousands of others. Dr. W. W. Hunter had written a book on the subject, *The Indian Mussulmans: Are they bound in conscience to rebel against the Queen?* Sir Sayyid reviewed this book in the *Pioneer* and reprinted his articles in *Aligarh Institute Gazette*. He thus did a great deal to win over even the stern Wahhabis. His attempts at modernizing Islam, his modernistic commentaries on the Qur'an, and his lectures earned for him the curses and the condemnation of the orthodox Ulema, but Sir Sayyid carried on. He now gathered round him a band of sincere and talented Muslims like Mohsin ul-Mulk and Wiqar ul-Mulk, writers like Nazir Ahmad, Altaf Hussain, and Zakaullah, and turned his attention to arousing the Muslims' interest in education. He opened first a school at Aligarh. Later it grew into the Muhammadan Anglo-Oriental College, later still into the Muslim University. This was a great step forward. He had been to England, his views had broadened further, his courage and humanity had always been remarkable and his enthusiasm had no limits. This one man turned the course of events for the Muslims of India, and under his guidance and that of his associates, who all wrote, spoke, advised and exhorted, the Muslims woke up and accepted life. The result was that a rebirth of Muslim culture occurred and so by the time the century ended the Indian Muslims were on their feet.

CHAPTER 14

ISLAM IN
THE TWENTIETH CENTURY

The Muslims in 1900. The twentieth century saw the Muslim rulers with their crowns either lost or in danger of being lost. It also saw the Muslim people struggling to find a voice of their own. Everywhere they were trying to think for themselves in political, social, and spiritual matters. So far the Muslim world had been led by priests and kings; the common man had followed. He could ask for patronage, but he had no rights of his own. He had not been allowed to exercise his right to think for himself where affairs of his society and his state were concerned. His thinking had been done for him. Now, when he came into contact with the West, he found that his rulers were neither equipped materially to meet the challenge of the West, nor open enough in mind to accept their own backwardness nor willing to make efforts to make up their deficiency. The educated Muslim therefore began to think and speak for himself. The leaders of orthodox thought feared that the common man would be dazzled by the material progress, the material power, and the political might of the Western nations and would give up his own beliefs, and lose his pride, becoming a mere worshipper of the West. All these things happened.

The Gain and Loss. There was loss in this contact with the West. The Muslim states began to fall before the advancing Europeans. North, West, and Central Africa were already under either French or British power. India was gone. Afghanistan was under England's thumb; the north of Persia was under the stern influence of Russia and the south was under British control. The Shah ruled in his capital, but his finances, his army, and his resources were all under foreign direction. The Ottomans had suffered many defeats and were gasping for life. Indonesia was under Dutch domination and had been so for two hundred years. The Muslim rulers of these lands had lost power and prestige everywhere. The people, on the other hand, were fighting for democratic principles, for social justice, for education, for other social services; this was the gain. Indeed, it was the impact of the West that inspired the people in all Muslim lands. But the people had also their losses. They were losing their respect for Islamic traditions, forgetting their past, and ignoring Islamic thought. Their questioning attitude was not wrong. It stimulated their minds, but it was leading them further and further away from their own customs, beliefs, and traditions. This danger was realized by many Muslim thinkers in the twentieth century. The most prominent of them was Dr. Sir Muhammad Iqbal of India, who devoted the last thirty years of his life to giving the Muslims of the world a new evaluation of Islam, and a correct interpretation and perspective. Iqbal and similar thinkers, however, would have achieved little if the times had not produced an audience ready to listen to them, to understand them, and to act on their ideas.

The Ottomans—Macedonia (1902). The greatest awakening was in Turkey. Newspapers like *Iqdam*, and new writers were experimenting with ideas of self-determination. When the Macedonians rose in 1902 and the Sultan put down the rising, the European powers intervened. The aim of these powers was that the Balkans should be free. Russia and Austria now met and announced the Mürsteg Reforms for Macedonia, which meant that the Sultan might continue to be the suzerain, but that Macedonia would be free. When the Sultan did not agree, the European allies sent their fleets into the Aegean and occupied the Turkish island of Lemnos, and in 1905 the Sultan had to yield. The following year there was a dispute between England and Turkey over the border between Egypt and Palestine. The British issued an ultimatum and the Sultan yielded again.

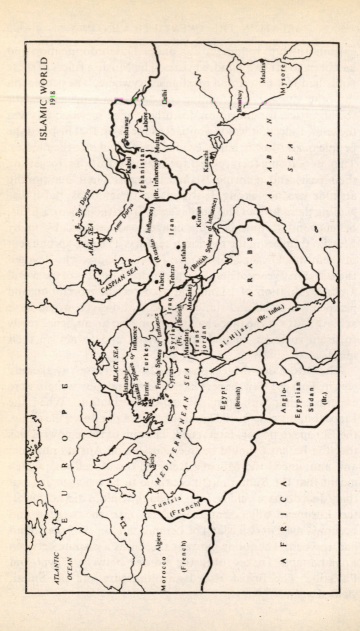

ISLAMIC WORLD
1918

The Young Turks—Committee of Union and Progress. This humiliation of the Turks roused the Young Turks again. These progressive nationalists, though banished from their native land for holding opinions different from those of the autocratic Sultan, had kept in touch with each other. They now met in Paris in December 1907 and drew up a programme. They decided to increase their influence in Turkey by contacting officers of the Turkish army. They also established Masonic Lodges in various towns of the Empire. When the Czar met King Edward VII of England in 1908, apparently to discuss the granting of more reforms to Macedonia, but really to come to an understanding about Turkey, the Young Turks grew alarmed. They realized that the European powers, especially Russia and England, were bent on cutting up the Ottoman Empire. They therefore organized in 1908 a Committee of Union and Progress (*Ittehad-aur-Taraqqi*) making Niazi Bey its chief organizer. These new nationalists now organized a rising at Resna in Macedonia. The army sent against them went over to the Young Turks, and on the demand of the Young Turks the Sultan was forced to restore the Constitution of 1876.

Anglo-Russian Understanding—Muhammad V (1909-1918). The next few years brought more misfortune for the Turks. In October 1908 Austria quietly moved her forces into Bosnia and Herzegovina, and Bulgaria, banking on the support of Austria and Russia, declared her independence. The Turks were in no position to fight Russia so they tried to negotiate, but here too they found no answer to their problem, as the European powers were not in agreement over the Balkan issue. To make matters worse, Crete, so far a Turkish possession, now proclaimed her independence and decided to join Greece. Considering this Balkan muddle, the powers agreed to attend a conference called in London in October 1908. The Turkish Parliament then deposed Sultan Abdul Hamid II in 1909 and put Sultan Muhammad V on the throne. The conference in London decided that Austria should retain Bosnia and Herzegovina. Turkey was to be given compensation for her loss of suzerainty. Serbia did not like the state of affairs at all and mobilized, but found no support from anybody. She submitted, but her hatred of Austria grew.

The First Balkan War. In the next four years the Turks were forced to see other parts of their empire falling from their grasp. First occurred a revolt in Albania, which was put down, much blood being shed in the process. Consequently the feelings between the Albanians and the Turks became more bitter. Then there was considerable unrest in Arabia; that too was suppressed and again feelings became aggravated. In 1911 Italy invaded Tripoli and Turkey sent an army across, but Italy was near and her forces were better equipped. The Turks fought on and Italy therefore sent her fleet to the Dardanelles and conquered Rhodes and the Dodecanese islands. Seeing Turkey engaged in this unequal war, Bulgaria sent a note to Turkey, asking her to give home rule to Macedonia: the other Balkan powers joined Bulgaria and their forces defeated a Turkish army at Lale Burgas in November 1912: even Adrianople fell. At this time the Turkish Government stood helpless, so the Group of Enver Pasha, containing Talaat Pasha and Jemal Pasha, organized a *coup d'état* in January 1913 and overthrew the government. By the Lausanne Treaty Turkey had already lost Tripoli to Italy and also Thrace and the island of Crete to Greece, so when Enver Pasha took over, Turkey was finished as a European and an African power.

The Second Balkan War (1913). Enver, Talaat, and Jemal tried to get the situation under control, but they soon had another war on their hands. The Balkan powers differed again. Serbia and Greece joined against Bulgaria, because Bulgaria had refused to give more of Macedonia to Serbia. General Savov of Bulgaria now attacked the Serbo-Greek positions. At this stage Turkey joined Rumania against Bulgaria. There was unrest throughout the Balkans. After a few exchanges, advances and retreats, in which the Turks took back Adrianople, the war ended in the Treaty of Bucharest on 10 August 1913. As a result, the boundaries between the Balkan powers were slightly changed. By the Treaty of Constantinople which followed on 29 September 1913 the Turks retained Adrianople and their western boundary was fixed on the Maritza River. After this loss, in which every European power had done her worst against Turkey, the three men at the top, Enver, Talaat, and Jemal, decided to call a German Military Mission to reorganize their army. Germany was the only European state, which had as yet done no harm to Turkey. She sent General Liman von Sanders to rebuild their army, but this did not please the other Europeans, especially Russia. Later France and England joined Russia in insisting that the Turks should remove General von Sanders from the command. Turkey had to submit, but this event showed to what extent her ancient enemies would go to ensure that she remained helpless and weak. The secret alliance which she contracted with Germany was the reason why Turkey joined Germany against England, France, and Russia in the First World War. The painful history of five hundred years was behind the choice of the Turks.

Persia (1900-1914)—Liberal Government. The political awakening in Turkey was not a solitary incident. Similar events were taking place at the time in Egypt, Persia, and even in India. The East was waking up. New ideas of the liberty of the individual, the rights of man, and the sovereignty of the people were working like a political ferment everywhere. In Persia, the liberal movement started by Jamaluddin Afghani had spread widely. The Shah had appointed Ayn ud-Daulah as Chief Minister in 1903 and he had proved very corrupt. The people suspected that he took money from foreign powers to increase their influence in the country. There were demonstrations against him everywhere. The Shah however, treated the demands of the people with disdain and suppressed the demonstrations with harshness. In order to escape the Shah's soldiers, the people fled in thousands to the British Legation and the indignation increased. The British intervened and the Great Bast (Agreement) between the Shah and the people resulted: the Shah was forced to dismiss Ayn ud-Daulah on 5 August 1906. The Persian Parliament, the Majlis, was now called. It met at Tehran on 7 October and drew up a constitution. The Shah died soon after and was succeeded by his son Muhammad Ali Shah (1907-1909). The new Shah was bitterly opposed to the reforms and he and his minister, Atabeg-i-Azam, determined to oppose the constitution. But the people were fully awake now. The result of the reactionary policy of the Shah was the death of Atabeg, who was assassinated in August 1907. A new liberal ministry under Nasir ul-Mulk was sworn in, but the Shah persisted in his unwise policy.

Foreign Influence in Persia. The Shah attempted a *coup d'état* and imprisoned Nasir ul-Mulk in December 1907. This led to popular risings all over the country which forced the Shah to release the liberal Premier. But he was an obstinate man and continued to entertain thoughts of crushing the people's movement. He conspired with the Russian Legation and with the help of the Cossack Brigade shut down the Majlis, killed many of the liberal leaders, and proclaimed Martial Law in Tehran. He did not, however, succeed everywhere. At Tabriz the people seized power into their own hands and shut their gates against the army that the Shah sent against them. The Shah appealed to Russia, who sent an army and conquered Tabriz. Encouraged by the Shah, the Russians treated the people of Tabriz in a very brutal manner. This angered the Persians. There was extreme unrest everywhere and three months later Ali Quli Khan, the leader of the Bakhtiari tribe, marched on Tehran, captured it and deposed the Shah. He set Sultan Ahmad, the twelve-year-old son of the Shah, on the throne and restored the constitutional government. The same year the Anglo-Persian Oil Company was formed. A pipe-line was constructed from the oilfields to Abadan in Shatt-ul-Arab and oil refineries were set up there. Persia soon became a great oil-producing country.

Foreign Influences. The constitutional government was restored, but foreign influences did not decrease. In 1911 W. Morgan Schuster, an American financier, arrived at the request of the government to reorganize the finances of the country. Schuster was given great powers and a special guard was organized to protect him and the treasury. The ex-Shah, who had fled to Russia, was given an army by the Czar and landed at Astrabad on the Caspian Sea, though the Government's forces soon put an end to his pretensions. In reply Russia invaded Persia and on 24 December 1911 the leading statesmen of the country declared a State of Emergency, closed the Majlis and formed a Directory to cope with the situation. Russian influence began to increase, and Persia was in this unhappy state when the First World War started.

Egypt (1900-1914). The British were in full possession of Egypt and the Sudan when the century dawned. The Khedive was a mere figurehead. The Aswan Dam on the Upper Nile was completed and opened officially in December 1902. Two years later, the British finally accepted the Suez Convention by which the Suez Canal was to be free and open to merchant and war vessels of all powers in war as well as in peace. This convention gave the Sultan of Turkey and the Khedive of Egypt power 'to take such measures as they might find necessary for securing by their own forces the defence of Egypt and the maintenance of public order.' The British did not, however, let Egypt exercise this last power for fifty years. In 1906 the British gave an ultimatum to the Sultan asking him to renounce claims to the Sinai Peninsula. Since the Sultan was by now almost powerless, the peninsula became Egyptian territory, and therefore came under British influence.

Egyptians and Foreign Rule. The people of Egypt were not happy, and hated every day of foreign rule. Since, however, the Khedive had not allowed them to develop any public institutions, they could do nothing. In June 1906 a shooting accident caused the death of some villagers and an Englishman. The British caught the 'culprits' and punished them severely. This affair caught the attention of the public and it was discussed in newspapers all over the country. Violent speeches were delivered and excited articles written against the British, who had given special privileges to members of their own nationality. The national feeling, which had gradually been created by such liberal thinkers as Shaikh Muhammad Abduh, the Rector of al-Azhar University, and by writers like Mustafa Kamil who had started a movement called *Hizb ul-Watan* and who, since 1900, had been editing the national paper *al-Liwa* (The Banner), was strengthened. On the forceful representation of Mustafa Kamil, Cromer, the Consul-General, was withdrawn and Sir Eldon Gorst was sent instead. But the new Consul-General was no better. He supported the Khedive against all reforms, so Mustafa Kamil and his party of Liberals turned against him, too. They called a National Congress in 1907 and in its sessions raised the cry of 'Egypt for the Egyptians'. The movement slowly gained ground and though suppressed did not weaken or die. After Gorst, Lord Kitchener became the Consul-General (1911) and he was even more severe against the 'agitators'. Both he and the Khedive tried all measures to crush the movement, but did not succeed. At last in July 1913, Lord Kitchener's Government had to introduce a new electoral law and a new constitutional system. The old Assembly was abolished and some popular authority was given to the new Assembly. It was given power to initiate legislation and to supervise the budget. The Assembly met early in 1914. On 6 November 1914, Egypt proclaimed a state of war with Turkey and on 16 December 1914 was declared a British protectorate. The following day the Khedive Abbas II was deposed, because he had pro-Turkish leanings. An uncle of Abbas II, Hussain Kamil, was seated on the throne in his place (1914-1917), though he had no say in state affairs.

Al-Maghrib and Ifriqiya. By the turn of the century, France was in possession of the whole of north-west Africa, except for part of Morocco. She now came into conflict with Kaiser William II, who, realizing that Germany had been left out of North Africa, started diplomatic relations with the Sultan of Morocco. He went so far as to visit the Sultan in 1905. The French grew afraid of German influence in this area and offered a port to the Germans in Morocco, and other economic concessions, but the Kaiser was no friend of the French; he refused all the offers. An international conference, called in 1906, gave equal economic opportunity to all Europeans in the country. The tribal people hated the French, and caused continual trouble. This gave France the excuse to occupy north Morocco in 1907. In 1909 France and Germany came to another agreement over economic concessions, but this agreement did not last. The following year the Riff tribesmen rose in Spanish Morocco under their leader Raisuli. France had now an excuse to declare to the other European nations that she was needed to maintain order in Morocco. Since the other powers had agreed already not to interfere, Morocco became a French Protectorate in 1912.

India (1900-1914)—Muslim Awakening. In India, Muslims had begun to take part in politics, after the Aligarh movement of Sir Sayyid had been accepted by the people. There was still opposition from very old-fashioned and narrow-minded Ulema, but the Muslims had realized by the end of the nineteenth century that it was foolish to isolate themselves. New education was therefore being welcomed by most of them. National bodies like the *Anjuman-i-Himayat-i-Islam* of Lahore had come into being in many places and private effort was assisting the efforts of the Government in educating the Muslims. With education came employment in Government offices, then the most coveted form of service, and with education and service came political consciousness. The Muslims brought out their own newspapers, both in English and Urdu; they began to educate public opinion and journalists like Abul Kalam Azad, Zafar Ali Khan, and Maulana Muhammad Ali became national heroes for the Muslims.

Congress and Hindi. The Indian National Congress was first organized in 1885 and met annually to discuss particular proposals and later on, questions of the government's general policy. The Hindus were in a majority, since most Muslims, acting on advice, did not support the Congress. The word 'national' was very popular with the Hindus because it covered the very large majority of the Hindus everywhere in India. They now started to clamour for Hindi as their 'national' language. This language existed only on paper as yet, and was spoken as a crude dialect in the countryside in the United Provinces only, but the far-sighted Hindus claimed that they had nothing to do with Urdu. The extremists even said that they could never accept it as it was written in the Arabic script. This was a fallacious argument, but popular sentiment is never logical. So loud was their claim that early in the first decade of the century Hindi was accepted on an equal footing with Urdu in the United Provinces.

Muslim League. Leaders of Muslim opinion, among whom must be counted the then young, very energetic, and liberal-minded Agha Khan, joined to form the Muslim League in 1906. Membership of the Muslim League was long confined to either titled Muslim notables or *jagirdars* and big landlords or highly placed Muslim officials, and its policy was on the whole pro-British, but it began to serve a useful purpose early in its life. For instance, it demanded separate electorates for Muslims in the promised reforms. The British saw the point, and separate electorates were given to Muslims in the Morley-Minto Reforms of 1909. With the introduction of these reforms Indian members came to be appointed to the Viceroy's Council too. With Muslim representation on the Councils started the second stage of the education of the Indian Muslims in political matters. They could now not only impress on the Government their views on national and communal issues, but also protest strongly to the Government, as they did, against the dismemberment of Turkey. Things were in this stage when the First World War started, but the National Movement continued its activities, in spite of the repressive measures of the Government.

Indonesia—The Coming of Islam. Indonesia, as such, did not exist in 1900, as it was then known as the Dutch East Indies. Muslim traders from West India, mostly from Gujarat, had started coming to these islands in the fifteenth century. At first, they started small trading concerns, but since they were honest in their dealings and were a link with the Middle East and even Europe, they were welcomed by the local traders and the local Rajas; some of whom accepted Islam. A Raja of Borneo is recorded to have been converted in 1510. When the famous Portuguese navigator Magellan touched Borneo in his round-the-world voyage, he recorded having met Muslims there. Gradually the Muslims settled in little pockets on the coasts of Sumatra and Java. They inter-married with the Indonesians and learnt the language of the people. In the course of time their vigour and industry won power for them. They established little principalities of their own in all the islands. It was not very long afterwards that they built powerful kingdoms of their own, like those of Demak and Malacca.

The Europeans—The Dutch. In the sixteenth century the Portuguese began to take an interest in the islands. They came in search of spices, but finding the islanders poorly equipped with weapons of defence, began to think of conquest. After them came the Dutch and then the British. These two powers fought for supremacy in this area during the seventeenth and eighteenth centuries. By the beginning of the nineteenth century, the islands had come into Dutch hands. The Dutch wanted to exploit the people and the islands for their own benefit; they had therefore no idea of developing the country for the good of the people. In 1830, they introduced the Forced Culture System, by which they controlled the crops and fixed the prices to suit themselves. Forty years later, they gave new Sugar Laws to the people, and even new Agrarian Laws, by which they relaxed the control over crops and prices which had been in force for so long. This state of affairs continued for another forty years. Meanwhile the British got control of North Borneo and the Dutch of the remaining islands of the group. But the Dutch, like the British in India, needed educated natives to work for them in subordinate posts, or to be middlemen between them and the farmers, to bring raw materials for their factories. They could not stop the richer ones from going abroad. Schools were being developed too, and people were becoming aware of what the subject nations of the Europeans in Asia and Africa were doing to win reforms and political rights. They began to express themselves in their national newspapers and by the time the First World War started were demanding political representation in the legislatures of their country. At last the Dutch decided to give a Legislative Council to the East Indies. It was to have twenty-four elected and twenty-four nominated members, though it had no legislative powers. It could only advise the government on political issues and discuss the budget. This is always the first stage of political reforms, granted to any subject people; so a point had been gained.

World War I—(1914-1919). The First World War concerned the Muslims only in the part played in it by the Turks. Persia was occupied early in the war by Russia and Great Britain and later by Great Britain alone. Afghanistan had as yet no real independence and could not go to war with any country without British approval. So the only Muslim power which still had any political life was Turkey. Her 'empire' existed only on the strength of the Arab countries of Iraq, Syria, Palestine, and al-Hijaz. Nejd was removed from all political influences, shut off as it was by deserts on all sides. Since the Turks had chosen to ally themselves with Germany, the British attempted to break up the rest of the Ottoman Empire. They sent a British Expeditionary Force, which was strongly reinforced by Indian regiments, many of them containing large percentages of Muslims, some even wholly Muslim in character, against the Turks who fought the British on three fronts, Mesopotamia, Palestine, and the Dardanelles. After a few advances and retreats, the British forces were successful on the lower fronts. Early in the war the Turks under one of their younger military commanders, Mustafa Kemal by name, fought heroically to defend Gallipoli against the British force which had landed there. In this engagement the Turks fought as they had done centuries before and drove the British from their coasts. They had some victories to their credit in Mesopotamia and Palestine, but the British succeeded in rousing the Arabs everywhere against their overlords the Turks.

The Revolt of the Arabs. The Arabs were promised independence if they joined the British. Helped by the Arabs, the British began to push forward both in Mesopotamia and in Palestine and finally in Syria. Baghdad and Damascus fell and the war ended in the defeat of the Central Powers. Turkey was now at the mercy of the European Allies and they showed no mercy. After the war, Palestine, Transjordan, and Mesopotamia were given to the British as mandates for twenty years, and Syria to the French. The Sharif of Mecca, who had helped the British, was given al-Hijaz and his sons the thrones of the other British Mandates. Istanbul was occupied by an international army. What remained of Turkey was divided into four spheres of influence. The western coast of Asia Minor went to Greece, the northern to Russia, the southern to France and Italy. Only the central plateau of Anatolia was not given away: it was so barren that nobody accepted it. Turkey was supposed to be finished. After six hundred years the Turks were no longer a power. The last sovereign state of Islam was gone and the West had won a complete victory over the East.

Post-War Muslim World (1918-1939)—Turkey. 1919 was a terrible year for Turkey. The Sultan was a mere puppet in the hands of the Western powers, but during that year a leader rose among the defeated and dispirited Turks who was to liberate Turkey. He was Mustafa Kemal, the hero of Gallipoli and a leader of the Young Turks. He organized a Nationalist Congress at Erzerum and produced a National Pact which was brought before the Parliament and passed. It included, among other things, abolition of capitulations and self-determination for the Turks. The Allies objected and sent General Milne to occupy Istanbul. The Nationalists retorted by setting up a provisional government at Angora (Ankara) on 23 April 1920, with Mustafa Kemal as President.

Mustafa Kemal as Liberator. The National Government worked fast. Combining force with diplomacy it succeeded in making separate treaties with Russia, France, and Italy. The Russians and the Italians withdrew. The Greeks were, however, very hostile and since they had the support of Lloyd George, the British Prime Minister, began a war of conquest. They defeated the Turks at Alashehr, occupied Adrianople in Thrace and Brusa in Asiatic Turkey. The Sultan was then made to accept the Treaty of Sévres in August 1920, by which the Turks had officially to give up all claims to non-Turkish lands, but Mustafa Kemal did not submit. He planned his campaigns with the same vigour as he would have done had he had enormous resources. Nothing could have been more ill-equipped than the Nationalist army, but it had a great commander. The Greeks defeated the Turks more than once, but by August 1921 Mustafa Kemal was pushing back the Greeks. A year later he defeated them and forced them to quit Smyrna, to which they set fire when they left. The allied powers threatened Turkey, but Mustafa Kemal stood firm. At last at the Council of Mudania (October 1922) the Allies accepted Mustafa Kemal and his New Turkey. Thrace was returned to Turkey and the Dardanelles and the Bosphorus were declared neutral. After this, Mustafa Kemal turned to the internal affairs of his country and abolished the Sultanate. A year later he dissolved the Caliphate too and declared Turkey a republic. He now cut himself off completely from the past, which had choked the life out of his country, and he made changes in every field of life. He declared Turkey to be a secular state; he adopted the Latin script, he abolished purdah, polygamy, and the Muslim law. He adopted European systems of criminal and civil law and began to modernize his country on European lines. At first he met with a lot of opposition, both internal and external, but he was a strong man and he knew how to fight. He had some very loyal comrades and worked like a dozen men himself. In the fifteen years of his presidentship he completely revolutionized Turkey, and made it secure and progressive. By the time he died, he was accepted in the whole Islamic world as a great man. He was known everywhere as Ata-türk, that is, the father of the Turks. He died in 1938 and was succeeded by his old companion and friend Ismet Inönü who had been the first Premier of the Republic of Turkey. Ismet Inönü's great achievement was that he continued to work steadily at building up the country, kept Turkey out of the Second World War and made it emerge stronger in 1945 than it had been in 1939 when the war exploded.

Ismet was re-elected in 1939, 1943, and 1946, but was defeated in 1950 and was succeeded by Celal Bayar. In October 1939, Turkey concluded mutual assistance pacts with Britain and France, but remained neutral during most of the Second World War. On 23 February 1945 she declared war on Germany and Japan, but did not take any active part in the conflict. Soviet Russia put pressure on her after the war for a share in the control of the Dardanelles, but Turkey did not yield and instead accepted military aid from the U.S.A. in 1947, to modernize her armed forces. She also received aid under the

European Recovery Programme and was accepted as a full member of NATO in 1952. Turkey's armed forces were fully modernized and her economy greatly improved. Her dynamic Premier, Adnan Menderes, the then Premier started various projects for modernizing her towns, especially Istanbul, and his party (the Democrats) again returned to power. In February 1955, Turkey signed in Baghdad a defence treaty with Iraq, which was joined later by Pakistan, Iran, and Great Britain and was called the Baghdad Pact. It was a defence alliance to combat Communist aggression.

Persia. Persia had declared herself neutral in the First World War, but she had, in fact, no say in her foreign policy. Russia therefore occupied most of the towns in the north and the British those in the south, and later the central zone. The Shah had only one choice left; to ask for German aid. The German officials in Persia came forward to advise him and this made England anxious. General Sir Percy Sykes was sent to Persia. He organized the South Persian Rifles and marched with his troops to Isfahan. When the Russians withdrew from Persia after the Bolshevik Russian Revolution of 1917, British influence was supreme over the whole country. It remained so during the war, but after 1919, England again acknowledged the independence of Persia. She promised a loan and other concessions in return for more privileges especially oil concessions. The Shah agreed, but the Majlis refused to ratify the agreement. Persia was now in a hopeless state, and needed a leader as badly as Turkey had done. Here, too, the leader came from the people. He was an officer in the Cossack Brigade, called Reza Khan.

The Pahlavis come to Power (February 1921). The Russians continued to interfere in Persia, even after the Revolution. In 1919, the Bolsheviks occupied Enzali, Resht, and the province of Gilan. The Persian Cossack Brigade went up to meet them, but was defeated. The British now reorganized the brigade. One of the senior officers was Reza Khan. He was an intelligent and resourceful man, capable of great energy and patriotism. In February 1921, he set to work to remove the Russian officers from the brigade. When that was done, he negotiated with Sayyid Ziyauddin, a famous Persian writer and reformer. After coming to an understanding with him, he marched on Tehran with 3,000 Cossacks and set up a new government there in which Ziyauddin was Prime Minister and General Reza Khan War Minister and Commander-in-Chief. General Reza's first move was to come to terms with the Bolsheviks, who agreed to withdraw from Persia, cancel all debts, and abolish capitulations and indemnities. They did this in order to strengthen Persia, so that the British influence might be weakened, but the agreement was also to Persia's advantage. In 1922 Reza Khan called in an American financial expert to reorganize the country's finances. He strengthened the army, suppressed a revolt in Gilan and brought Azerbaijan, which was showing separatist tendencies, under control. In 1923, he became Premier and the Shah left for Europe never to return. Later that year General Reza Khan had to subdue the powerful Bakhtiari tribes of the south who had risen in revolt. He ran the government very capably, and introduced many progressive measures. In February 1925 the Majlis invested him with the powers of a dictator. A few months later the Shah was declared deposed, and on 25 April 1926 General Reza Khan was proclaimed king as Reza Shah Pahlavi.

Reza Shah as King. Reza Shah was as progressive as Mustafa Kemal, though not so radical. He restored order in the country, rebuilt the defence forces, and began construction work on railways and other public works. Education and contact with the West were encouraged. As in Turkey, a new judicial system based on French law was introduced and the capitulations were abolished. He inaugurated the National Bank of Persia the same year and later nationalized the lines of the Indo-European Telegraph Company. In 1932 the Persian navy was founded. The following year a new agreement was signed with the Anglo-Persian Oil Company, by which the royalties to Persia were increased. Reza Shah now established friendly relations with Afghanistan, Iraq, and Turkey. It is unfortunate that such a progressive monarch was not allowed to remain neutral in the Second World War. In August 1941 the Allies (Great Britain and Russia) removed the Shah from the throne and occupied Iran, putting his son, Muhammad Reza Pahlavi, on the throne instead. During the war Iran served as a strategic base for the Allies.

In November 1945, the Soviets inspired a movement for self-government in Azerbaijan, the north-western province of Iran, and even sent troops to help the Communists who had won power there. Iran protested to the United Nations and the Russians had to remove their troops, which they did in May 1946. In 1950 Ali Razmara became Premier, but was assassinated a year later. Then Dr. Mohammad Mossadeq, who had strong sympathies with the Iranian Communists, the Tudeh Party, came to power. Mossadeq nationalized the oil industry and forced the British to evacuate the Abadan oil fields on 3 October 1951. All negotiations between Iran and Great Britain failed and though Mossadeq won his case at the World Court, he was ousted in August 1953 in a *coup d'état* led by Fazollah Zahedi, who was then appointed Premier. The oil dispute was settled in August 1954 and on 7 April 1955, Zahedi was succeeded by Husain Ala. Iran joined the Baghdad Pact in 1956 and thus became an integral link in the defensive belt between Soviet Russia and the Arab World. This pact also made her safe from Soviet threats, which had been a feature of her past for two hundred years.

Egypt (1919-1957). During the First World War the Nationalist movement in Egypt had become strong, mainly because the Egyptians were forced to serve the larger interests of the British Empire. The attitude of the people stiffened and the Nationalists combined to make a new party, the Wafd. The chief organizer and mainstay of the party was the great patriot

Saad Zaghlul Pasha, who had the gifts of honesty, sincerity, intelligence, and leadership. He organized public opinion and made repeated representations to the British, who, feeling that Saad Zaghlul and his party were becoming a great nuisance, arrested them and sent them to Malta. Their arrest was widely resented and led to many riots. These riots were put down with such severity by Marshal Allenby that the British Commander-in-Chief of the Egyptian Army, Sir Lee Stack, was assassinated. The British now insisted on wholesale punishments to which Saad Zaghlul could not agree. Since the British continued to insist, he resigned from office, but in the elections which followed Saad's party was again victorious. Saad Zaghlul now became President of the Chamber and blocked all measures proposed by the government. At last, according to a treaty signed in 1927, the British agreed to end the military occupation of Egypt by 1937. Zaghlul died soon afterwards and was succeeded by his lieutenant Mustafa Nahas Pasha.

Democratic Progress in Egypt. After Zaghlul's death, the King began to interfere more and more in the affairs of state; he introduced a new constitution, which reduced the powers of the two Legislative Chambers. He had the backing of England, so he persisted in his policy in spite of public opposition, riots and intense popular resentment. After some more years of political struggle the constitution was restored in December 1935. Four months later the King died and his sixteen-year-old son, Farouk, came to the throne. The elections were now due and again Nahas Pasha and his Wafdists came to power. In August 1936 a new treaty was signed between Egypt and England, by which the British were to withdraw their forces from Egypt except for 10,000 troops which they would maintain in the Canal Zone. England was to keep a naval base in Alexandria for another eight years. A year later the capitulations were abolished too. But the young king now began to have despotic ideas of his own. He dissolved the parliament on 2 February

1938, even though it still had a large Wafd majority. When the new elections were called the government party won a victory. The new government wanted to embark on a military expansion plan, but the Second World War broke out and Egypt again came under military occupation. After the war, British troops were evacuated from Cairo and Alexandria in 1946, but negotiations between Egypt and Great Britain over the revision of the 1936 treaty broke down, as Great Britain refused to recognize Egyptian sovereignty over the Anglo-Egyptian Sudan. In 1951, therefore, Egypt abrogated the treaty and there were riots in the Suez Canal area over the Egyptians' insistent demand that the British should evacuate the Canal Zone. The tension reached its height in January 1952 and on 22 July 1952, the army, led by Major General Mohammad Neguib, seized power. King Farouk abdicated in favour of his infant son, but in June 1953, General Neguib declared Egypt a republic, Neguib becoming the President, as well as the Premier. The latter post was handed over on 18 April 1954 to Colonel Gamal Abdul Nasser, the leader of the ruling military clique. Gamal Nasser deposed Neguib on 14 November, 1954 and became head of the state. He was confirmed as President in a popular referendum held on 23 June 1956. President Nasser soon began to take over the leadership of the Arab World, by showing a pronounced militant bias. Nasser resented the Anglo-American influence in the Middle East and, making use of the Arab sentiment against Israel, took a very firm stand over the Suez Canal, which he nationalized in July 1956. This was his retort to the withdrawal of the offer of America and Britain to help Egypt in building the new dam at Aswan on the Nile. The whole world protested, but Nasser stood firm. Since negotiations led to nothing, except that Nasser offered to pay for all the remaining Suez Canal shares and the likely dividends, and Egypt rejected the eighteen-nation proposal of international control of the canal, Britain, France, and Israel invaded Egypt in October 1956. The combined armies and air forces of the three countries smashed Egyptian resistance and overran Sinai. The city of Port Said was captured and Cairo bombarded. Egypt retaliated by sinking old ships in the Canal and blocking it, and by cutting the oil pipelines which ran through her ally Syria's territory. The United Nations Assembly met and ordered an immediate cease-fire.

Gradually the British, French, and Israeli forces withdrew and by April 1957, the Canal was again in use. Nasser had won his point.

India (1916-1939). In India, the National Movement had continued to do vigorous work during the war and as a consequence most of the leaders had been arrested, tried, and imprisoned. Muhammad Ali and Shaukat Ali, who had until then fought for the Congress, were also imprisoned. The Muslim League and the Congress had made a pact, the Lucknow Pact of 1916, by which the Hindu and Muslim leaders had agreed to work together in future. The British had been upset at this joining of forces and had tried to placate the leaders by promising reforms after the war if the two political bodies helped the war effort. When the war ended in 1918 and no change occurred in the attitude of the government there was violent reaction in the country. The government now did a foolish thing; it passed the Rowlatt Acts by which political workers could be arrested without assigning cause, and imprisoned without trial. The country broke into protest at these despotic ways, but the government declared Martial Law in a number of towns and indescribable barbarities were committed on defenceless, unarmed crowds and assemblies, and in the Punjab even on peaceful citizens of various towns. But cruelty never solves such problems. When the mood of the people did not change, the government was forced to introduce new reforms, the Montagu-Chelmsford Reforms of 1919. Under these reforms a system of diarchy was introduced. Some minor ministries, like Education, Health and Lands, and Local Self-Government were given to Indians, but Finance, Defence,

Communications, Law, etc., were reserved for the British. The Legislative Councils were to have 70 per cent elected seats. The leaders were released, but Mahatma Gandhi, the new Congress Leader, was not satisfied. He decided on a non-co-operation movement. The Muslims, who were burning under a sense of grievance at what Europe had done to the Muslim world, began the Khilafat movement and demanded the restoration of the Caliphate. The Congress and Khilafat parties now joined hands in a non-violent non-co-operation movement, but this friendship did not last long. The Hindus, being in the majority and for historical reasons never very friendly with the Muslims, began to show a desire to make use of the Muslims and later to dominate them. Riots therefore broke out in a number of places and communal feelings became estranged.

The Muslims separate—Sir Muhammad Iqbal. The famous Ali brothers, who had been the most sincere followers of Mahatma Gandhi so far, were now shocked into a sense of stern reality. They broke away from the Congress and joined the Muslim League. From now on, the Muslims began to walk a separate path. They began to cherish their language, rediscover their culture and re-interpret their religion. This was the period when Sir Muhammad Iqbal spread his nationalist ideas and began to address the Muslims. In his two stirring poems *Khizr-i-Rah* and *Tulu-i-Islam* (1921-1922) he called on the Muslims to awake. In 1922 his remarkable *Masnavis*, *Asrar-i-Khudi* and *Rumuz-i-Bekhudi* came out, followed two years later by his first collection of Urdu poems, *Bang-i-Dira*. These poems fired the imagination of the younger generation. A new ferment began to work in the mind and blood of the Muslims. Other leaders like Sir Muhammad Shafi, Sir Fazli Husain, and the Raja of Mahmudabad began to inspire the people with fresh political aims. A new political star also appeared on the horizon, Muhammad Ali Jinnah, a famous barrister of Bombay. As yet a Congressite and at best a liberal in politics, he now began to lean towards the Muslim League.

With his keen brain he began to guide the councils of the Muslim political leaders. Never impassioned, always cool, his deep insight in political matters soon came to be appreciated. Iqbal the great seer realized Jinnah's greatness; there was much communication between them. The Agha Khan offered very valuable guidance · and active help. When the Indian Government found that differences between Hindus and Muslims were growing and no solution was in sight, it called a series of Round Table Conferences in London, for which the Muslims unanimously selected the Agha Khan as their spokesman. These conferences were attended by Allama Iqbal, as well as by Maulana Muhammad Ali who, though very ill, did not hesitate to work for the Muslims. Mr. Jinnah offered his famous Fourteen Points which were discussed by the Muslim representatives in London. The result of all these negotiations was that the British Government passed the *Government of India Act, 1935* which was a landmark in the liberation of India. By it Burma and Aden were cut off from India. The type of government chosen for India was federal with autonomy for the provinces. The Frontier Province was made a Governor's Province and Sind was separated from Bombay. The Governor-General retained only Defence, Finance, Foreign Affairs, and Communications. Soon after this the Second World War started.

World War II—UN. The Second World War does not concern the Muslims much, as Turkey, Arabia, Iran, and Afghanistan, the only independent Muslim countries at the time, did not participate in it. The Indian Muslims fought in the Indian army on various fronts, but they fought for the British cause. The Turks remained neutral and Iran was again occupied by the Allies. Egypt became the headquarters of the Middle-East Command, and North Africa a battleground. The Japanese conquered the Dutch East Indies and during their occupation encouraged the Muslims of those islands to think in terms of political independence. Japan conquered British

Malaya too, which is essentially a Muslim land, but here she could not prevail against the local Sultans who, like the Nawabs and Rajas of India in the British times, were firm allies of the British. The Second World War, however, benefited the Muslim world as much as the first had done. Out of the war-weary post-1918 world had emerged a new Turkey, a new Iran, a new Arabia, and a new Afghanistan. Out of the chaos after the Second World War period, emerged more independent Muslim countries: Pakistan, Egypt, Libya, Indonesia, and the Arab kingdoms and states of north Arabia—Iraq, Syria, Transjordan, and Lebanon. One other effect of the Second World War was the emergence of the United Nations Organization. It is a much stronger body than the League of Nations; it has a better foundation, better aims, more resources, and it has already achieved more results. It is a forum of world opinion and can work for the good of mankind. Smaller nations take their troubles to it and have an opportunity to present their points of view, influence world opinion, and ask for help. Help has been extended in a number of cases. Much more help is being rendered in the subordinate economic, educational, health, and other bodies, which have been fostered by the parent United Nations Organization.

The World of Islam after 1945—Pakistan (1947). The most important event of this period was the emergence of Pakistan. The Muslim League and the Congress had drifted farther and farther apart during the war and seeing that the Hindus were dreaming of Swaraj and Ram Rajya, that is of unquestioned dominance in a future set-up, Muslim opinion became crystallized into the Two Nation Theory which was first propounded by Allama Iqbal in 1930 but was now taken up officially by the Quaid-i-Azam, Muhammad Ali Jinnah, who was now the undisputed head of the Muslim League and therefore of the Muslims of India. The League itself had broadened and become a popular body. In the Lahore Resolution of March 1940, the League officially announced its goal to be Pakistan. Both Hindus and the British made many attempts to break the stand of the Muslims, but the Quaid was firm and would hear of no compromise. At last the British Government agreed. *The Indian Independence Act, 1947* was passed and India was divided. Pakistan became a sovereign state, and a member of the British Commonwealth of Nations. There was trouble over the partition and especially over the boundary dispute, which was referred to arbitration. Hundreds of thousands of Muslims were massacred, tens of thousands of women abducted, and thousands of children murdered. But Pakistan was achieved and that was the reward the Muslims wanted. No nation achieves anything without sacrifice and Pakistan paid the price of her liberty. On the transfer of power to India and Pakistan in August 1947, Muhammad Ali Jinnah became the first Governor-General of Pakistan, with Liaquat Ali Khan as the Premier. Soon after, Pakistan was faced with four formidable problems. The first of these was the transfer of population which resulted in violent clashes with the Sikhs in East Punjab and the Hindus in and around Delhi resulting in a butchery of lakhs of Muslim men, women and children. A few months later, the Raja of Kashmir opted for India, without consulting his people, and India moved her army into Kashmir to protect the Raja's interests. The Muslims of the border, the tribesmen, raided the western approaches of the state. The people of Punchh, the western sub-state in Kashmir, rose and Pakistan moved some troops to the frontier. There were fears of a major conflict, when the Security Council of the United Nations Organization ordered a cease-fire. The third calamity was the Radcliffe Award, by which the district of Gurdaspur although a Muslim majority area went to India, and the fourth was the 'police action' of India against Hyderabad. Pakistan was battling against these problems when the Quaid died on 11 September 1948. Three years later, on 16 October 1951, Liaquat Ali Khan, the foremost man in the new State, was assassinated. Liaquat was succeeded by Nazimuddin as

Premier with Mr. Ghulam Mohammad as Governor-General, Mr. Ghulam Mohammad acting arbitrarily dismissed the Constituent Assembly but in co-operation with East Pakistan leaders like Mr. Husain Shaheed Suhrawardy. He succeeded in getting the constitution of Pakistan passed by which the provinces of West Pakistan were united, the country having thus two provinces of West and East Pakistan with parity at the centre. Ch. Mohammad Ali, an ex-civil service official, was the Premier at that time. Ghulam Mohammad, whose health had failed, was succeeded by Major-General Iskander Mirza in September 1955 and the country was proclaimed a Republic on 23 March 1956, with Iskander Mirza as President. The standard of conduct of public affairs deteriorated rapidly. On 7 October 1958 the President proclaimed Martial Law, abrogated the constitution, dismissed the central and provincial governments and dissolved the legislative assembly. Associated with him in this was Mohammed Ayub Khan, Commander and Chief Martial Law Administrator. A week later General Ayub was made Premier also, and an advisory council was appointed. On 27 October Iskander Mirza was made to resign and General Ayub became President. Many new plans were promised and the country's affairs began to settle down. The country became a member of the Baghdad Pact and the South-East Asia Treaty Organization, but a long period of non-civil governments was thus ushered.

Arabia—The House of Saud. Sharif Husain, who had been the hereditary governor of Hijaz under the Ottomans, was proclaimed King of the Arabs on 29 October 1916, but did not rule long. There had been great rivalry between the Sharifs of Mecca and the House of Saud, since the eighteenth century. The part that King Husain had played during the First World War had not been popular with all Muslims; the House of Saud had not approved of it. The ruler of Nejd at this time was Abdul Aziz ibn Saud. He was a very forceful man and had definite views about how the government of al-Hijaz should be organized. He had been strengthening his position in eastern Arabia since 1913, and had made a treaty of friendship with Great Britain in December 1916. At this time the British wanted as many allies against the Turks as possible. But when Amir Abdul Aziz found that Husain and his family had become dominant in all the countries to the west, north, and north-east of Nejd, he decided to start a campaign. He took Asir in August 1920, and then annexed Hail, the seat of the Rashid Dynasty. In 1922 he took Jauf, the home of the Shalan Dynasty. In 1923, strengthened and secure in Central Arabia, he invaded al-Hijaz. He took Taif in August 1924, Mecca on 3 October, and a year later Jeddah and Medina. On 8 January 1926, Sultan Ibn Saud was proclaimed king of al-Hijaz. In February he added al-Hijaz to his kingdom and within six years he was the ruler of Saudi Arabia.

King Ibn Saud. It was not long before King Ibn Saud had treaties with Great Britain and her Arab Mandates in the north, and, after a lot of trouble, with the Imam of Yemen. Ibn Saud was a very resourceful monarch; he was lucky too. Oil was discovered in Nejd and a profitable oil concession was given to an American concern; Riyadh, the ancestral home of the Sauds, soon becoming the centre of a new industry. Wealth began to pour in and the standard of life in Arabia began to improve. Ibn Saud introduced many reforms. He lightened many of the taxes on pilgrims, provided facilities, built roads, motorized transport, and tried to modernize Saudi Arabia. He took an independent view of international affairs, but when the Arab League idea was proposed, he agreed whole-heartedly to join it and for the rest of his life he remained a staunch supporter of the Arab cause.

Saudi Arabia remained neutral during most of the war and was one of the original members of the United Nations Organization. King Ibn Saud died on 9 November 1953 and was succeeded by the Crown Prince, Saud. Saudi Arabia is virtually an absolute monarchy, though a Council of Ministers, headed by the Prime Minister, was formed in October 1953. Hijaz and Nejd have separate administrations and tribal organizations wield a great deal of influence. Saudi Arabia is rich in oil, and the Aramco (Arab-American Oil Company), with its centre at the popular airport Dhahran, yields a steady and solid income. King Saud took part in world politics, having shown his sympathy with the Democratic bloc. He displayed considerable diplomatic flair and was respected for his views. The country's chief importance still lies in the holy cities of Mecca and Medina, and King Saud elicited respect from most Muslims of the world for his guardianship of these two towns. The annual Hajj has been bringing to Mecca and Medina Muslims from all over the world in increasing proportions.

The Hashimite Kingdoms. As mentioned earlier, Great Britain obtained the Mandates for Iraq, Palestine, and Transjordan after the First World War. To all these places the sons of King Husain of al-Hijaz were nominated. Emir Faisal, who was originally selected as King of Syria, was finally proclaimed King of Iraq on 23 August 1921. There were revolts in the north under Shaikh Mahmud, the Chief of the Kurds, but gradually these disturbances were brought under control. There was considerable trouble with Turkey over the oil-bearing Mosul area which the Allies had taken away from Turkey and given to Iraq, but at last even this question was settled, in June 1926. In return for three air bases given to England, Iraq was promised ultimate independence and admission to the League of Nations. When King Faisal died he was succeeded by his youthful son Ghazi (1933-1939). In 1935 the Mosul oil pipelines to the Mediterranean ports of Tripoli and Haifa were completed. A party of National Reform was formed in 1935 and the country started to learn about democratic government. King Ghazi having died in a motor accident in 1939, his infant son Faisal was proclaimed king, though King Ghazi's brother Prince Abdul Ilah became the Regent and remained so till Prince Faisal came of age.

Palestine and Transjordan—The Jews. Before the Second World War Hitler's campaign against the Jews was forcing large numbers of them to flee from Europe and to fulfil their old prophecy of return to the ancient home of Israel in Palestine. In return for Jewish support during the First World War, Lord Balfour, the British Foreign Minister, had promised his support to the establishment of a national home for the Jews in Palestine, provided that 'this did not harm the rights and privileges of the existing Arab population'. After the war, the Jews were permitted to emigrate to Palestine. They were highly advanced technically, more resourceful than the Arabs, and had the backing of the rich Jews of the world, especially of the Jews of the United States. They began to offer the Arabs large sums of money for their farms and other areas. The Arabs, when they saw how the Jews had been able to improve the land they had bought, felt cheated, and began to fight back. There were many riots and in spite of the efforts of the government the tension grew. There were many attempts at a solution, but no just solution could be arrived at. In sheer self-defence the Arabs formed the Arab High Committee in 1936, to safeguard their interests in the entire Arab world. At last Great Britain appointed a commission to look into the matter and this commission suggested a partition of Palestine. This was acceptable neither to the Arabs nor to the Jews. Much unrest resulted, and the Arabs started an agitation headed by the Grand Mufti of Jerusalem, but nothing came of their protests. This was the state of affairs at the beginning of the Second World War. The Arabs and the Jews co-operated with each other during the war, but when the war ended, friction grew. In 1945 the Arab League was founded, representing all the Arab nations. The League protested strongly against the illegal immigration of Jews into Palestine. The British Mandate ended on 14 May 1948, but when the British forces withdrew, violence increased. Arabs and Jews began to fight each other and the Jewish National Council proclaimed an independent

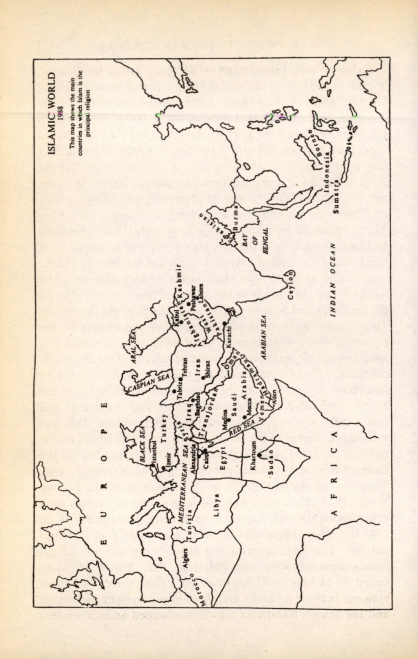

ISLAMIC WORLD
1958

This map shows the main
countries in which Islam is the
principal religion

state of Israel. The Arab nations, except for Saudi Arabia and Iraq, sent in their troops, but the Jews fought back strongly. There was a short truce in June 1948, but a month later, hostilities were resumed. The Jews now began to advance on all fronts. The United Nations Organization at last managed to call a cease-fire on 7 January 1949. During the short war, however, the Jews lost none of the territories allotted to them under the Partition Plan, and in fact acquired about fifty per cent more land. In 1950 Jordan annexed eastern and central Palestine, including the old city of Jerusalem, and Palestine ceased to exist as a separate land. King Abdullah of Jordan was assassinated on 20 June 1951 and his son Talal, who was pronouncedly anti-British, was deposed on 11 August 1952, because he was alleged to be mentally ill. King Talal's young son Hussain, who was studying in the United Kingdom, was recalled and seated on the throne. King Hussain had in the beginning a difficult time, because of uneasy relations with Israel and the hostile attitude of Egypt and Syria, who had been showing a marked pro-Soviet bias for some time. King Hussain, however, showed open friendship with the democratic bloc, accepted aid from U.S.A. and Saudi Arabia, and faced his enemies boldly.

Syria. In 1930 France had recognized Syria as an independent republic, but it was still subject to the mandate. In 1939 the nationalists made demonstrations and there was rioting. As a result, the French High Commission suspended the Syrian constitution. During the war Syria was an Allied base, but in 1945 there were nationalist demonstrations again and the British troops had to restore order. The Syrian forces participated in the 1948 action against Israel, but met with a number of reverses. In March 1949 Husni Zagim organized a *coup d'état* and thereafter there were many such *coups d'état*, that of November 1951, by Colonel Adib Shishakly being the most successful one. Shishakly was elected President in July 1953, but was overthrown in February 1954. On 18 August

1955 Shukri al-Kuwatly was elected President. Al-Kuwatly's policy was pro-Soviet and the country began by having a strong alliance with Egypt, whose President is acknowledged as the head of this axis. On 1 February 1958, Syria joined Egypt to form the United Arab Republic though the alliance did not last long.

Afghanistan. Afghanistan had remained neutral in the First World War, but the Amir, Habibullah, was a friend of the British and was in regular receipt of subsidies from the Government of India, in order that he should reject German offers of alliance. The Afghans objected to this pro-British attitude and, perhaps as a result of this, the Amir was assassinated in February 1919. He was succeeded by his younger son Amanullah (1919-1929) who was Governor of Kabul and had the support of the army. There was now a wave of anti-British feeling in the country and the Afghans invaded India. There was a desultory war for a few months, but in August 1919 the Treaty of Rawalpindi put an end to it. Afghanistan was declared independent and British subsidies stopped. King Amanullah was a man of liberal views and tried to introduce political and social reforms in his country, but he did not prepare the ground for these reforms and when he promulgated the Fundamental Law in 1923, which gave a constitution and other reforms to the country, he raised much opposition. There was a revolt led by a bandit, Bacha Saqa, who marched with the malcotents on Kabul and captured it; he also forced Amanullah to flee. Bacha Saqa reigned for a year and then General Nadir Khan, a very able man, arrived from Europe. He assembled an army and defeated Bacha Saqa, took Kabul on 8 October 1929, and was proclaimed king on 16 October. He reigned for four years only, but laid down the lines on which his country was to run. He was succeeded by his son, Zahir Shah, but the powers behind the throne, and the actual rulers of the country, were the brothers of the late king, who were led by Sardar Hashim Khan. Afghanistan remained neutral during World War II, and was admitted to the United Nations in November 1946. It became an ally of India when the British left that country, and began to agitate for the tribal area of Pakistan's north-western frontier, declaring it to be a part of larger Afghanistan, which it named Pakhtoonistan. The country accepted aid from Soviet Russia and began to develop its resources. Relations between Afghanistan and Pakistan remained strained.

Indonesia. There had been progress in the East Indies also. A Legislative Council had been created in 1916 and it met in 1918. Half of the forty-eight members were elected. It was as yet an advisory body, but it was a step in the right direction. Six years later, it became a real legislative assembly and its assent was now made necessary for all government measures. The Assembly was enlarged in 1929 with thirty East Indian members out of a strength of sixty. A National Indonesian Party now came into being and in 1937 the *Volksraad*, as the assembly was called, voted unanimously for Dominion Status. The war now intervened, but in August 1945, two days after the Japanese surrender, Dr. Sukarno and Dr. Muhammad Hatta, the Indonesian leaders, proclaimed the Republic of Indonesia. The British and Dutch troops which had arrived to supervise the repatriation of the Japanese troops, turned on the army of the new republic, and there was some fighting, but the Indonesians stood firm. The Dutch offered to negotiate and proposed that Indonesia should become a Dominion of Holland, but the Indonesians did not agree. Fighting continued, till the Indonesian Republic was recognized by the Cheribon Agreement of 15 November 1946. There were still differences and even fighting between the Indonesians and the Dutch, so the matter was referred to the UN. Negotiations were started between officials of the UN and both the parties. A truce was signed in January 1948 and the matter went to the Security Council. Complete agreement was at last reached in November 1949 and in August 1950 the Republic of Indonesia was accepted as an independent sovereign state. After attaining independence, the leaders strove to set the country's affairs in order; this was necessary, as the country had had no peace since the Japanese occupied the islands during the war. As was natural, there were a number of economic, financial, and political crises, but in the hands of Dr. Sukarno, the President, the country began to settle down. Dr. Hatta was succeeded by Dr. Ali Sastromidjojo as Premier, but Sukarno began to show a more and more pronounced leaning towards the Indian Premier, Mr. Nehru's, 'neutral' policy, which meant taking advantage of both the Democratic and the Soviet world blocs. He frankly declared that he believed in guided democracy. Having failed to get the issue of West New Guinea settled, he ordered in December 1957 that all Dutch concerns in Indonesia should be nationalized. There had been disturbances already in the country, the Nationals, the Masjumi (Muslims) and the Communists being evenly balanced. The new Premier, Djunda, forced Sukarno to retire for a time and he was succeeded by Acting President Dr. Sartono, the Parliament Speaker. Sukarno returned as President after a few months.

The Yemen. The Yemen became independent after 1918, before which the Turks had occupied the kingdom. It made treaties with Saudi Arabia and with Great Britain in 1934 and was admitted to the United Nations in 1947. There was a rising in the country in 1948, during which the ruler, the Imam of Yemen, was assassinated. Imam Ahmad, succeeded him in March 1948. To the south-east of the Yemen lay the British Protectorate of Aden. The Yemenites soon had differences with the British over their borders, but on the whole the country remained settled and prosperous. The Yemen had a strong ally in Saudi Arabia.

Morocco and al-Maghrib. The Tangier Statute, which was concluded by England, France, and Spain in 1923, had created an international zone in and around Tangier, which was permanently demilitarized. During the Second World War

Spain occupied the zone, apparently to restore order, but was forced to evacuate in 1945. Morocco was under the Vichy Government during part of the war, but three days after the landing of the Allies in 1942, it came under Allied control. After the war, Sidi Muhammad bin Youssef, who had been Sultan of Morocco under the French since 1927, began to assert himself. His differences with the Resident General grew, but finding the nation behind him, he continued his policy of independent action. The French therefore removed him on 20 August 1953 and exiled him to Madagascar. His uncle, Moulay Mohammad bin Arafa, was placed on the throne, but there was such determined national resistance against him that Sidi Muhammad bin Youssef had to be recalled. In 1956, Morocco gained her independence and it was not long before the progressive Sultan Muhammad began to play a leading role in the Muslim politics of al-Maghrib. He accepted aid from the United States and worked hard to introduce social and political reforms in the country. Soon there were signs of considerable economic progress and diplomatic efforts in conjunction with Mr. Habib Bourgiba, the President of Tunisia, to find a solution to the problems of war-torn Algeria were appreciated. The national movement in Algeria grew in strength and the nationalists began to fight France and her armed might doggedly and desperately. This went on for many years.

Libya and Tunisia. After the war another new Muslim state came into being when Tripoli, the land which lies between Tunisia and Egypt, now reconquered from Italy, had to be given a new government. The UN decided that it should be made into an independent Muslim state and that its sovereignty should be given to the House of Senussi Shaikhs who had helped the Allies during the war. Consequently Shaikh Idris el-Senussi was raised to the throne of Libya. To the west the Tunisians had been working hard for political rights, but the French had stood firm. However, a determined people generally succeeds and since the Tunisians persisted in the face of severe persecution, the French first gave Home Rule to Tunisia, and later made it independent on 20 March 1956, with Mohammad Lamine Pasha Bey as the ruler. A month later Mr. Habib Bourguiba, the leader of the Neo-Dastour party, was made Premier. The party did not agree with the Bey on most problems and so on 25 July 1957, Bourguiba declared the country a republic and deposed the Bey. Bourguiba, the President and Premier, was an enlightened statesman of moderate views and a sincere patriot. He had been striving hard to make his country economically strong. He began to work for a solution of the Algerian problem. The people of Algeria continued to fight for their independence. They were till 1960 the only Muslim people of note who were still under foreign domination.

The World of Islam around 1960. Islam had at last awakened from a long sleep. Muslims began to think again and tried to understand their responsibilities. The world had changed since the days of early Islam, and so they began to realize that they cannot impose an old pattern, whether social or political, on the new world. They must march with the times, understand the problems which face them and learn to cope with them. Every country will have her difficulties, but they must be met and overcome. Faced with courage, determination, and intelligence such difficulties never prove formidable. Fortunately the Arab-Asian countries are learning to think together. The Afro-Asian countries have made attempts to discuss their problems in a conference. This has been a step in the right direction. Small nations have no place in the modern world, either politically, economically, or technically. The only solution for the Muslims is to come together, and plan a joint economy, which will be beneficial to all. Their culture is basically the same, their languages are not dissimilar, so there is no reason why they should not work together and move forward to a brighter future.

This is apparent to all thinking Muslims, in nearly all Muslim countries, but political conventions, social bonds, traditional loyalties, and the rule of dogma still prevails. Democratic ideas take long to mature and the common man has to fight for his basic rights. In Muslim lands the doctrine that sovereignty rests in the people is taking long to germinate and flourish. But time keeps the determined.

CHAPTER 15

THE WORLD OF ISLAM
1960-86

Notable Events and The Islamic Conference. The World of Islam can be said to have advanced in recent times in self-consciousness, self-determination, co-operation, and the vital impulse. The worldwide Islamic Conference, the first co-ordinating factor in the Muslim World today, has already met four times: in 1969 at Rabat, Morocco; 1974 at Lahore, Pakistan; 1981 at Mecca and Taif, Saudi Arabia; and Casablanca, Morocco in 1984. At Mecca it was decided that the Islamic Summit should meet every three years.

Conference of Foreign Ministers. The Conference of Foreign Ministers of the Islamic States meets annually to consider ways and means of carrying out the policies of the Organization. An extraordinary session was called in January 1980 to discuss the Afghanistan problem. Since the issue was an acute one and the liberty of a Muslim State was threatened, the Foreign Ministers met again in July, September, and October 1980. Resolutions were passed, proposals made, and efforts to find a political solution to the problem of millions of refugees, who had flooded Pakistan and Iran and who moved back by secret ways to take part in the resistance movement organized by the *Mujahids* in Afghanistan, were stressed.

The United Nations passed resolution after resolution urging for a peaceful settlement of the issue. It has recently passed another one with overwhelming majority. Mr. Dego Cordovez, the Special Envoy of the UN Secretary-General, has met top level representatives of the countries involved. There have been seven Geneva Conferences to solve the issue and much has been achieved so far. Mr. Cordovez as well as the world is quite hopeful.

The Islamic Conference Secretariat. The Secretariat of the Conference is established at Mecca. It is headed by a Secretary-General. The aims of the Islamic Conference Secretariat are:

a. To promote better understanding and build up more solid relations among the Islamic countries.

b. To develop and increase better and more effective economic, social, cultural, and scientific relations among Muslims and co-operate, as far as possible in all vital fields, whether of research or discovery.

c. To remove all colour and racial bars as the Prophet advised in his sermon on the occasion of the Last Hajj. He had said: 'My people, you have one Allah and He is the All-Father. Therefore, no Arab can claim superiority over any non-Arab, or a White over a Black or Red, in birth or social distinction. Only he is best among you who is more righteous'.

d. To take the required steps to promote international peace and security founded on justice.

e. To help all Muslim nations in order to safeguard their dignity, independence, and national rights.

f. To join and make every effort to protect the Holy Places and to support the struggle of the people of Palestine.

The Arab League. The Arab World came under Ottoman rule in the sixteenth century. For two hundred years (sixteenth and seventeenth centuries) when the World of Islam gloried in three great empires that of the Ottomans in Eastern Europe, Western Asia, and Northern Africa; the Safavids in Persia; and the Moghuls in the Indo-Pakistan sub-continent, the Arab World lay quiescent. During the eighteenth century, the century of decline, the Muslim psyche woke to life. In Arabia Abdul Wahhab, in Persia Mohammad Ali Bab, and in the sub-continent Shah Waliullah began to breathe new life into the inert body of the Muslim World. The Arabs who had preserved their identity as a separate ethnic group, under the Ottomans, began to revive the memories of their great past.

They began to stress a common cultural past and heritage. Ideas of revival awakened and came to fruition during World War I, when the Arabs revolted against Turkey. They joined the Allies and were promised freedom. Colonel T.E. Lawrence, who liaised with the Sharif of Mecca and made promises in the name of the Allies, has recorded in his books, *The Revolt of the Arabs* and *The Seven Pillars of Wisdom*, how the Arabs were betrayed. In the Peace Settlement of 1919, the Arab World was split into a number of mandates, under British and French domination. Only Saudi Arabia and Yemen escaped.

The Mandatory States Win Freedom. In 1943, seven of these mandated countries achieved independence. An Arab Conference was then called at Alexandria in October 1944. At this Conference a policy was chalked out, called 'The Alexandria Protocol'. It was decided that a league of sovereign Arab States should be formed. A covenant establishing the Arab League was signed in Cairo on 22 March 1945, by representatives of Egypt, Iraq, Saudi Arabia, Lebanon, Syria, Jordan, and Yemen. By 1980 there were 21 members of the League, namely Algeria, Bahrain, Djibouti, Iraq, Jordan, Kuwait, Lebanon, Libya, Mauritania, Morocco, Oman, Somalia, Sudan, Syria, Tunisia, United Arab Emirates, People's Democratic Republic of Yemen, Yemen Arab Republic, the Palestine Liberation Organization, and Saudi Arabia. Egypt was suspended because of Anwar Saadat's unilateral peace treaty with Israel, but at the Islamic Summit Conference of 1984, General Mohammad Zia-ul-Haq of Pakistan and others succeeded in persuading members to re-admit Egypt to the League.

League's Functions. The function of the League is to promote Arab interests, prestige, and power in the world. The League does not admit, much less encourage any difference or dispute among the members. Mediation is the first requisite of such an alliance. It has a Council, a number of special committees, and a permanent Secretariat. Each member has a vote on the Council. The Council can meet in the capital of any Arab country. It has a Political Committee, consisting of the Foreign Ministers of the Arab States. The League calls itself a regional organization within the framework of the United Nations. The Secretary-General of the League is an acknowledged observer at all sessions of the UN.

The Arab Common Market. Some members of the League decided to have a common market. An agreement to this effect was signed between Iraq, Jordan, Syria, and Egypt on 13 August 1964. According to it, customs duties among the members of the market were to be abolished on agricultural produce and natural resources within five years; tarriff rates and customs duties on industrial products reduced annually by 20 and 10 per cent respectively. It was also agreed that there would be no restriction on the free movement of capital between member countries. It was envisaged that in course of time there would be common external tariffs and co-ordination in policies of economic development, even to the extent of the framing of a common foreign economic policy. The Arab Common Market began to function on 1 January 1965.

The Gulf Co-operative Council. The establishment of the Gulf Co-operative Council with headquarters at Riyadh in 1981, on the pattern of the European Common Market has been much more effective. Six South Arab countries joined the Council—Saudi Arabia, Kuwait, United Arab Emirates, Oman, Qatar, and Bahrain. Within two years of its inception attempts were nearly complete to issue a common passport. In 1982, the Gulf Investment Council was instituted. The capital of this Council is 12.1 billion dollars, to which every member will contribute 350 million dollars. An Oil Refinery has already been set up by the Council in Oman. In 1981 a resolution was passed by which no restriction will be placed on the free movement of labour and capital between the member countries. A joint tarriff is contemplated. The co-operative spirit is so active that in 1982 alone the trade between Saudi

Arabia and the Arab Emirates amounted to 136 million Saudi Riyals and by 1984, it had risen to 1401.6 million. This means that it had gone up 100 per cent—an extremely good sign. It is believed that soon this co-operation will extend to a military alliance.

The RCD. Three other Muslim countries, Turkey, Iran, and Pakistan decided in 1961-2 to enter into a Regional Co-operative Development Project (RCD). The idea was to develop a common infrastructure which would facilitate easy movement of manpower, material, and marketable produce. A Secretary-General, an Iranian, was appointed. Much planning was done. Representatives of the three member countries met. An RCD journal bringing out the common cultural and economic links between the three countries was published. Ayub Khan, the Shah of Iran, and the Turkish Prime Minister all took keen interest in the scheme. There was to be a joint air, land, and sea link. A Common Market was planned. For various reasons the plan met with little success.

Signs of Vitality. That the Muslim World was drained of its vitality by its long subjection to European Powers is denied by three facts. The first is the long and heroic fight of the Palestinians to recover their homeland. The second is the sturdy *Mujahidin* of Afghanistan who have been fighting undauntingly for the restoration of their rights. The third is the solitary Don Quixote of the Islamic World, Colonel Qaddafi who is busy defying the gigantic might of America. This is enough to show that Islam is still a living force in the world.

The Four Castes. Till a few years ago, there were three worlds. Now there is a fourth. The first belongs to the two Super Powers America and Russia: each moves in its own orbit, now and then the lines cut across and sparks fly high. The second, nearly as high is Europe: a highly advanced area; rich in culture and steeped in pride; intelligent and exclusive. To this world now belongs Japan, which despite being atomically targeted and saturatedly bombed, is today a technological giant. The third, the emerging Asian nations: China, India, Korea, Taiwan, Hong Kong, and Singapore: these countries are developing fast. India is already putting forward its claim to be a Mini Super Power and is throwing its weight about in the South-East Asian Zone. Moreover it claims to be the fountain-head of all Indo-European wisdom. The fourth, the semi-tropical belt extending from Indonesia to Senegal and Gambia which, except for Burma and India, is peopled by Muslims— the Islamic World: mostly oil-rich, but hide-bound, disturbed, and in place convulsed by new ideas and new loyalties. Here the past pulls one way and old practices hold the position of unalterable law, whereas the present challenges it at every step. The second—Latin America: which is an American Preserve under the Monroe Doctrine. The third—the newly liberated African countries: they are on the starting line and keen and eager for the whistle to blow. They have both brain and brawn and the past does not shackle them.

The Middle East dilemma. The Muslims are beset by two main problems. If they accept modernization, their manner and method, means and ways, and behavioural patterns will change. Advance means adoption of highly sophisticated technological practices behind which lies the thinking and ideas of the entire western civilization. To achieve the required expertise they have to send young men, the best that the countries produce, abroad to get higher education and acquire higher skills. Thousands go to other countries and only 20 to 25 per cent return. This brain drain is impoverishing the countries. And many of those who come back sneer at everything that is considered good by the older generation, because it is traditional. Consequently, the richer countries engage foreigners to modernize their centuries-old habit of work and thought. This is a new kind of bondage—a subtle kind of colonialism. Since their own past holds them in rigid bonds, their minds are befogged by the conflict of ideologies. Iran threw overboard many of the traditions and practices of the past. The result has been disastrous for modernizers. The Islamic Revolution there has changed the entire pattern of life. Turkey under Ata-türk became modern and old ways were swept away. The country is yet under military control. Egypt under Nasser claimed to be the country of the Pharaohs and even the present Head of State is a Lieutenant General. In the majority of Muslim countries from Bengal to Indonesia military commanders have assumed office. Does it mean that the newly liberated people of the Muslim World are not capable of meeting the challenges of the modern times and have to be drilled and dragooned to toe the line? It cannot be denied that the Western world is psychologically and even fundamentally, therefore, socially very much different from the 'East' and especially from the Islamic Way of life, but it does not mean that it is better or more exalted in everything. The emphasis that the Qur'an lays in filial piety, relationships, neighbours, and care of the poor, speaks of moral values nowhere else found in the world. How Islam meets this challenge remains to be seen.

The Four Groups of the Muslim World. The Muslim States divide themselves into four groups. The first, comprises the West African Muslim States: Morocco, Mauritania, Algeria, Tunisia, Senegal, Gambia, Mali, Niger, Nigeria, and Chad. The second, the North-Eastern African areas: Libya, Egypt, Sudan, Somalia, and Djibouti. The third, the largest in number if not in area extends from Albania, Cyprus, Turkey to the two Yemen Republics: Syria, Jordan, Lebanon, Iraq, Kuwait, Saudi Arabia, Qatar, Bahrain, the United Arab Emirates, and Oman. The fourth encompasses Afghanistan, Iran, Pakistan, Bangladesh, Malaysia, Brunei, and Indonesia.

The rest lie in the Soviet belt, they are: the Central Asian Soviet Republics of Kazhakistan, Turkmenistan, Uzbekistan, Kirghizistan, and Tadzikistan.

North-Western African Group: Morocco. From 1912 to 1950 Morocco had been divided into a French Protectorate and a Spanish Protectorate. There was besides, the International Zone of Tangier. On 12 March 1956, Morocco won its Independence. On 7 April Tangier was handed over to the Sultan and international control over the Tangier Zone was abandoned. Still a part of Morocco, called the Spanish Sahara, was under Spanish control. By a tripartite agreement between Spain, Morocco, and Mauritania, Spanish Sahara was handed over to Morocco and Mauritania on 28 February 1975. But a province called Wad Ed Dahab was under dispute. On 14 August 1979 it was handed over to Mauritania in return for Tiris El Gharbia, another province of Morocco. King Hassan II succeeded his father Mohammed V who had reigned (under foreign tutelage) from 1927 to 1961. Morocco is rich in mineral wealth and agriculturally it is self-sufficient. Morocco is an active member of the Islamic Conference and two of the four Summit Conferences held so far have been held in Morocco. European ideas and practices, mostly French, have influenced the social and political institutions, but the character and tone of public life have not lost their traditional Islamic colouring. Morocco is making use of its natural resources and is building up its economy steadily.

Mauritania. Mauritania became a French Protectorate in 1903 and a colony in 1920. It became an autonomous republic within the French Community in 1958 and was made independent in 1960. Under its first President, Mokhtar Ould Daddah, it became a one-party state in 1964. But he was ousted by a military *coup* on 10 July 1978 and the ruling party was dissolved. When Spain withdrew from Western Sahara in 1976, Mauritania took possession of the southern area naming it Tiris El Gharbia but in August 1979, Mauritania negotiated an exchange of areas with Morocco. Since the military *coup* of 10 July 1979, a Military Committee for National Recovery has held power. After the military *coup* Colonel Mustafa Ould Saleh assumed the Presidency and on 6 April 1979, the Military Committee for National Recovery was re-named Military

Committee for National Salvation. There was, however, soon another change. Colonel Saleh was replaced by Lieutenant Colonel Mohammad Mahmud Ould Ahmed Towly who was in turn overthrown by his Prime Minister, Lieutenant Colonel Khonna Ould Haydalla. This was on 4 January 1980. Mauritania has rich deposits of copper, sulphur, and other minerals.

Algeria. The national movement in Algeria had been very strong. In 1954, the National Liberation Front (FLN) started to fight for independence, forming a free Algerian Government in September 1958, with Farhat Abbas as Provisional President. A referendum held in France and Algeria on 6 to 8 January 1961, under orders of President de Gaulle approved the independence of Algeria by a clear majority. There was, however, much opposition to the idea still and a secret organization (OAS) organized by anti-Gaullist army officers took to terrorist measures. Torture of Algerian men and women freedom fighters—killing and burning continued for a year or more, till a cease-fire agreement was concluded between the national hero Ben Bella and the French Government on 18 March 1962. Even then the OAS massacres of Algerian resistance fighters continued for a few more months.

On 7 April 1962, a cabinet of 12 members was formed with Abdur Rahman Fares as Chairman. Next day a referendum on the Algerian issue was held in France and was approved by a vast majority. On 3 July 1962 President de Gaulle proclaimed the Independence of Algeria. A national referendum held on 15 September 1963 elected Ben Bella, the only candidate as President. A junta of military officers, however, overthrew the government on 19 June 1965 and established a Revolutionary Council under Colonel Houri Boumedienne. Under his rule elections were held on 25 February 1977. On Boumedienne's death, Colonel Bendjidid Chadli became President of the Republic and the General Secretary of FLN with Colonel Mohammad Benahmad Abdul Ghani as Prime Minister.

Algeria is rich in oil and there is considerable mineral wealth in this fairly large country. With French help these resources are being explored and exploited in the national interest. Algeria, however, adopts a non-interference policy. Age-old strained relations with Morocco have been smoothened out. Only Ben Bella, the Liberator, was confined and languished in prison for 12 years. He was released when Chadli came to power.

Tunisia. Tunisia which had been made a French Protectorate in 1881 gained its Independence on 20 March 1956. The Constituent Assembly which was formed on 25 March abolished the monarchy and Tunisia became a Republic on 25 July 1957, with Habib Bourguiba as President. He was re-elected in 1959, and again in November 1964 and 1969. He was finally elected life President in November 1974. Tunisia is a self-contained little country and has strong affiliations with France. Education level is high and Bourguiba, a sane and level-headed ruler, has given the Tunisians firmness, confidence, and economic stability—it is Tunisia which has given shelter to the storm-driven PLO and its leader, Yasser Arafat. Mr. Bourguiba has now been overthrown and the Tunisian Prime Minister has assumed power.

Senegal. The Republic of Senegal became independent on 20 August 1960. It too had long been in French possession, but had been made a member of the French Community on 25 November 1958. From January 1959 to 20 August 1960 it was a member of the Federation of Mali. The Republic is governed by a Council of 7 members and 2 Secretaries of State. There are in addition 8 ministers. There is a National Assembly of 100 members. Elections are held every five years by universal suffrage. French influences dominate, but Senegal has a say in the Islamic Conference. The President of Senegal was a member of the committee formed by the Islamic Conference to negotiate a cease-fire between Iraq and Iran. Over 80 per cent of the population are Muslim and have a progressive outlook.

The present Head of State is Abdon Diouf. He came to power in 1981 and got re-elected in 1983.

Gambia. Gambia was discovered by the Portuguese navigators in the fifteenth century but no settlement was made in it at the time. During the seventeenth century various foreign companies of merchants established trading centres along the river Gambia. They were controlled from Sierra Leone from 1807. In 1843 Gambia was made a Crown Colony by the British. For a few years it was even a part of West African Settlements. In December 1888 it was again made a Crown Colony. Gambia was given internal self-government in 1963 and became an independent member of the British Commonwealth on 18 February 1965. Two referendums were held to determine whether it should declare itself a republic or not, and finally in April 1970 Gambia became a Republic within the Commonwealth. At the general elections held on 5 April 1977, the People's Progressive Party (PPP) won a majority of seats. About 70 per cent of the population are Muslim. Gambia called 'The Gambia' joined Senegal in a Confederation on 1 February 1982. General elections were held on 4-5 May 1982. The President, Sir Dawda Kharrufa Jawara, is a man of progressive views and is trying to bring the people out of the slough of primitivism. Heavy minerals have been found in the land and are being developed. At present the chief exports are groundnuts, palm kernels, dried and smoked fish, hides and skins, and ground-nut oil.

Mali. Mali, like most of the territories in West Africa, was annexed by France in the middle of the nineteenth century. Till 1958 it had formed part of the area called French Sudan. It became an autonomous state within the French Community on 24 November 1958. On 4 April 1959 it joined Senegal to form the Federation of Mali. This Confederation gained its Independence in June 1960, but Senegal left the Confederation on 22 August 1960. The National Assembly was dissolved by President Modibo Keita on 17 January 1988. President Keita assumed absolute powers, but was overthrown by an army coup on 19 November. The Republic of Mali became independent on 22 September 1960 and was soon admitted to the UN. The Military Committee for National Liberation remained in power for five years. Gradually the Democratic Party of the People of Mali forged ahead (30 March 1979). On 18 May 1979 General Moussa Traore was elected President, unopposed, for a six-year term. The official language remains French, though the native language Bambura is the language of 60 per cent of the natives. Mali has a long history. There was a mighty Mali Empire in the Middle Ages. It is a rich country, both in agricultural produce and natural resources. There is a National Assembly of 82 members. It is directly elected. Elections were last held in 1982.

Niger. Niger is a land-locked country. On the north lie Algeria and Libya. There is Chad in the East and to the South is Nigeria. South-West lie Dahomey and Upper Volta. It is bounded by Mali to the West. The Republic of Niger gained Independence on 3 August 1960. It had been a territory of French West Africa since 1904. 85 per cent of the population is Muslim. There are 20,000 Christians. As in Nigeria, the Christians are supported by the Christian Missionary Organizations abroad and are encouraged and abetted by them when they cause trouble. On 15 April 1974 President Hamani was overthrown by a military coup. The Constitution was suspended and Lieutenant Colonel Seyni Konntehe (now Major General) who headed the coup dissolved the National Assembly and banned all political parties. He rules now as Head of State. Niger is not without good natural resources and there is considerable cultivation in the land.

Nigeria. The Federal Republic of Nigeria consists of a number of regions, formerly administered separately. Lagos had been ceded to Great Britain in August 1861 by King Dosnnmu and had been placed under Sierra Leone in 1866. In 1874 it was detached and joined with Gold Coast Colony. It remained so till 1886. Meanwhile, the United African Company had established powerful British commercial interests in the Niger Valley. In July 1886 the Company obtained a Charter and became the Royal Niger Company. The Company was taken over by the Crown on 31 December 1899. On 1 January 1900 the greater part of its territories was formed into the Protectorate of Northern Nigeria.

Nigeria became Independent on 1 October 1960 and a member of the British Commonwealth. By the Constitution passed in 1978, it became a Federal Republic comprising 19 States. The Head of the State is the President and he is the Executive Head too. The President and Vice-President are directly elected. The Republic is mostly Muslim, but the Southern Zone is predominantly Christian and as in Chad or Niger or Lebanon there have been instances of trouble between the two sections. The late President Al-Haj Shehu Shagari took office on 1 October 1979. Nigeria is an extremely rich country. Its agricultural, forest, oil, and mineral wealth give it opportunities of rapid development, of which the government is taking full advantage. Great emphasis is being put on education, both technical and general and industry is getting a fillip. The present Head of State is Major General Ibrahim Babanjiba. He came to power in 1985. Most members of his cabinet are army officers.

Chad. France made Chad a Protectorate on 5 September 1900. In 1908 it was made a part of French Equitorial Africa. It became a separate colony in March 1920. In 1946 it was made the fourth member of French Equitorial Africa, but in January 1959 it was given an autonomous status, within the French Community. It became fully independent on 11 May 1960, though the northern province of Borkon-Ennedi-Tibeste continued to be under French military administration till 1965. The upper regions are peopled mostly by Muslims and the southern, as in all these regions, by Christians, who continue to get support through the missionaries of European Christian communities and are a constant thorn in the side of the rather undeveloped Muslim communities. There is thus occasional friction between the two. A rather long civil disturbance of this nature ended on 21 August 1979, when a peace treaty was signed at Lagas between 11 warring factions. A 22-member Transitional Government of National Unity was formed in November 1979 and general elections were held in 1981 but trouble started two years later in which Libya got involved. Better conditions prevail now. A Supreme Military Council under the Presidency of General Felix Mallowane ruled until 29 August 1978, when the Council was dissolved. The reconciliation broke down in April 1980 and civil war spurted up again. This lasted till June 1982, when the military forces named Forces Armees du Nord (FAN) led by Hissene Habre, assumed control. The land is rich in oil, salt mines, and other minerals, hence the turmoil.

North East Africa: Libya. Libya was known as Trablas in Muslim History. In 1911, the year of the dissolution of the Turkish Empire in Europe, Italy conquered it, but after the expulsion of the Italians and Germans from the area in 1943, two of its parts, Tripolitania and Cyrenaica, were placed under the British, and Fezzan, under French army administration. In 1949, however, the British placed Amir Mohammad Idris al-Sanussi on the throne of Cyrenaica as its Amir. In 1951 the country was given the name of Libya. In 1969, however, a group of army officers, who had formed a Revolutionary Command Council took over and Amir Idris was deposed. The Revolutionary Command Council continues to rule with the assistance of a mainly civilian cabinet. The real source of power is Colonel Moammar Qaddafi. He has ostensibly no official status and holds very progressive views and wants his country to jog forward instead of walking towards an honourable place under the sun. A very sincere and energetic ruler, his one aim is to make his country a significant member of the Arab League. Rich in oil, the country has resources to meet most demands.

Colonel Qaddafi has resisted and defied American imperialistic moves in the Middle East and in April 1986, the exasperated Americans attacked Libya, bombarded Tripoli as well as Bengazi, demolished the palace of Colonel Qaddafi, killed his daughter and caused many casualties. But he remains firm and continues to maintain an independent stand. He is a vital force in Arab politics.

Egypt. On 1 February 1958, President Gamal Nasser of Egypt and, President Kwatly of Syria, proclaimed in Cairo that their two countries would unite under one Head of State with a common legislature, one flag, and a unified army. On 8 March the then Kingdom of Yemen joined to form the United Arab States. Three years later (19 August 1961) Syria broke away and resumed independence. President Nasser, therefore, dissolved the union with Yemen too. In August 1964, Egypt, Iraq, Kuwait, Jordan, and Syria joined to form an Arab Common Market. The aim was that the Arab countries should come together in some sort of a firm alliance. To begin with economic co-operation would be best. In this way there would be free movement of currency and products of member countries. The scheme did not flourish but the idea that the Muslims should unite is, however, there.

After the disastrous effects of the 1967 Israeli invasion, Egypt had a setback, especially after the death of a towering personality like Gamal Nasser (1970). He was succeeded by Colonel Mohammad Anwar Saadat. This was in October 1970. Under him the Provisional Constitution of 25 March 1964 was amended (11 September 1971). According to it, freedom of religion, and of the press, and free public education were guaranteed. In May 1980 further amendments were made. General elections took place on 7 and 14 June 1979. The National Democratic Party won 84 per cent of the seats. Meanwhile, Israeli occupation of the Sinai Peninsula which Israel had occupied after the 1967 War was causing a lot of unrest in Egypt. Consequently, in the War of 1971, the Egyptian forces pushed back the Israeli forces and regained control of the Suez Canal. Under American pressure, Anwar Saadat agreed to come to terms with Israel. In September 1978 at Camp David in America, there was an agreement between Egypt and Israel. Egypt accepted Israel as a sovereign country, and Israel agreed to evacuate the Sinai Peninsula. There was a Summit Conference and a Peace Treaty between Egypt and Israel was signed in Washington on 26 March 1979. It was ratified in Sinai on 20 April 1979. This cut off Egypt from the Arab World. The Arabs resented this defection and called the Egyptian action a stab in the back of the Arab cause. The Islamic Brotherhood (the Jamaat-i-Islami of the Arab World) openly cursed Anwar Saadat who was assassinated in October 1981. He was succeeded by another army officer Lieutenant General Hosni Mubarak. Egypt had been thrown out of the Arab League as well as the Islamic Conference, but at the Fourth Summit Meeting of the Islamic Conference at Casablanca (Morocco) in 1984, Egypt was re-admitted to both the organizations. Egypt has a viable economy and a liberal outlook. It refuses to be tied to the past and believes in progress, but the Islamic tone and temper remain. Egypt has rich natural resources, with considerable oil reserves and mineral deposits. Agriculturally the Valley of the Nile has been since ages, a very fertile region.

Sudan. Sudan was declared a sovereign independent Republic on 1 January 1956. The condominion (U.K., Egypt, and Sudan) had ceased to exist on 31 December 1955. A Council of State took over the administration temporarily. On 8 July 1965, the Constituent Assembly elected El Azhari as President of the Supreme Council. There was a coalition cabinet, but differences grew between the members and the Prime Minister Mohammad Ahmad Mahgoup, resigned on 23 April 1969. A 10-man Revolutionary Council headed by

Colonel Jaafer M. al-Nemery took over. The Council was, however, dissolved in 1972 and General Nemery began to reign supreme.

A new Constitution was proclaimed in 1973. It was further amended in 1975. Sudan has a Peoples' Assembly of 304 members. The President nominates 30 and 274 are elected. There is universal suffrage and elections take place every four years. President Nemery adopted a policy of rapid Islamization in order to placate the orthodox groups and went to extremes, especially in the imposition of penal regulations. This made him unpopular outside and especially in America, which threatened to stop the aid being given if Nemery did not moderate his excessive zeal. But instead of moderation he became more dictatorial. The result was that while on a visit to U.S.A. in 1984, a military *coup* upset his apple cart and Nemery was ousted. General Abdul Rahman Sawar El Dahab became President on 6 April 1985.

Sudan has two clear divisions. The northern part is wholly Muslim but in the south live many tribes in a semi-barbarous state and are a perpetual source of trouble. Sudan has been trying to come up to the level of Egypt of which it was a part for a fairly long time, but since the past holds Sudan in its grip the progress is slow. However, there are many enlightened and forward looking divines in the country who are pulling their weight.

Somalia. The Somali Republic came into being on 1 July 1960, when the British Somaliland Protectorate and the Italian territory of Somalia were merged into one country, called the Somalia Republic. In the beginning, administrative practices followed old patterns but gradually the people began to demand a Constitution. Consequently, a New Constitution was approved by a referendum held on 23 August 1979. It came into force on 23 September. The sole legal party in the country is the Somali Revolutionary Socialist Party. It had been formed in July 1976. Somalia is yet undeveloped and its economy has not been systematized. The present Head of State is Major General Mohammad Siad Barre. He has been in power for quite some time.

Djibouti. Djibouti had been a French possession like most of Upper Africa. At a referendum held on 19 March 1967, 60 per cent of the electorate vote for continued association with France. This is not surprising. The people in most African possessions had been kept at such a low level of political awareness that they could not readily conceive of a way of life in which they could stand on their own feet. However, the yeast of self-determination was working and in January 1976 the national leader, Ali Aref, had a conference with President Giscard d'Estiang of France and it was announced that France had agreed to grant independence to the country in the near future. Elections were organized on 27 May 1977 and the Republic of Djibouti became a sovereign State.

Djibouti is situated in the Gulf of Aden between the Somali Republic and Ethiopia. It has an area of 8,880 square miles. In May 1977 a 65-member Chamber of Deputies (Legislative Assembly) was elected. Hassan Gouled Aptidou is President and Burkat Conrad Hamadon is Prime Minister. The Port of Djibouti is the trade gateway of Ethiopia and the trade that flows through it is the mainstay of Djibouti. This small republic exports hides, cattle and coffee, but has to import cotton goods, sugar, flour, and cement. Djibouti is starting late but hopes to catch up with the other newly liberated African possessions of France.

The Heart of the Arab World: Albania. It is rather anomalous to begin an account of the Heart of the Arab World with the story of non-Arab Albania, a country where officially no Muslim exists, as in the Central Asian Sovietized Muslim States. But, as in Bulgaria recently hundreds of Muslims were shot because they refused to change their Muslim names, and just as all the Muslims of Central Asia have had to Russianize their names and their official religion, similarly there are only

Communists in Albania that is, the population has been converted to Communism, which is their only creed now. During the First World War it was decided by the Allies by the secret 'Pact of London' to partition Albania, but on 3 June 1917, the Italian Commander-in-Chief changed his mind and decided to give independence to the country. In 1925 a Republic was proclaimed. On 1 September 1928 Ahmed Beg Zagn, the President, became King and ruled the country as such till 1939. When the Italians again occupied the country, during the Second World War, Albania was overrun by the Axis Powers and it was only after the War that Albania won its independence again (November 1944).

On 10 November 1945, Britain, United States, and the U.S.S.R., recognized the Provisional Government of General Enver Hoxtra on the understanding that free elections would soon be held. On 2 December 1945, when the results came out, it was found that the Communists had won a majority of seats, so Albania declared itself a Republic on 11 June 1946 and was admitted to the UN on 15 December 1955. Albanian Communists were pro-Stalin and sided with China, so U.S.S.R., broke off diplomatic relations with Albania, but in 1977 China severed its diplomatic relations with it because Albania spoke against the post-Mao Chinese policy of closer liaison with the Democratic West. China cut off its aid to Albania (1978). In 1981, the Prime Minister, Mehmet Shehu, committed suicide. His successor General Hoxtra, a staunch Communist, accused Shehu of being a foreign agent and killed a number of Shehu's associates (1982). The present Head of State is Ramiz Alia. He replaced Hoxtra in December 1982.

Cyprus. Cyprus had been a Greek colony since 2000-1000 B.C. The Turks conquered it in 1571. In the nineteenth century when the Turks were losing their hold over most of their dominions, Great Britain by a treaty with the Sultan (4 June 1878) got control of the administration in Cyprus. It was finally annexed by Britain on 5 November 1914 and became a Crown

Colony on 1 May 1925. Thirty years later (1955) the Greek Cypriots rebelled. On 19 February 1959, at a conference held at Zurich, between the Greek and Turkish Prime Ministers and Great Britain, a treaty was signed in London (August 1960) by which Cyprus became independent, though Great Britain continued to retain its military bases on the island. By 1963 the Greek Cypriots and the Turkish Cypriots began to clash. As the Greek Cypriots were in majority they wanted to hold the mastery in the island. The Turkish Cypriots did not agree and the island entered on an era of continual political bickering. A UN Peace Force had to be sent to the island to maintain order. But the proposals made by the UN which favoured the Greek element were not acceptable to the Turks, who wanted a separate political status. The President, Archbishop Makarios, was adamant in the Greek cause. The Turkish Cypriots sought the help of Turkey and Turkish forces came into action. The Turks occupied about 40 per cent of the northern part of Cyprus. About 200,000 Greek Cypriots had to evacuate. The UN General Assembly, as was expected, resolved that the Turkish forces should withdraw. The Turks refused. On 13 February 1975 the Turkish Cypriots proclaimed an autonomous Turkish Cypriot Federated State with Rauf Denktash as President. President Makarios denounced this move but it was accepted by the Turkish Prime Minister. The Turkish Cypriots now rule over their own part of the island and maintain close relations with all Muslim countries. In 1984 the UN Secretary-General invited both parties to agree to a federal state, but the talks failed.

Turkey. The Democratic Party which had come into power in Turkey in the late fifties was overthrown by the National Unity Committee under the leadership of General Gemal Gursel (27 May 1960). The National Assembly was dissolved and political activities were suspended, but political pressure was too strong and so party activities were legalized on 12 January 1961. A new Constitution was framed and approved by a referendum held on 9 July 1961. Under it, general elections were held later the same year. The New Constitution consolidated all modernizing reforms which the Democratic Party had halted. The old style of religious education (learning by rote all traditional ideas) and the Oriental head gear was banned. Dervish orders were ruled out. The Western civil code was legalized as against the Shariah; polygamy was officially banned; and the Latin script was to continue to be used. All old style titles (like Pasha and Beg) were also abolished. Women were given full franchise. Western style surnames were to be used. Islam ceased to be the official state religion. All these 'reforms' had already been passed, they were now consolidated.

On 12 September 1980 the Turkish armed forces again came into action and overthrew the Demarel government of the Justice Party. Parliament was dissolved and all political activities were suspended. A new Constituent Assembly was convened and in 1981 a New Constitution was adopted. It was enforced on 7 November 1982 after a national referendum. New regulations regarding political activities and elections were given out in 1983. Executive power is now vested in the Head of the State and his Council of Ministers. He is also the Chairman of the National Security Council as well as the Chief of the General Staff of the Turkish Armed Forces.

Turkey is the most 'modern' of the Muslim countries. The Turks who perform Hajj every year number tens of thousands. The Turks are actually trying a fusion of Eastern (Islamic) and Western cultures. They have not cut themselves from the past but they do not let it ride them like an incubus.

Syria. On 28 September 1961, Syria broke away from the union with Egypt (The United Arab Republic of Egypt and Syria). President Nasser acknowledged the separation. Syria was re-admitted to the UN on 13 October as a separate member. The Arab League did the same. In March 1963 the National Council of Revolution came to power. It is believed that this was done in collusion with the revolutionary (Baath

Party) party in Iraq. Lieutenant General Hafiz Al-Asad seized power on 16 November and formed his own cabinet on 21 November 1970. A Provisional Constitution was framed on 16 February 1971. There was to be a People's Council of 173 members, all of whom were nominated by the President, Lieutenant General Al-Asad, who was sworn in as President, on 14 March 1971. A plebiscite was held and the New Constitution approved. Hafiz Al-Asad has a firm hold over Syrian affairs and has taken an active part in the Lebanon crisis. The Syrians are a self-contained people and insist on their distinct political entity. Though not oil-rich Syria has a viable economy.

Jordan. Amir Abdullah, a son of the Shareef of Mecca, had become King of Transjordan in May 1946. By a new Anglo-Transjordan Treaty (15 March 1948) which was to remain in force for 20 years, the name Transjordan was changed to the 'Hashimite Kingdom of Jordan'. This Treaty was terminated by mutual agreement on 13 March 1957. King Hussain, the grandson of King Abdullah, now ascended the throne. He has been the King of Jordan ever since. There is a legislature of two Houses. The Lower House has 60 members, elected by universal suffrage (30 from East Jordan and 30 from West Jordan). There is also a Senate of 30 members, all nominated by the King. Jordan includes parts of the dismembered Palestine and the ex-patriate Palestinians have not been very happy in their forced political status. Jordan is not rich in oil. Oil pipelines, however, pass through the country and pay toll. Jordan needs and gets aid from many sources to make both ends meet. King Hussain has by now become an astute diplomat and is consulted on most Middle East issues.

Iraq. A junta of young army officers effected a *coup* in July 1958 and overthrew the British orientated Ruling House. In the *coup* the innocent young King Faisal II, his uncle Prince Ilah, and the Prime Minister, Nuri As Said, were killed. Till 1962 General Qasim headed the military regime, but then a younger group of army and air force officers headed by Colonel Aref overthrew General Qasim's government. General Qasim lost his life in this *coup* (February 1963). On 4 May 1964 Iraq was declared an Arab Islamic Independent and Sovereign Republic. The aim was complete Arab unity. A National Council for the Revolutionary Command took control of the administration on 8 February 1963 and accepted the sovereignty of Kuwait, which had been disputed by General Qasim. It also settled the long and lingering demands of the Kurds in the north. But affairs were not yet settled. Another military *coup* on 18 November 1963 occurred. This was the result of the increasing influence of the Baath (Socialist) group of the government party. In April 1966 the then Head of State, Field Marshal Abdus Salam Aref died in an air accident. His brother, Abdur Rahman Aref, was then elected President by the National Defence Council. The Kurds gave trouble again and peace was finally made by a constitutional settlement with them in March 1970, whereby the Kurds were given autonomy. A new Constitution was passed in 1970 and was twice amended in 1973 and 1974. The supreme power now vests in the Revolutionary Council headed by Saddam Husain, which elects the President and the Vice-President. The President is also the Head of the Armed Forces.

In 1979 started the disastrous war with Iran. Tremendous losses have occurred and irreparable damage done to both sides. Yet the war goes on. The Islamic Conference as well as the UN have tried to negotiate a peaceful settlement of the issue, and whether it is religious, ethnic, economic, political, ideological, personal or national, engineered or spontaneous, there appears to be no abatement of the fury on either side. Iraq is rich in oil and agricultural produce but is also given aid by other Arab countries.

Kuwait. Kuwait, an extremely prosperous little country, lies just below Iraq. The Ruling House was founded by Shaikh

Sabah Al-Awwal (Sabah I) in 1756 who ruled for sixteen years (1772). In 1899, Sheikh Mubarak, the then Sultan, made a treaty with Great Britain whereby in return for protection the Sheikh promised not to part with any of his territory on any terms without the concurrence of Great Britain. In 1914 Britain recognized the independence of Kuwait, under the canopy of Great Britain's protection. On 19 June 1961, Kuwait was granted a sovereign status. Elections for a National Assembly of 50 members were held in January 1975, but this spurt of liberty did not last. In August 1976, the Amir dissolved the Assembly. Under pressure from an awakening people elections were again held in February 1981, but all important offices continue to be held by the Ruling House.

Saudi Arabia. Sultan Abdul Aziz Ibn Saud, the ruler of Nejd, had conquered Hejaz in 1924. Great Britain had recognized the independence of the dominions of Ibn Saud in May 1927. The name of the Saudi territories was changed to Saudi Arabia on 23 September 1932. Sultan Abdul Aziz was succeeded by his eldest son, Saud, who with the able assistance of his younger brother, Prince Faisal, continued to develop the oil resources of the country through ARAMCO, a joint company run by American technocrats.

In 1962 Saudi Arabia and Jordan agreed to co-operate in the military and economic fields. Saud had been succeeded by Prince Faisal, a most sagacious and farsighted statesman who initiated the use of the oil-weapon. He wanted to influence public opinion in the West, so that the Palestinian issue be adequately and justly solved. King Faisal sponsored the Second Summit of the Islamic Conference in Lahore in 1974. He also gave enormous funds to build an Islamic Research Centre around a spacious mosque—The Shah Faisal Mosque in Islamabad. King Faisal was assassinated and succeeded by his younger brother, Prince Khalid, who was ably assisted by another brother, Prince Fahd, who is now King.

King Fahd is a ruler with progressive ideas. He has built in Riyadh, the capital, a university complex. Annual awards are awarded to great scholars and researchers for their excellence in the fields of religion, humanism, science, technology, and art. Extensions have been constructed to Harm-i-Sharif and the Prophet's mosque. Jeddah has been made into a very modern port town. Saudi Arabia is fast achieving the stage which is termed economic 'take-off'. The House of Saud is most liberal in giving aid to other Muslim countries. The aid given to Pakistan for the maintenance of the millions of Afghan refugees in Pakistan is without parallel.

Yemen Arab Republic. On the death of Imam Ahmad, the ruler of Yemen, on 18 September 1962, army officers seized power, deposed the heir, Imam Saif al-Islam al-Badr, and proclaimed a Republic. The revolutionary republican regime was supported by President Nasser of Egypt, and the royalist party sought aid from King Faisal of Saudi Arabia. On 24 August 1965, King Faisal and President Nasser signed an agreement according to which both decided to support a plebiscite which should determine the future of Yemen. But this proposal came to nothing. Fighting went on and in August 1967 King Faisal and President Nasser agreed to withdraw their forces. At that time there were 50,000 Egyptian soldiers in the field and they were holding Sanaa the capital. Only the mountainous areas were in the hands of the royalists. By the end of 1967, however, the Egyptian forces were withdrawn.

The Revolutionary Council tried its hands at a workable constitution and from 1962-5 interim constitutions were issued. It was on 28 December 1970, at last, when a permanent Constitution was announced. According to it, there was to be a Council of 179 members, 120 of which were to be nominated by the President, and 69 elected. In February 1979, fighting started between the Yemen Arab Republic and the People's Democratic Republic of South Yemen (with Aden as capital and the whole southern coastal region once called Hadramaut in its jurisdiction). A cease-fire was concluded on 31 March 1979. Meanwhile, on 8 February 1978, a 99-man People's Constituent Assembly was established to decide on all constitutional matters in future. Colonel Ali Abdullah Saleh who speared the uprising against the age-old Zaidi dynasty of Yemen (whose last scion was Imam Badr) remained at the head of the Yemen Arab Republic.

South Yemen—The People's Democratic Republic of Yemen. After the bitter civil war between Imam al-Badr and the socialist group led by Colonel Saleh, Yemen was split. The southern part was made into a separate republic named 'The People's Democratic Republic of Yemen'. Between August and October 1967, the 17 tiny Sultanates of South Arabia were overrun by the forces of the National Liberation Front (FLN) and the rulers deposed. The British who had their old naval installations at Aden, sided with the FLN forces. The U.A.R. sided with the opposite faction calling itself 'Front of the Liberation of Occupied South Yemen' (FLOSSY). In November 1967, however, U.A.R. withdrew its support and the FLN triumphed. The British also agreed to withdraw and troops left Aden on 29-30 September. Now South Yemen People's Republic, a socialist regime, proclaimed its independence. The Constitution was consequently re-drafted and the amended version approved by the Supreme Council on 31 October 1978. The Secretary-General of the Yemen Socialist Party, as well as the Chairman of the Presidium of the Supreme People's Council is Prime Minister Ali Nasser Mohammad.

The People's Democratic Republic of Yemen has three islands in its jurisdiction, two in the Red Sea and one in the Arabian Sea, besides the entire southern coast of Arabia to the borders of Oman:

1. Kaneoran which has an area of 70 square miles was in British occupation from 1915 to 1967, but the inhabitants opted for the South Yemen Republic.

2. Perin came into British hands in 1709 but was abandoned a little later. In 1851 Britain again started using it as a coaling station. In November 1967 it too opted for the Republic.

3. Socotra lies to the east of the Horn of Africa in the Arabian Sea. It has an area of 1400 square miles. It was formerly part of the Sultanate of Oman and Qishu but like the other islands, it too, joined the Republic in 1967.

Lebanon. Lebanon an age-old battleground of nations has again been convulsed with passions and fierce hatreds. On this ground fought the Philistines and early Hebrews. These Philistines were the first global navigators who built the mighty Carthaginian maritime Empire and gave their name to Palestine. Then the Jews and Romans came into conflict, later the Crusaders and the Muslims. At present there is a triangular struggle going on which borders on self-annihilation.

In May 1958, in opposition to the then President Chamoun's policies, the Muslims (pro-Nasserites then) rose and for five months the Muslim quarters of Beirut, Sidon, Tripoli, and northern Beekaa were in the hands of the insurgents. Chamoun sought the help of America and triumphed. In later elections, General Fauad Chehab replaced Chamoun. He did not come into conflict with Muslims, who were a little over 50 per cent of the population with the influx of the Palestinian refugees. In 1970 Suleman Frange became President for a six-year term. It was in his time that Israeli attacks on the Muslims started. The Palestinians who had taken refuge in Lebanon were targeted. By November 1976 over 40,000 people had been killed. Two years later, Israel openly invaded South Lebanon as a reprisal for an alleged sea-raid by PLO guerillas. A UN Peace Force arrived, but the situation did not ease. The situation worsened when Reagan became President of the U.S.A., because he declared the PLO a terrorist organization. Inimical forces bent on destroying the Palestinian cause managed to create a split in the Palestine Liberation Organization. The PLO forces were hounded out of Lebanon and Muslim resistance in Lebanon was pulverized by the combined forces of Israel and its great ally, America. PLO headquarters shifted to Tunisia.

According to Lebanon's written and accepted Constitution the President of the Republic is to be a Maronite Christian, the Prime Minister a Sunni Muslim, and the Speaker of the Legislature a Shia Muslim. This administrative formula was adequately and sanely balanced. On 23 August 1982 Bachir Gemayel (Bashir Jamal) was elected President but only a month later he was assassinated. His brother, Amin Gemayel, replaced him. A week later, on 21 September 1982, under pressure from the United States the Israeli forces started to withdraw from Lebanon to be completely gone by February 1985. Lebanon has been perhaps the most advanced of the Arab countries, the University of Beirut rivalling the great centres of modern learning, and Beirut being a tourists' paradise. Lebanon had led the Arab intellectual renaissance and taken great strides forward in Arabic scholarship and literary creativity.

The Gulf States: Bahrain. The growing interest of Great Britain in the Middle East overwhelmed the Gulf States. Britain was a World Power in the nineteenth century. It was easy to persuade the petty Sultans of the Trucial States, as they were called then, to enter into treaty with a power like Great Britain. With Bahrain Britain had treaties first in 1862, second in 1892, and a third still later, in the name of friendship and protection. The Trucial States were told that Great Britain would look after their foreign relations, which meant 'hands-off' to other European powers.

The Bahrain islands are situated between the Qatar Peninsula and the mainland of Saudi Arabia. The capital is at Manama. The population does not exceed 300,000. A sort of Constitution exists. There is a National Assembly too. Bahrain is administered by a Cabinet. The ruling family holds all the key posts. The Khalifa House has been in power since 1782. Though elections took place in 1973, the Amir H.H. Sir Isa bin

Salman al Khalifah dissolved the Assembly in August 1975 and since then ruled through his cabinet. Oil is the mainstay of the country as it is that of other States in the Gulf.

Qatar. The State of Qatar extends on the landward side from Khor al Odeid to the boundaries of Saudi Arabia. There are only 200,000 people in the state. The capital is at Doha. On 9 February 1977, six years after Qatar gained its independence (1 September 1971), it gained control over its two natural resources, oil and gas, by signing an agreement with Shell Qatar. On 16 October 1976 the Qatar Petroleum Producing Authority (QPPA) was founded to act as the administrative body of the QPPA. The north-west Dome oilfield is now being developed. It contains 12 per cent of the known world reserves of gas. H.H. Khalifa bin Ahmed al-Thani assumed power on 22 February 1972 and rules supreme. The people have no say in the government.

United Arab Emirates. From Sha'am, 35 miles south-west of Ras Musum for nearly 400 miles to Khor al Odeid at the south-eastern end of the Qatar peninsula, the coastal area in the south of the Gulf, which was formerly known as the Trucial Coast of the Gulf, is the country now called the United Arab Emirates. It also includes about 50 miles of the coast of the Gulf of Oman. It belongs to the rulers of seven Trucial States. They are: Abu Dhabi, Dubai, Sharjah, Ajman, Umm al-Qwaim, Ras al-Khaimah, and Fujairah. Ras al-Khaimah joined the U.A.E., in February 1972 and the small state of Kalba had joined Sharjah in 1952.

The British influence in this area started in the first quarter of the nineteenth century, after the end of the Napoleonic Wars. In 1820, five years after the Battle of Waterloo, the rulers of these States were made to enter into a treaty with Great Britain. The reason given was that Britain would guarantee peace in the region and suppress slavery. There were further agreements giving more and more concessions to Britain. There was in March 1892, an Exclusive Agreement, by which the Shaikhs pledged themselves and their heirs, not to enter into any agreement with any other Power and to receive no foreign agents, or cede, sell or lend any part of their possessions to any other country.

The British forces withdrew from the area at the end of 1971. The old treaties were terminated. A new Treaty of Friendship between Britain and the Emirates was drawn on 2 December 1971. The Emirates are now a federation. They are headed by a Supreme Council, composed of the 7 rulers. The Supreme Council appoints a Council of Ministers. The ministers draft legislation and prepare the federal budget.

The Emirates are enormously rich. Their wealth is built on oil and gas and trade. Dubai, especially, is a very big trade centre. Fisheries are bringing in a lot of money. Sharjah excels in this industry. The fertile Buraini oasis, known as Al-Ain largely belongs to Dubai. It is being developed for intensive agriculture on scientific lines.

The Emirates are playing an important role in the affairs of the entire area. The President of the Supreme Council, for some years, has been H.H. Shaikh Zayed bin Sultan al-Nahyan, the ruler of Abu Dhabi. He is a very enlightened monarch, with a contained, confident, and forceful personality. He has been very friendly with and helpful to Pakistan. His state is run on most efficient 'modern' lines.

Oman. The Sultanate of Oman, until 1970 the Sultanate of Muscat and Oman, is an independent sovereign state. It lies in the south-east corner of the Arabian Peninsula. There is a plateau along the coast with an average height of 1,000 feet, the highest peak rising to 9,998 feet. There is some vegetation here, the rest of the area except for the oases being barren. In the valleys of the interior, however, and in the area known as Batinah, there is intensive cultivation of dates—the average yield being not less than 50,000 tons per year. There are two important towns—Muscat, the capital and Matrah, the starting point of trade routes into the interior. The population of both towns has become a mixed one. There are, of course, the pure Arabs but Indians (Khojas from Kutch and Hindus from Gujarat and Bombay), Pakistanis (Khojas and others), and Negroes are also there in a considerable number. The port of Gwadar and a small tract of country on the Baluchistan coast was handed over to Pakistan on 8 September 1958. The present ruler is Sultan Qabus bin Said. He succeeded his father, Said bin Taimur, on 23 July 1970. There is a treaty between the United Kingdom and Oman for commerce and navigation facilities as Oman lies in a strategic position in the very mouth of the Gulf. Because of the recent Soviet menace in Afghanistan, American interest has increased in this area. There is plenty of oil in Oman too.

East of Middle East: Afghanistan. Afghanistan was a source of anxiety to the British when they ruled India. Czarist Russia had annexed Central Asia after the middle of the nineteenth century. The next step was feared to be Afghanistan. Great Britain's policy was to keep Afghanistan either a friendly state or under British protection. At least it should be a Buffer State. Hence the four Afghan Wars and finally the conquest of the country by General Roberts who was awarded with an earldom and was made Earl Roberts of Qandhar.

A military *coup* conducted by Sardar Mohammad Dawood, the cousin and brother-in-law of King Zahir Shah of Afghanistan (17 July 1973) ushered in an era of blood and butchery. Dawood declared Afghanistan a Republic and openly maintained that the Afghans had a righteous claim over any area which held Pushto-speaking people. He did not disguise the fact that he meant the region from Torkham to Attock. Dawood was killed in another military *coup* in 1978. This *coup* was engineered by Nur Mohammad Turkai who had pronounced Communist leanings. Turkai now became the Head of the People's Democratic Party of Afghanistan and the President of the country. Turkai was succeeded by Hafizullah Amin another fire-brand, but he was liquidated and Babrak Karmal was installed as Head of State. Karmal's measures were so stringent that the anti-Communist population began to leave the country. The migration started in December 1978. It soon became a flood. But the rightist Afghans started a resistance movement. This movement gained volume and strength and the commoners began to flee from the country through open and secret ways. Lakhs poured into neighbouring Pakistan and Iran. Hundreds of thousands Afghan men, women and children, young and old, wounded and pale, sought refuge in Pakistan and by 1984 there were 3 million of them.

In 1964 a Constitution had been given to the people. This was abolished by Dawood and in February 1977, a new Constitution was adopted by the *Loya Jirga* Grand Assembly. This Constitution was abrogated by Nur Mohammad Turkai in April 1978. Turkai was ousted but not before a so-called Treaty of Friendship was thrust on Afghanistan by Soviet Russia in December 1978. This resulted in a constant flow of Russian troops, by air and land, into Afghanistan till by March 1981, there were nearly 100,000 Soviet troops in the country. By 1984, the country was nearly bled dry. Apart from the dead and wounded there were by that year 3 million Afghan refugees in Pakistan and 1.5 million in Iran. The entire Free World protested. Resolution after resolution was passed by the UN Assembly and the Security Council begged Russia to withdraw its armies and let the *Muhajirin* return to their homes in safety, but so far in spite of the efforts of Mr. Dego Cordovez, the Special Representative of the UN Secretary-General, and seven Geneva Conferences, the issue hangs in the balance. With Karmal also gone (1986) and replaced by Dr. Najibullah, the fight goes on. There are signs now that Russia may agree to withdraw her troops in a year's time. The *Muhajirin* will then return to their homes and a non-aligned government established in Afghanistan.

Iran. The preceding chapter accounted for the rise of Reza Shah Pahlavi. His son Mohammad Reza Shah had succeeded him in 1941. He was a progressive monarch, and wanted to revive the ancient glories of the days of Cyrus and Darius the Great, and Anushirvan, the Sassanian ruler of legendary fame. He embarked on the policy of rapid modernization, with Japan as his model. His extreme measures first gave rise to a communist surge under Dr. Mosaddeq, his one-time Prime Minister. When he had finished with his country's leftists, he began to suppress the Rightists. His secret police, the notorious Savak, outdid the Gestapo. In defiance of the opinions of the Islamic, at least the Arab World, he employed Israeli techno-crats in his oilfields and refineries and Americans in other industrial enterprises. His policies did not make him very popular and the orthodox elements started an anti-Shah movement. The leader was Ayatullah Rohulla Khameini whom he banished in 1964. But the movement against him gained ground and hundreds of patriots were killed on Black Friday in the Jaleh Square. Martial Law was proclaimed in September 1978. In November 1978, the Shah appointed Dr. Shahpur Bakhtyar, a moderate statesman as Prime Minister, but even he could not control the situation and the Shah had to flee the country with his family on 11 January 1979. He was by now a sick man and sought asylum in Egypt. He breathed his last on 27 July 1980 and was buried in that country. His glory disappeared in smoke.

Ayatullah Rohulla Khameini, now Imam Khameini, came back to Iran in January 1979 and was immediately accepted as the saviour of Iran. He held a referendum in April 1979 as a result of which Iran was declared an Islamic Republic. Imam Khameini was acclaimed as the Imam. The Islamic Revolution in Iran he brought into being has astonished the world. Its overwhelming success, its planned policies, the capable execu-tion, the availability of capable administrators, and above all, the total identification of the Iranians with the policies of Imam Khameini, appear to be an unusual phenomena. The efforts of all bodies working for restoration of liberty and human rights, like the Committee for the Defence of Liberty, which had been established in 1978 and which had suffered at the hands of Savak, now bore fruit. Dr. Beni Sadr was elected President and general elections were held in January 1980. But trouble raised its head. Iraq invaded Iran, ostensibly to gain control of Shatt-ul-Arab, the silted delta of the twin rivers of Iraq, Euphrates and Iraq, a long-disputed area. The war continues in spite of the efforts of the entire Muslim World and even the UN.

Pakistan. Pakistan has suffered from a political malaise since 1960. The sixties were the era of Field Marshal Ayub Khan, who brought in a Presidential form of government and gave the country an electoral body in the shape of Basic Democrats. His successor, General Yahya Khan, who re-clamped Martial Law in the land, undid most of the good of the previous regime. He rescinded the Parity between the two Wings of Pakistan. He held general elections in December 1970. Sheikh Mujib, the leader of East Pakistani malcotents, won nearly all the seats from there and a clear majority in the All-Pakistan Centre. Mr. Bhutto won a majority of seats in West Pakistan with his Party named Pakistan People's Party (PPP). Mr. Bhutto and General Yahya Khan attempted a coalition but Sheikh Mujib-ur-Rehman would not agree. Things soon went out of hand. East Pakistanis rebelled and Martial Law was imposed there. Mujib took to conspiracy with India, and was arrested. His lieutenants fled to India and sought help from the Indian government. With superior numbers, better weapons, and clear lines of communication they won their way to Dacca. The Pakistan Army surrendered on 17 December 1971. 93,000 army and civilian personnel were taken to India and imprisoned there. Yahya Khan resigned, and Mr. Bhutto assumed the office of President as Civil Martial Law Administrator. His rule lasted five and a half years (January 1972 to July 1977).

Mr. Bhutto started well. He gave the people pride, dignity, awareness, and a sense of direction. But his political measures were not so popular. He gave a Constitution to the country to which all parties agreed (August 1973). Meanwhile trouble raised its head in Baluchistan and the Frontier. The Baluchis accustomed to the age-old Sardari system refused to be democratized and revolted. The army was sent to quell the rising. The Baluchis fled to the hills. Governor's Rule was therefore imposed in 1975 but it did not work. In the N.W.F.P. also, there was unrest, mostly against the dictatorial practices of Mr. Bhutto and the N.W.F.P. government was made to resign. The opposition parties now united to form an alliance called Pakistan National Alliance (PNA). They started a campaign in the name of Nizam-i-Mustafa, a convenient and oft-used slogan. There were demonstrations and great unrest. Clashes between PPP workers and PNA volunteers became frequent. Law and order were affected. Mr. Bhutto imposed Martial Law in Karachi, Hyderabad, and Lahore. The PNA volunteers defied military rule. There was firing, hundreds died and thousands were arrested. So Mr. Bhutto was forced to negotiate with PNA. This was further aggravated by the 1977 general elections which were alleged to have been rigged. The PNA demanded new elections, strict observance of the 1973 Constitution, guarantee of non-interference by the Centre in the provincial administration, and resignation of Mr. Bhutto. The ever watchful army, witnessing the struggle between the PPP and PNA who had now begun to arm themselves, stepped in. Mr. Bhutto was arrested, his government overthrown, the Constitution suspended, the Parliament dissolved, and Martial Law clamped on the land on 5 July 1977.

The Chief of Army Staff, General Mohammad Zia-ul-Haq, assumed the office of the Chief Martial Law Administrator. In a broadcast the same evening, he assured the nation that he had done so in the interest of the people, and had no intentions of running the government, and was resolved to hold elections within ninety days. He had meant what he said, but, some powerful political groups demanded that he should first hold an enquiry into the 'misdeeds' of the Bhutto regime. 'First Reckoning, then Elections' was the cry. This made the General pause. Moreover, Begum Nusrat Bhutto lodged a suit against him accusing him of treason, on grounds of declaring Martial Law when there was no provision as such in the 1973 Constitution. The military government had to defend its position and the case was hotly contested. The Supreme Court at last dismissed the case ruling that under the '*Doctrine of Necessity*' it was permissible to overrule constitutional guarantees if there was danger of anarchy or civil war.

Meanwhile, Mr. Bhutto was alleged to have caused the murder of a political opponent. The case lingered on for months. Mr. Bhutto was found guilty and hanged in 1979. The influx of Afghan refugees who came in thousands every day, till by 1984, there were 3 million of them in Pakistan and posed potential hazards. India, though appeased temporarily by the Simla Pact negotiated by Mr. Bhutto in 1974, by which Mr. Bhutto had managed to repatriate the 93,000 Pakistani army and civilian personnel imprisoned in India after the fall of Dacca, was making threatening gestures on the eastern borders. Elections could not be held under these conditions and they were further postponed.

General Mohammad Zia-ul-Haq tried many measures to give representation to the people in the government of their country. He formed 'cabinets' of chosen military officers and agreeable civilians. Even the PNA co-operated with him for some eight months, but after Mr. Bhutto's end the PNA withdrew its support. Local bodies elections were held on a non-party basis. A Majlis-i-Shoora, was constituted. These measures did not bear fruit. Nine and more parties joined to initiate the movement for the 'Restoration of Democracy' (MRD). It even started a civil disobedience campaign as a result of which several political bodies had been interned and hundreds of political workers had been jailed.

Such was the pressure that on 14 August 1983, the Chief Martial Law Administrator announced that he would definitely hold elections in about eighteen months, but, on a non-party basis. In January 1985 the exact date of the elections was pronounced—5 February 1985. Before the elections however, the President passed a Provisional Constitution Order (PCO) by which he retained most of his powers even when Martial Law was lifted. The President appointed Mr. Mohammad Khan Junejo of Sind, as Prime Minister. The Chief Ministers of the provinces were similarly appointed.

On 1 January 1986 Martial Law was lifted amidst great rejoicing and a new democratic era was ushered in, but not before the 1973 Constitution had been 'suitably' amended. The President who had already obtained a term of five years as Head of State through a referendum conducted on Islamic lines, also retained the office of Supreme Commander of the Armed Forces as also the right of issuing Ordinances in moments of necessity. A new phase has begun in Pakistan's political history with the emergence of Miss Benazir Bhutto, the Acting Chairman of PPP. The future is full of possibilities.

Bangladesh. As a result of the general elections held in Pakistan in December 1970, Sheikh Mujib-ur-Rahman, the leader of the Awami League, had won nearly all the seats in East Pakistan and an overall majority (167 out of 300) in the National Assembly. Mr. Zulfiqar Ali Bhutto had secured 80 seats, a majority from the West Pakistan side. Mujib now demanded the right to form the government. He had already proclaimed that if he came to power, he would leave only two subjects to the Centre, Defence and Foreign Relations. East Pakistan would have its own Auxiliary Force, currency, and fiscal policy. Neither President General Yahya Khan nor Mr. Bhutto would permit this or agree to it. Negotiations led to no positive result.

Sheikh Mujib-ur-Rahman, began on the one hand to have secret negotiations with India and on the other, to get his ardent workers trained in guerrilla fighting and subversive tactics. President Yahya Khan appointed Rear Admiral Ahsan, an East Pakistani, as Governor to see if he could bring round Sheikh Mujib but his efforts failed and Sheikh Mujib's followers organized a terrorist group called *Mukti Bahini*, and took to marauding. People were asked not to pay taxes in districts or sub-divisions where West Pakistani civil servants were posted. The East Pakistani regiments were asked to revolt. These units killed their West Pakistani Officers. The Border Force also revolted and threw the border open to armed infiltrators. Mujib had begun to run a parallel government. He was, therefore, arrested and flown to West Pakistan and a case for treasonable conspiracy lodged against him in Ayub Khan's time was reviewed. His Mukti Bahini now went on the rampage. Martial Law was imposed. Admiral Ahsan the Governor, and Major General Yaqub Ali Khan, the Martial Law Administrator, tried to effect some sort of a political compromise but the situation had gone beyond control and Awami League leaders had escaped to India to set up the Bangladesh government in exile. They sought help from Mrs. Indira Gandhi, the Indian Prime Minister, who welcomed the appeal, promised military aid, and sent a well-equipped and highly trained army to help the insurgents. The Pakistan Army led by Lieutenant General A.K. Niazi fought but had to retreat before a stronger force till Dacca was surrounded by the Indian troops and General Niazi laid down his arms. 90,000 Pakistani soldiers, officers, and men surrendered and coupled with 3,000 civilian government officials were taken prisoner and sent to India. Dacca fell on 30 December 1971. The Awami League leaders in 'exile' returned in triumph. In the West, General Yahya resigned and Mr. Bhutto assumed power as President and Civil Martial Law Administrator. He immediately released Sheikh Mujib and had him flown to London from where he came to Dacca to proclaim the Independence of Bangladesh in January 1972. India recognized it promptly and so did Britain, at which Mr. Bhutto withdrew from the British Commonwealth.

A Constitution was soon framed on a parliamentary pattern. But this sunny state of affairs did not last long. For his pronounced leaning towards India, and other policies, Shelkh Mujib-ur-Rahman and his family were killed in a military *coup* on 15 August 1975.

Martial Law was declared. Mr. K.M. Ahmad was made President but was soon replaced by a former Chief Justice, Mr. A.M. Sayem. Political parties were abolished. Elections were promised and held in 1976. Major General Ziaur Rahman who had headed the *coup* became Chief Martial Law Administrator. He made the Air and Naval Chiefs of Staff, his Deputies. On 21 April 1977 General Ziaur Rahman became President. A new Constitution was now framed. In a general election, Ziaur Rahman was elected as President and Justice Sayem was retired. Martial Law was ended. Two years later, however, General Ziaur Rahman was murdered by a group of army officers and Justice Abdus Sattar was installed as Acting President. He was elected President in 1981. On 23 August 1983 there was another military *coup* and Lieutenant General Hossein Ahmad Ershad emerged as Chief Martial Law Administrator. He instantly dissolved the Parliament and suspended the Constitution. He assumed the office of President on 11 December 1983. Mrs. Hassena Wajid, daughter of Sheikh Mujib-ur-Rahman is leading the Awami League and Mrs. Ziaur Rahman is the leader of the National Democratic Party. Elections were held early in May 1986 but the results have been disputed. General Ershad continues as President but there is considerable unrest in the country.

The country is not without ample natural resources. Even gas has been found in it. The people are active and politically very conscious and only time is required to make Bangladesh a rich country.

Malaysia. Malaysia was known as British Malaya till 1963, when Great Britain decided to give it independence. On 16 September 1963, the Federation of Malaya, the State of Singapore, and the Colonies of North Borneo (renamed Sabah) and Sarawak were united to form the new country of Malaysia. These four countries signed an agreement to this effect on 4 July. For a time Indonesia contested the Borneo possessions but gave up its claim later. Two years later (9 March 1965) Singapore seceded from Malaysia and became a sovereign state on its own.

There are eleven rulers of the Malay States, all tiny but all conserving their rights. The Constitution had to have peculiar features. One of the rulers has to be elected to be the Yang di Pertuan Agong (Supreme Head of the Federation). He is chosen to be the constitutional Head of the State for five years. A Deputy Supreme Head is similarly elected. The executive head is then appointed from among the scions of the Ruling Houses. Elections are held every five years and conducted in peace. The people are a mixture of Malays, Chinese, and Cholas. The Cholas are the descendants of those South Indians, who came over from the Deccan during the days of the Chola Empire (tenth to fourteenth centuries A.D.). In those centuries the Cholas were a great maritime power and had extended their political and cultural influence as far as Vietnam and the East Indies. The people of Bali Island in Indonesia are still Hindus. The Cholas of Malaysia accepted Islam long since. The language of Malaysia is Bahasa Malay. Bahasa is the same word as Hindi Bhasha. The Federation is economically self-sufficient; rubber, tin, and palm-oil being the chief products. Oil is said to have been discovered in Sabah and Sarawak. The country refuses to be fossilized.

Brunei. The Sultanate of Brunei has a long history. It was once a powerful state. In the sixteenth century, Brunei was the sovereign of the whole island of Borneo and even parts of Safn

Islands. Its sway extended over parts of Phillipines. The Europeans, Portuguese, Dutch, and English, all overran these islands, and gradually took their possession. By the nineteenth century, Great Britain gained the upper hand and with the Rajah of Sarawak and the British North Borneo Company became the masters of the large island of Borneo. The State of Brunei was reduced to a small area. In 1847 a treaty was signed between Great Britain and the Sultan, ostensibly to promote trade and suppress piracy. In 1888, by another treaty, the State became a British Protectorate. Although the people of Brunei are of the Malay race, they did not join the Federation of Malaysia in 1963, as oil had been struck in large quantities and it did not suit British commercial interests to allow Brunei to do so. Brunei was, at last, granted Independence in 1985. The Sultan of Brunei had given his people a Constitution as early as 1959. There is a Privy Council, a Legislature, and an Executive. The Constitution was shelved in 1965. The Sultan, H.M. Sir Musa Hassanal Balkish, began to negotiate with Great Britain for new terms and according to the Treaty of 1979, Brunei was to become a sovereign state in 1983. Independence came in 1985 and was grandly celebrated. The official language is Malay but English is used as a second language. With oil gushers working night and day Brunei is fast becoming very rich.

Indonesia. In the sixteenth century, when the Portuguese after finding the Cape route burst on South Asia, the East-Asian islands became their pasture. The Phillipine islands were named after King Phillip IV of Spain. Soon the Dutch and the British joined in. In 1602 the Netherlands East India Company took over the island and continued to rule till 1798 when the Company was dissolved and the Netherland (Dutch) Government assumed the administration. This went on till 1941 when the Japanese conquered the islands. On the fall of Japan (1945) the nationalists led by Dr. Sukarno and Dr. Hatta proclaimed a Republic (17 August 1945) as mentioned in the preceding chapter. It achieved complete sovereignty on 27 December 1949 and took the name of Indonesia (formerly Dutch East Indies). In 1963, Indonesia also got possession of Western New Guinea. During the fifties the federal system introduced on the occasion of its independence was abolished and Indonesia became a Unitary State.

On 12 January 1960, President Sukarno issued a decree enabling him to control the political parties with the power to dissolve them. Three months later, he prorogued the Parliament as it had been elected on the basis of the 1945 Constitution. A Communist rising which very nearly overthrew the government in 1965 was ruthlessly suppressed. The Communists had killed six generals and many officers and a great number of men of the armed forces, but were themselves decimated in very large numbers.

There were differences with Malaysia too. Hostilities were started and continued for three years, but were at last terminated and Indonesia abandoned its claims on North Borneo. The country had not yet settled on a democratic pattern and as has happened in most other Muslim countries the military commanders took over, here under the leadership of Lieutenant General Suharto on 11-12 March 1966. The Communist Party and the National Front organized by Sukarno were dissolved. On 22 February 1967 Dr. Sukarno was made to hand over Presidentship to General Suharto. Dr. Sukarno the Liberator fled from the scene. There is a People's Consultative Assembly (a sort of Majlis-i-Shura) and General Suharto remains in power. Indonesia is very rich in natural resources including oil and other minerals. The Indonesians do not take sides in the political turmoil which affects the Muslim World now and then.

The Maldive Islands. The smallest Muslim state in the world is the group of Maldive Islands to the south-west of Sri Lanka. It had been under British domination for as long as the rest of the sub-continent, Burma, Ceylon, Malaya, or Singapore. It is not a very rich country but it is self-sufficient. Its main produce being Copra (dried coconut) and its oil as well as fisheries. It gained its independence in 1972. It is now a Republic within the British Commonwealth (1982). The President, H.E. Maumoon Abdul Gayoom, is also the Head of the Army being the Minister of Defence. President Zia-ul-Haq visited Maldive Islands a couple of years back and established very cordial relations with the people who gave him a generous welcome.

The Central Asian Muslim World. Soviet Central Asia comprises five Soviet Muslim Republics. On the west (east of the Caspian Sea) lies Kazhakistan; the largest of these states called the Kazhak Soviet Socialist Republic; Uzbekistan: Soviet Socialist Uzbek Republic; and Turkmenistan: The Turkmen Soviet Socialist Republic. At the top to the right of Turkmenistan and west of Sinkiang, the Chinese Muslim province, is Kirghizistan: Kirghiz Soviet Socialist Republic; and to the south immediately to the north of Afghanistan is Tadzikistan: Tadzik Soviet Socialist Republic. All this area was known as Turkestan for centuries. It was conquered by Russia in 1860s. In 1966 Tashkent was occupied. In 1868, Samarqand and in 1870, Bokhara and Khiva. Until 1917, however, Central Asia was divided into Khanates and Emirates; the Khanate of Khiva, the Emirate of Bokhara, and the Governor-Generalship of Turkestan. But after the Bolshevik Revolution of 1917, things began to change rapidly. The Khan of Khiva was deposed in February 1920 and a People's Republic was set up there. Six months later the Emir of Bokhara met with a similar fate. The large northern Governor-Generalship of Turkestan was first made into an autonomous Soviet Socialist Republic on 11 April 1921, within Soviet Russia. Three years later there was further dismemberment and re-distribution of areas. By 1925 the new states of Uzbekistan, Turkmenistan, and Tadzikistan had been established. The remaining districts of Turkmenistan populated by Kazhaks were joined with Kazhakistan, the largest of these states, where gradually the Muslim population has been reduced to 40 per cent. Kirghizia lying next to Chinese Sinkiang was the last to be Sovietized. It became a Soviet Socialist Republic in 1936.

Kazhakistan. Kazhakistan became a constituent republic of the U.S.S.R. on 5 December 1936. The capital is Alma-Ata, formally Verney, and one time Khorezm. The seat of a mighty Khwarizshahi Sultanate, the area had a glorious past. It has now as the other republics a Supreme Soviet (The National Assembly). Elections were held in 1980. It has 510 deputies (1 per 20,000 persons). 182 are women, 189 urbanites, and 218 from the rural areas. Kazhakistan has now one state religion like the other Central Asian States, which is Communism. The names everywhere have been Sovietized. Till lately Muslim institutions were frowned upon and even old mosques could not be repaired. Things have improved now. Better educational facilities are provided and development projects and systematic farming have been started. Better schooling is also available and there is no dearth of skilled labour now.

Uzbekistan. The semi-independent Khanates of Khiva and Bokhara were first transformed into Peoples Republics (1920) and three years later made into full-fledged Soviet Socialist Republics. Thus the Uzbek Soviet Socialist Republic became a constituent member of the U.S.S.R. in 1925. The Uzbek Republic comprises of a large part of the Samarqand region, the southern part of the Syr Darya, Western Ferghana (the birthplace of Babar the First Moghul), the western plains of Bokhara, and the Uzbek regions of old Khorezm. The Supreme Soviet elected in 1980 has 510 deputies (1 per 5000 persons); 178 women and 346 Communists. There are no parties in the U.S.S.R. The Sovietization process with emphasis on industrial development and modern education on progressive lines is going on here too and it must be admitted that the people are not standing still. The attitude to life, as a field of personal endeavour, is the gift of modern Russia. Better schooling, better housing, and higher skills are among the benefits too.

Turkmenistan. The Turkmen Soviet Socialist Republic was formed on 27 October 1924 and covers the territory of the former Trans-Caspian Region of Turkestan, the Charjnii Villayet of Bokhara, and a part of old Khiva, situated on the right bank of the Oxus (Amu Darya). In May 1925, the Turkmen Republics entered the Soviet Union as one of its constituent republics. 66 per cent of the population are Turkmen most of whom were nomads before World War I; 14.5 per cent Russians are urbanites; 8.3 per cent Uzbeks; and 3.2 per cent Kazhaks. There are small minorities of Tartars, Ukrainians, and Americans. This mixture is a political safeguard. The capital is Ashkabad. The Supreme Soviet in the 1980 elections had 330 deputies (1 per 5000 population). 107 are women and 224 Communists. Rapid changes are being made in the milieu in the name of progress, which undeniably is genuine.

Tadzikistan. The Tadzik (Tajik) Soviet Socialist Republic comprises of regions of Lower Bokhara and Turkestan, where the main ethnic group was that of Tadziks. It was admitted as a constituent republic of the Soviet Union on 5 December 1929. It lies to the south of Amu Darya and is mostly mountainous, the tallest peak being over 23,000 feet high. Even the lowest valleys of the plateau of this part of the Pamir Range is nearly 5000 feet above sea level. There are huge glaciers in the land and rivers, all falling into Amu Darya and making the valleys rich in vegetation and yielding great electric power by means of hydro-electric schemes. The people, the most advanced of the Central Asian folk, speak Persian. The capital Doshamba has a famous university where the latest method of teaching and research are practiced. The intellectual output is therefore high. The script is changed to Russian and it is said that it facilitates reading and writing. The main occupation of the people is farming. There are 43,000 kilometres long irrigation canals. Fruit farming, fruit preserving, cattle breeding, and dairy farming flourish. Tadzikistan's Supreme Soviet has 349 members, 123 women and 238 Communists. There are rich mineral deposits in the mountains.

Kirghizia. In 1924 when Central Asia was being re-organized territorially, on ethnic lines, Kirghizia was separated from Turkestan and formed into an autonomous region within Russia. In 1936, however, Kirghizia became the Kirghiz Soviet Socialist Republic and was incorporated into the U.S.S.R. Its Supreme Soviet elected like that of other Central Asian States in 1980 consists of 350 members, 126 women and 243 Communists. Kirghizia is famous for its livestock breeding, pigs, sheep, and goats. Yaks are bred for meat and dairy milk. Kirghizia raises sufficient wheat for its own use as well as other crops for fodder.

The Dream. The entire Muslim World dreams of one World of Islam and yet ideas of nationhood, of ethnic, linguistic, and cultural groupings have nearly undermined the dream of an Islamic Ummah. Sayyid Jamaluddin Afghani in the nineteenth century and Sir Mohammad Iqbal in the twentieth spoke of this One World. It still remains a dream, though attempts have been made at political unification and economic co-operation. Some of them have failed; others are working slowly. The sap is there, it needs time to bear fruit. The principle behind *Juma* congregation, Eid Prayers, *Namaz Janaza*, and Hajj is to bring Muslims together. The world is no longer as small as it was in the days of the Prophet and yet it is smaller. If we could know how each one of us lives, eats, drinks, dresses, houses, marries, attains fatherhood or motherhood, becomes a citizen and what our customs, cultural and behavioural patterns are, from Sinkiang to Sudan, West-Irian to Gambia, Albania or Kirghizia to Somalia, we could recognize each other, understand each other, and come nearer to each other. A Turk is different from a native of Maldive Islands in the Indian Ocean, but both are Muslims, both hear the Call to Prayer chanted in the same language as does a Cantonese Muslim or a Yugoslavian Musalman.

The Islamic Conference Secretariat could well take the lead in planning and organizing a Cultural Division where scholars could conduct research on anthropological and aesthetic aspects, arrange study-groups, and learn and record for others basic behavioural patterns in all Muslim lands. It would keep alive the spirit and soul of the Muslim Ummah as it shines through its daily life.

Since the Muslims continue to call the *Azan*, say their prayers, join annually for Hajj, whether they are in China or Denmark, there is hope that one day there will emerge a Commonwealth of Muslim nations.

INDEX

A

Abaga, son of Hulagu, 171, 200, 201
Abbas I, Shah of Persia, 212, 213, 214, 215, 220, 256
Abbas II, Khedive, 332-3
Abbas ibn Abdul Muttalib, 6-7
Abbasid Caliphs, 54-5, 64, 70 ff., 79, 89, 92, 93, 98, 102 ff., 120 ff., 161, 210, 270; decline of, 129 ff., 142; second line, 169-70, 236
Abdalis, the, 217, 219, 297-8, 313
Abdul Abbas, 70
Abdul Aziz, Sultan, 309
Abdul Aziz ibn Saud, King of Arabia, 350 f.
Abdul Fadl ibn al-Naqid, 174
Abdul Halim Kara Yaziji, 256
Abdul Hamid, Sultan, 310
Abdul Hamid II, 310 f., 327
Abdul Malik, 58, 59 ff., 67, 69
Abdul Mumin, 92 ff.
Abdul Muttalib, 6, 7
Abdul Nabi, Shaikh, 284
Abdul Qadir al-Jilani, Sayyid, 151
Abdul Qadir, of Mascara, 312
Abdul Rahim, 284-5
Abdul Rahman I, 71, 79 ff., 89
Abdul Rahman II, 83
Abdul Rahman III, 84 ff., 88
Abdul Rahman IV, 88
Abdul Rahman ibn Abdullah, 67 f.
Abdullah, King of Transjordan, 355
Abdullah II, Uzbeg king, 213
Abdullah ibn Abi Sarh, 53
Abdullah ibn Tahir, 114, 134-5
Abdullah ibn Yasin, 91
Abdullah ibn al-Zubair, 45, 58, 59
Abdullah al-Rasibi, 41
Abdur Rahman ibn Muhammad, 61
Aboukir Bay, battle of, 300
Abu Ali ibn Sina, *see* Avicenna
Abu Ayyub al-Ansari, 54
Abu Bakr, 13, 14, 27 ff., 42, 57
Abu Dhabi, 390, 391
Abu Futrus, fort, 71

Abu Hanifa, Imam, 123
Abu Muslim al-Khorasani, 68, 70, 104, 106
Abu Obaidah ibn al-Jarrah, 30, 32
Abu Said, 208
Abu Said ibn Bahram al-Tannabi, 132
Abu Sufyan, 6, 12, 16, 18, 27
Abu Talib, 6, 7, 12
Abu Yusuf Yaqub, al-Mansur, 93
Abul Kalam Azad, 334
Abul Muzaffar Alauddin Bahman Shah, 196
Abyssinians, 193
Acre, 163, 167, 172, 300, 303
Adana, 303
Aden, 4, 239, 347, 358
Adham Khan, 284
Adrianople, 226, 230, 231, 303, 328, 329, 338; Treaty of, 303
Adud ul-Daulah, 140 ff.
Afghanistan and Afghans, 53, 135, 147, 215 ff., 274 ff., 280 ff., 298, 313, 314 f., 324, 336, 342, 362, 368, 392
Africa, *see* Ifriqiya
Afshar dynasty, 215 ff., 219
Afshin, General, 117 f.
Agha Khan, the, 334, 347
Agha Muhammad, Shah of Iran, 313
Aghlabid dynasty, 83, 84, 89 ff., 95 f., 109, 115
Agra, 190, 277, 280, 282, 289, 291, 292
Agriculture and irrigation, 82, 86, 145, 185
Ahadith (Traditions) of the Prophet, 123
Ahl al-Bait, 27, 43, 44, 47, 70
Ahl al-Kitab, 34
Ahmad, grandson of Hulagu, 201
Ahmad, Sayyid, of Bareilly, 322
Ahmad ibn Buwayh, 140
Ahmad ibn Hanbal, 119, 123
Ahmad ibn al-Maimandi, 139
Ahmad ibn Tulun, 130
Ahmad Khan, Sir Sayyid, 299, 322 ff., 333
Ahmad, K.M., 400

Ahmad, Nazir, 323
Ahmad Shah, 194
Ahmad Shah Abdali, 298, 318
Ahmadabad, 194
Ahmadnagar, 197, 285, 288 ff.
Aisha, Lady, 36, 39, 57
Ajmer, 177, 178, 281, 283
Akbar the Great, 195, 280 ff., 283 ff., 290, 292, 297
Akhis, the, 226
Ala, Husain, 342
al-Ala ibn Mughith, 80
Alam Khan, 275, 278
Alam Shah, 298
Alashehr, battle of, 338
Alauddin II, Bahmani, 196
Alauddin II, of Konya, 223
Alauddin Ali Shah, 192
Alauddin Husain Shah, 193
Alauddin Jahansoz, 177
Alauddin Juwayni, 209
Alauddin Khalji, 182 ff., 187, 194
Alauddin Muhammad, 147, 148
Albania, 227, 230, 234 f., 328, 368, 379, 380, 407
Albuquerque, 195
Aleppo, 142, 145, 160
Alexandretta, battle of, 303
Alexandria, 34, 305
Algeria, 53, 62, 85, 90, 93, 242, 359 ff., 364, 368, 370, 371, 373; Beylerbey of, 241; taken by France, 299, 312. *See also* al-Maghrib
Ali ibn Abu Talib, 13, 26 f., 37 ff., 43, 44, 47 ff., 71, 75, 104, 140; cursing of, 66
Ali ibn Husain (Zain-ul-Abidin), 48
Ali ibn Isa, General, 112
Ali ibn al-Nafia, 174
Ali Muhammad, Sayyid (the *Bab*), 315
Ali, Muhammad and Shaukat, 345, 346
Ali, Mohammad, 350
Ali Pasha (Lepanto), 241, 242
Ali Pasha (statesman), 309, 310
Ali Quli Khan, 330
Ali al-Rida, 48, 113, 214
Alid dynasty, 66, 68, 89, 103, 104, 112 f., 270
Aligarh, Muslim University, 323
Alivardi Khan, 297
Allenby, Marshal, 343
Alma River, battle of, 309

Al Nahyan, Shaikh Zayed bin Sultan, 391
Alp Arsalan, 144 f.
Alphonso VI, 89, 91
Alptigin, 136
Alwar, 278
Amanullah, King of Afghanistan, 356
America, discovered, 240, 366, 376, 378, 380, 388, 389
Amiens, Treaty of, 300
al-Amin, 111
Amorium, siege of, 118
Amorsia, 256
Amr ibn al-As, 29, 33, 36, 37, 41, 42, 43, 55
Anatolia, 144, 155, 157, 226, 232, 244, 257, 268, 271, 301, 303, 337 (Anadolu)
Ancyra, battle of, 117
Andalusia, 93
Anglo-Iranian Oil Co., 317
Anglo-Persian Oil Co., 331, 342
Ankara (Angora), 337
Anna, Empress, 225
Ansar, the, 26, 27
Antioch, 158, 161, 163
Anushtigin, 145, 147
Apafy, 261
Aptidou, Hassan Gouled, 379
Arab-American Oil Co., 352
Arab Common Market, 365, 376
Arab High Committee, 353
Arab League, the, 351, 353, 363, 375, 382
Arabia and Arabs, 1 ff., 42, 90, 91, 348, 350 ff., and *passim*; Saudi Arabia, 350 ff., 352 ff., 358; revolt against Turks, 337; culture, 1, 3 ff., 7, 8, 34 ff., 72 ff., 86, 102, 107, 108, 110, 115, 150; Arabic, 62, 72, 83
Arabian Nights, the, 106, 108, 152
Arabian Peninsula, 391
Arbitration, the, 40 f.
Arafat, Yasser, 371
Architecture, Muslim; early, 62, 65; in Spain, 72, 82, 86, 97, 98 ff.; in Egypt, 174 f.; in India, 179, 180, 187 f., 203; Turkish, 240
Aref, Ali, 379
Arkad, fall of, 170
Armenia, 157, 171, 235, 272; revolt, 311
Army organization, 122, 181, 184, 213, 224, 228, 246, 248 ff., 257, 261, 264, 290 f., 300 f.
Arqabah, battle of, 28

Asadi Tusi, 139
Asaf Jah Nizam ul-Mulk, 297
Asaf Khan, 288
Ashnas, 119
al-Ashraf, Sultan, 172
Ashraf Shah, Sultan, 216
Asia Minor wars, 105, 107, 108, 144, 223 ff., and *passim*
Asirgarh, fort, 285
Asjadi, 139
Askari, Prince, 279, 280, 281
Assam, 293
Assassins, 132, 146, 149, 162, 170; Alamut, 146, 149
Astrabad, 216
Astronomy, 115, 122, 141, 152, 177, 202, 207
Aswan Dam, 331, 341
Atabeg-i-Azam, 330
Ataturk, *see* Kemal, Mustafa
Attock, battle of, 148
Auckland, Lord, 318
Aurangzeb, 285, 288, 290, 291 ff.
Austria, wars against Ottomans, 237, 241, 255 ff., 261 ff., 265 f., 269 f.; cf. 301, 309, 327 f; Don John of, 241, 242; war of Austrian Succession, 268. *See also* Vienna. Holy Roman Empire
Averroes, 95
Avicenna, 135, 151
Avignon, fall of, 68
Awami League, 348 f.
Awqaf, 170
Ayn Jalut, battle of, 169
Ayn ud-Daulah, 329 f.
Ayyubid Empire, 161 ff., 165 f., 167, 168
Azerbaijan, 114, 149, 203, 208, 254, 256, 341
al-Azhar University, 332
al-Aziz, Caliph, 98
Azov, 264, 265, 266, 267

B

Baalbek, 161
Baath Party, 382 f.
Bab, Mohammad Ali, 363
Bab, the, 315
Baba Farid, 198
Babak, 113, 114, 117
Babanjiba, Ibrahim, 374
Bab-i-Ali, 'The Sublime Porte', 235
Babiliyun, siege of, 33

Babism, 315
Bacha Saqa, 356
Badr, battle of, 15 f.
Badruddin Arif, Shaikh, 182
Badruddin Mahmud, 229
Baghavand, battle of, 218
Baghdad, 110, 113 f., 257; founded 105 f., 107; attacked, 129, 143, 149, 152, 169, 215, 223, 256; architecture 105 f.; Caliphs of, 80, 92, 98; cultural centre, 105 f., 115, 141, 145 f., 150, 204; hospital, 141; Nizamiyah University, 150; observatory, 115; taken by British, 337
Baghdad Pact, 340, 342, 350
Bahadur Shah, grandson of Mahmud Beghara, 195, 278 f.
Bahadur Shah I (Moghul), 297
Bahadur Shah (Mutiny), 320
Bahadurpur, battle of, 292
Baha'ism, 315
Bahauddin Zakariya, Shaikh, 182, 198
Bahaullah, 315
Bahmani Kingdom, 195 f., 274
Bahrain, 138, 364, 365, 368, 389
Bairam ibn Masud, 139
Bairam Khan, 282 f.
Bajaur, 274 f.
Bakhtiari tribes, 330, 341
Bakhtiyar Khalji, General, 179
Bakhtyar Shahpur, 394
Baku, 216, 217, 314
Balaclava, battle of, 309
Baldwin, Count, 156, 157, 171
Balfour, Lord, 353
Balj ibn Bashr, 79, 80
Balkan Wars, 328 f., cf. 310, 325
Baluchistan, 60
Bangladesh, 368, 398, 400
Banks; Imperial Bank of Persia, 316; Imperial Ottoman Bank, 309; National Bank of Persia, 341
Baqi, 247
Barcelona, sack of, 88
Barmakis, the, 106 f., 109 f., 114
Barquq, 172, 174
Barre, Mohammad Siad, 379
al-Basasiri, 143
Barslay, Sultan, 173
Basra, 34, 39, 73 f., 102, 130; British Concession, 219
Bathory, Prince Sigismund, 255
Batinis, the, 49

al-Battani, 122
Bayar, Celal, 339
Bayazid I, 170, 206, 228 ff., 270
Bayazid II, 235 f.
Bayazid Bustami, Shaikh, 134
Baybars, Sultan, 169 f., 200
al-Baytari, 174
Beirut, 388, 389
Bektashiya Order, 271 f.
Belgrade, 234, 237, 264, 266, 270; Treaty of, 266, 267
Benares, 177, 192
Ben Bella, 370, 371
Bengal, 179, 180, 185, 187, 189, 192, 198, 279, 282, 291, 297, 298
Berar, 197
Berbers, the, 61 f., 62, 79, 89, 91 f., 92, 142
Bernard of Clairvaux, 160
al-Beruni, 139, 151
Bessarabia, 266, 270, 309
Beylerbeys, 244, 246, 271
Beys, 244, 246, 311
Bhakti Movement, 198 f., 294 f.
Bhera, 275
Bhim Dev, Raja, 179
Bhojpur, 181
Bhutto, Benazir, 398
Bhutto, Zulfiqar Ali, 395, 397, 398, 400
Bidar, 197
Bihar, 187, 190, 192, 193, 278, 279, 282
Bihzad, 221
Bijapur, 197, 274, 290, 295, 296
Bikaner, 285
Bilgram, 280
Black Banner Movement, 69, 70
Black Sea, neutral zone, 309
Black Stone, 133
Bocskay, Stephen, 255
Bodyguards, power of, 88, 98, 117, 140, 172, 193, 253. See also Janissaries, Mamluks
Bohemund, Count, 157; II, 161
Bokhara, 53, 61, 135, 142, 147, 218, 275, 404, 406
Bombay, 346
Borneo, 335, 368, 401, 402
Bosnia, 228, 231, 234, 270, 327
Bosphorus, 339
Bourgiba, Mr. Habib, 359, 360, 371
Brahmins, 191, 286, 296
Bridge, battle of the, 30
British, in Africa, 299; in Egypt, 299,

306 ff., 311, 342 ff.; in Far East, 335 ff; in India, 199, 298, 299, 318 ff., 345 ff.; in Persia, 219, 313 f., 324, 330 f., 336 f., 340 f.; Mandates, 337, 351, 352, cf. 358 f. See also 300, 302, 303, 309, 312, 327, 380, 385, 402
British East India Co., 298, 318 f., 321
Brunei, 368, 401, 402
Brusa, 224, 338
Bucharest, Treaty of, 301, 329
Buda, 239, 256, 264
Buddhists, 266 f.
Bugeaud, Marshal, 312
Bughra Khan, 181
Bulgaria and Bulgars, 225, 226 ff., 264, 272, 310 f., 327 f.
Burma, 347, 367, 403
Bushire, British concessions, 219 cf. 316
Buwayhids, the, 139 ff., 143
Buxar, battle of, 298
Byana, 189
Byzantine Empire, 4, 28 ff., 33, 35, 43, 53 f., 61, 65, 105 f., 107 ff., 116, 130, 144 f., 154, 223 ff., cf. 55, 96, 102, 212. See also Christians, Constantinople, Papacy.

C

Cairo, (al-Qahirah), 98, 165, 170, 236, 364; mosques, 98, 172; Nasiriya College, 172, 174
Caliphate, 13 f., 27 ff., 71 ff., 119 ff., 170, 244, 270 f., 299, 305; mantle of Prophet, 244, 270. See also Abbasids, Omayyads, and passim
Camel, battle of the, 39
Campbell, Sir Colin, 320
Cantacuzene, 225 f.
Carpets and fabrics, 220 f., 221
Casablanca, 362
Castlereagh, Lord, 301
Catherine the Great, 267, 268 ff.
Caucasia, 216, 217, 314
Cawnpore, 320
Ceramics and glass, 99, 220 f.
Chad, 368, 373, 374
Chadli, Bendjidid, 370
Chaghatai Khan, 205
Chaldibran, battle of, 212
Chalukyas, the, 176

Chanderi, 183, 189, 195; 281
Charlemagne, 80 f., 108
Charles Gustavus of Sweden, 265
Charles V, Hapsburg, 238
Charles of Lorraine, 263
Chaunsa, battle of, 279
Cheribon Agreement, 357
Chesme, battle of, 269
Chilianwala, battle of, 318
China, 202, 207, 367, 380, 408
Chittagong, 293
Chittor, 183, 195, 278
Chosroes, Shah of Persia, 4, 28, 31, 107
Christianity and Christians, 4, 7; converts, 29; Crusades, 154 ff., 163, 223, 226 ff.; influenced by Muslims, 159; Orthodox, 233, 308; Protestant, 286; Reformed, 240; Regiments of Sultans, 257; Roman Catholic, 286; Spanish, 79 ff., 84 ff., 86 f., 94; Sultanas, 243, 259 f.; treatment by Muslims, 35, 311, cf. 82 f. See also Byzantine Empire, Missionaries, Mozarabs, Muwallads, Papacy
Chunar, 278, 279
Cid, the, 92
Cilicia, 65, 117, 121, 130
Civil Service, Turkish, 271
Communism, 340, 342
Constantinople (later Istanbul), 54, 55, 156; crusade against, 165; Turkish siege of, 210, 226, 229, 230, 232 ff.; cf. 65, 118; Treaty of, 329. See also Byzantine Empire, Istanbul
Cooch Behar, 193
Cordova, 79, 80, 86 f., 88; palace at, 86
Cordovez, Dego, 362, 393
Cossacks, 262, 263; Brigade, 316, 330, 340
Crete, 83, 90, 115, 258, 262, 265, 266, 305; rising, 311; joins Greece, 327, 328
Crimea, 264, 265, 267, 269 f.; Crimean War, 308 f.
Croatia, 234, 264, 265
Crusades, the, 93, 98, 145, 154 ff., 223; against Turks, 226 f., 229, 230 f., 235 f.
Currency, Arabic, 62; in India, 186
Cyprus, 35, 43, 173, 360, 380, 381; and Venice, 236, 241, 242; occupied by British, 313
Cyrenaica, 90, 375

D

Dacca, 399
Daddah, Mokhtar, Ould, 369
Dadrah, battle of, 278
Daghestan, 216
Dahir, Raja, 60, 176
Dahomey, 373
Dalhousie, Lord, 318, 319
Dalmatia, 234, 265
Damascus, 31; attacks on, 160, 201, 256, 304; capital city, 44, 55 58, 64, 102, 121, 170; university, 96, 173; taken by British, 337
Damietta (Dimyat), 121, 166, 168
Dante, 96
Dara Shikoh, Prince, 291 ff.
Dardanelles, 299, 303, 328, 337, 339
Dariyah, 304
Data Ganj Bakhsh, 198
Daud al-Qaysari, 224
Daulatabad (Deogri), 186
Dayalpur, 291
Deccan, the, 176, 182 ff., 195 f., 274, 285, 288 ff.; 297, 320
de Gaulle, General Charles A.J.M., 370
de Lesseps, Ferdinand, 306
Delhi, 177 ff., 186 f., 189, 206, 275, 282, 288, 289, 291, 298, 320; Kotwal of, 184; Red Fort, 289; Sultan of, 187 f., 190, 191, 194, 274. See also Lodhis
Demak, 335
Democracy, 299, 309, 310 f., 325, 327
Demotika, 226
Denmark, 408
Deorai, battle of, 292
Dera Ghazi Khan, 274
Derbent, 216, 217, 314
Derebays, the, 267, 268, 301
de Reuter, Baron, 316
Dervishes, 210, 271, 382
Dhahhak ibn Qais, 58
Dhar, 183
Dhimmis, 72
Dholpur, 189
Dini-i-Ilahi, 286
Dipalpur, 275
Diu, 195
Diyar Bekr, 142, 143, 203, 208, 210, 212, 214, 256
Djibouti, 364, 368, 379
Djunda, Mr., 358

Doab, the, 277
Doctrine of Lapse, 318 f.
Doctrine of Necessity, 397
Doroshenko, 262
Dorylaeum, battle of, 157
Dost Muhammad, Amir, 316
Dragut, Admiral, 242
Druses, the, 49, 256, 272
Dubai, 390, 391
Dutch, 325, 335 ff., 357

E

Edessa, 256
Education, 82, 86 f., 95 f., 115 f., 121, 139, 141, 146, 172, 181 f., 188 f., 196, 197 f., 205, 224 f., 235, cf. 150
Edward I of England, 200
Egypt, conquest by Muslims, 33 f., 41 f., 53; Fatimid rule, 90 f., 95 ff., 115, 119, 142, 143 f.; Mongol invasion, 169, 173; Salahuddin Sultan of, 161 f., 165; Burji Mamluk Empire, 172 ff., 195, 236; Turkish conquest, 237, cf. 331, 332; Napoleon in, 300; under Muhammad Ali, 302 ff., 310; British in, 299, 305, 306 ff.; 311, 331 ff., 342 ff., 347 ff., and U.S.S.R., 355, 356. See also 364, 365, 368, 376, 377, 382
El-Arish, Convention of, 300
Enver Pasha, 328, 329
Enzali, 340
Epirus, 230
Erivan, 214, 215, 257, 314
Ershad, Hossein Ahmad, 400
Ertoghrul (Turkey), 223
Ertughrul (Persia), 207
Erzerum, Treaty of, 314
Erzerum, Congress of, 338
Erzinjan, 207, cf. 235
Eski Baba, battle of, 226
Estiang, Giscard d', 379
Eugene of Savoy, 265, 266, 267
Europe, 366
European Common Market, 365
Evliya Chelebi, 272

F

Fahd, Prince, 385
Faisal, Emir, 352
Faisal, Prince, 385

Fakhruddin, Prince, 256
al-Farabi, 122
al-Farazi, 122
Farhad Pasha, General, 213
Farid Shakar Ganj, Shaikh, 182
Farishta, 196
Farouk, King, 343
Farrukhi, 139
Fars, 203
Fath Ali Shah, 313, 314
Fatima, the Lady, 21, 85, 90
Fatimid dynasty, 84 f., 87, 90 f., 95 ff., 132, 142, 143, 144, 154, 161
Ferghana, 61, 274, 275
Firdausi, 135, 139
Firuz Tughluq, 187 f., 191 f., 193
Forced Culture System, 336
Fourteen Points, 347
France and Franks (French); wars against Muslims, 66, 67 f., 171, 262, 264, 268, cf. 243; and North Africa, 299, 311, 312 f.; 324, 333, 358; and Suez, 344; Syrian Mandate, 337, 355 f.; French Revolution, 302. See also 300, 302, 309, 370, 374, 379
Frederick Barbarossa, 163
Frederick II, 97, 167
Freedmen, 73, 145 f., 179 ff. See also Slaves
Freemasonry, 327
Friday Prayers, 122
Fuad Pasha, 309
Fujairah, 390
al-Fustat, 34, 102
Fuzuli, 247

G

Galatia, 65
Galicia, 88, 89
Gallipoli, 226, 227, 229
Gambia, 367, 368, 372, 407
Gandhi, Mahatma, 346
Ganja, battle of, 314
Gardens, 98, 188
Gaur, 192, 279
Genghis Khan, 148 f., 170, 205 f.
Geneva Conference, 362
Genoa, 158, 166, 225, 227, 233, 234
Georgia, 254, 256, 269, 314
Germany, 329, 333, 337, 339, 340
Ghakkars, the, 281
Ghalib, Shaikh, 272

Ghassanid dynasty, 4, 29 f.
Ghaur Khan, 147
al-Ghauri, 175, 178
Ghaurids, 147, 177 ff., 223
Ghazan (Mongol), 172
Ghazan Mahmud, 201 f.
Ghazi, King, 352
Ghaznavid dynasty, 129, 136 f., 143, 147, 177
Ghazni, 136, 138, 139, 147, 177, 179
Ghazwahs, 53, 55, 59, 68, 88, 105, 122, 138, 142, 169, 224, 279
al-Ghazzali, Imam, 146, 150
Ghiathuddin, 178, 179
Ghiathuddin Azam, Shah, 179
Ghiathuddin Balban, 180 ff.
Ghiathuddin Tughluq, 183, 185
Gibraltar (Jabal-i-Tariq), 63
Gilan, 216, 217, 340
Goa, 196, 197
Gobind Singh, 294
Godfrey of Bouillon, 156, 158, 163
Golconda, 197, 274, 290, 296
Golden Horde, the, 170
Gordon, General, 306, 307
Gorst, Sir Eldon, 332
Goths, the, 82
Granada, 234
Greece and Greeks; ancient Greek culture, 94 f., 102, 154, cf. 235; Muslim invasion, 90, 227, 229; Orthodox Church, 235, 308; War of Independence, 301 f., cf. 327, 328; war with Turkey, 338, 339. *See also* Byzantine Empire
Greek Fire, 54
Gujarat, 176, 183, 187, 194 f., 278, 335
Gulf Co-operative Council, 365
Gulf Investment Council, 365
Gulistan, Treaty of, 314
Gulnabad, battle of, 215
Gurdaspur, 349
Gurkhas, the, 320
Gursel, Gemal, 381
Guy of Lusignan, 163, 173
Gwadar, 392
Gwalior, 189, 192, 283, 292

H

Habibullah, Amir, 356
Hadith, 74
Hadramaut, 2, 386

Hafiz, 192, 204 f., 209; *Diwan*, 205
Hajib, the (Muhammad ibn Abi' Amir), 87 f.
Hajj, the, 17 f.
al-Hajjaj ibn Yusuf, 58 ff., 64, 176
al-Hakam, 82, 115
al-Hakam II, 86 f.
Haldighat, battle of, 285
Hamadan, 216, 217, 257
Hamdanids, the, 141, 142
Hamid, 228
Hamida, Bano, Empress, 280, 283
Hammudids, the, 88
Hamza, 6, 13
'Harem Rule', 215, 254, 257, 259; cf. 253, 255
Harrah, battle of, 57
Harun al-Rashid, 81, 90, 106, 108 ff.
al-Hasan, Imam, 37, 43, 47, 53, 89, 103, 104
Hasan al-Askari, 48
Hasan al-Basri, 74
Hasan Ghaznavi, Sayed, 139
Hasan ibn al-Naaman, 61, 62
Hasan ibn Sabah, 132, 146 f., cf. 162
Hashim, the Bani, 5, 12, 13, 37, 44, 57, 80
Hashim Khan, Sardar, 356
Hatta, Muhammad, 357, 402
Hatt-i-Humayun, the, 309
Havelock, General, 320
Haydalla, Khonna Ould, 370
Hazaraspids, the, 204
al-Hazen, 99
Hazrat Ali, 88
Hebrews, *see* Jews
Hemu, 282, 283
Herat, 203, 207, 213, 216, 219, 221, 280
Heresies, 106, 107, 229; cf. 131 f., 225 f. *See also* Babak
Herodotus, 2
Herzegovina, 234, 328
Hibatullah ibn Jumay, 174
'Hidden Imam', the, 90 f., 132
Hijaz, 2, 5, 57 ff., 98, 133, 145, 161, 304 f., 337, 350 ff.
Hijrah, the, 14, 16
Hims, battles of, 171, 172
Himyar, *see* Yemen
Hindal, Prince, 278, 281
Hisham, 67
History and historians, 108, 110, 174, 209 f., 272 f.

Hittin, battle of, 162
Hizb ul-Watan, 332
Holy Leagues (anti-Muslim), 238, 241, 264
Holy Roman Empire, 240 f., 260 f. *See also* Austria
Holy Wars, *see Ghazwahs*
Hong Kong, 367
Hospitallers, Order of, 169
Hoxtra, General Enver, 380
Hudaibiya, Pact of, 17 f.
Hulagu Khan, 149, 152, 169, 170, 171, 172, 200 f., 209
Humayun, Emperor, 195, 213, 278 ff., 282, 284
Hungary, 229 ff., 230 ff., 234 f., 237, 239 f., 255, 261, 263, 264 f., 308, 310; Ferdinand of, 237, 239; Louis of, 237
Hunyadi, John, 230 f., 234
al-Hurr ibn Abdul Rahman, 66, 67
Hurr ibn Yezid Tamimi, 45
Husain, Sharif, 350
al-Husain, Imam, 37, 44 ff., 47, 57, 104, 131; tomb of, 119 ff., cf. 203, 304
Husain, Sir Fazli, 346
Husain ibn Numayr, 57
Hussain, Altaf, 323
Hussain Kamil, 333
Hussain, King of Jordan, 355
Hyder Ali, 298
Hyderabad, 297, 320, 349

I

Ibadat Khana, 286
Ibn Abi al-Mahasin, 174
Ibn Abi Usaibiah, 174
Ibn Arabi, 95
Ibn Bajjah, 95
Ibn Battutah, 96, 185
Ibn Hawqal, 152
Ibn al-Haytham, *see* al-Hazen
Ibn Hazm, 95
Ibn Hisham, 123
Ibn Khaldun, 96
Ibn Khallikan, 89, 174
Ibn Musa ibn Babuwaihi (Ibn Babuya), 48
Ibn Rushd, *see* Averroes
Ibn Sina, *see* Avicenna
Ibn Taiyima, Imam, 173 f., 304
Ibn Tufail, 95

Ibn Tumart, 92
Ibrahim I, 258
Ibrahim al-Abbasi, 70, cf. 104
Ibrahim ibn al-Aghlab, 90, 109
Ibrahim ibn Muhammad Ali, 303, 305
Iconium, *see* Konya
Iconoclasts, 86, 119 f., 140, 190, 304 f.
Idolatry, 304
al-Idrisi, 95
Ifriqiya, 53, 58, 61, 79 f., 82, 85, 90, 93, 109, 115, 142
Ijtihad, 316
Ikhshidids, the, 97 f.
Ikhwan us-safa, 141
Il Khans, the, 200 ff., 204 f., 210, 223. *See also* Hulagu Khan
Iltutmash, 180
Ilyas Shah, 192
Imams, the, 47 f., 113
India, Muslim conquests in, 60 f., 105, 136 ff., 154, 176 ff., 206 f., 274 ff., 317 ff., 352, cf. 270, 319; British in, 299, 317 ff., 321 ff., 345 f., 348 ff.; caste, 96; culture, 102, 176; Missions, 319; Mutiny, 319 f.; Independence Act, 349; Hindus and Hinduism, 136 f., 184 f., 188, 190 f., 197, 286 f., 319; revolts, 293, 296 ff., 321 f., 333 f.; Congress, 334, 345 ff., 348 ff. *See also* 367.
Indonesia, 325, 335, 348, 357 f., 367, 368, 402
Industry and Commerce, 86, 118, 140, 220
Inkerman, battle of, 309
Inonu, Ismet, 339
Iqbal, Sir Muhammad, 209, 325, 346 f., 407
Iran *see* Persia. *See also* 362, 366, 367, 368, 393
Iraq, 4, 342; campaigns in, 30 f., 34, 42, 59 f.; under Muslim rule, 57, 67, 69, 73 f., 132, 147; conquered by Timur, 206; by Ismail, 210; by Turks, 215, 223, 237, 310; Wahhabis in, 303 ff.; after World War II, 348, 355; British Mandate, 352. *See also* 364, 365, 368, 376, 383
Irene, Empress, 107, 108
Isfahan, 140, 145, 204, 213, 215
Islam, *passim*; faith of, 21 ff.; persecutions in India, 317 f., cf. 293 f.; Muslim law, 34, 48 f., 65 f., 74, 76,

82, 123 f., 170, 173 f., 250; values, 123 f.
Islamic Conference, 362, 371; Secretariat, 363, 408
Ismail, Khedive, 306 f.
Ismail Safavi, 208, 210 ff., 236, 275; Safavids, 363
Ismailis, the, 48, 90, 129, 132 f., 146 f.
Israel, 344 f., 353 ff., 364, 376, 377. *See also* Jews.
Istanbul (formerly Constantinople), 236, 256, 264, 269, 301, 303; Sancta Sophia, 234; Universities, 309, 317. *See also* Constantinople
Italy, states of, 155, 241, 242; in North Africa, 312 f., 328, cf. 337, 338. *See also* Genoa, Venice
Ivan the Terrible, 267

J

Jabir ibn Hayyan, 122
Ja'far al-Sadiq, 48, 131
Jai Singh, Raja, 295
Jaichand, Raja, 179
Jains, 286
Jaipal, Raja, 136
Jaipur, 285
Jaisselmer, 285
Jalaluddin, Khalji, Sultan, 182
Jalaluddin, Prince of Khiva, 148 f., 180
Jalaluddin Rumi, 208 f., 247, 271
Jalaluddin Tabrizi, 198
Jalayr Dynasty, 203
Jalula, battle of, 31
Jamaluddin Afghani, Sayyid, 299, 306 f., 316 f., 329, 407
Jammu, 178
Janbulad, Kurd, 256
Janissaries, 224, 225, 253, 256, 257, 258, 259, 266 f., 300 ff.
Japan, 347, 357, 358, 366
Jassy, Treaty of, 270
Jaswant Singh, General, 291, 294, 296
Jats, *see* Zotts
Jaunpur, 187, 188, 189, 191, 278, 279
Jawara, Dawda Kharrufa, 372
Jawhar, Fatimid General, 98
Jazirat-ul-Arab, *see* Arabia
Jeddah, 304, 351
Jehangir, 287 ff., 293
Jemal Pasha, 328, 329
Jerusalem, 32, 33, 62, 158, 162 ff., 165, 167, 353 ff. *See also* Crusades

Jews, the, 5, 7, 10, 17, 29, 34, 224, 240 f.; return to Israel, 353 ff.
Jhansi, 318, 320 f.
Jilan, 203
Jinnah, Muhammad Ali, 346, 348 f.
Jizya, the (tax), 295
Jocelin II, Count, 161
Jodhpur State, 294
Jordan, 4, 29, 364, 365, 368, 376
Judaism, *see* Jews
Juna, 'Mad' Prince, *see* Muhammad Tughluq
Junaid, 176
Junaid, Shaikh (Dervish), 210
Junejo, Mohammad Khan, 398

K

Kaaba, the, 5 ff., 18, 57, 170
Kalb, Bani, 142
Kabul, 53, 61, 135, 136, 179, 181, 190, 193, 206, 217, 218, 223, 274, 275, 282, 285, 292, 356
Kalbites or Himyarites, 67, 69, 79, 97, 114
Kalilah wa Dimnah, 139
Kalinjar, fall of, 179
Kamal Devi, Rani, 183
Kamal Reis, 236
al-Kamil, 165, 166
Kamil, Mustafa, 332
Kampil, 181
Kamran, Prince, 279, 280
Kanauj, 177, 179
Kandahar, 218, 278, 280, 290, 292
Kaneoran, 387
Kara Mustafa (Grand Vizier to 1642), 258
Kara Mustafa (1678-1689), 263
Karbala, 121, 203, 304; battle of, 46
Karim Khan, 219
Karjahisar (Melangnore), 224
Karlowitz, Treaty of, 265
Karmal, Babrak, 392
Karman, 140, 147, 204, 206
Karmanshah, 216, 217
Kars, 214, 219, 254, 256, 309
Kashmir, 187, 318, 349
Kastamuni, 206
Kathiawar, 138, 194
Kayseri, 206
Kazakhistan, 368, 404, 406
Keita, Modibo, 372
Kemal, Mustafa, 337, 338 ff., 368

Kereoztes, battle of, 255
Kermia, 228
Kertch, 269
Khadijah, Muhammad's wife, 10, 21
Khairuddin Barbarossa, Admiral, 238, 242 f.,
Khalid ibn al-Walid, 16, 18, 20, 28 ff., 31 ff.
Khalid, Prince, 385
Khaljis, the, 182 ff., 194
Khameini, Ayatullah Rohulla, 394
Khan, Field-Marshal Mohammed Ayub, 350, 366, 395
Khan, General Nadir, 356
Khan, General Yahya, 395
Khandesh, 285
Kharijites, the, 106, 114
Khartoum, 307, 308
Khanua, battle of, 277
Khawarij (Puritan) Rebellion, 41
Kherla, 193
Khids Khan, see Sayyids
Khilafat Party, 346
Khiva, 218, 404, 406
Khokhars, the, 179
Khorasan, 34, 42, 46, 53, 59, 70, 104, 105, 114, 134, 143, 147, 207, 212, 216, 275, 313
Khurram, Prince (Shah Jehan), 288 ff., 293
Khusro, Amir, 181
Khusro Khan, 184
Khwaja Gesu Daraz, 198
Khwaja Jahan, 191
Khwaja Maruf al-Karkhi, 134
Khwaja Moinuddin Ajmer, 198
Khwaja Qutbuddin Bakhtiyar Kaki, 182, 198
Khwarizm Shahs, 61, 144, 145, 147, 148, 204, 209
Khuzistan, 133, 140
Kinburn, 269
al-Kindi, 122
Kirghizia, 407
Kirghizistan, 368, 404
Kirkuk, battle of, 217
Kitchener, General, 307, 332
Kizilbashes, 210, 213
Kleber, General, 300
Koil, 189
Konntehe, Seyni, 373
Konya, 145, 209, 223, 303
Koprulu, Ahmad, 260, 263; Muhammad, 259 ff; Mustafa, 264

Korea, 367
Kossovo, battle of, 227 ff.; 2nd battle, 260 ff.
Kuchuk, Treaty of, 269
Kufa, 34, 37 ff., 43, 44 f., 57, 59, 73 ff., 102, 103
Kurdistan, 147, 212
Kurds, 256, 352
Kutlugh Shah, Prince, 201
Kuwait, 364, 365, 368, 376, 384, 385
al-Kuwatly, Shukri, 356

L

Lahore, 177 ff., 181, 189, 190, 218, 275, 280, 289, 292, 362; Anjuman-i-Himayat-i-Islam, 333; Fort, 289; Resolution, 348
Lale Burgas, battle of, 328
Lausanne Treaty, 328
Law, 123 ff., 173, 235, 240, 246, 271
Lawrence, T.E., 364
League of Nations, 348, 352
Lebanon, 348, 364, 368, 389
Lemnos, 260, 325
Leo, Byzantine General, 65
Leon, Kingdom of, 84, 85, 86, 88
Leopold I, 263
Lepanto, 236; battle of, 240 ff., 254, 258
Liaquat Ali Khan, 349
Liberalism, 299, 309, 316 f., 329 ff.
Libya, 348, 364, 368, 373, 375, 376
Light Brigade, Charge of, 309
Literature, 72, 89, 94, 107, 108, 110, 139, 145, 152 f., 204, 249 ff.
Lloyd George, David, 338
Lodhi dynasty, 189 ff., 198, 275, 278
London, Treaty of, 305; 2nd Treaty, 309
Louis of Baden, 264
Louis, St., King of France, 168
Louis XIV of France, 261
Lucknow, 278, 320; Pact, 345
Lutf Ali Khan, 219

M

al-Ma'arri, 141
Macedonia, 227, 311, 325, 327, 328
Magellan, 335
al-Maghrib, 62, 63, 96, 109, 234 f., 311 f., 358 f.
Mahabat Khan, 289, 290, 292
Mahabharata, the, 191, 193

Mahadoji Scindhia, 298
Maham Anga, 283, 284
al-Mahdi, 107 ff., 110
Mahdi, Imam, 48
Mahmud, Shaikh, 352
Mahdi of the Sudan, 307 f.
Mahmud the Great, 136, 138, 139
Mahmud II (Ottoman), 301
Mahmud Beghara, 195
Mahmud Gawan, 196, 197
Mahmud Khan Khalji, 193 ff.
Mahmud Sami, 307
Mahmud Shah of Bengal, 279
Mahmudabad, Raja of, 346
Mahrattas, 199, 288, 294 ff., 297, 298
Majlis, the, 330, 331, 340, 341
Makarios, Archbishop, 381
Makhdum Jahanian Jahan Gasht, 198
Malaya, 299, 403
Malaysia, 368, 401
Maldev, 284
Maldive Islands, 403, 404, 407
Mali, 368, 372, 373
Malik Ambar, 288, 290
Malik al-Ashtar, 37, 39
Malik ibn Anas, Imam, 123
Malik Kafur, 183
Malikshah, 144 f., 146, 147, 160
Mallowane, Felix, 375
Malta, 90, 115
Malwa, 176, 180, 187, 193 f., 279, 281, 284; Khans of, 193
Mamluks, the, 169, 170, 200 ff., 300; Bahri, 73, 169 ff., 172; Burji, 73, 169, 172 ff., 195, 236
al-Mamun, 111 ff., 116, 117
Man Singh, Raja, 192
Mandu, 183
al-Mansur, 80, 104 ff., 112, 113
Mansur al-Hallaj, 134
Manzikert, battle of, 144
al-Maqdisi, 152
Marj Rahit, battle of, 29 f., 58
Marj al-Saffar, battle of, 172, 201
Marrakesh, 91, 93
Marwan, II, 69, 70, 104
Marwan ibn al-Hakam, 36, 57 f.
Marwanids, the, 57, 142
Masjid Atala, the, 191
Maslamah, General, 67
Masnad Ali Khan, 190
Masts, battle of the, 53
Masud, Sultan, 139

al-Masudi, 123
Mathematics, 122, 146, 152, 176
Mauritania, 364, 368, 369
Mawali, the, 66, 69, 72, 102
Maximilian, Emperor, 241
Mazandaran, 134, 216, 217
Mazdakites, the, 106
Mecca, 3, 4, 5, 12, 14 ff., 18, 29, 45, 57, 58, 59, 133, 145, 350, 352, 362; cultural centre, 102; Sharifs of, 236, 278, 279, 350, 364, 383
Medicine and Science, 72, 94, 95, 98, 99, 110, 115, 122, 135, 141, 145, 151, 171, 174, 176, 189, 196, 235
Medina (Yathrib) 2, 5, 13, 14 ff., 21 ff., 34 ff., 38 ff., 43, 44, 57, 102, 104, 145, 304, 351, 352
Meerut, 320
Mehr un-Nisa (Nur Jehan), 288
Menderes, Adnan, 340
Merv, 207
Meshhed, 113, 207, 214, 216
Mesopotamia, 214, 239, 337
Metternich, Count, 301
Mevleviya Order, 271
Mewar, 194, 275, 281, 285
Midhat Pasha, 310 f.
Mir Jumla, 293
Mir Mahmud, 215
Mir Shayista Khan, 293
Mir Vais, 215
Mirdasids (Bani Kalb), 142
Mirkhond, 209
Mirza, Major-General Iskander, 350
Mirza, Shah, 190
Mirza Muhammad Hakim, 285
Mirza Haidar, 275
Mirza Taqi Khan, 314 f.
Missionaries in India, 319
Missolonghi, 302
Modarites, see Qaisites
Moghuls, the, 187, 190 ff., 196, 200, 209, 213, 218, 221, 274 ff., 281, 319, 363; culture, 287. See also Zahirud-din Babar
Mohacs, battle of, 237; 2nd battle of, 264
Mohammad, Mr. Ghulam, 350
Mohammed ibn Abdul Wahhab, 2, 173 f., 303 f. See also Wahhabis
Mohan Roy, Raja, 321
Mohsin ul-Mulk, 323
Moldavia, 268, 270, 303, 308

Monasteries, 91

Mongols, 129, 148 ff., 169 f., 174, 180 ff., 208 f., 223, 227; conversion to Islam, 170 f.

Montagu-Chelmsford Reforms, 345 f.

Montecucculi, 262

Moorish culture, 82 ff., 94 ff.

Morea, the, 242, 264, 265, 266, 301

Morley-Minto Reforms, 334

Morocco, 53, 62, 63, 71, 87, 89, 91, 92, 358 f., 362, 364, 368, 369; French Protectorate, 299, 333, 358-9. *See also* al-Maghrib, Moscow, Duchy of, 267

Mossadeq, Dr. Mohammad, 342, 394

Mosul, 142 ff., 157, 160, 203, 208, 214, 256, 352

Moulay Mohammad bin Arafa, 359

Mozarabs, the, 83, 92

Muawiyah, Amir, 6, 18, 38 ff., 53 ff., 69, 71

Mubarak, Hosni, 377

Mubarak Shah, 189

Mudania, Council of, 338

Muhajirin, 26

Muhammad, the Prophet, 6-20, 21, 47, 155, 247

Muhammad I (Ottoman), 229 f.

Muhammad II, Conqueror, 232 ff., 239, 251, 270

Muhammad III, 255

Muhammad IV, 260, 264

Muhammad V, 327

Muhammad III, Bahmani, 196, 197

Muhammad the Abbasid, 68, 70

Muhammad Abduh, 317, 332

Muhammad Ahmad. *see* Mahdi of the Sudan

Muhammad Ali (Egypt), 299, 303 ff.

Muhammad Ali, Maulana, 334

Muhammad Baqir, 48

Muhammad ibn Abu Bakr, 37, 39

Muhammad ibn Balban, 181

Muhammad ibn Hasan al-Tusi, 49

Muhammad ibn Ismail al-Bokhari, Imam, 124

Muhammad ibn al-Qasim, 60 f., 64, 65, 176

Muhammad ibn Saud, 304

Muhammad ibn Yaqub al-Kulaini, 48

Muhammad Khudabanda, 254

Muhammad Lamine Pasha Bey, 360

Muhammad Said, Khedive, 306

Muhammad Shah, Emperor of Delhi, 218, 297 f.

Muhammad Shah of Persia, 314

Muhammad Sokolli, 241, 243 ff.

Muhammad al-Taqi, 48

Muhammad Tughluq, 185 ff., 190, 195

Muhammad Zaman, Mirza, 278

Mujahids, 362

Mujibur Rehman, Sheikh, 395, 398, 400

Mukti Bahini, 399

Mullahs, 246, 271, 321

Multan, 176, 178, 179, 181, 182, 274, 278, 282

al-Muqanna, *see* Babak

al-Muqtadir, 133, 134

al-Muqtafi, 130 f.

Murabits, the, 89, 91 ff., 92

Murad I (Ottoman), 226 ff.

Murad II, 230 ff., 239, 247

Murad III, 254

Murad IV, 215, 257 f.

Murad, son of Shah Jehan, 291, 292

Mursteg Reforms, 325

Musa al-Kazim, 48, 131

Musa ibn Maimun, 95

Musa ibn Nusayr, 58, 62 ff., 65 f.

Mus'ab ibn al-Zubair, 57

Musailimah, revolt of, 28

Muscat, 391

Music, 83, 159, 189

Muslim ibn Aqil, 45

Muslim ibn al-Hajjaj, Imam, 124

Muslim ibn Quraysh, Sultan, 142

Muslim ibn Uqbah, 57

Muslim League, 334 f., 346 f., 348 f.

Mustafa, Uncle of Murad II, 230

Mustafa, Sultan, 264

Mustafa III, 268

Mustafa IV, 301

al-Mustakfi, Caliph, 140

al-Mutadid, 130

al-Mutamid (Abbasid Caliph), 129 f.

al-Mutamid (Seville), 89, 91 f.

al-Mutanabbi, 141, 142

al-Mutasim, 116

al-Mutawakkil, 119 ff., 129

Mu'tazila school of thought, 74, 115, 119. *See also* Rationalism

al-Muwaffiq, 130

Muwahhids, the, 86, 89, 93

Muwallads, 83

Muzaffaruddin, Shah of Persia, 317

Muzaffarids, the 204 f.
Mysticism, 74, 94, 96, 133 f.

N

Nadir Kuli Khan, Shah of Persia, 216 ff., 218, 298
Nagpur, 318
Nahas, Pasha, Mustafa, 343 ff.
Nahrawan, battle of, 41
Namik Kamal, 309
Nana Sahib, 320
Napoleon, 300, 301
al-Naqi, 48
Naqshbandiya Order, 272
al-Nasir, 172, 174
Nasir Khusro, 146
Nasir ul-Mulk, 330
Nasiruddin of Bengal, 193
Nasiruddin Mahmud, 180, 181
Nasiruddin Qabacha, 179, 180
Nasiruddin Shah of Persia, 314 ff.
Nasiruddin Tusi, 149, 152, 200
Nasser, Col. Gamal Abdul, 344 f., 368, 376, 386
Nassi, Joseph, 240 f.
Nationalist Movement, 306 f.
NATO, 340
Navarino, battle of, 302
Navarre, 85, 86
Navy, Muslim, 35, 42, 43, 53, 54, 90 ff., 170; Turkish, 236, 237, 238 ff., 240 ff., 243, 244, 258, 268 f.
Nazimuddin, Mr., 349
Nedim, 247
Nefi, 247
Negroponte, 234 f.
Neguib, General Mohammed, 344
Nehru, Mr., 358
Nejd, 2, 132, 304, 337, 350, 351, 352
Nelson, Admiral Lord, 300
Neo-Muslims (Muwallads), 82, 83 f.
Nezib, battle of, 305
Nicephorus I, 108 f.
Nicholson, Sir John, 320
Nicodemia, 224
Niger, 368, 373
Nigeria, 368, 374
Nightingale, Florence, 309
Nihavand, battle of, 31
Nile Valley, 306
Nish, 227, 231
Nishapur Sabzwar, 213
Nisibin, battle of, 104

Nizam ul-Mulk, 146, 147
Nizami, Shaikh, 139
Nizamshahi, the, 289
Nizamuddin Aulia, Shaikh, 198
Normans, the, 97
Nubia, 170
Numidia, 90
Nur Jehan, see Mehr un-Nisa
Nusairids, 49
Nusrat Shah, 193

O

Obaidullah ibn Ziyad, 45, 47, 57, 103
Obaidullah al-Mahdi, 131, 132
Obrenovich, Milosh, 301
Oczakov, 270
Oltenitza, battle of, 308
Oman, 364, 365, 368
Omar ibn Abdul Aziz, 66
Omar ibn Hafsun, 84
Omar ibn al-Khattab, 13, 27, 30 ff., 42 f., 66
Omar ibn Saad, 45
Omar Khayyam, 146, 152
Omayyads, the, 5, 6, 12, 27, 36, 38, 53 ff., 102 f., 111; in Spain 80, 85, 90; murder of, 70
Omdurman, battle of, 308
Optics, 99, 174
Orissa, 192, 193
Orkhan I, 224 ff., 228, 270
Orthodox Caliphs, 26 ff.
Osman, 223
Osman I, 223, 228
Osman II, 255
Osman ibn Affan, 35 ff., 42, 53
Osmanlis, see Turks, Ottoman
Oudh, 297, 318 f., 320

P

Padmini, Rani, 183
Pahlavis, the, 340 ff.
Painting, 214, cf. 287
Pakistan, 105, 136, 274, 348 ff., 357, 362, 366, 368, 395
Paleologus, John, 225, 227
Palermo, 96 f.
Palestine, 5, 32 f., 226, 304, 336, Christian pilgrimages, 154 f.; British Mandate, 352. See also Israel, Jerusalem, Jews

Palestine Liberation Organization, 364, 388
Palmerston, Lord, 305
Pamplona, 85
Panchayat system, 191
Panipat, 1st battle of, 190, 275; 2nd battle, 282 f.; 3rd battle, 298
Pan-Islamism, 317, cf. 360
Papacy and Popes, 83, 97, 156 ff., 165, 166, 167, 171, 200, 227, 229 f., 235, 236, 238, 241, 261, 264. *See also* Christians, Crusades
Paros, 260
Partap, Rana, 285
Passarowitz, Treaty of, 266
Pathans, the, 293, 294
Patna, 277
Peace Settlement, 1919, 364
Pergamos, 61
Perin, 388
Persia, 3, 4, 31, 42, 68, 70, 74, 90, 133, 147, 203 ff., 223, 299, 310, 313 ff., 363; culture, 102, 135 f., 139 f., 182, 191, 218 ff., 272; Turkish wars, 234 ff., 238, 239, 254, 257, 266, 267, cf. 314; and Moghuls, 290 f; and Russia, 329 ff.; and British, 341, 348; since World War I, 340 ff.
Peshawar, 136, 178, 218
Peter the Great, 215, 265
Peterwarden, battle of, 266
Petrovich, George, 301
Philadelphia, 229
Philippopolis, 226
Phillipines, 402
Philokrene, battle of, 224
Philosophy, 87, 94 ff., 110, 122, 135, 150, 247, cf. 176
Physics, 99
Pirates, 173, 312; Barbary, 312
Piri Reis, Admiral, 247
Plassey, battle of, 298
Podolia, 262, 265
Poetry, 89, 135, 139, 141, 146, 150, 182, 189, 205, 209, 215; Persian, 221, 246 f., 272 f.; Turkish, 246 f., 272 f.
Poland, 231, 262, 264, 265, 267, 268
Police, 184, 282
Polo, Marco, 201
Poltava, battle of, 265
Portuguese, the, 195, 240, 335
Postal services, 62, 170, 316ι
Potemkin, General, 269

Pratiharas, the, 176
Prithvi Raj, 177, 178
Prophet's House, the, 103
Prussia, 269
Pruth, Treaty of, 266
Pugachev, revolt of, 269
Punjab, the, 136, 176 ff., 182 f., 278, 281, 282, 284, 298, 317 f., 318, 320, 348 f.
Puritan Party, 38, 41, 44, 55, 86, 93, 184

Q

Qaddafi, Moammar, 375, 376
Qadis, the, 187, 202, 246
Qadisiya, battle of, 31
Qairawan, 53, 61 f., 102; Mosque, 90
Qaisites (Mazharites), 67, 69, 109, 114
Qait Bay, 174
Qajar Party (Persia), 219, 299, 313 f.
Qalawun, Sultan, 171 f., 174
Qarmatians, the, 49, 129, 130 ff.
Qatar, 365, 368, 390
Qatar Peninsula, 389
Qilij Sultan, 157
Quraish, the Bani, 5, 26
Qur'an, the, 14, 20, 23, 24 f., 31, 42, 50, 51, 52, 76, 77, 123, 132, 173, 184, 292, 304 f.; 323; codified, 36, 42
Qurrat-ul-Ain, 315
Qutaybah ibn Muslim, 61
Qutbuddin Aybak, 179
Qutbuddin Mubarak, 184
Qutlugh Khan, 183
Qutub Minar, 179, 180

R

Rabat, 362
Radcliffe Award, 349
Radsin, Treaty of, 263
Rafi ibn Layth, 109
Raghib Pasha, 268
Ragusa, 235
Rahman, General Ziaur, 400
Railways, 310, 316, 341
Raisuli, 333
Rajatrangini, the, 191
Rajputs and Rajputana, 176, 181, 183, 189 ff., 195, 275 ff., 278, 281, 284 ff., 288 ff., 294 f.
Rakoczy, George, 261
Ranjit Singh, 318

Ranthambor, 180, 183
Ras al-Khaimah, 390
Rashid dynasty, 351
Rashid Pasha, General, 302
Rashiduddin Fadlullah, 202, 209
Rationalism, 76, 119
Rawalpindi, Treaty of, 356
Raymond, Count, 156, 158, 171
al-Razi, 122, 135
Raziya, Sultana, 180
Razmara, Ali, 342
Reformation, the, 240
Reginald of Chatillon, 162
Regional Co-operative Development (RCD), 366
Religious Orders, 133, 151, 271 f. 304
Renaissance, the, 97, 240
Resht, 216, 340
Reza Khan, 340 f.
Rhodes, 54, 173, 237 f., 328
Richard Lionheart, 163 f.
Riyadh, 365
Roderick of Spain, 63
Roger II of Sicily, 95
Rohillas, the, 297
Roland (*Chanson de Roland*), 81
Romans, the, 2
Roncesvalles, battle of, 81
Rose, Sir Hugh, 320
Rowlatt Acts, 345
Roxelana, 237, 239
al-Ruha, siege, 160, 161
Rum, Seljuks of, 144 f., 150, 154, 157, 247
Rumania, 328
Rumeli Hissar, fort, 232
Rumelia, 271
Russia, 215, 216, 217, 227, 234, 254, 255; wars against, 263, 264, 265, 267, 269 ff.; Protector of Christians, 269, 308, 309; and European powers, 299, 300 ff.. 302 f.; 308 ff., 327; and Egypt, 355; and Afghanistan, 356; and Persia, 313 ff., 324, 329 ff., 336, 340 ff.; and Turkey, 338, 339; Revolution in, 340. *See also* 366, 380, 392, 404

S

Saadat, Anwar, 376, 377
Saad ibn Abu Waqqas, 31, 45
Saadat Khan, 297
Saadi, Shaikh, 182

Sabir Kalyari, 198
Sa'di (Muslihuddin), 204, 209
Sadr, Beni, 395
Sa'duddin, 273
Safavids, the, 208, 210 f., 213, 215, 220, 256, 266
al-Saffah, 103 f.
al-Saffar, 135
Saffarids, the, 135
Safi al-Din of Ardabil, Shaikh, 210
Sahih al-Bokhari, 124
Sahih Muslim, 124
St. Gotthard, battle of, 262
St. John, Order of, 171, 173, 238
Saints, 151, 304, cf. 197 f.
Sajah, rebel, 28
Salem Kemen, battle of, 264
Salgharids, the, 203 f.
Salahuddin, Sultan, 93, 95, 161 ff., 169, 174
Saleh, Mustafa Ould, 369, 370
al-Salih, Sultan, 167, 168
Salim Shah, 282
Salonika, 230
Samanids, the, 135 f.
Samarqand, 109, 135, 147, 205 ff., 206, 221, 274, 275, 404
Samarra, 117, 118, 130
Sambhal, 278
Sambaji, 296
San Esteban, 85
Sanga, Rana, 275 f., 284
Sanjaks, 246 ff.
Sanjar, Sultan, 144, 147
Sanskrit, 139, 151, 176, 188
Sardinia, 90, 91, 115, 156, 243, 309
Sardis, 61
Satara, 318
Sartono, Mr., 358
Sastromidjojo, Ali, 358
Saud, House of, 350 f.
Saud ibn Abdul Aziz, 304 f.
Saudi Arabia, 362, 364, 365, 366, 368, 386, 389
Saudis, the, 304
Savov, General, 328
Sayyid dynasty, 189
Schuster, W. M., 331
Science, *see* Medicine
Sebastian, General, 300
Sebastopolis, 61
Secret Societies, 70, 133. *See also* Qarmatians
Selim I, 212, 235 ff., 239, 270

Selim II, 240 ff., 244, 254
Selim III, 301
Senegal, 367, 368, 371
Senussi Shaikhs, the, 359
Seringapatam, battle of, 298
Serbia and Serbs, 225 f., 227 ff., 234, 267, 308, 328; rising, 300 f.
Seven Years War, 268
Seville, 64, 82; the Giralda, 93; Kingdom of, 89, 91
Sevres, Treaty of, 338
Shafi, Sir Muhammad, 346
al-Shafii, Imam, 123
Shagari, Al-Haj Shehu, 374
Shah Jehan, see Khurram, Prince
Shah Rukh, Prince, 207
Shah Wali-Ullah, 272, 363
Shahabuddin Muhammad al-Ghauri, 178 ff., 180
Shahid, Ismail, 322 f.
Shahji Bhonsle, 288, 290, 295
Shaikh-ul-Jabal (Old Man of the Mountains) see Hasan ibn Sabah
Shaki, 314
Shalan dynasty, 351
Shamsuddin, Shah, 192
Shamsuddin of Tabriz, 209
Sharaf ul-Daulah, 141
Shariah, 244, 271, 382
Sharjah, 390
Sharqi Kingdom, 188, 191 f.
Shaybani Khan, 274, 275
Shehu, Mehmet, 380
Sher Shah Suri, 193, 195, 279 f., 281 f.
Shihabuddin Muhammad of Nisa, 209
Shiites and their creed, 47 f., 85, 89 ff., 98, 110, 113, 115 f., 119 ff., 123 f., 131 f., 140, 142 f., 147, 150, 162, 212 f., 219, 268, 271 f., 286, 389; Rasail, 141. See also Qarmatians
Shimr ibn Zil-Joshan, 46
Shiraz, 140, 192, 203, 205, 209, 219
Shirkuh, 161
Shirley, Anthony and Robert, 213
Shirvan, 214, 216, 254, 256, 314
Shishakly, Col. Adib, 355
Shujah, 291
Shurahbil ibn Hasanah, 29
Sicily, 90, 91, 95 ff., 115, 167, 243, Norman Kingdom, 160
'Sick Man of Europe' (nineteenth century Turkey), the, 254
Sidi Muhammad bin Youssef, 359
Siffin, battle of, 40

Sikander But Shikan, 190, 198
Sikander Lodhi, 189 f., 198
Sikander Shah, 192
Sikha-Shahi, 318
Sikhs, 199, 287, 294, 297, 298, 317 f., 320, 349
Simla Pact, 397
Sinai Peninsula, 331, 345, 376
Sind, 60, 176 f., 179, 187, 218, 274, 280, 282, 292, 297, 319, 347
Singapore, 367, 403
Sinkiang, 407
Sistova, Treaty of, 270
Sivaji, 288, 295 f.
Sivas, 206
Slave dynasty, 179 ff.
Slaves and slave trade, 73, 123 f., 243, 312; revolt, 130, cf. 179 ff.; school for, 235
Slavonia, 265
Smyrna, 338
Sobieski, John, 262 ff.
Sobraon, battle of, 318
Socotra, 388
Sofia, 227, 231
Sogund, 223
Somalia, 364, 368, 378, 407
Somnath, 138
South-East Asia Treaty Organization, 350
Spain and the Spanish, 62, 67, 79 ff., 103, 115, 119, 156, 240, 242 f., 369
Sri Lanka, 103
Subuktigin, 136, 138
Sudan, the, 306 ff., 331, 344, 364, 368, 372, 377, 378, 407
Suez, 303; Canal, 306, 310, 331, 377; Crisis, 344
Sufis, the, 133 f., 150 f., 209
Sukarno, Dr., 357 f., 402, 403
Sulaiman, 64, 65 f.
Sulaiman (son of Orkhan I), 225 f.
Sulaiman the Magnificent, 236 f.
Sulaiman III, 264
Sulaiman, Prince, 228
Sulaiman Chelebi, 247
Sultaniya, 203
Sumatra, 335
Sunnah, the, 304
Sunnis, the 47 f., 69, 92, 98, 110, 114, 115, 116, 123, 131, 133, 134, 138, 142 f., 150 f., 161, 212, 215 ff., 268, 304, 389
Supa, battle of, 285